CARY GRANT
In Name Only

CARY GRANT
In Name Only

Gary Morecambe and Martin Sterling

ROBSON BOOKS

First published in Great Britain in 2001 by Robson Books, 10 Blenheim Court, Brewery Road, London N7 9NY

A member of the Chrysalis Group plc

British Library Cataloguing in Publication Data
A catalogue record for this title is available from the British Library.

ISBN 1 86105 466 1

Typeset in 11/13pt Times by FiSH Books, London WC1
Printed by Mackays of Chatham, Kent

I saw him often, so often that I ceased,
Almost, to notice him. So now I visualize
A photograph or something like a still
From an old movie, shot in black-and-white...

From 'Matches' by Vernon Scannell

Contents

Acknowledgements

There are so many people we wish to thank for co-operating in the production of this book. For their time and effort, Roger Moore, Sheridan Morley, Ruth Leon, Doris Spriggs, Michael Sellers, Sarah Debenham and Lauren Leboyer. For his hours spent in research, Jack Bartholomew. For arranging present-day photography of Monaco and the south of France, Neill Tughan. For his unstinting and invaluable help in providing background research, the film historian Chris Boxall. For providing a private family photograph for the book, Joan Morecambe. For her editorial skills, Dorothy Twist. For his provision of accommodation in London, David Coupe. For his support and enthusiasm for the project, Graham McCann. For her continued support on all our literary endeavours, our special agent, Jennifer Luithlen. Thank you to Jeremy, Jo, Kate, Anthea and all at Robson Books for making this project so enjoyable.

A special thank you to Barbara Grant Cohen for her good wishes.

And finally our families, who have spent the last year living with Cary Grant (they wish!).

Authors' note

While many of Cary Grant's films have been comprehensively examined in this book, the authors, in order to keep the main body of the story flowing, have tended to be brief about some of those films that are widely regarded as less significant in this actor's vast repertoire. The authors have, however, given detailed analysis on the films they believe to have remained most memorable to the wider viewing public, with particular attention to all Grant's collaborations with the director Alfred Hitchcock. There is a complete filmography at the back of this book.

Foreword

'How old Cary Grant?'

'Old Cary Grant fine, how you?'

The 1930s telephone exchange is quoted more than most because it instantly established two things: a perennial interest in Grant's age, and the speed of the man's wit at a time when Hollywood was more usually at its wits' end.

This admirable new biography will tell you the facts of his life: the Bristol birth of Archie Leach (how many of us recall now that, like Bob Hope and Liz Taylor, this apparently most American of movie stars was in fact born over here?), the move to Hollywood, the new name, the five marriages and seventy movies, especially those for Hitchcock, hallmarked as they were by the snobbery with violence that became his stock in trade.

But what concerns me is his enduring legacy. Grant was by no means the only Hollywood charmer of his generation – but who now recalls as easily George Sanders, or Claude Rains, or Charles Boyer, or even Rex Harrison or David Niven?

The truth is that Grant was always the leader of that super-elegant generation of gentlemen actors, the one who defined the style others could only follow. All the more surprising when you consider he was a boy from the back streets of Bristol; but then again, the greatest movie Englishman of them all, Leslie Howard, was in fact mainly Hungarian. To play the perfect English gentleman on screen, it helped not to be one, and Grant in any case soon slipped into mid-Atlantic mode, one brilliantly parodied by Tony Curtis in *Some Like it Hot*.

Was he gay? And if so, does it really matter? Certainly he shared a beach house with Randolph Scott and certainly theirs was an address where Noel Coward always stayed on his brief visits to California. But the evidence has always been shaky. Was he into LSD? He certainly denied it, but then withdrew a lawsuit against the journalist who had first run with the story.

In truth he was a private man, haunted as had been Chaplin (another refugee from the wrong side of the English tracks, with a mentally disturbed mother) by the contrast between early childhood poverty and later Hollywood affluence only achieved, it seemed, at the cost of cutting off all his family roots.

But what matters is what he left behind: *The Philadelphia Story*, *To Catch A Thief*, *Indiscreet*, *An Affair To Remember*, *North by Northwest* and dozens more, in almost all of which his debonair, throwaway style was as perfectly suited to elegant light comedy as to Hitchcock thrillers.

And think of what he did for the stars he worked with: Katharine and Audrey Hepburn, Grace Kelly, Deborah Kerr; all shone brighter in his reflected limelight, for Grant had almost no jealousy and believed, unlike virtually every other male star of his time, that the better you made your co-star look, the better you looked yourself.

Grant stands and speaks alone for a time when Hollywood cared about style, about elegance, about timing, about grace under pressure and about men with carnations in their dinner jackets. Now that the world has gone rough and ready, Grant's legacy matters all the more: by sleight of hand he took audiences out of the troubles of the Depression or the Second World War and gave them a couple of hours of utter escapism. He was Fred Astaire without the dancing.

He was also untouchable, unbeatable, unmissable. He learned very early on one of the great tricks of his trade, which was to always hold something back. Let the camera come and find you, don't go out to meet it close up, and let the audience think there is always something else going on behind the eyes, beyond the heart. Leave a little something unknown, whether it be about your birthplace or your sexuality or your life, and you will remain a subject of intrigue and interest. Grant was not a man who ever let it all hang out, but in his own curious, clenched, buttoned-up way he was perhaps the most romantic of them all.

When Cole Porter had to find an actor to play him on screen, he found Cary, for he, too, was at the top, and he too had known what it was like to be down in the depths on the 93rd floor. 'Cary Grant is not supposed to die,' wrote the *New York Times*, when he did in November 1986; but then again, he never really has. He will live as long as any of us have the strength to slip one of his movies into the video recorder or DVD player, and that should be quite a while yet. His passport has several centuries to run.

Sheridan Morley
June, 2001

CARY GRANT: IN NAME ONLY

First Introduction

I was brought up on a movie-diet of Cary Grant, Fred Astaire, the Marx Brothers, Laurel and Hardy, Jimmy Cagney and Phil Silvers – probably in that order – all interwoven with Morecambe and Wise shows. The advent of the video machine, which appeared in our home in 1975 – we were considered trend-setters! – ensured that hardly a week would pass without a showing of *Father Goose, Bringing Up Baby, Suspicion, Arsenic and Old Lace, North By Northwest, Charade* and a handful of other firm favourites from the Grant canon, which my father had managed to capture on tape.

We weren't compelled to watch Cary Grant movies but were drawn in by my father's delight and Grant's unique screen presence. He was one of my father's very few heroes, and sold to me at an early, impressionable age. From my personal viewpoint, I suppose it is one of those things where it could have gone either way, but I found myself enchanted by the film star; more so as my father, a huge icon himself, saw fit to adulate him and let it be known openly that he adulated him. And I realised, very quickly, that with Cary Grant I was watching someone quite remarkable...unique. As I grew older, I began to analyse the reasons and this, to a large degree, has culminated in the writing of this book.

So much of what Grant did seemed effortless, which disguised the hard work he put in to being the Cary Grant we wanted and expected. I had witnessed this with my own father – the endless rehearsals to make the final product appear ad-libbed.

In my teens, I discovered my father and Grant were friends – Grant being a great lover of the British comedians who had emerged around the latter part of the era of the music halls, and early radio shows – and had known each other for many years. Whenever Cary Grant saw my father, he would call him 'Sir Eric!' My mother, Joan, says that they were never sure if he really thought my father had been knighted, or if it was just a fun thing to show how much he appreciated and admired his comic skills.

A phase followed when I would brainwash my father into inviting Grant to our house. I knew they occasionally met up through Grant's association with the Fabergé company, which brought him over to London. Indeed, Grant even had an anecdote about my father from one such luncheon. It concluded with Grant saying, 'After the meal, we [Eric and Grant] visited the men's room together. While we were there, a man came in, recognised Eric and asked whatever happened to Wilson, Kepple and Betty. Eric replied, "Not a lot. Two of them died." That just finished me off. I fell about laughing.' And how my father would have enjoyed making his *own* hero laugh. But in response to my request to invite him home, he would just smile and say, 'What would he want to come here for? He's based in America, and anyway, he's too busy.' So my opportunity of meeting the great screen icon was denied me: my remaining incentive is to at least take this opportunity of associating myself with him via the printed word.

What follows from Martin Sterling and myself is a serious and, hopefully, objective examination of someone who has on numerous occasions been described as the world's greatest leading man.

Gary Morecambe
Somerset, 2001

Second Introduction

Shortly before her premature death in 1998, the writer and director Jan Butlin directed a rehearsed reading of my play *Before PM* in London.

Jan, who was one of the youngest people ever to go to RADA and who once had the distinction of having three plays that she had directed running simultaneously in the West End – an achievement yet to be equalled by so young a woman – had a commitment to helping young actors and writers. During a break from rehearsals, I asked Jan what was the single most important piece of advice she could give to any aspiring actor.

'That's easy,' she said. 'I tell them to rent six Cary Grant movies and study them.'

Initially, that struck me as odd. Cary Grant had then (in 1997) already been dead eleven years and had not made a film for thirty-one years. I myself was still a toddler when his final film, *Walk, Don't Run*, was released in the summer of 1966: so what could drama students on the threshold of the new millennium possibly learn from watching his old movies?

But the more I thought about it, the more I realised Jan was right. To watch any classic Cary Grant film is to witness a performance as vibrant and fresh as the day he made it.

Actors usually become great stars by playing the same role over and over again. Typically, Grant bucked this trend by pulling off the greatest sleight-of-hand in acting history, one that fooled many. His obituary in *The Times* in 1986 said that he had a limited range. That is absurd. His range was greater than any of his contemporaries in Hollywood but the failure of some critics to recognise how good an actor he was *is* understandable.

One of the shrewdest businessmen ever to operate in Hollywood, Grant understood perfectly that the 'Cary Grant' brand he had created was the most commercial movie franchise for many years. But disguised beneath commercial expediency, he was able to deliver performances of astonishing subtlety and variety that remain incredibly relevant today. His style, which he created and which was personal to him, has a timelessness no other actor can match.

To study Grant is to have a master class in acting. So subtle was his technique that casual observers might conclude he had no technique at all. And there is no such thing as a 'typical' Cary Grant performance. If we take Jan Butlin's advice and select six classic Cary Grant films at random, each performance can be seen to be very different once we look beneath the 'Cary Grant' patina. Roger Thornhill from *North By Northwest* is diametrically different from *Charade*'s Peter Joshua; the nerdish David Huxley of *Bringing Up Baby* is not the same man at all as conniving Walter Burns in *His Girl Friday*; and what does Jerry Warriner in *The Awful Truth* have in common with the repressed Devlin of *Notorious*?

If Cary Grant the actor continually surprises us, Cary Grant the man remains an enigma. Critics who accused him of only playing himself were wrong for the simple reason that Grant – who had pulled off cinema's greatest feat of alchemy by moulding the golden 'Cary Grant' from the base metal that was Archie Leach – never truly knew just *who* he really was.

Biographers are often accused of trying to deconstruct their subjects, but an honest writer cannot ignore or shy away from negative characteristics if the portrait is to be in any way complete. Is this an accurate portrait of Cary Grant? Who knows? It is certainly an objective one. And if he, himself, didn't know who he was, no one will ever pin him down definitively.

All Hollywood idols have feet of clay because they are human, not gods. Cary Grant is no exception. He had faults and he had weaknesses. Sometimes he was foolish. The extraordinary thing, for me at least, is that, far from diminishing his status, these failings enhance him. Cary Grant was all too human, which makes his achievements even more remarkable.

Martin Sterling
Norfolk, 2001

Taken in 1982 – Joan Morecambe, Eric Morecambe (with arm around) Barbara Harris, Cary Grant. Caption by Cary Grant reads: 'You're not jealous are you Joan? Good. Neither am I! Happy thoughts. Cary.'

1 ———————————————————

'Remember that what you are told is really three-fold: shaped by the teller, reshaped by the listener, concealed from both by the dead man of the tale.'

Vladimir Nabokov (*The Real Life of Sebastian Knight*)

At the Cannes Film Festival in May 2000, the then 84-year-old Oscar-winning actor Gregory Peck gave a press conference during which he derided current Hollywood male stars.

Peck, one of the surviving emperors of Tinseltown's golden age, declared that the age of glamour was dead and said there was 'no way' modern stars could compare to his own generation in matters of style.

The press, worldwide, picked up on his comments and the resulting articles provided plenty of crowd-pleasing copy, as 'scruffy, fitness-obsessed' contemporary stars such as Brad Pitt, Leonardo DiCaprio and Tom Cruise were compared with 'gentlemen' stars from yesteryear – Peck himself, Humphrey Bogart, Clark Gable, David Niven and Errol Flynn. As the *Sunday Telegraph* observed: 'a paparazzo's picture of Tom Cruise arriving at a Beverly Hills gymnasium cannot compete with an image of Humphrey Bogart propping up a cocktail bar with Lauren Bacall.'

All good knock-about fun, of course. But the reality is much more complex than a simple then-and-now comparison.

'We lived in far more secrecy,' veteran actress Luise Rainer, a contemporary and friend of Peck's, said at the time of his Cannes outburst. 'That made us much more glamorous because people didn't know about our private lives. If they were interested, they just had to guess. Now the media crawls under people's skirts. That's what kills glamour.'

The truth is that the glamour of old Hollywood relied heavily on rigid studio control of stars, and the tuxedoed sophistication of Bogart and Gable was manufactured every bit as much as the designer scruffiness of their successors, as David Niven recalled when he described how MGM's publicity department 'created' him.

'Mother?' they asked.

'French,' Niven replied.

'Good, we can use that. Father?'

'Killed in the war.'

'Great! What rank?'

'Lieutenant.'

'Jesus, that's terrible. We'd better make him a general...'

There was, however, one movie icon whom Tinseltown's publicists didn't need to create because he was already his own creation.

More than Gable, more than Peck, even more than Bogart, he was highlighted in every article that followed Gregory Peck's attack at Cannes as the epitome of Hollywood's lost sophistication.

His name was Cary Grant.

A movie star for more than thirty years, Grant made over seventy films and was as popular as he'd ever been when finally retiring from acting in the mid-sixties.

Cary Grant was like no one else and, probably because of this, was never replaced. Nobody talked like he did. Nobody looked like he did. And nobody behaved like he did. He was, as one of his biographers Graham McCann described, a class apart. The actor and close friend of Grant, Tony Curtis, described him as 'one of the film industry's true superstars.'

Except Cary Grant wasn't real. He was entirely one man's invention: a man who was born Archie Leach in the prosaic setting of Bristol in the southwest of England.

He would live to be a very respectable 82 and the world he departed was very different from the one into which he had been born. Technological advances had changed lives forever. Medical advances had prolonged life and banished many diseases. Presidents and kings had come and gone. Two World Wars had seen the global map re-drawn again and again. But the most fundamental change in human history that occurred during his 82 years was the development and proliferation of mass communication, with Hollywood, a virtually unknown district of Los Angeles when Archie was born, becoming the single greatest influence on the way people looked, talked and thought.

And Archie Leach was destined to become one of its greatest exponents.

London's streets may still have been 'paved with gold' in the minds of many in 1904, but when Archie grew into adolescence and early manhood, Hollywood had already overtaken it as the real place of dreams. And when the studios came of age at more or less the same time as he did, they were hungry for leading men who could satisfy the fantasies of cinema-goers the world over.

The young Archie Leach certainly had the look that those early moguls craved. Indeed, he was blessed physically because he not only possessed a devastatingly handsome face, but he was fortunate to develop an athletic body; a result of nature and not, he claimed, honing or exercising. Both were to prove to be his passport out of a truly unprepossessing start in provincial, post-Victorian Britain.

Ever since D.W. Griffith made *In Old California* in Hollywood in 1910 – the first movie to be shot there – the place has never been short of pretty boys, a few of whom even made it as stars. But when Archie Leach metamorphosed into Cary Grant he was so much more than just an attractive face attached to a decent body.

Great actors can become great stars, but not every star is a great actor. Grant was both. Even in roles that were patently wrong for him – such as playing Cole Porter in *Night And Day* (1946), an hilarious piece of miscasting that rivalled John Wayne as Genghis Khan in *The Conqueror* (1955) – he somehow managed to convince.

The playwright Noel Coward, five years older than Grant and a friend from the 1930s until Coward's death in 1973, was another legend who was his own greatest creation. Indeed, Grant and Coward had much in common. Both had escaped unprepossessing English backgrounds to conquer America and the world, and Coward, arguably the first modern superstar – 'The Beatles of his era', according to John Lahr – epitomised urbane sophistication in the 1920s just as Grant was to do a decade or so later.

Noel Coward once succinctly explained the concept of 'star quality' to his godson Daniel Massey. 'You could put me on a stage with Olivier, Gielgud and Ralph Richardson,' he said, 'and they'd be acting me off the stage, down the aisle and out of the auditorium. But everyone in that audience would be looking at me.'

And Coward was unquestionably right. Cary Grant, too, had that same star quality. No one's eyes left Grant when he was on-screen. The difference between them was that nobody ever acted Grant off-screen. Beneath Grant's debonair screen persona lay a formidable acting talent that, like his physique, owed nothing to formal training. Grant often appeared to be doing nothing; but his style was deceptive.

And that is what he had: style. For, if the glamour of old Hollywood was largely manufactured, Grant still epitomises all that we seem to have lost. In September 2000, he came second only to the late Princess Diana in a list of the Best Dressed People of All Time compiled by *People Weekly*, America's best-selling celebrity magazine. Furthermore, no fewer than three of Grant's female co-stars made the top twenty list – Audrey Hepburn (5th), Grace Kelly (15th) and Katharine Hepburn (17th) – reinforcing Grant's claim to be the emperor of style because of his own image and the women with whom he was seen.

Conversely, beneath that urbane façade, there were doubts and insecurities and frustrations. When Archie Leach manufactured Cary Grant, he failed to exorcise all Archie's ghosts and left Grant with an Achilles heel of lingering uncertainty that would take a career and a final happy marriage to resolve. At the height of his success, Grant was assailed by a lack of self-confidence. This was to manifest itself particularly in his relationships with the opposite sex.

All that was ahead. When Archibald Alexander Leach was born on 18 January 1904 at 15 Hughenden Road, Horfield, in Bristol, Queen Victoria had been dead just three years and the twentieth century had yet to make much impact on Bristol.

In the wider world there were stirrings of what were to prove to be the prevailing themes and preoccupations of the last century of the millennium. Orville and Wilbur Wright had just made the headlines with their new flying machines – although the US Army insisted that heavier-than-air machines would have no practical military value. The Hon. Charles Rolls reached agreement with Henry Royce to make cars. On-going uprisings in Imperial Russia against the Tsar and rumblings in the Balkans presaged decades of horrific bloodshed to come. And in London, J.M. Barrie's new play *Peter Pan* opened at the Duke of York Theatre.

Many creative people were born in that year who would come to dominate the arts and entertainment in the new century: John Gielgud, Graham Greene, Glenn Miller, Bing Crosby, Johnny Weissmuller, Peter Lorre, Count Basie, Christopher Isherwood, Frederick Ashton and Cecil Beaton. And in the same year that these, and Grant, were born, Dan Leno – who might be called the patron saint of tortured clowns – died after having previously suffered a nervous breakdown.

Although almost forgotten by all but theatre historians today, Leno was a huge star in his time whose name would have been as familiar to Archie Leach's parents, Elsie and Elias, in 1904 as the name Cary Grant is to us today. At the peak of his comedic music-hall career in 1901, Leno became known as the King's Jester following a sensational royal command performance. But pressures of show-business fame – believed by many to be a modern psychosis – led to a decline and eventual insanity.

Grant was certainly familiar with Leno's story and the tragic end of his life and, as someone who regarded his fame with much caution, must have felt it was a salutary reminder of the downside of achieving it.

Although he would never approach the despair that Leno felt, Grant understood perfectly the demons that had haunted the clown. They are the demons that confront every major performer at some stage – particularly comedians – the fear of decline and failure. The sometimes terrifying expectations of the audience and the unremitting conflict between personal happiness and professional success press too hard. The history of entertainment is littered with casualties.

Personal happiness often eluded Grant, but then his parents had hardly set him a good example. If ever a family could be labelled dysfunctional, the Leach family could. They were lower middle-class, with little to single them out from the thousands of others in Edwardian England. Elias James Leach, Archie's father, purportedly half-Jewish but decidedly Anglicised by the time Archie was born, was the son of a local potter. He worked for most of his short life at Todd's Clothing Factory near Bristol's Portland Square. Elias was a noticeably fine-looking man, who took great pleasure singing the sentimental gallery-pleasing music-hall standards of the day. But he had no interest in a professional show-business career and it is unlikely that Elias's amateur singing had any influence in Archie's eventual entry into show business. When Archie turned to a show-business career, however, it might have created a certain empathy between father and son.

Elsie Leach was born Elsie Kingdon – often misspelt as 'Kingdom' – in February 1877. Though seemingly quiet and shy throughout childhood, she was known, by those people who knew her better, to have a ferocious temper. She was also fiercely ambitious. Her four brothers emigrated to Canada leaving her, at twenty-one, to look after her ageing parents. She seems to have seen marriage to Elias as an escape route, despite believing that she was marrying beneath herself since her father was a successful shipwright. They were married on 30 May 1898.

It was to be a marriage that knew little happiness. Their first home together, north of the city, was a rented house at 30 Brighton Street. It was a small and cramped affair and not conducive to an atmosphere of well-being.

Elsie's ambitious approach to life meant that Elias felt obliged to accept as much overtime as he was capable of doing at Todd's. He worked himself into the ground, but still he didn't make enough money to satisfy the status she was determined to attain.

Elsie became pregnant almost immediately and John William Elias Leach arrived on 9 February 1899. There is no suggestion that John was born prematurely, which means that since not quite nine months elapsed between the wedding and his birth – eight and a half months – it is possible that Elsie, although perhaps unaware of it, was pregnant on her wedding day.

This is the point at which the true problems and the flawed foundation stones of Cary Grant's upbringing start to appear. Elsie doted on John, showing him all the love and affection she rarely, if ever, showed to Elias. Sickly from the beginning – he had successive fevers and coughing attacks – he developed tubercular meningitis just before his first birthday. Like any good mother, she devoted herself to his nursing to the point of exhaustion. Her doctor ordered her to rest, which she did, but only awoke to find John was dead.

She blamed herself for his death, insisting that, had she stayed awake with him, he would have somehow survived. She began falling into a depressed state, which shifted her guilt onto Elias. He, in turn, looked for comfort in drinking heavily for the first time.

Of course, their tragedy was not unique: many families during this era lost children in their first year to one infant disease or another. (Grant's hero Noel Coward had lost an elder brother in almost exactly the same circumstances.)

Elsie and Elias must have been communicating on one basic level because in the spring of 1903, Elsie became pregnant with Archie. This prompted a move to a marginally larger home at 15 Hughenden Road. Elsie was, understandably, obsessed with preventing a repeat of the tragedy of their first child and, even when the midwife said Archie was a perfectly healthy baby, she refused to allow Elias to register the birth for seven weeks as she didn't wish to tempt fate.

Elsie wouldn't let Archie out of her sight. She thought that she had let John out of her sight with dire results and so created a cloying relationship with Archie. She shut everyone out of her life bar him. Elias, who was no doubt fairly disappointed at this situation, found his sole function was to bring in money to support them.

Elias worked as long as he could at the factory. It kept him away from Elsie who was prone to nagging him. But it also kept him from Archie making him a virtual stranger to the boy during this early period.

Once the relief of Archie's arrival and early years had subsided, the old familiar pattern of the Leach's marriage reasserted itself: bush fires of resentment and hostility broke out and, ultimately, Archie's birth did nothing to cement a flawed relationship between his parents. This instilled a guilt in the young boy's mind that would afflict him through the earlier years of manhood.

He certainly seems to have been aware of the awkward nature of the relationship from an early age, remembering, for instance, their grief on the morning that King Edward VII died (in May 1910 when Archie was just six) and how their 'shared common bond of sympathy' was 'a rare moment' in their marriage. An incident earlier than that was even more revealing of their relationship, and how, though only an infant, it formulated his own emotional stability.

'I recollect awakening in my crib during a thunderstorm,' he said, 'and seeing them outlined against the window by a flash of lightning. Their backs were toward me and their arms around each other's waists as they looked out at the rain. And now, today, as I think of it, I recall the intense feeling of being cut off from their unfamiliar unity.'

The clarity of Archie Leach's earliest memories was remarkable and their intensity indicative of the way his childhood impacted so dramatically on the rest of his life. His earliest memory was of being publicly bathed by his mother in a portable enamel bathtub in front of the kitchen fire at his grandmother's house: 'It was an old house that either had no bathroom or, more likely, was unheated and too cold for me to be there. I was just a squirming mass of protesting flesh; protesting against being dunked and washed all over in front of my grandmother. The enormity of such an offence. Now if that was my earliest memory why had I, a mere baby, such a sense of embarrassed shame?'

A more pertinent question for him to have asked himself would have been whether the instinctive discomfort he clearly felt at having been stripped and helpless before two women had had any bearing on his later need to control all the subsequent women in his life?

The Leach family moved several times in the years after Archie's birth and his earliest memory of one of these houses was of a long garden. 'In one section,' he recalled, 'there was a large patch of grass around a fine old apple tree near which my father lovingly sank strong, high, wooden supports for a swing. I took pride in that swing, the possession of it, but lacked the daring and abandon of a free swinger; and my father's rhythmic shoves, although gentle, seemed much too perilous. Either I've always lacked bravery or, as I prefer it, never been foolhardy.'

Grant remembered wild strawberry patches that led to open fields at the end of that garden. Those fields, long since covered by housing, were 'forbidden and unexplored territory' to the four-year-old Archie and he yearned to explore them: a foreshadowing of the wanderlust that was never to leave him. It was in that garden, too, that he first experienced injustice – something he grew to dislike intensely as an adult.

'We often ate under the shade of our apple tree,' he said, 'particularly on summer Sundays, on a trestle table set up for the occasion. My father jumped up and down every moment or so to inspect the progress of each item in his vegetable garden. I, on the other hand, was constantly told to sit still and stop bobbing up and down. I could never understand the equity of a rule that didn't also apply to one's parents.' Even at the age of four, Archie could recognise hypocrisy. And hypocrisy was one of the things he was to despise most of all in later life.

The frequent house moves weakened the Leach's financial resources and their increasingly impoverished state hardly helped to improve relations between Elias and Elsie. They bickered and sniped at each other constantly, though it seems that most of the bickering came from Elsie, who was not satisfied that her husband was providing the family with any real security.

Years later, examining a photograph of his parents, Grant said, 'My father was a handsome, tallish man with a fancy moustache but [the photograph] does not show that he possessed an outwardly cheerful sense of humour and to balance it, an inwardly sad acceptance of the dull life he had chosen. My mother was a delicate black-haired beauty, with olive skin, frail and feminine to look upon. What isn't apparent in the photograph is the extent of her strength and her will to control – a deep need to receive unreservedly the very affection she sought to control.'

Presumably as a consequence of their deteriorating relationship following Archie's safe arrival, Elias began a succession of affairs with other women and returned to drinking more heavily than he had done previously.

Archie started at Bishop Road Junior School in Bishopston, aged just four. He immediately struck his first teachers as an insular boy, one who connected neither with the world of adults nor other children.

'I had no opportunity to observe or associate with other adults,' he said. 'And although my father and mother came from large families and I had many aunts and uncles, few of them, as far as I could appreciate, glowed with the joy of life.'

But if Archie didn't identify with adults, he made few friends of his own age either. School did not change him much: he once confessed to having been 'stammeringly shy' in the presence of girls in the class.

Contrary to Elsie's high opinion of his academic potential, Archie's progress at the school was erratic, although he did excel at sports and at soccer particularly. He was an excellent goalkeeper. His teachers, though, found he had a tendency to daydream in class. These daydreams usually centred on the films he and Elias had recently taken in at the Metropole cinema. Archie adored the weekly serials that were hugely popular at this time and these trips to the cinema with his father seem to have been the happiest part of his childhood. Despite the intensity of Elsie's smothering, Archie still managed to bond with his father: sitting in the safety of the dark, watching Pauline imperilled week in, week out, was a wonderful antidote to the bleak tension forever present at home.

If Archie's earliest memory was one of embarrassment, others followed. He particularly recalled being awakened one evening by the noise of a party in the drawing-room below 'and of my father's coming up and carrying me downstairs on his shoulders to be shown off to the guests and to lisp unhappily and haltingly through the first poem I ever learned. There I was wrapped in a blanket reciting 'Up In A Balloon So

High' while my father, showing both pride and strength at the same time, held me at arm's length high above his head in the air. It was a high-ceilinged room and I remember being very close to the high, centre chandelier. I think my father was high, too.'

Given that the Leach household was hardly renowned for its parties, the sound that woke the infant Archie was more likely to have been drunken friends of Elias's from the pub. Nonetheless, the essential warmth of Archie's first memory of his father was in stark contrast to the first memory of his mother. Where he merely lisped 'unhappily and haltingly' through his poem for Elias, he was 'a squirming mass of protesting flesh' while being 'dunked and washed' by Elsie in front of his grandmother; and where the environment of his poetry recital is, essentially, warm – he is at a 'party' and 'wrapped in a blanket' – his bathtub experience took place against a harsh backdrop, 'an old house' that was 'unheated and too cold' and he was left humiliated.

Thus, from the outset, Archie seems to have instinctively gravitated towards Elias rather than Elsie and this may help to explain why, when he finally learned the truth about the terrible thing Elias later did to Elsie, Cary Grant never seemed to find it within himself to condemn his father for it.

Certainly Elsie resented the time Archie spent with Elias away from home. She made it clear that she disapproved of their trips to the cinema and, when Archie was about eight or nine, she began bringing pressure on him to apply himself more to his studies. She insisted that he must try and win a scholarship to a better school, which, eventually – and contrary to the expectations of his first teachers – he did.

Clearly a large part of Elsie's wanting Archie to excel at school was genuinely altruistic: she saw academic success as his chance to have a better life. But she also hoped to lessen Elias's influence over their son. Archie was becoming more and more a source of friction between his parents as Elsie tried to dominate every aspect of his life.

She even insisted that he wore shorts instead of long trousers, despite his being the last boy in Bristol to do so. It was as though she wanted to perpetuate his childhood as he represented everything in her life. In retrospect, he always seemed resentful of her for this.

'It seemed to me that I was kept in long baby clothes much longer than any other child,' he recalled. 'And perhaps, for a while, I wasn't sure whether I was a boy or a girl. Then, later, I was kept far too long, I swear to you, in short pants. I wore curls too long, too, and like most little boys I ached for the day they'd be cut off.'

Elias didn't approve of the way Elsie dressed Archie either but she took no notice of his complaints. Elias wasn't wholly without influence, though, and as well as taking Archie to the cinema it was he who really encouraged his son to excel at sports.

Then, in September 1911, when Archie was seven-and-a-half, one of those complex, simmering conflicts broke out that presaged the death throes of the 500-year-old Ottoman Empire: Italy declared war on Turkey for possession of Tripolitania.

Although Britain was not directly involved in the conflict, it provided sales opportunities for manufacturers of military equipment and supplies. It also gave Elias the perfect excuse to put some distance between himself and Elsie and he left the family home, ostensibly to take a better-paid job making military uniforms eighty miles away in Southampton.

The loss of a parent, however temporary, is usually a traumatic experience for any child but, significantly, Cary Grant would always claim he had no memory of his father's departure.

'Perhaps I felt guilty at being secretly pleased,' he once said. 'Now I had my mother to myself.' And he had the calm stability that the temporary separation would have left in its wake; a pleasant if short-lived experience.

With Elias in Southampton, the relationship between mother and son became even more intense. There were no other siblings to dilute her obsession. During Elias's absence, Archie and Elsie moved to 5 Seymour Avenue, Horfield, and two female cousins of Elsie's moved in with them. Their rent was a useful contribution towards what was a slightly larger house than the previous one.

Despite having little spare money, Elsie insisted on Archie taking piano lessons, as she had by now convinced herself he was a child prodigy and harboured ambitions for him to become a famous concert pianist. She took him for long walks along the River Avon to the affluent areas of Bristol, where she had been born, convincing him that success and wealth were his birthright. (Strangely enough, when decades later he achieved both, she hardly acknowledged the fact.)

Six months later, Elias was home. Though the job in Southampton paid well, the expense of maintaining two homes – and a double life with another woman – proved untenable. Absence had not made their hearts grow fonder. Back under the same roof, Elias and Elsie reverted to living separate existences, with Elias spending as little time at home as was feasible and Elsie continuing to berate him for failing to provide a better standard of living. When they were together, the atmosphere was, at best, icy. Elias was so constantly nagged that he would avoid going home and visit the pub instead. This was unfortunate, as alcohol was to be his eventual downfall.

The pair came to blows on more than one occasion. If Elias brought friends home, Elsie objected fiercely. But perhaps worse than the screaming fights was the ever-present brooding hostility that threatened to break out at any time. It is suggested that Elias grew depressed, which added to his desire to stay away from the house. This, in turn, fuelled Elsie's own, very real, depression. Both were slowly destroying each other and there would emerge only one survivor.

Talking about his parents many years later, Cary Grant commented: 'Since my parents did not seem particularly happy together anyway, the lack of money became an excuse for regular sessions of reproach...against which my father resignedly learned the futility of trying to defend himself. This is not to say who was right and who was wrong. They were both probably both. From my childish viewpoint I couldn't properly assess their emotions or their reasoning.'

This is an interesting remark because, despite his trying to see both sides of the argument and claiming he was too young to judge, Grant's memory of how Elias 'resignedly learned the futility of trying to defend himself' further indicates with whom young Archie's sympathies surely lay during this period.

As an only child, it must have been acutely distressing and not a little frightening for Archie to witness the disintegration of his parents' marriage.

'I seemed to be caught in a subtle battle,' he later recalled, 'which eventually took residence inside my own slowly-forming character. I doubt if I was a happy child because, like most people, I conveniently find it difficult to remember those early formative years...'

It is scarcely surprising that the mature Cary Grant would clutch at the rare straws of happiness from his childhood, and either re-invent or totally blot out virtually everything else. And he had good reason to do so. For there are signs that he was, for some of the time, partly a miscreant – presumably as a direct response to his unsettled state. On one occasion, when he was about eight, Archie and another young boy built themselves a trolley – basically, wooden planks supported by wheels. They set off without food or money on an adventure on their home-made vehicle that would take them to Bath (about twelve miles from Bristol). As Grant recalled, '. . . we decided to turn back. When we reached home, it was about three o'clock in the morning. My father was waiting up for me and the police were conducting a search.'

During this time, Elsie's mental state grew increasingly fragile and by 1913, when Archie was nine, it is very clear that she was unwell. The stress of her failing marriage coupled with their precarious finances provoked her into becoming more and more unpredictable. She had taken to hoarding food, scrubbing her hands incessantly with a hard brush, shouting out loud to no one and asking where her dancing shoes were.

Many years later, Cary Grant admitted that her behaviour at the time exhibited all the classic symptoms of the obsessive paranoiac close to breaking point. She may even have suffered post-natal depression when Grant was born – which doubtless would have gone unrecognised. She may also have suffered delayed trauma following the death of her first son, which, again, would have gone unrecognised, partly because of the normally high mortality rate of the era and also because it is unlikely such a disorder was widely understood.

Elias consulted the family doctor about his wife and then went to the magistrates to arrange to have Elsie sectioned. He told Archie nothing of this.

Elsie, quite literally, had reached the point of no return. When nine-year-old Archie said goodbye to his mother before heading off for school one fateful morning, he couldn't possibly have dreamt that the next time he would set eyes upon her he would be an adult and a film star. Archie returned at tea-time to an empty house. Elsie Leach had gone and no one seemed to know where. Archie was frantic. To compound matters, his two cousins thought it best to tell him his mother had died of a heart attack and had had to be buried immediately. A neighbour told him that she had gone on holiday to Weston-super-Mare. Elias told Archie that she would return shortly.

To Archie, it must have seemed like a spontaneous decision to disappear from his life. Ignorant of the full extent of her mental illness, his child's reasoning concluded that he was somehow the root cause and the shock was enormous. Just one year after he had embraced his father's absence from the family home because it had meant having his mother to himself, her presence in his life had disappeared as suddenly and effectively as a light being switched off.

Elsie might as well have died and left him no body to mourn for the effect it had on him. He did not see her again for over twenty years, during which time he had convinced himself she was surely dead. Elias never saw Elsie again.

The two cousins who had moved in with Archie and Elsie now moved out. This loss of rent meant that Elias couldn't keep the property and the two of them moved in with Elias's mother in Picton Street, near the centre of Bristol. Elias and Archie occupied a front room downstairs and a back bedroom.

Archie's grandmother was aloof and treated them virtually as boarders. She would deign to eat with them on Sundays but apart from that she virtually ignored them, especially Archie, as he was a mere child in an era when children were at best seen and not heard. Left to his own devices during the week – he cooked his own meals and put himself to bed – one can only guess at the deep loneliness he must have felt and the sorrow and confusion over his absent mother.

He took to wandering the streets and watching the departing ships at the quay, yearning for the day when he could be on one of them. This was also the time when he began to get into more trouble. He attempted to stow away on a ship, but his nerve failed him and he returned home to the monotony of his new life.

At a time when suffragettes were still fighting for the vote and divorce was so rare as to remain scandalous, Elias handled Elsie's sudden departure by ignoring it in public. For the neighbours, initially at least, Elias's and Archie's lives seemed to continue as though the nightmare had never happened.

It is unclear how Elias explained to Archie the permanent disappearance of his mother. If she had gone away for a while, then surely she would, at some point, return? Elias reportedly did confess to his son that she had 'gone for a rest' in a nearby resort – a not unusual thing to do in Edwardian times. The reality was she had been admitted to a mental asylum at a place called Fishponds.

Whatever internalised grief Archie carried with him following Elsie's departure, it was not shared by Elias. His overwhelming feeling was one of immense relief. Elsie had not been an easy or compliant woman with whom to live and her continued nagging had worn him into long periods of silence. Moreover, Elias had a steady mistress by then. Her name was Mabel Johnson and they would later enter into common-law marriage and produce another child.

The long-term effects on Archie will probably never be fully known, but Elias's indifference to Elsie coupled with Elsie's neurotic instability and disappearance – the ultimate rejection of a child by his mother – can surely be seen in Cary Grant's life. He was to carry a wariness of women throughout the whole of his domestically unsettled life – five marriages, countless affairs, and the honest recognition that he had never been truly happy despite fame and fortune.

One can see in Grant other parallels with another contemporary British star who conquered Hollywood – Charlie Chaplin. Just as Grant came from a poorer part of Bristol, had a father who would die of alcohol and a mother who lost her mind through a complete breakdown, Chaplin came from the East End of London, had an alcoholic father who died young, and a mother who lost her mind through sustained malnutrition. Both Grant and Chaplin put their mothers on pedestals when they were older, even if objective observers wondered if either woman really deserved such adoration. Both men spent their peak years coaxing their mothers to Hollywood and providing a comfort they couldn't have dreamt of. And this was something they shared with Noel Coward, who had an intense relationship with his mother, while virtually ignoring his ineffectual father and younger brother.

Meanwhile, despite the disappearance of his mother from his life, Archie still had his schooling. He won a scholarship to Fairfield Secondary School and started there at the beginning of the new term on 2 September 1915. He was eleven years of age. The school had a good reputation and had between 300 and 400 pupils. The headmaster at the time of Archie's arrival was Augustus Smith, known to everyone – as one would expect – as 'Gussie' Smith. Despite possessing a natural air of authority, 'Gussie' had surprisingly liberal views on corporal punishment, which he loathed administering, and on one occasion announced that 'the staff are more trouble than all the children.'

Doris Guest, the headmaster's clerk, herself only about seven years older than Archie, remembered the boy as 'a scruffy little boy; a pathetic little figure, but one who had something very endearing and fascinating about him. He had those big lovely eyes and he always seemed to be plastered in ink. He was lively, there's no doubt about that.'

One of Archie's contemporaries at Fairfield, Eddie Plunkett, also recalled his scruffiness. 'I remember him sitting more or less chin-on-knees,' he recalled. 'He was wearing short trousers, with socks halfway down his legs, and had a hole in his pants. I teased him about it.'

Generally speaking, those who knew him in these early years tended to paint a rosier picture of Archie's life than was the case. And it was an image Archie did little to dispel.

'We all had holes in our pants and socks,' said Plunkett. 'But we were happy kids.'

The truth, however, was that Archie Leach was not happy. Elsie's disappearance had devastated him and it began to show. Maybe the other kids *were* scruffy, but he was scruffier. Worse, he was very withdrawn and would wander the streets of Bristol for hours on end. Even at the age of eleven, Archie thought that life was a fairly pointless experience:

'There was a void in my life. A sadness of spirit that affected each daily activity with which I occupied myself in order to overcome it. But there was no further explanation of Mother's absence and I gradually got accustomed to the fact that she was not coming home. Nor, it transpired, was she expected to come home.'

Archie spent hours at the docks watching the ocean vessels coming in and going out, and also watching the thousands of young soldiers – many scarcely older than himself – embarking on troop ships bound for mud and death on the Western Front. Watching the vessels become microscopic on the horizon, he would surely have begun fantasising on what lay beyond Bristol.

Archie's story begins to read like a Dickens novel. We can see shades of Pip in *Great Expectations*, of the workhouse boy, Oliver, in *Oliver Twist* and definitely the young David Copperfield embarking on his long journey through life, which would take him from tragic tormented childhood and deliver him into dignified gentlemanly splendour in manhood.

Archie's desperately unhappy home life marked him out as 'different'. Children are renowned for the cruelty they can display towards those who don't fit in and, contrary to the reminiscences of other school contemporaries, a note of realism was sounded by Ted Morley in 1996, then the sole surviving member of Archie's class: 'He was very scruffy. An ugly duckling. Always poorly dressed. And we tended to ostracise him because of that.'

These were the things that as Cary Grant he would rectify for ever, for it is certain that the taunts of his fellows about the way he was compelled to dress – to look – provoked his later obsession for cleanliness, decorum and the general presentation of himself.

Bombarded by verbal abuse, it was at this point that his inferiority complex was undoubtedly born, and it was a complex that would manifest itself later particularly during his second marriage to the Woolworth heiress, Barbara Hutton.

They also made him appreciate just how necessary it was to escape from poverty and, presumably, his reputation for parsimony – for looking after the pennies – stems from this frugal era. He admitted in later years that he knew from a relatively young age just what he expected to get out of life.

What he wanted was what most people – particular those from a limited background – want out of life: money. But to that he added fame. 'You're insane as a pit bug if you don't go for the things you want in this life,' he once said – and he seemed uncannily aware, even as a teenager, that he was unlikely to find either in Bristol.

Elsie might have gone, but her influence remained. She had been determined that Archie was not to be like his father, whom she considered dissolute, and her relentless pushing had left its mark. While she may have had a negative impact on his emotional life, as he was to acknowledge many years later, in the matter of creating absolute determination and vision, she was hugely positive.

'Gussie' Smith found Archie an enigma. He was always in trouble, just one step away from being labelled a juvenile delinquent – which would have led to its own severe treatment – but, conversely, he was an excellent scholar, able to soak things up when he applied himself and was particularly good at art, geography, history and chemistry.

Good work at school – when he felt like it – was no substitute for his mother. He could not know that, far from being dead, Elsie had been institutionalised and he did not learn the truth until he was 32-years-old, when Elias finally confessed.

By that time, Archie was a movie star in Hollywood with a new name. As he himself said of the reunion with his mother, which was a profound shock to both of them, 'I was known to most of the world by sight and by name, yet not to my mother.'

That was because when Elsie was reunited with her little Archie after a 23-year absence, he had already completed his transformation into Cary Grant.

2

'I've often wondered whether destiny creates the course of
the man, or whether man creates the course of the destiny.
Probably both.'

Cary Grant

But the eventual reunion was all in the future.

With Elsie gone and Elias – who was otherwise preoccupied – a
detached father at best, Archie was, effectively, on his own: a latch-key
child, as Graham McCann puts it.

Archie did have one distraction: still too young for the army, he
served as a junior air-raid warden during out-of-school hours. He also
spent some time in the First Bristol Scout Troop, which he'd joined in
1913, just before the Great War.

Even with such possibilities of camaraderie Archie, like Chaplin
before, had few close friendships, if any. Chaplin at least had his
brother Sydney, who later became his manager, in whom he could
confide and share the frustrations of a tough life. Archie had no such
person and throughout his entire school career and some subsequent
time spent in the Boy Scouts there is no record of any close friend.
This, added to an overt shyness of girls, made him something of an
intense loner, who would grow to depend on his own instincts in all the
big decisions he made.

Academically, his chief interest was chemistry and he would hang
around the school laboratory, long after hours, talking to one of the
part-time laboratory assistants and asking questions. It was as though
the certainties of science gave succour to the young Archie Leach, a
contrast to the erratic and unstable nature of home life.

Bristol has always been a theatrical town. The Theatre Royal, which
opened in 1766, is the oldest theatre in the country in continuous use.
Today, it still retains much of the original auditorium, even if extensive
modernisation in the 1960s transformed the theatre into a complex.

However, Bristol's rich theatrical tradition appears not to have touched Archie until his teens – he never took an active part in the theatrical productions at school – but it was at this point that he began regular discussions with the science lab assistant.

There is so often a defining moment when a great actor, writer, film star or whoever, gets in touch with the art-form that will eventually change his or her life. Grant's 'moment' came through his introduction to the theatre world by this unnamed lab assistant whom he plagued with questions, because it also happened that this gentleman worked as an electrician at the Hippodrome, Bristol's newest music hall, opened to the public in 1912.

Presumably feeling a little sorry for this solitary youth, the electrician invited Archie to have a look round backstage at the Hippodrome. Archie accepted the offer and one Saturday afternoon stepped onto his own Road to Damascus. Backstage life was something Archie had never before encountered nor even remotely dreamt about. He'd been to the music hall in the audience, as most people of the era had, but backstage was something else entirely. However fleeting the moment, he was suddenly perceiving show business from within.

Maybe it was the camaraderie – a tightly knit community working together to one common goal – that appealed to him. It was certainly that for so many artistes who trod the boards in the early part of the twentieth century. What is clear is that, with his very first glimpse backstage, the young Archie Leach knew, at once, where his destiny lay. There would never, for a moment, be any diversion from his choice of career.

When reflecting on that first visit many years later, Grant said, 'What other life could there *be* but that of an actor?'

In this current era, which still embraces live performance but also has digital television, video, computers, DVD, multi-screen cinema, 3D surround-sound, numerous variations of screen games and home entertainment, it is difficult for modern audiences to appreciate the appeal of the Empires and the Hippodromes of the British music hall. With our multiplying forms of entertainment and a life expectancy and standard of living unthinkable just two generations ago, we struggle to understand how relentlessly harsh life could be for the vast majority. Harsh reality meant the question of survival, not the choice between buying the chest-freezer or the planned holiday in Florida, as it has become for most people in modern western society.

In 1904, the year of Archie's birth, it was reported that there were more paupers in Britain than at any time since 1888. There were 250,000 people living in workhouses, and it was estimated that one out of every 41 people in the country was able to survive only from hand-outs from the local parish. Britain might have been the richest country on earth but she still had ten million workmen living in conditions of appalling destitution. Swathes of the cities were filthy and the air was frequently foul with pollution.

The music halls offered an escape from all that, as J.B. Priestley's masterful novel, *Lost Empires*, published in 1965, demonstrated. *Lost Empires* was a superb evocation of that lost era of show business and, like the young Archie Leach, Richard Herncastle, Priestley's fictional protagonist, is on the threshold of manhood and effectively alone in the world. In the months before the First World War, Richard joins his Uncle Nick's illusionist act on the music hall stage. His impressions and observations of this showbiz fraternity – an eclectic mix of jugglers, mystics, acrobats, tenors and comedians – at the start of the novel convey for the reader a marvellous sense of period and must surely have been shared by Archie:

It was wonderful to leave the darkening and chilly streets of Newcastle and then find oneself sitting in the fourth row at The Empire. I think that the secret of all these music halls is that while they seemed big – and most of them were – at the same time they seemed warm, cosy, intimate.

A lot has been written about the magic of the playhouse, but it has always seemed to me very pale and thin compared with the warmer and deeper magic of the music hall, which attracted more men than women to itself just because there was something richly feminine about it, belonging half to some vast tolerant mother and half to some bewitching mistress.

I don't say I was putting all this into words as I stared about me that night, saw the orchestral players switch on their lights and try their instruments, noticed fat Mr Broadbent, no longer out of temper, bobbing up, first to smile at two people sitting just in front of me and then to tap with his baton, and heard his orchestra, with its desperate strings as usual fighting a losing battle with the woodwind and brass, scurrying through Grieg's *Norwegian Dances*; but I will swear some such thoughts were going through my head.

If there was, indeed, something of the vastly tolerant mother about the music hall, we can well understand what appealed to Archie about it: this was something he had hardly known when Elsie was around and not at all after she'd gone.

Archie followed up his first visit to the Bristol Hippodrome with a succession of regular visits, asking as many searching questions about theatre of the electrician-cum-lab-assistant as he had about chemistry back at school. Eventually, he introduced Archie to the manager of the Empire in Bristol 'possibly to get some relief from my constant questioning,' Grant once lightly remarked, and it was at the Empire that Archie began to learn the basic customs and rules of the theatre.

At the Empire, he worked for a while on the limelights but it proved a short-lived engagement: he ruined a magician's trick – a well-known performer who called himself The Great David Devant – and was dismissed. David Devant was the originator of many spectacular illusions practised by magicians to this day. Archie had been crouched beside the limelight man, watching Devant's intriguing act. While the limelight man took time out for a cigarette, Archie was given momentary control of the lamp. Unfortunately for the young lad, keen to see how the trick was managed, he allowed the lamp to slowly dip: suddenly, there was a flash of blinding light revealing hidden mirrors under a table. Devant's illusion was ruined – and so was Archie. He had to return to the Hippodrome, where he ran errands and generally made himself useful. For the first time in his life, he was truly happy. He felt at home among the theatrical entourage at the Hippodrome; they were the only real family he now had.

Up until his discovery of the theatre world, Archie's desperately unsettled family life had manifested itself in bouts of behavioural problems at school. One of his former teachers even reminded him of his truculence and difficult manner when, as the famous movie star Cary Grant, Archie returned to visit the school many years later.

Once Archie discovered the theatre, his behaviour noticeably improved. He had discovered something that totally satisfied him. Even the knowledge that boys just a couple of years his senior were being systematically slaughtered in the 'war to end all wars' in the fields of Europe did not intervene. That world was alien to him: nothing of real interest existed beyond the theatre and particularly the Bristol Hippodrome.

It was while running errands that Archie heard about Bob Pender, the manager of a troupe of young acrobats and the man who would be responsible for the transformation that Archie embarked upon. With the age of conscription at eighteen, Pender had an on-going problem sustaining his troupe, its members regularly being sent away to feed the British war machine. Archie was still only fourteen when he wrote to Pender. For the hitherto shy and restrained Archie, it was an unprecedented and bold move because he had had no experience as a performer, let alone a professional acrobat.

Archie's letter must have impressed Pender. Or maybe he was just forced to consider an application from any reasonably fit youth below the age of conscription. Whatever the reason, he wrote an encouraging reply, suggesting that Archie report to him in Norwich – two hundred and thirty miles away.

It is revealing that Archie told Elias nothing about any of this. Instead, he simply stole away from Bristol in the dead of night and took the first available train for Norwich – generously paid for by Pender. 'I can't remember anything about the journey,' Grant always claimed. The journey was probably unadventurous in comparison to the adventure that awaited his arrival.

Like the hero in some simple-minded Hollywood yarn, Archie had, effectively, run away to join the circus. And the attitude of this fourteen-year-old boy in planning his escape is indicative of his life, and his relationship with Elias, at this time: 'My father and I often awoke and left the house at different hours without seeing each other, so I knew it would be quite some time before I would be missed.'

His behaviour is also indicative of his future life as a 'star', when he would so often do the unpredictable – against the wishes of others and against all natural logic – that would invariably turn out, surprisingly, to be totally sound and praiseworthy. This controlled risk-taking – this pure nerve he possessed – played a major part in his being worth sixty million dollars at the time of his death in 1986.

Understandable though it is, perhaps Archie misjudged the depth of his father's care for him. Elias, seemingly flawed in so many ways, put aside his drinking and his relationship with Mabel Johnson to go in search of his missing son.

Archie and Pender hit it off at once and Archie and *Mrs* Pender, equally hit it off. Mrs Margaret Pender was an established dancer whom Bob Pender had met when she was ballet mistress at the famous *Folies Bergère* in Paris.

As Cary Grant, Archie would undoubtedly sign far more lucrative contracts, but the buzz he received out of that first contract – one sheet of ordinary notepaper stating he was to have the opportunity to learn a profession – allegedly remained unsurpassed. He moved into the same digs as the Penders and two or three of the younger members of the company, who also received a little preferential treatment from the proprietor, presumably because of their age and lack of worldliness.

It wasn't the beginning of a great rise to stardom – if that's what Archie had been expecting or hoping. The reality was that he found the work depressingly difficult. But the clumsiness and general awkwardness dissipated as the days went by and he began to take a pride in what he was achieving, which in turn helped his confidence.

One thing that took his interest and which he constantly practised was making-up in thick greasepaint. Ironically, in later years, he didn't wear any make-up at all, as if the memory took him so far back as to make him uncomfortable. And of course, in much later years, he had such a perpetual suntan, that make-up would not have been compulsory when under the lights.

A week after Archie disappeared, Elias caught up with him in Norwich. How he managed this has never been made entirely clear, but presumably he made the connection with Pender and was then able to trace the theatre in which the man operated.

'Luckily, Bob Pender was just coming out of his nearby dressing-room,' recalled Grant, 'and I managed to introduce them to one another before Father and I were able to exchange too many unamusing words which we might later regret.'

Although Elias had spent a distraught week, it is to both Pender's and Elias's credit that the situation was handled in a mature and calm manner and was resolved very quickly. Also, it is possible that Elias, as a man who struggled all his short life to earn a quick buck, saw the theatre as a wonderful opportunity for his only child. Had he been able to have his time again, perhaps Elias himself might have chosen the same career.

It was agreed that Archie could join Pender's troupe, but that he must first return to school – he wasn't yet old enough to leave legally – and complete his basic education. With much reluctance, Archie returned to school – but not for long. Having escaped to theatre-land once, he wasn't inclined to buckle down to the dreariness of school life and that truculent bad behaviour that he'd happily left behind.

Archie was expelled from Fairfield on 13 March 1918. Typically of the way he would later bend facts to suit the re-invention of himself, Cary Grant once claimed he was expelled because he was discovered in the girls' toilets, suggesting the kind of high jinks in keeping with a man-of-the-world image. Certainly nothing to be ashamed of. The reality, however, was not something one could so easily smirk about and it didn't emerge until 1996.

Archie Leach was expelled for stealing from a church. He had brought shame on Fairfield and 'Gussie' Smith expelled him in front of the whole school. 'Gussie', so it is recorded, had tears in his eyes during the expulsion. Sentimental though this sounds, it is entirely believable because it was the first time in the school's history that a pupil had been expelled.

The whole affair was witnessed by Archie's contemporary Ted Morley: 'To be honest, you couldn't describe it as a break-in at all. It was a prank that went wrong. Archie and two other lads were on an excursion for the day. The church was always open to the public and they just walked in. It wasn't premeditated. No criminal act was contemplated and they didn't do it for profit or gain. I think their only satisfaction was knowing they had perpetrated a prank.'

But it was the fourteen-year-old Archie's remarkable conduct at the expulsion that stuck in Morley's mind.

'He showed absolutely no emotion. He just took out a silver cigarette case, tapped a cigarette on the case – he didn't light it or put it in his mouth – and just said, "Can I get my books?" I believe that was the Cary Grant character coming out for the first time.'

It is also possible to believe that Archie Leach was feeling fairly smug at having contrived a way to return to Pender at the earliest possible moment. If so, it was the first recorded example of one of his strongest characteristics. Again and again throughout his adult life, he would demonstrate a determination to remain doggedly focused on anything he became fixated on.

As well as the abrupt end of his schooldays, he may have managed a quick return to Norwich by nagging his father – as any ambitious teenager is likely to do – until his father finally threw up his arms in despair and told him to do whatever he wanted to do, if only he would stop going on about it.

Within a short time, he was training and performing for Pender's troupe. These next two years were to be the most important years in

Archie's development. Although he later claimed that he never enjoyed acrobatic work and saw it merely as a means to an end – that of becoming an actor – Archie's relish for the twice-weekly work-outs in the gymnasium was obvious to everyone in the troupe. This is interesting because it contradicts Cary Grant's repeated assertion that he had never taken, or had, interest in regular exercise in his life.

Bob Pender, a versatile and accomplished comedian in his own right, was a superlative teacher, and Archie learned how to fall, how to dance and how to walk on stilts. But maybe the most essential lessons were the lessons in mime through which Archie absorbed the skill of acting out moods without the use of dialogue. In his later career, Cary Grant would be unique in Hollywood for his visible reactions to his co-stars and whatever was going on around him: he was the greatest on-screen listener in the history of the movies. If he owed anyone anything for that, it was Bob Pender.

Pender's troupe also taught him the importance of discipline to a performer – something he would never lose. Bob Pender instilled in his young charges the principle that team spirit in a tightly-knit troupe such as theirs was paramount to continued success. It was under Pender's influence that Archie first learned how to behave well, to get along with anyone and to take direction from those giving it.

This was all to pay dividends in Hollywood and add lustre to Cary Grant's star image. The name Cary Grant became synonymous with good behaviour, manners and style – both inside and outside the film industry. Again, Grant had good reason to thank Pender for his early tuition.

Another essential part of Archie's development during this time was the dissolving of his regional accent into something altogether different. Grant's mid-Atlantic accent was always impossible to place and it was one of his greatest strengths as a star. Essentially classless, while still educated and vaguely privileged, Grant's accent meant he never had to be typecast. Grant could play an American just as comfortably as he could play an Englishman. Wherever his accent was finally fixed, there was little trace of the West Country cadences and rhythms of his childhood. Touring for Pender would give him the opportunity to hear many dialects and some people have remarked on the noticeable hint of London East End cockney in some of his words.

Archie turned sixteen in January 1920 and shortly afterwards, while the troupe were touring England, he was to make the most important trip of his life. Pender had reached an agreement with Charles Dillingham, an impresario in New York, for his troupe to appear in a show called *Good Times*. Like the rest of his fellow acrobats, Archie was terribly excited by the prospect of his first trip abroad. But there was one snag: there were twelve boys in Pender's troupe and the New York contract required just eight.

Archie had worked extremely hard since joining Pender – he always worked hard at his profession – and had settled remarkably well. Perhaps the troupe, presided over by Pender and his wife, was the family he had never truly had. Whatever the reason, Pender had come to regard Archie as one of his best performers and duly selected him as one of the fortunate eight.

On 21 July 1920, Archie Leach joined Pender and the team on board the *Titanic*'s sister ship, the *Olympic*, to set sail for New York and an unexpectedly monumental future. The *Olympic*, like her doomed, legendary sister, was a lavish palace on water, with restaurants, bars and ballrooms, all giving Archie a glimpse of a life he could only have hitherto imagined. If that wasn't enough, even before he reached America, he got his first taste of Hollywood glamour because Douglas Fairbanks and Mary Pickford were also on board.

Fairbanks and Pickford – the then current King and Queen of Tinseltown – were arguably the most famous and celebrated couple in the world, although they divorced fifteen years later. Pickford, a Canadian who had been acting on stage since the age of five and was brought into the movies by D.W. Griffith, was then 27 years old and known as 'the world's sweetheart'. Reputed to earn 100,000 dollars a year, which was a massive sum in 1920, Pickford had consolidated her wealth in April of the previous year by co-founding United Artists with Fairbanks, Griffith and Charlie Chaplin. The purpose of this partnership was to ensure they received a fair share of the massive profits made from their films. This, coupled with the shrewd handling of her own career, had made Pickford one of the richest women in America.

Fairbanks, ten years older than his wife, was the swashbuckling, energetic hero of countless silent costume romps and that year, 1920, was to see the release of, arguably, his definitive performance in *The Mask Of Zorro*. His real name was Douglas Elton Ulman, and he was born on 23 May 1883 in Denver, Colorado. His successful film career lasted from 1915 to 1934. As well as starring in most of his films, he produced, directed and wrote, a little in the manner of his best friend, Charles Chaplin. A natural athlete – and an acrobat, himself, despite being of a surprisingly short and stocky build – it was inevitable that he would be drawn to Pender's young troupe during the course of the voyage.

It was much to Archie's delighted amazement that he not only met Douglas Fairbanks, but had a photograph taken with him. (Grant later starred with Fairbanks's son, Douglas Fairbanks Jnr in *Gunga Din* in 1939.)

'What impressed me most about Douglas Fairbanks was his tan,' recalled Cary Grant, years later. 'I decided then that having a tan made you look good, no matter how you felt underneath. I always kept a tan after that.'

As the *Olympic* serenely approached New York, one of Archie's first sights, following a sleepless night for fear of missing his first glimpse of America, was the imposing Woolworth building. He would not have believed it if someone had told him, there and then, that one day he would marry the heiress to the Woolworth fortune. But that's exactly what would happen – one day.

New York had already established itself as one of the most thrilling cities in the world, and, to this strapping sixteen-year-old boy from Bristol, England, it wasn't about to disappoint.

Ten months later, in May 1921, another young Englishman, and Archie Leach's hero, was to make the same journey across the Atlantic, this time on the *Aquitania*. This was Noel Coward and, like Archie, he was eventually revered across the 'New World'. Coward, who had already established himself in British theatrical society, had been seduced by what he'd heard of New York and was determined to see his name in lights out there: 'Its gigantic sky-signs dazzled my dreams,' he later wrote, 'flashing with unfailing regularity the two words "Noel Coward".'

As Coward's biographer, Philip Hoare, wrote: 'In the post-war world, America promised fame and fortune and romance and Coward hoped to experience all three.' This would be a hope undoubtedly shared by Archie Leach.

To Englishmen – even someone like Coward who lived in London and frequented the West End – the sheer unrelenting energy of New York was mind-blowing and, in later years, Grant and Coward would compare their first impressions of the city in the early 1920s. New York never stopped. Everywhere, there were people rushing around: cars, trams and trains; rolling streams of humanity searching individually and in packs for that much-promised success. All it took was guts and hard work. It creates, in the mind's eye, a modern-day prospecting site, where hordes arrived with the dream of finding vast, untapped riches. Coward recalled crossing Times Square, 'the very hub of Broadway. It was just at the time in the early evening when the famous lights were being switched on and it took away what breath I had left…'

Grant agreed with this, and once remarked about his own first impressions of New York, that 'the first thing I loved about America, was how fast it all seemed.' From the first moment he stepped onto American soil, Archie felt at home. England and Bristol, with its painful memories of a disaffected, unspectacular childhood, was literally an ocean away from his new life – new beginning – in New York. What a place and opportunity to re-invent oneself.

The blistering heat of a New York summer – a heat that those who could, escaped – delighted Archie. He had always loathed the cold of Bristol and the dankness of the family home whose only source of warmth was from inadequate bedroom fires. He once said that one of his overriding childhood memories was the way the cold would penetrate him to the bone and that he had long dreamt of staying somewhere that remained warm for the whole year round. He was half-way to realising that dream. The full realisation would come in California and he grew quickly to love the West Coast climate. He later cited the climate as one of the main reasons for his putting down roots in America (he became an American citizen in 1942). Certainly, as a sun-worshipper, once settled in California, his skin developed the walnut complexion it was to maintain for the rest of his life and would add to his 'star' image – as with Fairbanks Snr before him.

There is a certain irony that Archie, as part of Bob Pender's troupe in New York, was back working at a Hippodrome. But this Hippodrome was on Sixth Avenue, between 43rd and 44th Streets. If Archie needed any reminding of the size of this huge continent, the Hippodrome provided it: it was vast and, with a seating capacity of ten thousand, the largest theatre in the world.

The show they were in, *Good Times*, was a great success and ran for 455 performances. At the end of the run, it was obvious to Pender that Archie, along with a couple of others from the troupe, had no intention of returning to England. Archie was particularly vociferous on this point, and no persuasion from Pender, or his wife, could sway him. His mind was made up.

Pender understood Archie well enough by now to know that further argument was futile. He later remarked in a letter to Elias Leach, explaining the situation, that Archie needed money, spent money and wanted to lead an expensive glamorous life. Whether this fell on deaf ears one can only speculate, but it is the kind of dream, had circumstances been different, that would undoubtedly have appealed to Elias himself.

In a generous gesture – surely not the first – Pender gave Archie and the others who wished to remain behind the cash-equivalent of their fare home. But from now on they would be on their own. It was the summer of 1922. Archie Leach was eighteen, alone in a new continent he desperately wanted to adopt as his home, and looking for a 'goldmine' along with the millions of other 'prospectors'.

3

'Everybody wants to be Cary Grant. Even *I* want to be Cary Grant.'

Cary Grant

By electing to stay in New York, Archie had taken hold of his own destiny boldly, but he appears to have had few definite career plans beyond trying his hand in the USA. If the acrobatic work had not really interested him, other than as a means to an end, this was the period during which he would really knuckle down to make that end. It is the era when his pragmatism – a word that became synonymous with Grant – and sheer motivation and guts would make the impossible possible.

However, for the next five years, he struggled to bring any kind of structure to his working life. 'Before I made my way to some measure of success,' Grant recollected, 'I had many tough times, but I was always lucky.'

It was his luck that somehow always kept him from starving and, when his big break finally came, meant that he was in the right place at the right time.

Nevertheless, the search for vaudeville work in the first months after Pender's troupe had returned to England was endless and frustrating.

'If I hadn't been badgered, cajoled, dared, bullied and helped into walking those high stilts when I was a boy in the Pender troupe,' he recalled of this time, 'I might have starved that summer – or gone back to Bristol.'

Some of Archie's jobs in these first months and years in America can hardly be described as vaudevillian bookings at all. One job had him back on stilts as an elongated living advert. He could be seen striding back and forth across the entrance of Steeplechase Park, which was owned by George Tilyew and situated on Coney Island.

At some point, he met up with a couple of other former Pender employees. Whether they were the original ones he had worked with or, by pure coincidence, were former Pender men who had happened to settle out there, is not altogether clear. The former is more likely, as the mutual struggle they all must have experienced on their separation from Bob Pender would, quite probably, have driven them along the same tracks.

Archie and his former colleagues perfected a vaudeville act that they could perform at the Hippodrome, back in New York. The act was successful enough for them to tour it along the West Coast – where Archie fell in love with the Californian climate – and even across the border into Canada.

But by 1927, aged twenty-three, Archie came to realise that his striving to find employment in vaudeville was leading him nowhere and he returned to New York determined to become a legitimate actor. This was not as presumptuous as it might seem. Even though he had worked primarily as a vaudevillian, Archie had met enough actors by now to know his way around the profession.

Where Archie was fortunate – and always would be, even when a star – was in his appearance. Although he had always been attractive as a boy and as a man, Archie's features and one-time lanky body had suddenly matured. He was now exceptional – instantly noticeable, and unlikely to be forgotten in a crowd of faces trying to get on the road to stardom. The looks were coupled with a natural charm – almost a mischievousness – a combination that opened many otherwise closed doors.

Furthermore, his looks ensured that, despite being a virtual nonentity in the world of show business, he was invited to any number of exclusive parties. This gave him the opportunity to introduce himself to theatrical movers and shakers of 1920s Broadway – and even impose all six foot one inch of himself upon them.

Archie's sex life at this point remains shrouded in some mystery, but there's no doubt that this superbly handsome, charming young Englishman was compellingly attractive to New York women of varying ages. And if he was a little diffident... well, maybe that just made him all the more attractive.

Though nothing has ever been proved, it is possible he was assumed to be gay by those directors and producers of a similar nature. If so, it is possible that the persistent rumours about his being gay – which dogged him in later years, and which he denied with increasing weariness – originated at this time, only to be fuelled later in Hollywood.

Archie's decision to return to New York was vindicated when he was introduced to Reggie Hammerstein, brother to Oscar Hammerstein II. Oscar, one of the greatest lyricists of all time, was then collaborating with Jerome Kern and was to go on to even greater glories with Richard Rodgers. But it is easy to forget now that Oscar and Reggie came from a very important theatrical family: their grandfather, Oscar Hammerstein I, having made a fortune in industry, was one of New York's leading impresarios and founder of the Manhattan Opera; their father, William, was manager of New York's Victoria theatre; and their uncle, Arthur, was a Broadway producer.

Archie's introduction to Reggie was, therefore, a lucky chance to say the least. Better yet, Reggie introduced Archie to his uncle, Arthur, who promptly gave Archie an audition.

When he left Bob Pender's acrobat troupe, Archie hadn't uttered a single line on stage – although he had, of course, appeared in front of many audiences – and he had never had a formal acting lesson in his life. (Nor did he; and he remained forever sceptical about the merits of supposedly 'learning' to do something which was, as he saw it, a natural talent one either had or did not have.)

At the audition, Arthur Hammerstein watched a raw talent go through its paces, as he had, no doubt, done on countless occasions before. Archie had enough stage presence coupled with good looks to convince Hammerstein to put him under contract.

Arthur Hammerstein specialised in operettas and so Archie had a good idea where his immediate employment was likely to be concentrated. Being a man who always possessed an excellent sense of humour, he must have found the notion of acrobat becoming operatic performer highly amusing. But he was game for anything. He hurriedly took voice lessons and soon found himself cast in the minor role of an Australian prisoner of war in a production called *Golden Dawn*. It was a moderate success, running for 184 performances.

Hammerstein cast him next in the revival of the American farce *Polly With A Past*, written by Guy Bolton and George Middleton. Archie was cast in the role of Clay Collins – a role Noel Coward had played in the London production – which was, essentially, a 'feed' to the main stars.

Archie didn't remain in the role for too long. Hammerstein replaced him before the show went on Broadway. He had concluded that the young actor's physical presence outweighed his vocal presence.

These were tough times for Archie Leach. The actress Leslie Caron recalled him telling her that during that era 'he was very poor and would sell ties out of a suitcase looking for the police. If he saw a cop, he would quickly close the case and run.'

However, not making it to Broadway proved only a minor setback. Marilyn Miller, a major Broadway star at that time, selected Archie to replace her leading man in her hit show *Rosalie.* To put himself in a position where he could accept this offer, he had, firstly, to persuade Hammerstein to release him from his contract. Hammerstein, not altogether thrilled by the idea, took some persuading, but agreed eventually, if reluctantly, and Archie's contract was picked up by Jacob J. Shubert. Assuming that Archie had done most of the persuading himself, it shows the great tenacity of the young man. Even without a definite goal, he continually displayed a drive that kept the graph of his career climbing upward.

The Shuberts – Jacob produced in partnership with his brother Lee – were arguably the most influential, if erratic, impresarios in New York, and it did Archie's reputation no harm at all to be taken up by them. Nor did co-starring in *Rosalie*.

With the unlikely combination of George Gershwin and Sigmund Romberg composing the score, *Rosalie*, which had opened at the New Amsterdam Theatre on Broadway in January 1928, could also boast lyrics by Ira Gershwin and P.G. Wodehouse. It was, by any measure, a formidable team and an indication of the strength of the score of *Rosalie* is that one of its songs written by the Gershwins: 'How Long Has This Been Going On?' was to become one of their future standards.

The show's book, written by William Anthony McGuire and Guy Bolton (who had co-written *Polly With A Past*), centred on the American obsession with pioneering aviators and was inspired by Charles Lindbergh, whose record-breaking flight to Paris in May 1927 was still fresh in the minds of the public. The association with Lindbergh's triumph boosted the box-office for *Rosalie*, and it ran on Broadway for nearly a year.

This show was the most expensive and prestigious production Archie had been involved with thus far and the role of Lieutenant Richard Fay, a West Point flyer who risks his life to fly across the

Atlantic to be with his true love, was a tremendous showcase for any talented young actor.

The role was certainly of its moment: by the time MGM made the film version in 1938, interest in aviation pioneers had waned and the hero, played by Nelson Eddy, was changed from a pilot to a college football hero! This MGM film also jettisoned the entire original score and substituted one written by Cole Porter, whom Cary Grant would later portray in *Night And Day* (1946).

A good run in *Rosalie*, followed by decent roles in subsequent Shubert productions, gave Archie a level of comfort unknown to him hitherto. He was hardly a star but he was not short of material comforts and was generally regarded as a competent stage performer with possibly great potential.

After a show in which he had been appearing for the Shuberts closed, Archie decided it was time to take a holiday. At least, that's what he told everyone. But his choice of destination was deliberate: Hollywood. Unknown to all but himself, this was more than just a break from New York, this was a scouting trip.

By now, the movies – thanks to *The Jazz Singer* (1927) – had sound and a revolution had taken place. Some stars' careers had literally been destroyed overnight by their inability to adapt to the studios' new demands. Even Douglas Fairbanks, one of the world's major silent stars when young Archie had encountered him aboard the *Olympic* in 1920, saw his star wane.

But if sound had destroyed, damaged and altered some careers, for others it began providing opportunities. And Archie, never slow off the mark, perhaps recalling nights at the picture house in Bristol with Elias, wondered – hoped – if his might be the right face in the right place at the right time.

How did Hollywood emerge as a film-making centre and still continue to exist as the centre of film-making nearly a century later? Nine years before Archie Leach was born, Frenchman Louis Lumière invented the motion picture camera (1895). His first film was of the arrival of an express train at Lyons station in central France. His cinematographes – something totally new in a world where the only mass entertainment was the theatre – soon captured the interest of the world. In April 1896 the first theatre in New York to take money for filmed entertainment opened – the most significant date in the beginnings of the film industry, according to screenwriter William

Goldman. As Goldman says, by 1910 'there were over nine *thousand* theatres in operation across the country'.

The demand for new product virtually assured that the early efforts being produced in Hollywood would transform that town into being the major centre of film industry in the world. The chief benefactor was Thomas Edison as the motion picture itself was his invention and he was paid a fee by all the major studios for the right to make films.

Producer and director D.W. Griffith was one of the industry's first moguls. David Wark Griffith, 1875–1948, helped to develop many of the basic techniques in film-making. He based himself in the then little-known Hollywood, primarily because of the opportunities afforded him through the consistency of the climate in that region: his ground-breaking epic *Birth of a Nation* (1915) signalled the real birth of the film industry as we know it.

Silent film shorts were the prevailing format in the burgeoning movie business for the next twenty years and were regarded as little more than a hobby: certainly making movies was not the huge industry it rapidly became. From 1910, the films grew marginally longer to cater for increasingly well-structured plots. By then, when Archie was just starting at school, Chaplin had arrived and was making such silent shorts to increasingly great acclaim. In 1927, sound arrived. Although Chaplin opted to stay with the silent film for a few more years, he was the only big film-maker to succeed in a medium that was soon considered dead.

As well as the coming of sound, the other burning issue of the time was the censorship struggle. In 1922, the film industry attempted self-regulation, which brought the Presbyterian and former Postmaster General, Will Hays, into the argument. The Hays Office persuaded studios to insert 'morality clauses' into their contracts for actors and actresses. The clean-up was slow and it could be fairly argued that it still remains a grey area nearly one hundred years on.

The scientist Albert Einstein, besides directing his talents to the construction of the nuclear bomb, also developed the idea of film editing and montage. D.W. Griffith embraced this discovery and was the first to use parallel editing in a film.

When Archie Leach arrived in America to begin what would be his new life, the big American studios had already started to form: Paramount Pictures (1912), Columbia Pictures (1920), Warner Brothers (1923), Metro-Goldwyn-Mayer (1924) and, a little later, 20th-

Century Fox (1935). The great irony about the bastions of the film industry – and very in-keeping with the American dream – is that they were virtually all founded by German-Jewish immigrants, or their descendants. For example, William Fox of 20th-Century Fox, was actually Wilhelm Fried. All but RKO were founded by immigrants, or first-generation Americans.

These vast studios, which re-created Hollywood from a hick village into a world-renowned centre for film-making, used big stars, taken under binding contracts, to churn out film after film. This was the reason why Cary Grant would make so many films in his early career: twenty-five per cent of his entire output was produced in the three years between 1932 and 1935. Stars were not free to seek their own contracts during this era – which is interesting in relation to the stance that Grant eventually took – and often these stars would be loaned out by one studio to another. Essentially, the studio controlled the star and not vice versa.

It is impossible, at this juncture, not to mention the studio system's greatest advocate, and the film industry's recognised *wunderkind*, Irving G. Thalberg. He was born in New York City in May 1899 and he was barely twenty-one when he was reorganising Universal's Hollywood studios. Thalberg was an icon of Hollywood, admired and respected by everyone with whom he came into contact, even the Marx Brothers, although they went out of their way to give him a hard time, including stripping off all their clothes and warming themselves by a fire on the floor of his office!

At MGM, Thalberg worked directly for Louis B. Mayer, and is largely credited for establishing the studio with a string of successes. His greatest gift was being able to get the best out of all who worked with him, and always seeming to back a winning film.

Sadly, Thalberg had been born with a very weak constitution, and the film business wasn't the place to offer it gentle nourishment. He died in 1936, while in pre-production of the Marx Brothers movie *A Day At The Races*, a legend who departed this life a mere thirty-seven years of age. Like Dan Leno, Thalberg had paid a heavy price for success in the entertainment business and such salutary lessons were not lost on Cary Grant even in these embryonic years of his stardom.

Hollywood – a place that had such an effect on the imagination of the public that people would sell up their houses and move there just to inhale the same air as the 'stars'. Many hoped they would be 'spotted' by a producer or director. It sometimes happened, as in the case of Rock Hudson to name but one but inevitably most returned home, dreams dashed.

One of the most cynical insights of 1930s Hollywood came from Joe Adamson and is worth relating as, beneath the acerbic wit, there is more than a grain of truth:

Hollywood in 1931, before civilization, pollution, and inhibition set in together, was a mad town, mad in its extraordinary ability to inflate all the most limited concerns into the unlimited obsessions; mad in its freedom from taboos, so that everybody could be liberated enough to imitate everybody else; mad in its exorbitant outgrowths of piddly thoughts. Los Angeles has always been famous because whatever it displayed, it displayed it prodigiously, just as it now displays the industrialist's disrespect for the balance of nature prodigiously.

Don't ever let anyone tell you that Hollywood is anything but a land of make-believe, where pink clouds billow, fairies dance, and the sun always shines. Because that part about the fairies is true. The film industry itself is no more crass or commercialized than, say, the insurance business or the plumbing-goods trade. The fact that the studio czars resisted anything out of the ordinary in their relentless drive for homogenized entertainment, or that they couldn't regard the screen as one huge canvas because they regarded the audience as an overgrown Kansas, is circumstantial evidence...

While with the Shuberts, Archie Leach had been screen-tested by Paramount at their East Coast studio in Astoria, New York, even before his scouting trip to Hollywood. This had come to nothing as his first screen test report read: 'Good-looking. Neck too thick. No chance at all.' But in 1931, having returned to New York from Hollywood, he got another bite at the apple with Paramount when talent scouts from the West Coast spotted him in a Broadway play called *The Last Flight*. They offered him a small part as a brash young sailor in a ten-minute one-reeler called *Singapore Sue* (1932), which, again, was shot at Paramount's studio in Astoria, New York. He was paid $15 for his work on the film.

Singapore Sue was an inauspicious screen debut for the future Cary Grant and it was perhaps as well that he was credited as Archie Leach.

Seventy years on, the film is faintly embarrassing and Archie Leach is not so much stiff as arboreal. In fairness, though, the film's rudimentary production values – primitive even for 1931 – and abysmal script hardly helped and none of Grant's fellow performers, including Anna Chang and Millard Mitchell, fared any better. Mitchell, playing one of Leach's fellow sailors, went on to become a dependable character actor in the 1940s and 1950s and is perhaps best known for his role as the studio boss in *Singin' In The Rain* (1952), the musical film that starred Gene Kelly.

But Archie remained undeterred. Indeed, the experience encouraged him to explore further movie opportunities. But he knew that success in the movies was not guaranteed and certainly wouldn't come overnight. Shrewdly, then, he developed a two-track career: consolidating and developing his Broadway experience, while slipping in and out of Hollywood between theatre jobs to get himself known to the studios.

His strategy worked, although it was probably inevitable anyway that Archie Leach, who had a good Broadway pedigree by now, would be noticed. He was introduced to Marion Gering, a Polish-Russian director with extensive stage experience, who had emigrated to the USA in 1925 and was now working for Paramount.

Following a recommendation by Gering, Paramount agreed to screen-test Archie Leach again. Paramount liked what they saw this time and offered Archie a contract at $450 a week. He needed no encouragement, and signed the contract and moved to Hollywood without delay. There was one condition of his contract, however: the name Archie Leach had to go. No one at the studio who mattered, seemed to care for it – which is hardly surprising – and Archie didn't demur.

He readily discussed alternatives with Paramount for, as top man Adolph Zukor put it, 'Archibald Leach just isn't something you can put up outside a cinema.' Archie came up with the name Cary Lockwood: it held fond memories to him, for it was the name of the character he had played in John Monk Saunders' play *Nikki* in New York and the Cary part particularly appealed.

It is interesting to note in passing that the name Cary crops up in the names of several towns in the southwest of England (such as Castle Cary). Though possibly coincidental, as his first name is linked to a character he played, it might account for why the name should have appealed so greatly to him.

However, Paramount informed Archie that Lockwood was out: it was already taken (by Harold Lockwood). The studio provided a short-list of potential surnames, it generally being accepted that the Cary part was fine. The one that apparently jumped out at Archie was 'Grant'. Short names were very much in vogue and, more than that, it sounded American and could be pronounced in an American accent.

And so, Archie Leach was re-born as Cary Grant on 7 December 1931.

Grant was to find living behind a mask – indeed a complete invention, because with Paramount he had developed a new style of character with the new name – perplexing.

'If I couldn't see clearly out,' he said, 'how could anyone see in?'

It would be many years, virtually his lifetime in fact, before he could begin to separate the two identities of Archie Leach and Cary Grant and there are those who believe he never quite reconciled himself to this self-determined schizophrenia.

'I've spent the greater part of my life fluctuating between Archie Leach and Cary Grant,' he once said towards the end of his life. 'Unsure of either, suspecting each. Only recently have I begun to unify them into one person: the man and the boy in me; the hate and the love and all the degrees of each in me; and the power of God in me.'

Of course, Grant wasn't the first or last movie star to be left with feelings of confused identity after the studios got hold of them and redefined who and what they were. In his autobiography, Tony Curtis, a huge admirer and friend of Grant and later his co-star in *Operation Petticoat* (1959), recalled his difficulty in getting used to changing his name.

Curtis initially changed his name from Bernie Schwartz to Anthony Curtis. Then a girl shouted at him from across the street 'Tony of the movies!', an expression he loved, so he abbreviated the Anthony. But he continually had to remind himself he was Tony Curtis and not Bernie Schwartz.

'Not long after I changed it,' he wrote, 'I was at a cocktail party with Janet Leigh, and there was Cary Grant, my idol. Janet said, "Come on, we'll go over and meet him." So I went over to meet him and I was so nervous. I said, "Hi, my name is...Bernie Schwartz..."'

In his biography of James Mason, *Odd Man Out*, Sheridan Morley wrote: 'The most successful of the Californian British ceased to be particularly or noticeably British at all. Cary Grant and Elizabeth

Taylor as often as not played Americans, while one of the most triumphant of all the Hollywood Raj in terms of longevity and commercial profit virtually never appeared on-screen as anything but American: Bob Hope.'

If Grant wrestled internally with questions of identity, he had a pretty shrewd idea of what he had to project externally if he was to be successful in Hollywood. He knew Cary Grant had to be glamorous and masculine in a groomed, well-tailored way. And he must be international. Grant had no interest in being pigeon-holed as the guy from England who played only effete Lord of the Manor roles.

Later generations of British-born international superstars would get away with regional accents: Sean Connery can get away with playing characters from anywhere in the world with an Edinburgh burr, while all Michael Caine's characters have more than a lingering hint of Bermondsey. But an English accent in Hollywood in the 1930s was liable to limit an actor to playing either the villain or the buffoon. Basil Rathbone – his hugely popular Sherlock Holmes series for Universal notwithstanding – was Tinseltown's favourite villain *because* he was British, while C. Aubrey Smith had cornered the market in stereotyped crusty colonels. When Nigel Bruce wasn't playing Watson to Rathbone's Holmes (and playing him as a buffoon) he was playing a similar role in other films, including *Suspicion* with Cary Grant.

It could be argued that Laurence Olivier didn't change his accent to find Hollywood success, but then he played Englishmen in his biggest box-office successes: *Wuthering Heights, Rebecca* and *Pride and Prejudice*. Besides, Olivier came to Hollywood already an established star. Grant was far from that as yet and all the evidence suggested that the way he sounded would limit his potential.

To avoid that, Grant believed his accent had to change along with his name: 'I still spoke English English,' he said, 'and I knew that to get jobs I'd have to learn American English.' This, of course, was probably not hard work to a man who, since separating from Pender, had lived and breathed the American accent in its various forms. Add to that the actor in him, and the challenge of creating something he would maintain for life possibly took him no longer than a couple of days' hard work.

There was, however, more than just American in Grant's accent. His voice developed into a curious but appealing hybrid of American and English. On top of that was a little of his West Country upbringing and the various accents, chiefly cockney, he had come into contact with during his Pender days – enough to defy forever anyone to identify it. Not even Professor Henry Higgins could have placed Cary Grant's accent. Indeed, Grant's carefully crafted accent became so much a part of the persona he created for himself that there would be those in later years who were amazed to learn he came from England.

The character of Cary Grant, manufactured by himself and the studio, was a part he was to play on-screen and off for the rest of his long life. There's no doubt that Grant is a gentleman, yet he remains, essentially, classless. He is a man not so enmeshed in his past as one excited about his future: indeed, he rarely seems to have a past – or, if he has, it is one he rarely thinks about – and this gives Grant an ambiguity that audiences have always found compelling. Who is he, this man? Is he just, as he appears on the surface, a sophisticate in search of a better, a more fulfilling life? Or is there something more? A hint of selfishness, perhaps? A touch of the caddish? Something more sinister, even? Where did he come from? Apparently, nowhere.

As Grant grew in stature as a screen actor, these subtextual nuances became more subtle and assured and were exploited fully by directors – particularly Alfred Hitchcock in *Suspicion* (1941) and *Notorious* (1946), and by Stanley Donen in *Charade* (1963) – to leave a question mark over Grant's character. It lets them tease the audience with the question: is this man who he seems to be saying he is? Grant was great at ambiguity and these were the roles he played best: but then as Grant himself never seemed to establish who he really was in his own mind, it was a role he played full-time anyway.

'I pretended to be a certain kind of man on screen,' Grant told an interviewer, 'and I became that man in life. I became me.'

Richard Schickel wrote: 'But if Grant... never himself seemed to summon up the magic, if he always let it happen in the eye of the beholder, his scripts and his directors were encouraged to enhance it...'

Audiences embraced Cary Grant because he crossed all barriers. Overtly debonair, he might be, but he always gave the sense that he really preferred blue-collar company. Grant wasn't a snob and didn't kowtow to the elite; yet he could blend in effortlessly among the higher social echelon when the occasion arose. Essentially, he projected the image of a gentleman traveller seeking his moment; a man who could mix with all types without being partisan or judgemental; a chameleon who piqued your curiosity.

Grant's screen persona was, however, undoubtedly that of the good-looking, quick-witted, urbane sophisticate, oozing *savoir-faire*. Given that America was still recovering from, and haunted by, memories of the Depression, one might have expected American audiences in particular to have resented and loathed his image. But they didn't, as Graham McCann observed: 'They seemed to adore Grant. They did so because he represented a certain type of gentleman, a Hollywood gentleman who had the common touch. The Hollywood movies of the time tended to reflect certain ideas about elegance and luxury. The Hollywood gentleman was pictured as a breed apart: he played among the privileged without himself symbolising privilege; he lived with them but remained one of us.'

One columnist, writing about Grant as his Hollywood career began to take off, wrote: 'Cary Grant is a new and very important symbol. He is an Englishman but far removed from Ronald Colman and Leslie Howard, representative of a new type of Englishman on whom the influence of American civilization has been very strong...'

Every man is the sum of his experiences, and Cary Grant couldn't kill off Archie Leach in the literal sense. Archie was always at the core, as Graham McCann suggested: 'Cary Grant was not conceived as the contradiction of Archie Leach, but rather as the constitution of his desires. If Cary Grant succeeded, Archie Leach, more than anyone else, more than any other influence or ingredient, would be responsible. Cary Grant would always appreciate that fact.'

Grant internalised any conflicts between his true self and his actor self and always maintained an urbane self-confidence to outsiders. If Cary Grant was a mask, it was, at least, a marketable and increasingly successful one.

In his first year with Paramount – 1932 – he made seven films, in itself one-tenth of the total number of films he would make. His debut as a screen actor was *This is the Night*, starring Lily Damita. In his fourth outing, he found himself acting alongside the notorious Tallulah Bankhead, in *The Devil and the Deep*. Bankhead, who was born in Huntsville, Alabama on 31 January 1903, was *the* live-wire of the era. With quotes such as: 'I'll come up and make love to you at five o'clock. If I'm late, start without me,' she wasn't easy to ignore. She had embarked upon a very successful stage career at the age of fifteen. Over the years, she moved to New York then to London, developing quite a reputation as a hard-boozing, chain-smoking party-animal. Some of the parties she threw literally went on for days and days. Guests were encouraged to bring their pyjamas! Her swansong was her appearance as the Black Widow in the sixties television series, *Batman*.

On Grant's fifth outing, he played alongside Marlene Dietrich in *Blonde Venus*, with the leading director, Josef von Sternberg, at the helm. Marlene Dietrich was born Maria Magdalene Dietrich on 27 December 1901. She abridged her first names and in 1921 auditioned for the Max Reinhardt Drama School, where she took bit parts during 1922. She always credited Josef von Sternberg for 'discovering' her, as he contracted her to star in *The Blue Angel* (1930). She made a six-movie deal with Paramount, all of these pictures, except one, being directed by von Sternberg.

Josef von Sternberg was an Austrian-American, born in 1894 in Vienna. During the First World War, he served in the US Signal Corps, where he used his talent to make training films. In the early twenties, he came to America and settled in Hollywood, where he could pursue his love of film-making. He joined Paramount in 1927, and remained with them for eight years.

This appearance with the proven team of Dietrich and von Sternberg was a big moment in the development of Cary Grant's career, as through this association he started to be noticed. It was also von Sternberg who would do something very simple yet fundamental to the final metamorphosis of Leach into Grant: he very carefully brushed the actor's hair to alter his parting from a right-to-left to a left-to-right. It would remain that way always.

Although *Blonde Venus* was a major release, using top-drawer talent both in front of and behind the camera, it was a dreary, fragmented melodrama about a German café singer who marries an English research chemist. One critic said, 'The story has all the dramatic integrity of a sashweight murderer's tabloid autobiography.'

Nevertheless, Grant had good reason to be quietly satisfied with his first year at Paramount. The seven films had hardly stretched him as an actor and none of them was a masterpiece. But he'd worked hard and become comfortable performing in front of camera. He had also made new influential friends. He had no reason to believe that his contract would not be renewed.

Adolph Zukor, the Hungarian-born cinema pioneer who was then head of Paramount Studios, had other ideas. While reasonably satisfied with Grant's work, he wasn't particularly ecstatic about it and was ambivalent about keeping Grant on. But he reckoned without Cary Grant's lucky streak, which now ensured he was spotted – quite literally – by one of the most important women ever to appear in his life. She was to be the catalyst that finally made him a star.

She was Mae West.

4

'When I'm good I'm very good – and when I'm bad, I'm better.'

Mae West (*She Done Him Wrong,* 1933)

There was something entirely appropriate in Mae West's making Cary Grant a star. For, as Robert Osborne, an LA columnist says, she was every bit her own creation as he was:

I'm not sure there was a real Mae West. Whatever the five-year-old girl skipping along streets was before she invented this character she became, I'm not sure she existed anymore. I think Mae West became Mae West as Cary Grant totally became Cary Grant. He grew into that role because he played it so well and so often. That's what happened with Mae West.

West, the mistress of innuendo, would have shot herself rather than reveal her true age. But most film historians agree she was born Mary Jane West on 17 August 1893 in Brooklyn, where her father, John Patrick West – whose fiery temper led to his being known as 'Battling Jack' – kept a livery stable.

John West and his wife, Matilda, had two other children, but it was Mary Jane on whom Matilda doted. The very essence of the pushy stage mother, Matilda instilled into her daughter that she was made for the stage. She got young Mae into child roles in stock productions in Brooklyn and Queens and always did her best to make sure she was the centre of attention.

Matilda's determination rubbed off on Mae West, who soon came to believe in herself every bit as much as her mother did. From an early age, West was uncompromising. She worked hard in vaudeville throughout her childhood and early teens and was married at seventeen, though it was to be a short-lived affair.

She began to realise that to stand out she had to re-invent herself. Experimenting with her appearance, she dyed her hair red and then blonde. She also made her act more risqué, sensing that it would be a way to find her audience.

By 1911, she was on Broadway getting rave revues. In 1913, her act had grown so outrageous that the censors were scandalised – and the public loved her for it. The more the censors complained, the further West went. As one of her later publicists would recall, 'Mae didn't care what she did and what she said. And the audience was always a little bit titillated and slightly shocked by it, but they always laughed.'

But it was after the First World War and the 1920s world of prohibition and speakeasies in particular, that Mae West developed into an American phenomenon. If US moral guardians argued that unrestrained sex and booze were the greatest threat to the nation, Mae West was the personification of both, even if she was, in private, virtually teetotal.

In 1926, West wrote a play called, simply, *Sex* and she wrote it under the pseudonym of Jane Mast. A comedy drama, *Sex* was a massive box-office hit despite the refusal of the New York papers to carry ads for it because they balked at printing the title.

Urged on by the censors, the NYPD raided the theatre and closed the play for three days. Mae West was arrested on a charge of indecency and put in jail for ten days. And there she lived like a princess. The warden and his wife took her out to dinner every night and West would later claim that her spell in jail was the best week and a half of her life.

It was in 1928, and with her play *Diamond Lil* that West finally developed the character she was to play for the rest of her life: the wise-cracking bad girl with a heart of gold. The play consolidated her fame: *Diamond Lil* was a Broadway sensation and the must-see production of the season.

It was inevitable that West's success would be noticed by Hollywood and, in 1932, Adolph Zukor, head of Paramount Studios, ordered his executives to offer her a contract. When she met with Paramount's representative, West's first question was, 'How much does Adolph Zukor make?'

'Two hundred and fifty thousand dollars a year,' came the reply.

'Then I want two hundred and fifty-*one* thousand a year,' said West. 'I want to be the highest-paid person in this studio.'

Zukor was born in Hungary in 1873 and died in California in 1976, a remarkable 103 years of age. During his long life, he became a Hollywood legend. He put his entrepreneurial brain to good use when he decided to bring talent from the stage into his films. His clients included Mary Pickford, Douglas Fairbanks, Marion Davies and Gloria Swanson.

Mae West's first film at Zukor's Paramount Studios, was *Night After Night* with George Raft and Constance Cummings, but the film only comes alive when she is on-screen (her famous line 'goodness had nothing to do with it' comes from this movie) and she was the one who ensured it was a major box-office hit.

West chose as her next picture an adaptation of *Diamond Lil*. She wrote the screenplay herself, with help from Harry Thew and John Bright, and made only one concession to Paramount by agreeing to change the title to *She Done Him Wrong*. She not only had script approval, but also a major say in casting the movie. One day in 1933, while *She Done Him Wrong* was in pre-production, West was walking to her car with Zukor on the Paramount lot, when she spotted a tall young man.

'Who's the tall, dark, handsome gent?' she asked Zukor, nodding at Cary Grant.

'Just a bit player,' Zukor replied, somewhat ingenuously. 'His contract's about to expire.'

'If the guy can talk, he's my star,' West said.

Whatever his misgivings, Zukor had no option but to agree, albeit reluctantly. And this was the background to the meeting that would propel Cary Grant to a stardom that would even surpass Mae West's.

It was a most fortunate encounter, for as well as propelling Grant's career, *She Done Him Wrong* also reinforced Mae West's screen persona for millions of cinema-goers world-wide. It also proved the turning point for Paramount Studios who were – until the success of this picture – in dire financial straits.

She Done Him Wrong is set in the 'gay nineties'. Grant plays Captain Cummings (a typical uncompromising West double-entendre), an undercover cop who is after Lady Lou (West), a rough, tough woman who runs a Bowery saloon. As the late Leslie Halliwell, the doyen of British film historians, once wrote, *She Done Him Wrong* was, 'as near undiluted Mae West as Hollywood ever came: fast, funny, melodramatic and pretty sexy; also a very atmospheric and well-made movie.'

Grant was still undergoing a metamorphosis during the course of this film, so it is an embryonic Cary Grant – one still detaching itself from the solid clasp of Archie Leach – who fences verbally with West. If he seems subdued, maybe even a little nervous, in his scenes with her, it is because he was. In fact, he admitted years later that he had been somewhat intimidated by her reputation. He doubtless took comfort in knowing that most of the cast and crew were also scared of Mae West. It was her film – if his big break – and she called the shots.

They were also nervous about the film itself. West may have delighted in being provocative, but everyone else working on the picture knew it was potential dynamite. The Hays Office was by now beginning to flex its muscles, and the Hays Production Code, which propagated absurdities such as on-screen married couples having twin beds and characters keeping one foot on the floor while kissing, would scarcely approve of Mae West's screenplay crackling with outrageous double-entendres.

If Grant was anxious about working with West, he was equally as anxious about the material. He knew this was his most important film to date, and if the film proved too controversial, he might be tainted and, ultimately, damaged by it. It is difficult now to appreciate just how absurdly sensitive the censors could be then – and how deliberately provocative West's screenplay actually was. Seven decades on, *She Done Him Wrong* can still astonish in the way it delights in its own ambiguities and double-meanings, but in 1933 the movie was proof to many reactionaries of a terminal moral decline:

GRANT: You were wonderful tonight.
WEST: I'm always wonderful at night.
GRANT: Tonight you were especially good.
WEST: Well, when I'm good, I'm very good – and when I'm bad, I'm better.

Further evidence of how close to the wire the movie's screenplay actually got comes when one considers Mae West's famous catchphrase 'come up and see me sometime', which was to become her trademark.

As with James Cagney's supposed line 'you dirty rat' and Humphrey Bogart's 'play it again, Sam' and Grant's own 'Judy, Judy, Judy' – all misquotes – 'come up and see me sometime', which is also a misquote, was embraced by West. Ever the self-publicist, she would herself use the misquoted version, which had filtered into the public's consciousness, in subsequent stage appearances.

The actual line on which the misquote is based, from the movie *She Done Him Wrong*, is much more explicit. Grant, undercover cop, and West are at the bottom of her staircase.

> WEST: I always did like a man in uniform and that one fits you. Why don't you come up sometime and see me? I'm home every evening.
> GRANT: Yeah, but I'm busy every evening.
> WEST: Y'know, I've met your kind before. Why don't you come up sometime? Hmmm...?
> GRANT: Well, I...
> WEST: Don't be afraid. I won't tell.
> GRANT: But, er...
> WEST: Come up. I'll tell your fortune...

It may only be a question of semantics, but the shifting of the word 'sometime' renders the popular misquotation of the line much more innocuous than the line in West's script. West's emphasis is on 'come up' – which she repeats three times – and, coupled with the name of Grant's character, Cummings, her intention is undeniably sexual: bluntly, she is saying that if he can get an erection, she'd like him to visit her.

The misquote 'come up and see me sometime' shifts the emphasis, however subtly, away from that implication. No wonder Grant and the rest of the cast and crew on *She Done Him Wrong* were nervous, even if the star herself was gleefully unfazed.

But work on the film was not always fraught. Grant shared plenty of laughs with West. She was, apparently, impossible to dislike and, besides, had a thing for young Englishmen. Another who visited the set during production, Noel Coward, livened things up considerably.

Noel Coward, then arguably the world's most famous playwright and actor, had met Mae West before when he'd attended a performance of *Diamond Lil* in New York with Constance Collier and the impresario Charles Cochran. Afterwards, all three went backstage to meet West and Coward asked if she was writing another play.

'Sure I'm writ'n a noo play,' she told him.

'What's it about?' asked Coward.

'Wal, y'see, it's about this guy. He's a cocksucker, and...'

Constance Collier and Cochran were appalled but Coward remarked mildly, 'I've never heard a plot that began with such promise...'

Whatever misgivings Coward might have felt about West's carefully crafted vulgarity, there was always something he liked about her, as that remark suggests. Besides, Coward could scarcely claim the moral high ground. While Grant and West were working on the film, Paramount were also adapting Coward's most controversial play to date, *Design For Living*, for the screen.

So outrageous were the themes in *Design For Living* – bisexuality and sexual sharing – that Coward had had to circumvent the Lord Chamberlain's office which licensed plays in England (and which he knew would have rejected the play) by premiering it on Broadway. Even so, the *New York Times* thought it 'decadent' while another New York critic labelled it 'a disgusting, three-sided, erotic hotch-potch'.

Paramount's adaptation of *Design For Living* was rapid – it had only opened on Broadway in January 1933 – and its notoriety, like Mae West's play, convinced Zukor that it had box-office potential. But the amoral themes in it were too strong for the Production Code and the Legion of Decency and, in contrast to *She Done Him Wrong*, which was a pretty faithful screen version of *Diamond Lil*, the movie of *Design For Living* was emasculated. Its screen-writer, Ben Hecht, boasted that only one line from the original play remained in the film and jokily challenged Coward to 'see if you can find it'.

A publicity photograph of Grant, Coward and West taken on the set of *She Done Him Wrong* shows how Grant was still, at this point, an adjunct to the real stars. Coward and West only have eyes for each other, while Grant is standing somewhat superfluously looking on. And yet there is more than a hint of the themes of *Design For Living* in the photo. In the play – in which Coward performed with Alfred Lunt and Lynn Fontanne – the two male characters, Otto and Leo, both love the female lead, Gilda, and each other. In the photograph, West is between Coward and Grant. She is looking at Coward but Grant, her screen lover, is hovering. Was this meant to suggest that Mae West had her pick of the two men? As it was a publicity shot, the answer is a resounding 'yes' – albeit a tongue-in-cheek set-up by Paramount to neatly dovetail two of its premier films then in production.

If the analogy with *Design For Living* were to be applied a step further, the subtext could also suggest that there was something between Coward and Grant. There can be little doubt that Coward found Grant attractive. As Grant said of himself, 'I was tall, had black hair and white teeth, which I polished daily, I had all the semblance of what in those days was considered the leading man. I played in the kind of film where one was always polite and perfectly attired.' This was a role he was playing off-screen as well, and it made him irresistible to women – and, by implication, to gay men like Noel Coward.

Coward was already alleged to have had a fling with James Cagney and he was desperately attracted to Douglas Fairbanks Jnr (who politely rebuffed Coward's advances and, instead, became a lifelong friend) so there's no reason to doubt that he wouldn't have attempted to have an affair with Grant. This is conjecture, because we cannot, for sure, know how Grant stood on matters of sexuality. It's been a point of contention for years, despite the actor having married five times and enjoyed countless affairs with women.

It would have put Grant in a difficult position as he so admired Coward, even emulated him. Whatever happened between them – and there is no evidence that anything sexual *did* happen – it did nothing to sour relations. Grant and Coward were to remain friends until Coward's death from a heart attack in Jamaica in 1973.

Philip Hoare in his thorough biography *Noel Coward* repeats the theory that Coward's song 'Mad About The Boy', with its gay undertones, was written for James Cagney or as a serenade to Douglas Fairbanks Jnr. But he then makes a suggestion of his own: 'The song could also have been a comment on matinée idols who appeared heterosexual – not just Ivor Novello, but stars such as Valentino, Fred Astaire, Robert Taylor, Cary Grant and Errol Flynn.'

Was Grant gay? The question will now never be answered definitely. It's the wrong question anyway. Better to ask: 'Does it matter if Cary Grant was gay?' The answer to that, surely, is no. Knowing that Montgomery Clift or James Dean or Rock Hudson were gay does nothing to diminish our opinion of their work, while our knowledge of how their struggle to keep their orientation secret tormented them (Clift, in particular), somehow increases our admiration for them.

Admitting to homosexuality rightly no longer carries a stigma – except in Hollywood, which remains curiously nervous despite being run, allegedly, by a velvet mafia. Certainly, contemporary stars, such as

Tom Cruise and Richard Gere, have acted firmly and decisively to quash any suggestions that their orientation is anything but one hundred per cent heterosexual. Even Noel Coward, who was discreet but hardly closeted, ordered any mention of his being gay to be expunged from Sheridan Morley's 1969 biography of him. As Coward said, 'There are still a few old ladies in Worthing who don't know. I can't afford to offend their prejudice.'

Cary Grant joked that, when he once complained of being romantically linked by gossips with girls he had never actually met, he was told, 'It would be much worse if they printed that you were out with a different *boy* each night.' But, as his biographer Graham McCann noted caustically, 'the fact that a similar response was offered by Hollywood executives in 1995 when Hugh Grant was caught *in flagrante delicto* with the prostitute Divine Brown suggests that homophobia, in spite of the ubiquitous red ribbons sported at all Hollywood social occasions in the early 1990s, is still very real in the movie industry.'

So if Grant were gay, we can well understand his reluctance to admit it. The evidence that suggests that he was, however, is circumstantial and thin.

It is true that Grant had trouble in his relationships with women, which manifested itself in his seeming inability to totally commit himself to one person – or they to him. While this may possibly have its roots in some kind of sexual confusion, the more likely explanation is that he was wary of relationships because of his parents' disastrous marriage. He had witnessed both the rows between his parents and Elias's continual philandering. And when Elsie had walked out of his life without any explanation, it had surely planted the idea in his mind that, eventually, all women would walk out on him.

Grant's screen persona also muddied the issue. As a screen lover, he was curiously passive. Pauline Kael observed that he was 'the most publicly seduced male the world has ever known.' From the moment Mae West said 'You can be had' to Grant in *She Done Him Wrong*, time and again in his movies it is not he who is the sexual aggressor: often he is the victim of predatory women. His seeming passivity merely increased the fascination women had for him.

But the lingering rumours about Grant's alleged homosexuality refuse to die away. And, interestingly enough, some social historians insist that the first ever public use of the word 'gay' to refer to homosexuality was Grant's improvised line 'I just went *gay* all of a sudden' in *Bringing Up Baby.*

A film he made in 1935, *Sylvia Scarlett,* certainly did him no favours on the alleged homosexuality front. Grant's co-star in the film – which was directed by George Cukor, who was himself gay – was Katharine Hepburn, who once said, 'Everyone is called a homosexual in Hollywood.' Hepburn, whose on-screen persona was always somewhat ambiguous, played a girl pretending to be a man in order to escape from France. The ever absurd Legion of Decency condemned the film bitterly, attacking it for its coded homosexuality and a taint of lingering immorality clung to everyone involved for months afterwards.

The major piece of evidence that suggests Grant might have been gay has always been his close friendship with Randolph Scott, with whom he shared a house in Hollywood for a while. This domestic arrangement, which was, admittedly, somewhat unconventional, was probably a result of pragmatism rather than anything more intimate.

Grant, who was becoming less and less identifiable as an Englishman, deliberately avoided being pooled with the other ex-pats, or 'Hollywood Raj', living in the environs of Los Angeles. They had notoriously, if inevitably, become a microcosm of British society, with all its class-divisions, chippiness and snobbery.

Grant, who wanted none of it, was drawn more towards Americans like Randolph Scott, whose rugged good looks and masculinity – exploited to the full in countless outdoor films – were the antithesis of the effete Brits in Tinseltown.

When Grant and Scott lived together, the studio publicity machines swung into action, pushing the image of Hollywood's two most eligible bachelors living together under one roof. Only later did the darker suggestions start to fly, with the columnist Edith Gwynn suggesting that the two young stars were 'carrying the buddy business a bit too far'. She also famously invented a game for her readers whereby each movie star could represent a movie title: as an example, she put forward Cary Grant as *One Way Passage.*

Whatever the truth, Cary Grant throughout his life demonstrated time and again a pragmatic streak. So it is entirely likely that, as a single man, he simply thought it practical to share a house with another male friend who was also single. Self-exiled from the Hollywood Raj, sharing with Scott had to be better than the unavoidable loneliness that was the alternative. To that, we can add that Grant was notoriously tight with money – a fact never denied by the actor – so sharing the cost of living with a fellow-actor would have appealed greatly to him. Furthermore, for a short while he and Noel Coward shared a place when Coward was in Hollywood, yet this is conveniently overlooked when the hacks went for him and Scott.

The fact is that two male actors sharing a house was not unknown in Hollywood. James Stewart and Henry Fonda also co-habited for a time, and they, too, would face the same innuendos experienced by Grant and Scott, as would British actors Michael Wilding and Stewart Granger, who shared a yacht for a while in Cannes.

The gossip writer Hedda Hopper, convinced that Wilding and Granger had been lovers, told David Niven, 'I *know* what went on aboard that yacht.'

'So do I,' replied Niven. 'And it's a miracle the population of France didn't double.'

If such actors were homosexual, how logical is it really that they would disguise the fact by openly moving in with each other!

Grant rarely lost his temper when tackled about his sexuality, no matter how irritated he was privately, and this suggests that he really did have nothing to hide. 'If someone wants to say I'm gay, what can I do?' he once told an interviewer. 'I think it's probably said about every man who's been known to do well with women. I don't let that sort of thing bother me. What matters to me is that *I* know who I am.'

Grant had always warned his family about the 'dreadful things' that would be written about him after his death and he was proved to be right when, in 1989, three years after his death, the lurid rumours about him reached their apogee. Not only were the stale allegations about his supposed relationship with Scott given another airing, but also Dyan Cannons – his fourth wife – claims that he beat her while under the influence of LSD. These claims were made under oath during their bitter custody battle in the mid-sixties. They were now reported as if new evidence of a darker life. But these allegations were overshadowed by others, some particularly vile. The most amusing was that he wore women's underwear – something Grant openly admitted to as 'they are so easy to pack and wash'. Less amusing was the claim that he had taken part in gay orgies and rape. Most distasteful of all was that he had once had an arrangement with a Los Angeles undertaker to have sex with any dead women brought in to the morgue. Rather odd considering Grant had the pick of all the best 'live' women! A little-known actor Michael

St John substantiated the stories about Grant's supposed visits to the morgue and newspapers reported his further claims that he had been trussed up on a meat hook at a Hollywood party and gang-raped by Grant and the other men present. Grant was no longer around to defend himself, and it was left to others to stand up for him.

'Michael St John's assertions are nonsense,' said one veteran columnist. 'There's not a scrap of evidence to back them up.'

The actor James Coburn agreed, especially over the accusations of his 'relationship' with Scott. 'Cary and Randolph Scott were great friends,' he said, 'but there's no evidence they were lovers. I prefer *not* to believe vicious gossips out to make a fast buck.'

'When I was a young and popular star,' Grant once said, 'I'd meet a girl with a man and maybe she'd say something nice about me and the guy would say, "Yeah, but I hear he's really a fag." It's ridiculous but they say it about all of us. Now in fact, that guy is doing me a favour. Number one, he's expressed an insecurity about the girl. Number two, he's provoked curiosity about me in her. Number three, that girl *zeroes* in on my bed to see for herself, and the result is that the guy has created the exact situation he wanted to avoid.'

Cary Grant might have been many things, but he was never naive or stupid when it came to his public image, and if there is any remote truth in the allegations, then they are totally at odds with the image we know of the man – the image of a pragmatic person intent on behaving as the gentleman of his own creation.

Not surprisingly, Grant's fifth and final wife, Barbara Harris, was both furious and devastated by the unpleasant gossip, calling it 'a bunch of vicious lies'. Randolph Scott's widow, Patricia, went further: 'Barbara has told me these people are breaking her heart. But, like me, she is powerless to do anything about it. I hope they rot in hell.'

But it was Grant's beloved daughter, Jennifer, who was affected most by the rumours: 'I just lie awake at nights and cry,' she said. 'My father was a dear, sweet man.'

The only time Grant did strike back was, according to Graham McCann, in November 1980 when the comedian Chevy Chase remarked on the NBC *Tomorrow* show: 'Cary Grant was a great physical comic and I understand he was a homo. What a gal ... !'

Grant was reportedly, and uncharacteristically, furious. Quite why he reacted so angrily and publicly at this stage of his life – more than fourteen years after his last movie – is open to question, but react he certainly did. He issued a ten million dollar lawsuit, refuting the allegations as 'completely, totally and absolutely false' and insisting they had 'no basis whatsoever in fact'. Grant claimed he had been exposed to 'shame, ridicule and humiliation'. The lawsuit was settled out of court.

Possibly Grant reacted on this occasion because he was aware of getting older and he had seen how the memories of now deceased colleagues and contemporaries had been defiled posthumously. The situation gave him the chance to nail the matter while he was still around in person to do so.

But to his great credit, Grant rarely reacted when asked if he was gay, no matter how irritated he was privately, and, again, this suggests that he really did feel he had nothing to hide.

'If someone wants to say I'm gay, what can I do?' he once said. 'I can't control anyone's thoughts. I have enough trouble controlling my own.'

5

'The tough thing, the final thing, is to be yourself. That takes doing, and I should know. I used to be Noel Coward...'

Cary Grant

In Andrew Lloyd Webber's musical *Sunset Boulevard* (1993), based on Billy Wilder's classic movie, the faded silent-screen siren Norma Desmond recalled the birth of Hollywood with the lines:

We gave the world
New ways to dream.
Somehow we found
New ways to dream.

Norma Desmond was, of course, a fictional character, albeit based on several fifty-ish has-beens Wilder observed when writing the screenplay in 1950, but her assertions about Hollywood have the ring of authenticity. Supposedly Paramount's greatest star – 'Without me, there wouldn't be any Paramount Studio,' she says – Norma's assertion about movie pioneers teaching the world new ways to dream is spot on.

By the mid-1930s, Hollywood had changed how people all over the world spoke and dressed and ate and had altered forever the way non-communist populations viewed the world and interacted with those around them.

Just a quarter of a century after D.W. Griffith had made the first Hollywood film in 1910 in what was then the desert, the seven major Hollywood studios were booming with one, MGM, boasting it was turning out one feature film each week.

David Niven, another British ex-pat with whom Cary Grant was to share a long, if sometimes uneasy, friendship, recalled arriving in Hollywood at this time. Being driven round the back-lot of one studio, which spread over 200 acres, Niven saw 'the permanent sets, including New York streets, New England, French and Spanish villages, medieval castles, a railroad station complete with rolling stock...lakes with wave-making machines and rustic bridges, a university campus, an airliner, a section of jungle and another of pine forest, a Mississippi steamer, a three-masted schooner...a submarine, a stretch of desert with carefully dismantled streets, villages, cathedrals, mud huts, slums, southern plantations, and oriental palaces...'

Niven had discovered, as Grant had discovered, that Hollywood in the 1930s was an extraordinary place to be at an extraordinary time. For Grant, there would always be a passion for the back-lots, whatever the era. In the early 1960s the writer Michael Sellers, son of the legendary comic actor Peter Sellers, recalls Cary Grant taking 'great pleasure in driving my father and me around old Hollywood, telling us stories about the early days out there, and showing us the extent of the original MGM lot.' And the lots were highly necessary. Before the advent of easy, affordable air travel, films could rarely be made on location and so if a movie was set in, say, Dickensian London, all the props and sets needed to create an authentic image of that London were on hand without the need to move from the studio.

If the back-lots were an eye-popping microcosm of all history and experience, each studio itself resembled a 'mixture of the business district of a thriving small town and the maintenance area of a busy airport,' according to Niven, and was dominated by 'twenty or thirty towering, hangar-like, sound stages clustered together.'

The studios truly were, as Norma Desmond sings, huge Dream Factories. The studio system was in its heyday and the movie moguls reigned supreme. The positive spin put out by the studios was that anything was possible. But there was, inevitably, a downside: the star system tied actors to long contracts. These contracts could be very lucrative, but the strings attached were often frustrating and restricting.

The studios spent vast sums of money to sign established stars to long-term contracts and spent more money developing young unknowns who showed potential. The system offered protection and guaranteed employment to contracted actors but, in return, the studios expected absolute loyalty and if an actor, no matter how big a star, fell into disfavour, the studio could be ruthless. If, for example, an actor chose not to play a role for whatever reason, he would be suspended for the duration of filming – perhaps four months – then half that time again as further punishment. Then the entire period of perhaps six months was added to the end of the contract. Small wonder many actors came to resent their contracts and, feeling suffocated, rebelled. No matter how mink-lined it is, a prison is still a prison.

One of the major drawbacks for a contracted actor like Cary Grant was that he had very little say in the choice of roles he played. And the studios were thoroughly unadventurous. Once a performer had caught on, they would be assigned roles that would repeat their success. Paramount – perhaps with some justification – thought it had a pretty good idea of the sort of roles Cary Grant suited following *She Done Him Wrong*.

There was in fact some diversity in Grant's roles during the remainder of 1933, though the quality of the actual films varied enormously. The first film to be released after *She Done Him Wrong,* was an all-star adaptation of *Alice In Wonderland*. Theoretically, this should have been a sure-fire winner. In addition to Grant, who played the Mock Turtle, the cast included W.C. Fields as Humpty Dumpty and Gary Cooper as the White Knight. The film, alas, was an absurd and misguided project with all the famous actors hidden behind grotesque masks, which disguised them beyond all recognition.

The Eagle and the Hawk (1933) was a rather better film in which Grant co-starred with Frederic March and Carole Lombard. Set in France in 1918, Grant and March played two US Army pilots who loathed each other but enjoyed a typical Hollywood *rapprochement* by the final reel. The film was a good showcase for Grant and he had, in March and Lombard, two excellent co-stars. March, who had won an Oscar the previous year for Paramount's marvellous adaptation of *Dr. Jekyll and Mr. Hyde,* was one of America's most respected stage and screen actors, while Lombard – the third Mrs Clark Gable – was one of Hollywood's most versatile and gifted leading ladies, whose career was cut tragically short in a fatal plane crash in 1942.

Gambling Ship and *Woman Accused* did not match the quality of *The Eagle and the Hawk*. *Gambling Ship* was a potboiler, easily forgotten, while *Woman Accused*, a yarn about a woman (Nancy Carroll) who kills her ex-lover in a quarrel and goes on the run, was based on a magazine serial written by ten authors who had contributed a chapter each. The movie was as disjointed and episodic as might be expected from such a hotch-potch set-up.

If Grant felt any concern or disappointment his last film for

Paramount in 1933 must have raised his spirits enormously. *I'm No Angel* was his most fascinating role since *She Done Him Wrong* and this was appropriate since it once again teamed him with Mae West.

It would be wrong to believe that Hollywood playing safe by making sequels is a modern phenomenon: the major studios have tried to replicate proven success since the movies began. *She Done Him Wrong* had proved a smash hit and Adolph Zukor was determined to consolidate Mae West's obvious box-office appeal as quickly as possible. He threw everything into West's next production – originally entitled *It Ain't No Sin* – and, for good measure, insisted that Grant be in the picture as well. Zukor had good reason to play safe: *She Done Him Wrong* notwithstanding, Paramount had not enjoyed many successes recently and the studio was still suffering financially. Zukor desperately needed another hit.

Although Grant was actually billed third behind West and Edward Arnold, he is even more impressive and much more assured in *I'm No Angel*. He certainly no longer seems wary of West in their scenes together: the four films he had made, virtually back-to-back since last starring with her, had given him increasing screen presence and confidence.

If *She Done Him Wrong* was pure Mae West in that it was an excellent transfer of her 'Diamond Lil' stage persona onto the movie screen, *I'm No Angel* vies with it as West's best picture. With a laugh-a-minute script containing some of West's most ribald quips, the actual plot – all about a carnival dancer who gets off a murder charge and elbows her way into society – plays second fiddle to the sheer outrageousness of it all.

Paramount did everything in its power to promote the film. No one who had spent some time walking around on stilts to advertise a theme park on Coney Island could be surprised by the lengths the movie publicity departments would go, but, even so, Grant was amused by Paramount's parrots employed to push Mae West's latest picture.

The studio bought one hundred and fifty parrots while the film was still called *It Ain't No Sin*, and they were trained to imitate Mae West saying the film's title over and over again. The idea was to place the parrots in movie theatres and other public places at the time the film opened.

The parrots were duly trained and prepared for despatch when the Hays Office objected to the film's title. It was, they thought, too suggestive. Paramount had to change the title to *I'm No Angel*, and the parrots were given a crash course in the new title. All to no avail as the birds, confused, squawked out a succession of unintelligible sounds when placed in the various movie theatres and had to be hastily retrieved.

But the film – with or without parrots – was a smash hit. It is understandable that some writers claimed that Mae West had single-handedly rescued Paramount Studios from the brink of disaster with this one picture. It is certainly true that Zukor could breathe a sigh of relief when the coffers began filling.

The title of the movie was not the only casualty of the Hays Office. *I'm No Angel* proved to be the last hurrah of the unadulterated Mae West. After this film, she would be forced to tone down her act and, as Leslie Halliwell observed, this reduced her to 'the status of family entertainer,' which wasn't what the public expected or wanted from her. She went on to make the occasional amusing picture – such as *My Little Chickadee* with W.C. Fields, a film she never really wanted to do, but West had had her movie glory days.

It is interesting for Grant fans that he should have co-starred in both her massive successes. She had made him a star but he, ultimately, was to eclipse her. After *I'm No Angel* West made just seven more films in a ten-year period and then was not seen on the screen again until her grotesquely fascinating comeback in *Myra Breckinridge* (1970) and her appalling swansong, *Sextette* (1977). Not that quantity equals quality, but in sharp contrast, Cary Grant would star in almost sixty more movies, retaining legendary status for the rest of his life and beyond. And Grant grew a little tired with her perpetual public reminders of how she had made him a star. Indeed, his attitude towards her noticeably hardened over the years. At the time of filming *I'm No Angel*, Grant told a reporter: 'Mae knows so much. Her instinct is so true. Her timing so perfect. Her grasp of the situation so right. It's the tempo of the acting that counts rather than the sincerity of the characterisation. Her personality is so dominant that everyone with her becomes just a feeder.'

But over the next decade or so, as West's career waned while Grant's soared, he was at pains to point out that he had already made seven movies for Paramount before she had hired him for *She Done Him Wrong*, one of which, *Blonde Venus*, was directed by Josef von Sternberg and co-starred Marlene Dietrich, one of the biggest stars in the world. West, he protested, had hardly plucked him off the street. But then, as he went on, 'She always got a great deal of publicity for herself. I could never understand the woman. I thought she was brilliant with that one character she played. But she was an absolute fake as a person. I shuddered from it.'

The more cynical observer would spot the irony of Grant's words. West was no more a self-manufactured 'fake' than Cary Grant, but unlike Grant, who appears to have been universally popular and, for the most part, delightfully charming and thoughtful, West had a bit *too* much of Diamond Lil in her.

Grant was, by late 1933, exhausted. He had been making back-to-back movies for Zukor, without great pay (at least, great compared to what West had been receiving), and wanted a holiday. Zukor accepted his request, and Grant decided to return to England.

6

'Only half my life belongs to me; the other half belongs to those I shared it with.'

Cary Grant

Grant always acknowledged that his mother had damaged him when it came to relationships. Overcompensating for the loss of John, her first child, she had been terrified of losing Archie and had smothered him with stifling affection. In the event, of course, it was Elsie who left *him*.

She had hardly abandoned him. Indeed, her removal from the Leach household – and therefore from Archie's life – has always been regarded as something that was planned by others. The difficulty was, he hadn't known that. Unaware of the circumstances for more than twenty years, he assumed, understandably, she had deserted him.

So deep did these scars run that, when he was finally reunited with his mother, he was unsettled rather than joyful and, by his own admission, he found it hard to manufacture within himself the love he thought he should feel for her. This ambivalence, at various levels, was to remain with him for the rest of her life.

'Her stubbornness and independence frustrated me,' he said a couple of weeks after Elsie's death in 1973. 'She refused to acknowledge I was supporting her even in her later years. One time, I took her some fur coats. She said: "What do you want from me now?" "Nothing," I said. "It's just because I love you." She just said: "Oh." She couldn't accept that.'

One of Grant's lovers in the 1970s, Maureen Donaldson, said, 'Elsie didn't know how to give affection. And she didn't know how to receive it.'

Grant saying that he was frustrated by Elsie's independence is a telling remark. Independence in a woman was something he feared because it fuelled the deep-rooted anxiety within himself that, ultimately, a woman would become too independent and leave him.

Long after he knew the truth about what had really happened – how Elsie had been locked away – Grant's subconscious clearly was unable to rid itself of its core tenet, formed when he'd arrived home from school to an empty house, that no woman was to be trusted.

He said, 'I thought the moral was: if you depend on love and if you give love, you're stupid because love will turn around and kick you in the heart.'

This terrible, and tragic, emotional handicap manifested itself in Grant's erratic approach to all his relationships. But it was particularly apparent in all his marriages, bar the last, his fifth, to Barbara Harris. His first four wives had to endure his vacillations between controlling possessiveness and a lack of commitment. He was at least honest enough with himself to recognise that, for the most part, the fault clearly lay within himself. Speaking after the collapse of his third marriage in 1958, Grant said, 'Either something is wrong with me or, obviously, with the whole sociological and moralistic concepts of our civilization.'

Not only was he able to recognise, if not slay, his personal demons, he knew from whence they came: Elsie.

'My mother had a serious negative influence on my life,' Grant once admitted. 'I made the mistake of thinking that each of my wives was my mother, that there would never be a replacement once she left.'

Many years later, when he'd finally found contentment with Barbara Harris, he elaborated on his above remark.

'They all got bored with me. Tired of me. I made the mistake of thinking that each of my first four wives was a replacement for my mother, which is a burden no woman can maintain for long. I even found myself attracted to women who looked like my mother. My wives and I, until now, were never one. We played a different game and we were too much in competition.'

His candour about his marriages is all the more remarkable given that he was, essentially, a private man. No matter how much money publishers dangled in front of him, other than a lengthy, slightly sugary, piece he wrote for the papers, Grant would refuse all other offers to write his autobiography.

'I'm too busy living my life to write about it,' was his standard reply. 'Anyway, only half of my life belongs to me; the other half belongs to those I shared it with.' Always the gentleman.

The columnist Roderick Mann, who knew Grant for years and

interviewed him numerous times, recounted visiting Grant's home in Beverly Hills where, he learned, Grant kept his collection of memorabilia, including books full of jokes, stories and quotes, in a fireproof room.

'They'd be fun to publish,' remarked Mann.

'Nothing of mine is *ever* going to be published,' retorted Grant, uncharacteristically tetchy.

This probably explains his fury when, some years after their working relationship developed into something deeper, Sophia Loren wrote about their affair in her autobiography.

'Cary searched for perfection in all things,' said David Niven, 'Particularly in the three that meant the most to him: film-making, physical fitness and women. He found it without too much difficulty in the first two categories – but hit a few snags in the third.'

'The trick with women,' Grant explained, 'is to be relaxed. If you can attain true relaxation, you can make love forever.'

If Grant was not actually promiscuous, he certainly enjoyed an active sex life in and out of marriage. Casual partners usually found him a good lover, attentive and tender, and there were very few indeed who didn't adore him afterwards. His weakness was that he tended to rush in to each affair, blind to any potential problems, utterly convinced that, as Niven said, 'each romance was the one for which he had been put into the world.'

When an affair turned sour, as, inevitably, most of his did, he shouldered the blame entirely, saying he had been much too selfish to allow it to grow and succeed.

All his life, Grant had searched for peace, for identity, for a sense of belonging – and for his mother.

The precise date when Grant became aware Elsie was still alive and living in the institution at Fishponds remains unclear as Grant, himself, was deliberately vague on the facts for the rest of his life, but it can be pinpointed pretty accurately to late 1933.

Elias had resolutely had no contact with Elsie during this time and he didn't talk to Elsie's family either. Her family, the Kingdons, kept in constant touch with Elsie – something that not every family would have done in this harsher era – but they, in turn, had not seen Archie Leach for years.

'We used to go and visit Elsie,' one of Grant's cousins said. 'She'd write us beautiful letters asking why she couldn't be released. She also asked that her dancing shoes be sent to her because they had dances at the home. As for Archie, well, it was as though he'd fallen off the face of the earth.'

In fact, Elsie's family were utterly unaware of what had happened to Archie since his departure from Bristol... until he returned home in November 1933.

Grant's return to Bristol was nothing short of a sensation, which the local press milked for all it was worth. Although hardly the huge star he was going to become over the next decade, Grant's burgeoning Hollywood career in general and his two films with Mae West particularly (by the end of 1933, *I'm No Angel* had eclipsed even *She Done Him Wrong* at the box-office, grossing over three million dollars) made him a major local celebrity. The extent of their interest made Grant later come to an arrangement with the local press. Alston Thomas of the *Bristol Evening Post* said, 'We had always promised not to talk to his mother about anything to do with him.' He understandably wanted to shield Archie's unconventional past from that of Cary Grant's.

If we can only begin to guess at the astonishment of Elsie's family as they read about Cary Grant – the alter ego of Archie Leach of whom they had heard nothing since 1920 – being back in Bristol, we can surely understand why they were anxious to tell him of his mother's situation.

Fittingly, Grant's return to Bristol was triggered not by pangs of homesickness or a desire to pick up the threads with Elias, but the pursuit of a woman. This attractive young woman was Virginia Cherrill, a country girl by birth, having been born and raised on a farm. She had shot to fame as Charlie Chaplin's blind heroine in *City Lights* (1931) and starred with John Wayne in *Girls Demand Excitement* (1931). Wayne would later claim the latter was 'the worst motion picture in the history of the industry'. It is doubtful if that troubled Cherrill very much: she went on to become elevated into the nobility, through marriage, as the Countess of Jersey. Chaplin allegedly disliked her as a person, possibly because of her independent spirit and the fact she was able to stand up to his renowned demands and temperament.

Cherrill met Grant at the première of *Blonde Venus*, while putting an unpleasant divorce behind her. Prior to Chaplin discovering her, she had been a society figure, sometimes described, as Kenneth S. Lynn writes in his biography of Charles Chaplin, as 'a somewhat spoiled socialite from Chicago'.

High society, even in his early years – indeed, especially in his early years – as a handsome struggling actor needing contacts had held a certain attraction to Grant. In the second part of 1933, Grant and Cherrill were seen out together and were regarded as 'an item', although it was obvious, even then, to people who saw them in public together that theirs was an uneasy relationship. Nevertheless, gossips began to predict marriage – rumours that led Grant into an unusually angry denial to the press when the two were spotted together in Arizona: 'We are *not* going to marry!'

In October of 1933, Grant and Randolph Scott left California for England. In later life, Grant always seemed to play his motives down, suggesting the trip was almost a whim, but it seems more than likely that he was following Cherrill, whom he missed as soon as she'd departed for England.

Once he had caught up with her, Grant immediately made plans to return to Bristol. Quite how much he had thought about Bristol in the years since sailing for New York with Pender's troupe is unlikely ever to be known. Judging by the way he took to New York and, later, California, it was probably not very much.

He must have been very unsure of what his reception would be when he turned up in the town of his birth and childhood, with Cherrill and Scott in tow. He said that 'I'm just looking forward to having a quiet time with the folks and getting around some of my old haunts,' but he was received almost as a conquering hero. Touring Fairfield, his old school, no mention was made of the shocking reason for his expulsion nearly sixteen years earlier, and he and Scott were given a tour of the school by the headmaster who had succeeded 'Gussie' Smith. One or two of the staff who had bad memories of Archie were still there and were presented to him. On this occasion, all was smiles: smiles in considerable contrast to the expressions these same teachers had shown Archie Leach on the day of his expulsion.

Grant's reunion with his father, Elias, was unexpectedly warm and heartfelt, and it triggered a partial thaw, if not a true *rapprochement*, in relations between Elsie's family, the Kingdons, and Elias.

The Kingdons were invited to a huge party at the Picton Street house, Elias's mother's house, where he had taken the nine-year-old Archie after Elsie had been sectioned. The Kingdons were astonished to see 'many pictures all over the walls of Archie at all ages'.

Grant accompanied some members of his family on a somewhat

sentimental stroll round the backstreets he had last seen as a teenager. At one point, they passed a fish and chip shop. Grant – who always regarded fish and chips as 'the greatest meal in the world' – couldn't resist, and so spent part of his first visit to Bristol as a Hollywood star eating fish and chips out of newspaper in the street. One can only wonder what the all-American Randolph Scott made of such occurrences. In fact, Grant never lost his appetite for fundamentally English food, even after he had become an American citizen. After his retirement from the movies, he would sometimes return to 'the old country' and drive through the countryside, stopping off at pubs and enjoying ploughman's lunches or sausage and mash.

A priceless antique cupboard in his Beverly Hills bedroom, intended for his hand-made shirts and cashmere sweaters, housed, instead, Walnut Whips, Turkish Delight, Liquorice Allsorts and Kit-Kats! On one occasion, he was stopped by customs officers at Los Angeles airport when returning from London, and relieved of the pork sausages and bacon he was attempting to 'smuggle' into the country.

But behind all the happy reunions and the revisiting of favourite old haunts, there was one question neither Elias nor Elsie's family could put off. Elias dropped his bombshell and asked his son what he was going to do about Elsie. Grant announced that he would go and see her on her forthcoming birthday.

Previous biographers have tried to depict Grant's reunion with Elsie as some kind of climax to a Mills-and-Boon-style romance. One writer even went as far as to suggest it was 'easy', that 'twenty years seemed like twenty minutes', and that Elsie regarded Grant as 'still her little Archie'. However pleasant and deeply satisfying this romantic version of their reunion sounds, the reality was more complicated. By his own admission, Grant found meeting his mother again very difficult, and their subsequent relationship was frequently awkward.

The facts speak for themselves. Cary Grant was in Bristol in November 1933 but was back in London by 1 December, where he gave a press interview: 'I saw my father, my uncles, my cousins and my aunts and had a wonderful time.' No mention, there, of his mother.

He and Virginia Cherrill then returned to Bristol just before Christmas – where there was a big family party at the Grand Hotel – before spending the whole of January in London. He didn't visit Elsie until 8 February, just prior to his having to return to Hollywood: it was her fifty-seventh birthday.

In other words, at least ten weeks had elapsed between Grant finding out his mother was still alive and his going to visit her. Even allowing for the fact that he spent some days in a Fulham hospital undergoing a minor operation to correct an injury he had sustained during the shooting of *The Eagle and the Hawk* in March, the previous year, the delay is puzzling. This is not a criticism of Grant. It might well have been that he needed the time to get his mind around the whole notion of the resurrection of a 'dead' mother. But it does show that there was no gushing, fairy-tale coming-together of the two parties on his return to England.

There was also another major concern on his mind. He wanted to marry Virginia Cherrill. It might have only been a few months since Grant's angry denials, but he was often capricious when it came to matters of the heart. Seeing his extended family now prompted him to tell Cherrill that 'it would please me very much if we could be married in Bristol among my own folks.'

Grant's behaviour at this point displays the pattern of floundering between the need for control and indecision. Before Cherrill had had the chance to say 'yes' to a Bristol wedding, Grant withdrew the offer. A big family wedding would take too long to organise, he told her, and was out of the question. This argument may have been spurious, however, as Grant surely realised pretty quickly that the press would be out in force if he were to marry in Bristol. Returning to his *alma mater* was one thing; that was of local media interest only. But two Hollywood actors getting married in Bristol? A rare event, indeed.

Grant no doubt understood that every reporter in England would descend upon them if they went ahead with the big wedding. All his family would be on view – with the embarrassing exception of his mother. 'Where's your mother?' 'We had her put in an asylum!' How would *that* play back at Paramount? No, a local and big wedding was not a good idea. In any case, Grant had always detested a press *mêlée* and to be mobbed by reporters would cause him anxiety that could spoil his day. He toyed with the idea of their getting married on board ship on the way back to the USA – they were booked to depart Southampton on 9 February. This appealed to his romantic side, until he was informed that weddings conducted aboard ships were the stuff of movie scripts: such a marriage would not be recognised in California.

Eventually, Cary Grant and Virginia Cherrill tied the knot at Caxton Hall, London on 9 February 1934. Officially, Grant was still Archie

Leach in England and so, after a somewhat hurried, impersonal service, it was Mr and Mrs Leach who left London immediately after for Southampton, en route for a nostalgic trip to New York.

'We timed it deliberately to take place just before the boat-train left,' Grant said. His motive was clear: he had decided he wanted a quiet wedding 'without any ballyhoo'. But if he thought he would avoid a media frenzy by marrying 'quietly' at Caxton Hall, he was to be disappointed. Word quickly leaked out, and Grant and his new wife were besieged by the press and well-wishers. Grant was furious and when he yelled 'We're very happy' to the assembled throng awaiting them outside – his only public comment on the actual day – he was noticeably tetchy. His return home was beginning to take its emotional toll.

Whatever high hopes Grant had of his marriage to Virginia Cherrill, they were soon to be dashed. His decision to track her down and marry soon began to look like a capricious whim and some close to him claimed that he made it while he was coming round from his operation in the Fulham hospital. In the event, their marriage was destined to last less than seven months. Its failure was to plunge Grant into a depression and, some suspect – and he only ever vaguely denied it in an off-hand manner – a botched suicide attempt.

And yet, when Mr and Mrs Grant (as they would be known Stateside) arrived back in sunny Hollywood, they were, to all intents and purposes, the golden couple: fine-looking, young, successful, they seemed to have it all. Maybe only they, themselves, knew that the truth was very different.

The extended holiday had done Grant little good on the career front. With all the emotional baggage he was carrying – a new wife, a reunion with a 'lost' parent – he could hardly have even felt rested. He may have returned with a beautiful young wife, but he also came back carrying grievances against Paramount, especially Zukor, that he had left behind, unresolved, three months earlier. If anything, his belief that he was undervalued by Paramount coupled with his absolute conviction that he was tossed any script Gary Cooper didn't want to do, were more crystallised that ever. 'I see no reason why *Gary* and *Cary* should be confused,' he said with a touch of acerbic wit.

Grant later confessed that during this period he was moody, self-absorbed and impossible to live with, and this, naturally, would not have endeared him to his new wife. And it still was unknown by many that he had just endured a reunion with a mother he had assumed was dead for twenty years. Today, such an emotional shock would have meant his being a prime candidate for counselling, certainly a lengthy recuperation period. In 1934 it was expected of one merely to keep the chin up and get on with it.

Virginia – who, of course, *did* know what Grant was going through on both a private and professional level – was, slightly surprisingly, not inclined to feel much sympathy for her troubled husband, which suggests that she, who had in a sense been entrapped by Grant and coaxed into marriage, contributed, at least in part, to the speedy collapse of their relationship.

If Grant was currently self-absorbed, then so was Virginia. She had even been more than a little irritated that his brief stay in a London hospital had interrupted their time together. Virginia's increasing equivocation to Grant's feelings merely fuelled his anxieties: his behaviour towards her started to exhibit all the classic signs of his underlying insecurity. 'He was solemn and disagreeable and refused to pay my bills,' said the former Mrs Grant some time later.

This was not the marital bliss Virginia Cherrill had been promised – certainly not what the former socialite, whom the columnist Louella Parsons had dubbed 'the greatest beauty in Hollywood' and who could number the most eligible men in America among her previous escorts, was going to stand for from the unexpectedly truculent Cary Grant.

Virginia herself had retired from film-making on her marriage – indeed, it sometimes appeared to Grant that she had retired from doing anything at all – while Grant was, if reluctantly, back on the Paramount treadmill. He was continuing to work on a succession of scripts that he felt were beneath him and developed the habit of bringing his work frustrations home with him. But whenever he attempted to discuss how he was feeling, Virginia coolly informed him that she wasn't interested.

Grant's mood was not improved when he heard that Zukor had turned down a request from the great Irving Thalberg, who had asked for the loan of Grant to MGM for *Mutiny On The Bounty*. This film was the talk of Hollywood. It was going to be the movie of the year and everyone knew it. Thalberg was not offering Grant the lead – Clark Gable had already been signed – but that was of no concern to Grant. He was more than prepared to take one of the supporting leads, which were plentiful in a story about men on a ship at sea. Also, it had to be an improvement from the below-par formulaic stuff Paramount were tossing his way.

It was not to be. Zukor refused to release Grant, claiming that the actor was too busy. Grant was livid and, afterwards, could never quite bring himself to forgive Zukor. A break from Paramount once his contract expired was inevitable – just as inevitable as a break from his wife had become.

Rumours about the precarious state of their union had surfaced by early summer of 1934, but both had done their best to quell them. They had resolved to keep their differences within the confines of their home. Stories continued to circulate and proliferate that Virginia had left home several times to go to her mother's – and that Grant had had to go repeatedly to her and plead with her to come home.

In the middle of September, Virginia left Grant again and this time consulted a lawyer. As usual, he begged her to stay with him and, again, they somehow – if pointlessly – managed to paper over the cracks. The difference this time was that both of them found they were unable to continue to deny the rumours. This led to the beginning of the breakdown in their marriage being conducted via press statements.

'I hope we can make a go of our marriage,' Virginia told reporters, 'because I love my husband and have been very unhappy over our inability to adjust to our differences.'

Grant responded by denying the rumours that they were separated. 'We've just had a quarrel,' he explained, 'The kind of quarrel any married couple might have. I hope when I get home tonight Virginia will be waiting for me.'

Grant was outwardly as urbane as ever when he made such remarks to the press, but by then he knew their situation had deteriorated and was probably irredeemable. Also, despite his charm, Grant was never fully at ease with the opposite sex – again, the mother-son problem was the original instigator.

'In all those years in theatre, on the road and in New York, surrounded by all sorts of attractive girls,' he said, 'I never seemed able to fully communicate with them...'

With Virginia – because of Virginia – he now began to internalise all his frustrations, doubts, confusions, insecurities. Something had to give. And something *did* give six days later when Grant arrived home from the studio to find that Virginia was not there.

Quite what happened next isn't totally clear and has been muddied by seventy years of gossip and speculation. What *is* known is that in the early hours of 5 October, a servant found Grant slumped unconscious across the bed. There was, depending on which report you choose to believe, an empty bottle of pills beside the bed – or a full, unopened bottle of pills. The servant called an ambulance, the police and the press, in which order isn't clear, although it was certainly true that rumours were already flying around Hollywood that Grant had tried to commit suicide even as the doctors were using the stomach pump on him.

For his part, Grant claimed to have been vaguely aware of 'police crowding into my room and rushing me off to hospital', but, otherwise, played no active part in this particular drama.

Paramount and Grant played down the event afterwards. Publicists at Paramount insisted that Grant had been the victim of a cruel practical joke – just *whose*, they never said – while Grant himself gave his own version of events:

'I had been drinking most of the day before and all that day. I just passed out. You know what whisky does when you drink it all by yourself. It makes you very sad. I began calling people. I know I called Virginia. I don't know what I said to her, but things got hazier and hazier. The next thing I knew, they were carting me off to hospital.'

He made no mention of the bottle of pills, and neither did Paramount.

At least Virginia stayed loyal over this incident – and even gave her own interpretation. She confirmed that her husband had tried to call her that night but, refusing to say what, if anything, had been said, she referred to 'the incident', as she came to call it, rather curiously as 'nervous prostration' – whatever that means – and remained adamant that the whole thing was 'a mistake', a word that can be made very flexible in its interpretation. It was a 'mistake' if he accidentally drank too much *and* consumed pills – and a very different kind of a 'mistake' if he had decided to end his life.

Able to support Grant through this crisis, Virginia still wasn't prepared to delay the inevitable and, in November 1934, filed for divorce. It was granted in the Los Angeles Supreme Court on 26 March 1935. In addition to Virginia's oft-quoted line that Grant was 'sullen, disagreeable and refused to pay my bills', her lawyer further alleged during the hearing that he had drunk to excess, beaten her, threatened to kill her and ordered her to find work – only to throw tantrums when she did obtain acting jobs.

The failure of the marriage was, as Grant viewed it, a humiliation. He felt particularly battered by the divorce hearings during which he had had to listen to his character being destroyed with forensic skill by Virginia's lawyer. Afterwards, he told Randolph Scott, with whom he moved in again following the divorce, that he was never going to re-marry again.

The twelve months between November 1933 and November 1934 had been the worst he had endured since his departure from Pender's troupe. Typically, he blamed himself for the break-up of his marriage, even though it is evident Virginia had contributed to a lesser or greater degree. 'My possessiveness and fear of losing her brought about the very condition I feared – the loss of her,' he said.

As he contemplated life as a divorced man on his 31st birthday in January 1935, Grant could not know how marital happiness would elude him for over four more decades and four more wives. Only after that would he finally find the wife with whom he would at last discover the emotional contentment he craved.

7

'People who knew him terribly well said that a great storm
was going on inside.'

Douglas Fairbanks Junior

If Paramount believed that Grant had played any sort of significant part
in the success of *I'm No Angel*, they had a funny way of showing it, for
none of the films he was put in during 1934, were strictly worthy of his
proven talent. At least *Thirty-Day Princess* promised much: it was
scripted by Tinseltown's prevailing *wunderkind* Preston Sturges and
Marion Gering, Grant's original champion in Hollywood, was slated to
direct. But when Grant read the script, about an actress who
impersonates a princess, his heart must have sunk. The story was flat,
totally devoid of the light humour such a piece of fluff required and
nothing he, his co-star Sylvia Sidney, or the director Gering could do
was able to lift the uninspired nonsense.

Worse was to come. Having refused to loan Grant out to Irving G.
Thalberg for the prestigious *Mutiny On The Bounty,* Paramount were
now quite willing to loan him to 20th-Century Fox for *Born To Be Bad*
(1934), a truly idiotic melodrama that starred Loretta Young as a girl
who seduces the man (Grant) who has adopted her illegitimate son.

His relationship with Paramount was difficult in another specific
area – his contract. The studio offered him $2,500 per week and later
upped this offer to $3,500 per week. But Grant wanted script approval
and the right to turn down any role he didn't like. Only Mae West,
Marlene Dietrich and Gary Cooper had this at Paramount – and
Paramount refused to even discuss the issue with Grant. It is
understandable, therefore, that any sense of relief Grant may have
experienced on his return to Paramount was short-lived.

Also, as a contract player, Grant was expected to do publicity stunts
at the whim of the studio. One particularly embarrassing stunt had him
join a female midget on an open-deck bus. She was pretending to be

Mae West, saying to the real Grant, 'Come up and see me sometime.' Grant managed to force a smile and told her how like Mae West she truly was! Who sanctioned such ideas one can only guess, but it can't surely have been very beneficial for the star in question.

The next script he was required to perform was even shakier than *Born To Be Bad*. *Kiss And Make Up* was a well-below-par romantic comedy in which Grant played a beauty specialist in Paris, who forsakes a wealthy client in favour of his poor but loyal assistant.

Next up was *Ladies Should Listen* (1934), in which he plays a financier with romantic problems. *Enter Madam!* (1935) although a notch higher than his recent outings, was a fairly forgettable comic operetta. Grant plays a millionaire cut down to size after marrying a glamorous opera singer. This was followed by two more mundane outings: *Wings In The Dark* and *The Last Outpost*.

At least he was not a romantically-challenged banker in *The Last Outpost*, which was a *Boys' Own* yarn co-starring Claude Rains and Akim Tamiroff in which a British officer is captured by Kurds. Episodic and disjointed – Graham Green wrote 'half of it is remarkably good and half of it is quite abysmally bad: one can even put one's finger on the join' – *The Last Outpost* was at least a spirited piece and in Rains, Grant found someone to whom he could relate professionally.

Claude Rains was a British actor with masses of stage experience who, like Grant, spent his career in Hollywood. Unlike Grant, however, he remained essentially a character actor despite taking the title role in *The Phantom of the Opera* (1943), and appearing in some of Hollywood's most enduring classics, such as *Mr Smith Goes To Washington* (1942), *Here Comes Mr. Jordan* (1941) and, famously, *Casablanca* (1942). He was to appear with Grant again in *Notorious* in 1946.

As Grant celebrated his 31st birthday, he could be forgiven for feeling a slight sense of disappointment, certainly a feeling of unfulfilment. On the one hand, he was in constant employment as a movie star – something for which thousands of struggling actors his age would envy him – and enjoying a burgeoning popularity and a salary that his contemporaries back in Bristol couldn't contemplate, let alone attain. On the other hand, Paramount studios were hardly stretching him as an actor. As he looked back over his previous five films, he could see a rather disturbing pattern emerging. He was starting to be typecast.

For the most part, Grant was not a rebel. He had no intention of refusing to do a film or causing trouble on the set. He was far too centred and intelligent for that and whenever possible would disassociate himself from those who threw tantrums, or strutted about 'like they'd found a cure for cancer', as actor James Caan once put it. So Grant would bide his time and work through the remainder of his contract, doing his best in vehicles that were not always best for him.

When his contract expired, Grant wouldn't renew, no matter what Paramount might have offered. He had proved, beyond doubt, he could act alongside the biggest and that the camera loved him. He decided it would make better sense to remain a free agent, making his own decisions in future about what film and which roles were right or wrong for him.

Grant also turned down offers from other major studios, citing the same reason – the desire to retain personal control of his career. It is hard to recall a major up-and-coming star choosing to go it alone before. He was either very brave and not a little inspired in his decision, or very stupid and liable to have deep regrets.

Those who believed it was the latter, did not understand him very well, nor his struggle in elevating himself from a dysfunctional family in a poorish part of Bristol to the heights of Hollywood stardom. Most of his decisions – barring his relationships with the opposite sex – were reached in a pragmatic and reasoned manner, if seeming, at first sight, to be illogical. And because of the nature of his journey thus far, he came to the conclusion – logical to him – that he was far better equipped in taking charge of his own destiny.

David Niven recalled, 'Cary freely admitted that from the age of fourteen when he had run away from school to join an acrobatic troupe, he had been searching for peace within himself.' Grant hadn't found it yet, and he knew that peace wasn't to be found in staying under contract. Besides, two other aspects of Grant's personality played decisive parts in his decision to go it alone: 'Cary was a restless soul,' said Niven. '*And* an optimist.'

Restlessness and optimism make for odd bedfellows – particularly in the film industry – but they gave Grant that necessary thrust to make a momentous decision in his chosen career.

In fact, as Grant would be able to accept happily in retrospect, the banal clutch of films he had made for Paramount were not wasted: they were the foundations of the experience that he brought to his later, more dynamic, work. Pragmatic as he was, it is doubtful even Grant, himself, could see it that way at the time. In the fullness of his career, his output was prodigious, even by the standards of the contracted actor of the era. And he was learning constantly with each and every performance: nothing was missed, nothing was redundant to what would make Cary Grant a name of the fifties and sixties as well as the thirties and forties. Everything was scrutinised, the best bits retained and used in future performances.

At the conclusion of his contract with Paramount, he had made twenty-one films. If the embryonic Cary Grant had appeared in the first of these, that embryo had developed more and more over two years into the Cary Grant that lingers on in the consciousness almost a century after he was born. We can see now that in 1935, it just required the right film, the right part and, particularly, the right director to act as midwife.

His first film following Paramount's *The Last Outpost* was made for RKO and entitled *Sylvia Scarlett*. Based on the novel by Compton Mackenzie, this was an odd tale about a girl, played by Katharine Hepburn, pretending to be a boy so she can escape from France with her rascally father. A fortune in contraband diamonds motivates a Cockney adventurer (Grant) into action. On his way to getting his hands on the fortune, he takes time to romance Katharine Hepburn's character, bringing out her heavily suppressed feminine side. Until Grant appears on the scene, she has no time for feminine charm, jewellery or dresses. The film, directed by George Cukor and also co-starring Edmund Gwenn and Brian Ahern, was almost universally panned on release. The Legion of Decency attacked it for supposed coded homosexuality, while typical reviews called the film 'a sprawling and ineffective essay in dramatic chaos' and 'a tragic waste of time and screen talent'.

But for Grant, it was his turning point. He was to come out of this film an infinitely more enlightened man and actor. The critic Pauline Kael wrote about the Cary Grant who emerged: 'He became Cary Grant when he learned to project his feelings of absurdity through his characters and to make a style out of their feeling silly.'

Reassessing *Sylvia Scarlett* in 1978, *New Yorker* magazine believed it 'seems to go wrong in a million directions but it has unusually affecting qualities'. This was arguably an accurate judgement on a very peculiar film. Hepburn herself noted wryly in 1993 that *Sylvia Scarlett* is now regarded by the audience as a cult classic. 'Where were you when we needed you?' she demanded humorously of its modern-day fans.

No character was quite what he or she appeared and occasionally they spoke lines, or behaved, in a manner that not only was not in character but, sometimes, unrelated to the context of the entire piece.

'Our first picture together,' Hepburn wrote of this, the first of her films with Grant, 'and it was a strange experience. As we shot the picture, I began to wonder what Cukor was thinking. It just did not seem to me to work. It was just not funny. But Cary Grant's performance in this picture was magic. His energy was incredible, his laughter full and unguarded. Teddy Gwenn and I were his stooges. It was a great set-up, which didn't quite work.'

Hepburn made an interesting observation on Grant: 'He was chubbier, then. He became more thin and distinguished later. I think I preferred him as he used to be.'

Like a writer finding his voice, Grant found his screen persona with this film. And the difference had been working with George Cukor and, to a marginally lesser degree, Katharine Hepburn.

Cukor, who was born in 1899, had begun his directing career on Broadway and directed his first film in 1930. A sensitive, literate man, he had already proved himself a polished and intelligent director and had directed Hepburn in *Little Women* (1933) and, before *Sylvia Scarlett,* had directed the definitive all-star version of *David Copperfield,* a massive box-office smash.

Cukor, who died in 1983, also directed such unforgettable films as *A Star Is Born* (1954), *My Fair Lady* (1964), for which he won an Oscar, and *The Philadelphia Story* (1941), starring Grant and Hepburn again. Yet he was not universally popular with actors, mainly, many believe, because Cukor was one of Hollywood's most open, if publicly discreet, homosexuals. He was known as 'a woman's director', the code for saying he was gay.

A persistent rumour, which has become almost legendary, is that Clark Gable had had Cukor fired from *Gone With The Wind* – 'I want that fag fired' he's reported to have told producer David O. Selznick – because Cukor knew that Gable had once been a male prostitute who serviced homosexuals. David Thomson in his masterly biography of Selznick (*Showman: The Life Of David O. Selznick*), while writing that 'there is no evidence that Gable had been a paid lover to anyone', adds, 'though many people who became world famous as movie stars had "darker" pasts they were anxious to keep secret and which became the material of blackmail.' If Cukor did know anything about Gable's alleged past as a male hooker, to his credit, he always refused to be drawn on the matter and took any secrets to his grave.

If some of Tinseltown's biggest male stars were wary of Cukor because of his homosexuality, this merely adds to the belief that Grant truly had nothing to hide about his sexuality. He certainly had no qualms about working with Cukor: quite the reverse. He liked the director's intelligence and attention to detail and visibly relaxed throughout the making of *Sylvia Scarlett*. Fundamentally, Grant had never worked with a director of Cukor's ability up to now, and he enjoyed the experience immensely.

For his part, Cukor admitted that until *Sylvia Scarlett*, Cary Grant had been a good-looking leading man making a nice living, but he was without a distinct identity. According to Cukor, this was the film where he found it: 'He felt the ground under his feet,' as Cukor put it. This was encouraging, since Cukor had previously said that he had found Grant 'rather wooden and inexperienced'. Grant also had self-doubts, claiming that up to this moment he had been copying Noel Coward, Jack Buchanan and Hoagy Carmichael. (Interestingly, Carmichael was Ian Fleming's idea of the perfect actor to portray his fictional hero, James Bond – a role Grant himself was later offered.) One way he imitated them was to keep his hand in his pocket – 'but only because I was so nervous I couldn't pull it out again. It took me three years to get my hand out of there and they were three years wasted.'

Katharine Houghton Hepburn was born on 12 May 1907, at Hartford, Connecticut. Her career began in theatre, specifically in Baltimore, and her first film was *Bill of Divorcement* (1932). Though she had many long-term affairs with other men, it is her 27-year relationship with the actor Spencer Tracy that people remember. She made several films with Grant following *Sylvia Scarlett*, but it is perhaps for her co-starring role with Humphrey Bogart in the film *The African Queen* (1951) that she is best remembered.

Working with a feisty performer of Hepburn's stature only added to the making of *Sylvia Scarlett* and the evolution of Cary Grant, so it is rather ironic that the film was received so appallingly on its initial release that Grant felt obliged to offer to do another film for Cukor – for free. Not that Cukor had any intention of accepting the offer, as Grant had probably guessed. Nevertheless, Grant, Hepburn and Cukor would work together again with much greater success in the near future.

Grant went from the controversial disappointments of *Sylvia Scarlett* into a much lighter and accessible picture. *Big Brown Eyes* (1936), which co-starred Joan Bennett and Walter Pidgeon, had Grant playing a private detective who, together with his wisecracking girlfriend (Bennett), traps a jewel thief. Directed by Raoul Walsh, who also co-wrote the script with Bert Hanlon, *Big Brown Eyes* was agreeable nonsense but, ultimately, uninspired and derivative. Two years earlier, MGM had struck gold with *The Thin Man*, starring William Powell and Myrna Loy as the married sleuths Nick and Nora Charles, an adaptation of Dashiell Hammett's crime novel. So successful was the original that it spawned no less than five sequels between 1937 and 1946, with both Powell and Loy recreating their roles in each.

Given that Hollywood has never seen a bandwagon without wishing to jump on it, *Big Brown Eyes* was Paramount's attempt to initiate a *Thin Man*-type series, but the film was, alas, too mediocre to succeed. Nonetheless, audiences clearly enjoyed the interplay between Grant and Bennett, already a veteran of over thirty movies at the age of twenty-six, and Paramount quickly re-teamed them for *Wedding Present*, which was released after Grant's next film, *Suzy*, which he made for MGM.

Everything about *Suzy* reeked of class, and Grant was excited by the project – initially. Not only was his co-star the fabulously popular Jean Harlow, the fast-talking 'Platinum Blonde' who was to die so tragically the following year aged just twenty-six, but the script had been co-written by Dorothy Parker, no less.

Parker, the American writer and famed wit, who, with people such as Robert Benchley, Alexander Woollcott and Edna Ferber, was at the heart of New York's literati, was then at the height of her fame. Born in 1893, Parker reviewed for *Vanity Fair* and *New Yorker*. Often imitated, never bettered, her wit, which could be biting, is quoted to this day. She had damned a performance by Katharine Hepburn in a Broadway play with 'she ran the whole gamut of emotions from A to B', commented 'How can they tell?' when informed of the death of President Coolidge and coined the phrase 'Men seldom make passes at girls who wear glasses.'

But screenplays were probably the least distinguished of Parker's literary output and her largely disappointing years in Hollywood are typified by *Suzy*, a complicated comedy-drama which is never quite as good as it should be, nor quite as smart as it thinks it is.

Wedding Present, Grant's second film in 1936 co-starring Joan Bennett – this time they played laid-back newspaper reporters – was more amusing. It was based on a story by Paul Gallico, who had begun his literary career as a sports writer and had only just begun writing fiction. The film was directed by Richard Wallace and was a somewhat whimsical romantic comedy, but the on-screen rapport between Grant and Bennett, which had been so obvious in the otherwise routine *Big Brown Eyes*, gives the film a crackle it might otherwise have lacked.

Grant's next screen adventure was *When You're In Love* for Columbia, rechristened *For You Alone* in the UK. Written and directed by Robert Riskin, the film starred the American opera singer Grace Moore as a European opera singer who marries in order to stay in the United States. Moore, then thirty-six, gives a marvellous performance in the movie, while Grant does what he can with a somewhat underwritten role.

Grant then returned to England. This was to make the film *The Amazing Quest of Ernest Bliss* for the director Alfred Zeisler. Released in the US as *Romance and Riches*, Bliss's quest was not so amazing as the title would have one believe: he was a wealthy man who accepts a bet that he can live independently of his wealth for a whole year. Creaky even when released, Grant's first British film was if nothing else a salutary lesson demonstrating just how slickly smooth Tinseltown's Dream Factories really were.

But the film was to be memorable for very personal, and tragic, reasons. Shooting in London had scarcely been going on for a week when news reached Grant on 1 December 1935 that his father, Elias, had died in Bristol of 'extreme toxicity' – which one can loosely translate as 'alcohol poisoning'. However simplistic, clichéd and potentially incorrect it seems to suggest that Elias's heavy drinking began as a refuge from Elsie's increasingly unstable behaviour and constant nagging, all available evidence leads one to assume that this is what happened. His death was a legacy of his increasing dependency on alcohol.

Grant himself also inherited Elias's weakness for alcohol and, although he would never succumb to the dangers of drink in the way of his father – and his physique and health amazingly belied *any* suggestion of indulgence – he did indulge himself in weak moments.

He himself blamed his drugs overdose the previous year, when his marriage to Virginia Cherrill collapsed, on his being drunk on whisky. Whether it was a botched suicide bid or not – more likely not, if only because Grant tended to succeed at everything he set out to achieve – there is little doubt that intoxication had played a significant part in that particular drama. And more than three decades later, his supposed indulgence in drink and LSD was cited in Dyan Cannon's divorce proceedings against him in 1968.

Grant immediately suspended work on *The Amazing Quest of Ernest Bliss* and hurried to Bristol to mourn his father and make the funeral arrangements. He not only attended the funeral but delivered the eulogy, saying of Elias at one point, 'He was a wise and kindly man and I loved him very much.' A little later he added, 'I worshipped him and I learned a lot from him.'

Such a radical reinterpretation of his childhood was typical of Grant's attitude to his past. Those words simply do not square with the facts of Elias's remoteness during Grant's formative years, nor his running away to join Pender's troupe and his subsequent flight to a new life in America.

But Grant took emotional refuge in the 'truth' he concocted. Elias might have been a distant father to Archie Leach, but there was no reason why he had to be that way to Cary Grant. As there was no 'Cary Grant', whatever Grant said about his past *was* the truth as far as he was concerned – and who could argue with a figment of the imagination?

There was an unfortunate incident at the graveside when a press photographer tried to take a photograph of Grant. The actor was furious, and lashed out and he and the photographer became embroiled in a brief scuffle during which the photographer's camera was smashed on an adjacent headstone. This did nothing to endear the press to Grant, who had already expressed an intense dislike of journalists.

His father's passing not only took Grant back to Bristol, but it meant that he also had to face the question of his mother's future. Despite their earlier reunion, Grant appears to have been happy with the status quo – and clearly relieved that there was an ocean and continent between the problem and his everyday life in Los Angeles.

He should not necessarily be condemned for this. Projecting 21st century social mores onto the past is a mistake. Mental illness was still much misunderstood and a stigma not only for the person who was unfortunately ill, but also for their family. The sudden re-entry into his life of a mentally frail mother he had long believed dead was hardly something compatible with the slick image Cary Grant was carving out for himself in Hollywood. His own life had been emotionally turbulent in the intervening months since he'd seen her and the publicity, coinciding with his divorce and mysterious overdose, was not guaranteed to play well in Los Angeles. Also, those journalists who, even at this relatively early stage of his career, were already irritated by his reluctance to talk to them, would surely go to town if the truth were known.

Besides, there is clear evidence that, despite the Kingdon family's assertion that 'she is as normal as anyone', Elsie was seriously disturbed, if rendered harmless. Indeed, if she wasn't mentally ill before she was admitted, two decades in the Fishponds institution, with its notoriously harsh regime, was surely plenty enough to make anyone disturbed.

Whatever guilt he might have felt privately, Grant had other things on his mind between December 1933 and December 1935 and was happy enough to leave any decisions about Elsie's future to Elias. But Elias's death forced Grant into becoming involved. However much the Kingdon family professed to care about Elsie, as soon as Elias died, they made it quite plain that they expected Grant to take up the reins. As her only son, and a famous film star to boot, he was *expected* to support her, even though he and his mother were, effectively, still complete strangers.

To his credit, Grant acted quickly now. Elsie was released from Fishponds almost immediately after Elias's funeral, and Grant insisted she stay with him in London until he completed work on *The Amazing Quest of Ernest Bliss*.

During this time, he invited her to join him in California when he returned after the film was finished. Elsie refused. She would always refuse: Bristol was all she had ever known and it was where she wanted to stay. Grant's contemporary Charlie Chaplin had been in a very similar situation with his mother, Hannah, who had suffered mental illness – through malnutrition – for many years. Unlike Grant's mother, Chaplin's accepted the invitation to live in California. Chaplin's biographer, Kenneth S. Lynn, wrote that Chaplin had called off a rescheduled crossing his mother had been due to make 'out of fear that his mother's presence in California might depress him at a time when personal and professional unhappiness had already strained his nerves to the breaking point'. This reads as if it could have been lifted from a

Grant biography. Chaplin's mother did eventually arrive in California. An immigration official said, 'So you're the mother of the famous Charlie?' 'Yes,' she replied, 'and you are Jesus Christ!' This gives some indication of what Grant might have had to go through in the following years and, however much it was later claimed he had implored his mother to live with him in America, his real reaction to her refusal may have been one of intense relief.

Grant is on record as saying he never quite knew how he should treat his mother and what he should feel for her at this point in his life. Elsie was an awkward legacy from Archie's childhood and the only way Cary Grant could resolve it – and ultimately avoid actually having to confront his demons – was to be excessively generous towards her financially. He bought a house for her in Bristol, as close to her family as possible, and returned to California. Installed in her new home, Elsie's behaviour continually displayed her frail mental state. She was extremely nervous and had an irrational fear of men – 'I'm a virgin, I'm a virgin' she would claim repeatedly. She would bolt herself in the house – callers frequently had to plead with her through the letter-box to be allowed in – and at night would barricade herself in her bedroom, piling furniture up against the door.

When Grant sent her generous chests of food from America, Elsie would always refuse to open them. 'You never know,' she told friends. 'Cary might be hard up one day. I want to save them until they're really needed.' Not only is this interesting in itself, but it gives us quoted evidence that she now referred to her son by his screen name, and not the birth name that she and Elias had given him.

If a clearly bewildered Elsie living alone in a house in Bristol paid for by Grant wasn't the *ideal* solution for her, it was surely better for him than to have her with him in California, where she, and he, would have become a source of conjecture and ridicule among the gossip-columnists, Grant's colleagues and the studio heads. It was a story in the mould of some of his Paramount scripts – but true. It was better for Grant to maintain the distance between Bristol and Los Angeles, which had the added advantage that he could romanticise the true nature of her situation in his own mind. He could ponder lovingly about her without being harassed by her, imagine the happy times yet to come without their arriving on too regular a basis. Cary Grant would have liked this situation. He was always good at playing a part.

If his personal life was something of a roller-coaster between 1933 and 1937, the films he made during these years gave him the chance to develop; to show what he was capable of performing. And it is noticeable that the scripts after *Sylvia Scarlett* were, generally speaking, of an improving quality. What was becoming apparent on the studio floor and, ultimately, to cinema audiences around the world, was that Grant enjoyed and excelled at the light comedy roles in which his own ego and pompous persona could be punctured to humorous effect.

Howards Hawks, who directed three of Grant's next ten pictures, said of Grant's elevation into the premier league of leading men at this time: 'I've seen it happen time and again. A performer goes along for years and is never better than satisfactory. Then, suddenly, he becomes brilliant. It's a matter of confidence. Cary Grant became a star when he became confident of himself.'

Grant's confidence as a performer, ignited by his two box-office successes with Mae West, had really begun to grow during the making of the otherwise flawed *Sylvia Scarlett*. From 1937 onwards, he simply – or perhaps not so simply – upped another gear, and his career soared. Cary Grant was now well on his way to becoming the greatest leading man in the world.

8

'Right now, Cary is hot!'

Howard Hawks

The film that, possibly more than any other, finally proved what Cary Grant was capable of delivering was *The Awful Truth* (1937). Written and directed by Leo McCarey, the film epitomises the screwball comedies of the 1930s and remains extremely funny more than sixty years after it was made. As does the Marx Brothers film *Duck Soup* (1933), another film directed by Leo McCarey and with enormous script input by the director.

Born in Los Angeles in 1898, McCarey briefly practised law before trying songwriting. He gave up the former and failed at the latter. He broke into films in 1918 as an assistant to Tod Browning. His early years in the industry were spent working for Hal Roach, where he learned the art of creative comedy and directed many shorts, notably several starring Laurel and Hardy. McCarey was a great believer in entertaining audiences to the full, believing that films were an alternative world of escape – dream worlds.

The Awful Truth is that most difficult of genres, the cinematic soufflé. The picture co-starred Irene Dunne (with whom Grant again co-starred in *Penny Serenade* in 1941), Ralph Bellamy (who appeared in *His Girl Friday* in 1940) and Alexander d'Arcy. It has the most slender of plot lines: a divorced couple, fighting over the custody of their wire-haired fox terrier, are reconciled. The role of the dog was played by Asta, the same animal who was the canine companion of Nick and Nora Charles in the *Thin Man* series.

It could have gone horribly wrong – perhaps it deserved to with such a story-line – but, as *World Film News* noted: 'Among the ingredients the raising powder is the important thing and out of the oven comes a frothy bit of stuff that leaves no taste in the mouth and is easy on the stomach.'

The raising powder referred to is the sure touch of McCarey, who deservedly won the Oscar for best director. McCarey's script, Irene Dunne and Ralph Bellamy were also nominated for Oscars, as was the film itself for best picture. Strangely, but by now hardly unexpectedly, Cary Grant was again mysteriously overlooked. Everything he touched turned to gold, yet this gift was never formally recognised. (Not until the end of his career in an honorary award.) His is a superb performance in the film and surely should have been recognised. Is it possible that his talent was such that the powers-who-were believed he was going to pick up so many awards in due course that it was best to throw them at his lesser co-stars? Time after time, he would be the best thing in a film, only for his co-stars to get the nominations. Katharine Hepburn and James Stewart for *The Philadelphia Story* and Joan Fontaine for *Suspicion* are other notable examples.

'Thank you, Cary,' said Peter Stone when he collected the Oscar for best screenplay for *Father Goose,* Grant's penultimate movie, in March 1965. 'You keep winning these things for the rest of us.'

Grant was nominated only twice: for *Penny Serenade* in 1941 and *None But The Lonely Heart* in 1944 – both straight dramatic roles and atypical Cary Grant performances. Though he would publicly shrug off his unexplained exclusion, he was privately very disappointed by the neglect. The Academy of Motion Picture Arts and Sciences – presumably unwittingly – reinforced his paranoia about being an outsider. He believed that the movers and shakers of the industry didn't take him seriously – and for a man who had undergone a change of both name and character in an attempt to belong, this must have been most disconcerting.

Quite why the Academy never rewarded the most consummate screen actor of the century for a particular performance will probably never be fully explained. But the Academy Award historian, Bill Libby, has his own theory: 'There have been few greater sophisticated actors of comedy than Cary Grant. But his only two nominations came for serious roles... The master of perfect timing, he deserved an Oscar if anyone did. It was due to snobbery that he was denied one.'

There is probably a great deal of truth in Libby's theory. Hollywood, like the British honours system, has always rated the practitioners of serious, straight drama far higher than comedians, despite the universal truth, acknowledged by just about everyone in show business, that comedy is far harder to perform, as Grant himself once explained:

'The secret of comedy is doing it naturally under the most difficult circumstances. And film comedy is the most difficult of all. At least on stage you know right away if you're getting laughs or not. But making a movie, you have no way of knowing. So you try to time the thing for space and length and can only hope when it plays in the movie theatres months later that you have timed the thing right. It's difficult and it takes experience. I'll always remember the great actor, A.E. Matthews, who said on his death bed: "Dying's tough – but not as tough as comedy."'

Only in 1970, four years after his last film, did the Academy of Motion Pictures Arts and Sciences make it up to Grant by awarding him a special Oscar 'For his unique mastery of the art of screen acting with the respect and affection of his colleagues', presented by Frank Sinatra, Grant's co-star from *The Pride And The Passion*.

Sinatra, his words speaking for everyone who believed this was one award way overdue, did not hold back: 'This award,' he remarked, 'is made for sheer brilliance of acting. No one has brought more pleasure to more people than Cary has. And nobody has done so many things so well. Cary has so much skill that he makes it look easy.'

That it took the Academy well over thirty years to recognise that 'sheer brilliance' was nothing short of disgraceful and there were many who speculated that Grant would not turn up on the night of 7 April 1970 to collect his award. For the majority, this speculation was founded on the certain knowledge that Grant had come to loathe crowds and did everything to keep *out* of the limelight.

But there was another reason, known only to a few at the time, why Grant might stay away. Just before the Oscar ceremony, Grant had been informed that Cynthia Bouron, a former actress and call-girl, intended to sue him for the paternity of the baby she was carrying. Worse, there was the implied threat that she might announce her claim at the Academy Awards. To bolster her case, Ms Bouron said she would call the child 'Cary Grant' if it were a boy – and had already named her dog after him!

Grant had certainly met Bouron, but theirs was a casual acquaintance and unlikely to have been sexual. Bouron's reputation preceded her and, like everyone else in Hollywood, Grant was wary of her. Bouron's case hardly merited serious consideration. But, as Grant's lawyers pointed out, her instability was notorious and she was quite capable of carrying out her threat to subpoena him on prime-time television. If she did, he would be liable, under Californian law, which presumes alleged fathers guilty until proved innocent, for providing for the child until the case could be heard.

Acting on advice, Grant kept a very low profile before the ceremony, visiting Elsie in Bristol and then spending several days, well out of sight, with Noel Coward at Coward's retreat in Jamaica.

Matters came to a head three weeks before the ceremony, when the *Los Angeles Times* reported the birth of Bouron's girl child, whom she named Stephanie Andrea Grant. This proved the final straw for Grant who, even though knowing the child was not his, instructed the Academy to withdraw his name from the ceremony. Only the personal intervention of Howard Hughes and Gregory Peck persuaded him to change his mind, but Grant telephoned Princess Grace in Monaco, who was due to present him with the Oscar, asking her not to attend because he didn't want her embarrassed.

In the event, Bouron didn't show up, and her case was dropped the moment it came to court because, upon examination by the court officials, the child was found to be of mixed race! Three years later, in October 1973, Bouron's body was found in the boot of a car. She had been beaten to death with a hammer.

Grant accepted his Oscar with great dignity. With tears in his eyes, his voice heavy with emotion, he stepped up to accept the Oscar and thanked his colleagues. 'You know that I may never look at this without remembering the quiet patience of the directors who were so kind to me, who were kind enough to put up with me more than once, some of them even three or four times. I trust they and all the other directors, writers and producers and my leading women have forgiven me for what I didn't know. You know that I've never been a joiner or a member of any particular social set, but I've been privileged to be part of Hollywood's most glorious era.'

He received a standing ovation and Oscar historians agree that there was never a more popular presentation in the Academy's history. Grant himself was happy. He would later say that only the birth of his daughter, Jennifer, in 1966, and President Reagan awarding him the Presidential Medal in 1981, prevented the Oscar being the most memorable event in his life.

Nevertheless, that gracious acceptance speech – which he had rehearsed over and over again to himself the previous evening – was one he should have made many times before in Hollywood and perhaps the first time in 1937 for *The Awful Truth*.

The Awful Truth was re-made in 1953 by the director Alexander Hall as the musical *Let's Do It Again*, and it shouldn't have been. Jane Wyman and Ray Milland went through the motions all right, but the re-make only served to show how essential Grant and Dunne were to the original – as was Leo McCarey. As Joe Adamson wrote: 'McCarey was the type who was more amused by the subtleties and frailties of human behaviour than in the hyperbolic parables of man's innate lunacy... Two of his most choice achievements as a comedy director – the two-reel Laurel and Hardy silent *Big Business* and the Cary Grant–Irene Dunne divorce comedy *The Awful Truth* – are delightful comedic studies of the heated passions and cool tensions in the steady rise and fall of true human conflict.'

Grant's co-star, Ralph Bellamy, when he was interviewed in 1988, spoke of the time he worked with Grant and Dunne on the picture. 'At the end of the first day,' he recalled, 'Irene was crying and Cary was saying, "Let me out of this and I'll do another picture for nothing." Leo McCarey would come in with brown wrapping paper with notes saying, "You come in here, you come in there, the dog can run across the set." And that's the way we made the picture. We never had a script. Cary caught on quickly. It was right in his groove of humour.' The improvisational method, on this occasion, worked wonders. The film remains one of Grant's greatest achievements.

Grant made two other pictures in 1937, both of which were released before *The Awful Truth*. The first, *The Toast Of New York,* was, as one came to expect with Grant, entertaining enough, if not quite the toast of *anywhere*, but the other, like *The Awful Truth*, became one of the most popular and best-remembered films of his career: *Topper,* which he starred in for Hal Roach.

Derived from the novel *The Jovial Ghosts* by Thorne Smith, the film has a rather stuffy banker, played by Roland Young, who is haunted – none too terrifyingly – by the ghosts of his cosmopolitan friends, the Kirbys. The ghosts, played by Grant and Constance Bennett, exude a *joie de vivre* – or should that be a *joie de mort* – and are visible only to Topper. The witty blend of the supernatural with sophisticated comedy created a new genre and the themes in this film can be seen reflected in everything from Noel Coward's *Blithe Spirit* to Tim Burton's *Beetlejuice,* via the 1969 ATV (now ITC) series *Randall and Hopkirk (Deceased).*

Topper proved so popular with audiences that two sequels were made

– *Topper Takes A Trip* (1939) and *Topper Returns* (1941) – with Roland Young reprising his role as Topper in both. Constance Bennett also returned in the sequel but, by then, Hal Roach could no longer afford Cary Grant. Grant, ever-keen to take on new challenges, was not the 'sequel' type and his role was taken by a ghostly dog! This demonstrates more acutely than anything else, perhaps, the extraordinary upward curve of Grant's career from 1937 onwards. He was so difficult to replace that someone came up with the notion of a pet as opposed to another actor.

Another interesting footnote to *Topper* is that the *Los Angeles Times'* notorious gossip columnist Hedda Hopper made an appearance in the film. Grant, who cherished his privacy, loathed the malicious, often destructive, 'articles' that Hopper and Louella Parsons – for the *Los Angeles Examiner* – manufactured. But he was no fool. He was always courteous to both 'ladies' and even-handed when dealing with them separately, all too conscious of how destructive their columns could be and even more aware of the scalps they had already taken – Chaplin's in Hopper's case, Orson Welles' in Parsons'. They pursued relentlessly, if they felt petulance from their potential victims.

Louella Parsons very nearly didn't cause any star any problem whatsoever. In 1925 she contracted tuberculosis and was told she had six months to live. She decided to spend her final days in California, but the disease went into remission and she emerged as William Randolph Hearst's Hollywood columnist.

Other than *The Awful Truth* and *Topper* from this era, there came *Holiday* (1938) and *Bringing Up Baby* (1938), followed by *Only Angels Have Wings* (1939) with Jean Arthur and Rita Hayworth. These pictures have struck a chord with the public and remain memorable to this day, if only as four better-known titles from the Cary Grant canon.

Bringing Up Baby is rightly regarded as one of Cary Grant's most memorable pictures ironically, as he only got the part after Ray Milland, Robert Montgomery and Ronald Colman had turned it down. Described by *Empire Magazine* in 1998 as 'the definitive screen comedy', director Howard Hawks re-teamed Grant and Hepburn with considerably more success than *Sylvia Scarlett* two years earlier.

In *Bringing Up Baby,* Hepburn plays an eccentric millionairess who receives a friendly leopard called Baby from her brother. Meanwhile, she wants to get Grant, who plays a paleontologist, as interested in her as he is in a particular prehistoric bone. The bone and the leopard are the chief vehicles for the comedy to operate.

Hepburn enjoyed trying to build a relationship with the leopard, but 'Cary kept his distance whenever he could,' she said. Quite sensibly, it transpired, as the animal turned on Hepburn.

Nearly seventy years on, this film remains remarkably fresh: the lines are funny and delivered with great style, and Grant – boffinish and very American (we even get a couple of 'gee-whizzes') – responds with the right amount of anxiety to the accumulating difficulties he finds himself confronting. The direction is also sharp, and allows Grant plenty of scope to show his talents for the verbal and the visual elements of wit, while Hepburn underplays her role beautifully. Because of these two talents, enjoying verbal interplay yet never sending up, the film manages to avoid being a farce: it is something altogether cleverer than that and its longevity bears witness to the fact.

Central to the success of the film is that Grant and Hepburn, now at their considerable respective peaks, visibly relish the strength of the material the script gives them. One particular choice scene has Grant trying to avoid the amorous attentions of Hepburn and ending up flat on his face.

GRANT: Now just a moment, Susan. Don't think that I don't appreciate all you've done, but (*She tries to interrupt him*) just a moment, but there are limits to what a man can bear. Besides that, tomorrow afternoon I'm going to get married...

HEPBURN: (*Giggling*) What *for?*

GRANT: Well, because, bec... well, anyway, I'm going to get married, Susan, and don't interrupt. Now, my future wife has always regarded me as a man of some dignity (*Susan giggles*). Privately, I'm convinced that I *have* some dignity. Now it isn't that I don't *like* you, Susan, because, after all, in moments of quiet I'm strangely drawn to you. But, well, there haven't *been* any quiet moments. Our relationship has been a series of misadventures from beginning to end. So, if you *don't* mind, I'll see Mr. Peabody *alone* and *unarmed*...

HEPBURN: Without me?

GRANT: Definitely without you. Now, Susan, I'm going to say good*night*. And I hope that I never set eyes on you *again*...Goodnight...

With that, Grant slams her car door shut, turns, trips over the kerb and executes the most perfect pratfall – reminiscent, surely, of his Pender work – onto the pavement.

'*Bringing Up Baby* may well be the American movies' closest equivalent to Restoration comedy,' wrote Pauline Kael many years later. It was a perceptive observation because, like the best of Restoration comedy, *Bringing Up Baby* succeeds in entertaining a generation not born when it was made, just as evidently it entertained the generation for whom it *was* made.

So relevant did the film remain throughout the succeeding decades that Howard Hawks actually re-used parts of the script for the Rock Hudson vehicle *Man's Favourite Sport* in 1964 – prompting one critic to suggest that Hawks was 'savouring all his past jokes for one last time' – while Peter Bogdanovich used *Bringing Up Baby* as the template for his pastiche of screwball comedies, *What's Up Doc?*, starring Barbra Streisand and Ryan O'Neal, in 1972.

Grant's performance in the movie is extraordinarily assured. Straight-laced, slightly nerdish behind prop spectacles, he connects with the audience through both his vulnerability and – with Hepburn's 'help' – his being excessively accident-prone.

Grant responds with just the right amount of anxiety to the accumulating difficulties his character (Huxley) finds himself in. He clearly revels in Hawks's direction, which gave him plenty of scope to display his considerable talent for combining the verbal and visual elements of wit. And it is a tribute to Hepburn's skill that she is able to convince the viewer that she really is as feather-brained and irresponsible as her character, Susan Vance, is supposed to be.

Curiously, on its initial release, *Bringing Up Baby* was only a moderate success, which did nothing to alter Katharine Hepburn's reputation of being 'box-office poison', which is how many in Hollywood regarded her after the failure of *Sylvia Scarlett*.

The reviews had, largely, been very good, but the box-office returns disappointed RKO who had financed the picture. But that scarcely mattered to Cary Grant. With *Bringing Up Baby,* he had finally delineated the man for whom he had jettisoned Archie Leach. The metamorphosis was complete. He was now a confident movie star. As Howard Hawks put it: 'Right now, Cary is hot.'

In later life, Grant tried to define what had happened. 'I pretended to be somebody I wanted to be,' he said. 'And I finally became that person. Or he became me. Or we met at some point. It's a relationship.'

Pauline Kael wrote, 'He (Grant) became a performer in an era in which learning to entertain the public was a trade. He worked at his trade, progressed, and rose to the top.'

9

'Money is the sixth sense that enables us to enjoy the other five.'

Orson Welles

Hollywood was definitely the most glamorous place in the world in the latter years of the 1930s. The Depression was easing, but over in Europe storm clouds were gathering. Everyone seemed to sense that the onslaught of war was going to be instrumental in changing everything for ever.

Maybe that's why the social elite in Hollywood partied more flamboyantly and spent more conspicuously than ever before. And at the epicentre of Tinseltown's new elite was Cary Grant who, rumours notwithstanding, was regarded as one of the most eligible bachelors in America, even if he was a divorcee.

Grant and his friends – who at this point included Cole Porter, Noel Coward, David Niven and Irene M. Selznick – were all inveterate party-goers and party-givers and Grant was renowned for his wit, which was as lively in private as it was on-screen.

As Grant, himself, became more and more successful, he, in turn, became increasingly fascinated by very wealthy – and successful – businessmen. His origins in Bristol may have been modest to say the least, but Elsie's conviction, drummed into him on their walks together along the River Avon, that success and wealth were his birthright had obviously taken hold. As soon as he had established himself, Grant was mixing in the company of the mega-rich, of whom Elsie would have wholeheartedly approved. Yet he still, somehow, managed to retain the common touch – something of which *both* his parents would have approved. It was just one more of the ambiguities and contradictions which made up his life. He even dined with Barbara Hutton, granddaughter and heiress of the Woolworth founder, Frank Winfield, aboard the *Normandie* liner in 1938 – neither then knowing just how much closer they were to become four years later and the pain that would ensue from their disastrous second meeting.

Grant was a superb businessman himself – 'before computers went into general release,' said David Niven, 'Cary had one in his brain' – and he revelled in the company of tycoons like William Randolph Hearst and Aristotle Onassis. But the tycoon to whom he was, surprisingly, closest was the enigmatic Howard Hughes.

Hughes, whose later obsessive reclusiveness has tended to overshadow the flamboyant brilliance of his early years, could have been a character from the fiction of F. Scott Fitzgerald. Having inherited vast wealth, amassed from oil, at the age of eighteen from his father, Hughes went on to create a fabulous financial empire of his own. One of Hughes's passions was the movie business, and he produced and directed, among others, the classic *Hell's Angels* (1930), *Scarface* (1932) and Jane Russell's notorious debut, *The Outlaw* (1943).

A superb pilot, Hughes broke the air speed record in September 1935, reaching 347.5 mph, and set a new record for a round-the-world flight in July 1938 when he and a four-man crew circumnavigated the earth in three days, nineteen hours and seventeen minutes in a typically bravura stunt to publicise the World's Fair.

Hughes also designed aircraft, including the legendary all-wooden 'Spruce Goose', ran commercial airlines and invested shrewdly in Las Vegas real estate.

Grant had been introduced to Hughes, whose own sexuality has been called into question many times, by Randolph Scott in 1933, just after both had appeared in the Paramount programme *Hot Saturday*. Grant and Hughes established an immediate rapport and it wasn't long before Hughes was Grant's passport into the grandest and most glamorous parties in Hollywood.

Hughes was a frequent house-guest when Grant and Scott shared their third house together – a beach house at 1018 Ocean Front Road in Santa Monica – between 1935 and 1942, and there have, somewhat inevitably, been suggestions that Grant and Hughes had a more than intimate relationship at this time. All that's known for sure is that Hughes had a profound impact on Grant.

'Howard Hughes was a brilliant man,' said Grant. 'Way ahead of his time. I would listen to him for hours, not always understanding at the time exactly what he meant. But as time went by, his thoughts would be proven correct.'

Hughes's business activities certainly rubbed off on Grant – and quickly. By the time he came to make *Gunga Din* in 1939, Grant was already an astute operator with various commercial interests.

'Cary used to do a lot of arbitrage,' recalled *Gunga Din* co-star, Douglas Fairbanks Jnr. 'He'd buy Japanese yen and sell English pounds and buy Italian lire or German marks. He did that every morning before work on *Gunga Din*. He'd look over the paper and buy and sell things and send messages to buy so many pounds and then sell so many yen, and so forth. I was fascinated.'

Grant's business acumen enabled him to become one of Hollywood's first truly commercially minded stars. 'Acting was never really important to me,' he claimed, late in life. 'What really interested me was the economics of the film business. The profit and loss account.'

Practically the first major star to be a success as a freelance, Grant was also the first star to negotiate a ten per cent cut of the gross of his films. In 1937, just five years after arriving in Hollywood and being signed by Paramount for $450 a week, Grant had negotiated a deal with Harry Cohn to make four films for Columbia Pictures over the next two years. The deal was that Grant would be paid $50,000 for each of the first two movies and $75,000 for each of the second pair. Or in other words, he had, at the age of thirty-three, a deal for a quarter of a million dollars. And that was with just one studio.

Cary Grant tended to regard himself as 'Cary Grant Incorporated'. He was the product of his business and he knew exactly his own value. More to the point, he knew he had a developing power, control and clout in Hollywood. The contracts he negotiated were tough and entirely on his terms and they evolved as he did. As Graham McCann observed in his biography of Grant, 'each time something happened on a movie that he regarded as unacceptable, he remembered to cover that issue in the next agreement he made.'

The contracts for Grant's later films even included a clause that ownership of the negative transferred to him seven or eight years after the film was released – he refused to make a picture if ownership remained with the studio. This meant that Cary Grant owned his last ten films – the Hitchcock films excepted – as well as the negative of *Penny Serenade*, which he made in 1941. All of which made him huge sums of money when re-released or sold for broadcast on television.

Grant's clout was such that his influence spread far beyond his own performance. Stanley Donen, who directed Grant in four movies and with whom Grant set up a production company in the 1950s said:

'If you were trying to make a movie and you needed twenty million dollars, you'd have a hell of a time getting it. But if you could say, "I've got Cary Grant," there was no money trouble. But that meant Cary was entitled to have an opinion. He was more than the star. He was the reason the picture got made.'

But Grant was no megalomaniac star. He took his responsibilities very seriously and Stanley Fox, a lawyer-manager at agents MCA who eventually became Grant's most trusted business colleague, remembered 'Cary sitting day after day with a film editor. He wanted a film to move and didn't want it to run more than 120 minutes. His sense of good timing extended to the pace of the movie itself.'

It was also sound business sense but, as Fox explained, there were good reasons for Grant's evolution into producing the movies in which he appeared: 'Ninety per cent of Cary's income was taxed, but we never took advantage of any dodges. We thought the dangers involved in those deals could cost more money than the high taxes. So we formed different corporations for different situations. When Cary did a film, he was employed by the company. That was less than he could get if he were working for a studio. But he owned the picture. The company would get 75 per cent of the profits and the studios would get the other 25 per cent for putting up all the money and giving us whatever backing we needed. We got offices and an expense account.'

Peter Bogdanovich once said that he'd asked several of Grant's directors about how particular choice moments in his movies had been achieved and had received the usual reply of 'that was Cary's idea'. He became well known for his perfectionism on a movie set – indeed, in all aspects of his life. He would inspect every detail of the set and insist on changes if he felt they were called for. This didn't always go down well with the production staff – 'he was the biggest old woman I've ever worked with,' complained one cinematographer – and the production manager on *Night And Day* (1946) noted that 'I don't think there's a set on this picture that hasn't been changed by Cary and it's cost the studio a terrific amount of money.'

Graham McCann recounted the 'countless stories of Grant's insistence on minor and major changes to the dialogue, the costume

design and the decor: rooms that looked, he said, too small or too large, painting that needed to be replaced, doorknobs painted different colours, windows changed, camera angles altered, lenses switched...'
One reporter, interviewing Grant on the set of a movie on which he'd just started wrote that, 'he's the only star I've ever known who personally examines each extra before a scene to make sure they're dressed right.'

But then Grant knew what he was looking for. Edith Head, the *grande dame* of Hollywood costume designers who won eight Oscars for her work on films such as *All About Eve* (1950) and *The Sting* (1972), and whose first solo credit was *She Done Him Wrong,* thought Grant's taste was 'impeccable'.

'I consider him not only the most beautiful, but the most beautifully dressed man in the world,' she said. 'His is a discerning eye, a meticulous sense of detail. He has the greatest fashion sense of any actor I've ever worked with. He knows as much about women's clothes as he does about men's.'

Grant made no apologies for interfering with the look of a film. He told one reporter that 'it takes five hundred small details to add up to one favourable impression' and this was a philosophy he imposed as strictly on himself as anyone else.

If Grant controlled his career with an iron grip, he controlled his image just as assiduously. He refused to be photographed in close-up from the left side – 'I look dead' – and would measure the cut of his hand-made shirts or suits with a rule, sending them back if he felt measurements were out by as little as one-eighth of an inch.

Although Grant used the legendary Lew Wasserman at MCA and Stanley Fox to represent him on a deal – they split the ten per cent commission – he was, essentially, his own agent. He also invested in the Frank Vincent Agency and involved himself in the contract negotiations of other stars, including Greta Garbo and Rita Hayworth. Small wonder that, when the top agent Myron Selznick died in 1944, a columnist wrote: 'Now that Myron is gone, Cary Grant is the best agent in Hollywood.'

Some writers have tried to depict Grant as a man haunted by the poverty of his youth who had a morbid fear of being poor again. Others – Alexander Walker, for instance – take a more positive view and suggest that Grant was merely an exponent of self-reliance. Whatever his spur, Grant was tough at dealing with the studio bosses and, after what he considered to have been Paramount's shoddy treatment of him, he shared Charlie Chaplin's opinion that they were 'inconsiderate, unsympathetic and short-sighted'.

For their part, the studio bosses resented him for it and there can be little doubt that the rumours about Grant's meanness and obsession for money – though undeniably based in truth – were propagated by the movie moguls. This was picked up by certain columnists who, probably because he refused to co-operate with them, attacked him in print for being a social-climbing gold-digger. Grant couldn't have cared less. He worked hard and believed he was entitled to enjoy the rewards his career brought him and in the manner and style he so chose.

'I like money,' he once said. 'Anybody know anyone who doesn't?'

He would remain money-oriented to the end of his life but, to his credit, it was a characteristic he both recognised and, occasionally, mocked.

'I examine and add up the bill anywhere I go,' he said in the early 1980s. 'And so should anyone at today's prices. I'm not afraid to – I don't indulge in such insecurity. They say I still have the first nickel I ever earned and carry it around. But it's not true. If it were, I wouldn't carry it around. It would be in a case because it would be a collector's item and worth a whole lot more now.'

When an interviewer asked him if it was true that he cut off and saved the buttons from his old shirts, Grant confirmed and justified it by saying, 'It's perfectly sensible. I have special buttons made and when one falls off and gets lost, if I keep the old ones I can replace them at no extra cost. Besides, the cleaning lady uses my old shirts as dusters and if the buttons were still in place, they'd scratch the furniture.'

In spite of his comments – very tongue-in-cheek comments, it should be noted – the picture painted by some columnists in the late 1930s of Grant as the relentless social climber can be deemed a little unjust. Although he was fascinated by those who had achieved status through having great business acumen, the true litmus test of his friendships was whether people were good company or were interesting personalities who could feed his hungry imagination, such as Howard Hughes. If there were side benefits – it was Hughes, then dating Katharine Hepburn, who first suggested to director George Cukor that Grant would be the perfect lead in *Sylvia Scarlett* – then, so be it.

While Grant inevitably moved in affluent, privileged circles, he was always at ease with people from every level of society and, with a naturally friendly disposition, was quite able to put anyone at ease. Other than the fact that Grant was one of the very few Hollywood icons to disassociate himself from cliques, one close friendship that he formed in the mid-1930s and which was to last until his death in 1986 also blows away his supposed ruthless social climbing.

Albert Romolo ('Cubby') Broccoli may have gone on to establish cinema's longest-running and most successful franchise with the James Bond movies, starting in 1962, but when he arrived in Hollywood in the mid-1930s to join his cousin, Pat de Cicco – who was then working as an agent – he was just another 25-year-old from an Italian farming family looking for a slice of the action. Broccoli, who died in 1996, recounted his arrival at Pat de Cicco's house in Hollywood in 1934 in his biography, *When The Snow Melts,* which was published posthumously:

'I'm hardly there more than a few minutes when there's a ring at the door. "See who it is, Cubby, will you?" I open the door. It's Cary Grant. *The* Cary Grant, dropping by to borrow something from Pat. On the doorstep, smiling that famous matinee idol's smile. I call Pat and it's obvious he and Cary Grant are buddies. I'm knocked out at meeting this famous movie star.'

Broccoli described his cousin and himself as 'the suave wealthy man about town and his hick cousin' but Grant immediately warmed to the 'hick' cousin and grew very fond of the young Broccoli. It was reciprocated and in the 1950s Broccoli said that his two closest confidants were his cousin Pat and Cary Grant.

Apart from their friendship, formed on Broccoli's first day in Hollywood, Grant and Broccoli had a mutual friend in Howard Hughes. On Broccoli's second night in Hollywood, he visited the Colony Club and, being alone, was idly spinning a silver dollar. Another man, also alone, challenged him to 'Heads or Tails'. The stranger won the call, and three dollars, and Broccoli won a good friend for life – the stranger just happening to be Howard Hughes.

When Hughes had an appalling flying accident in 1946 while testing a military prototype aircraft he had spent six million dollars of his own money developing, Grant and Broccoli were among the handful of people allowed past the armed guards outside Hughes's room at the Good Samaritan Hospital.

Significantly, then, the friendships Grant made during the mid-to-late thirties proved to be enduring and were far from being the opportunistic kind he was accused of forging by the media at that time.

This was also true of the professional bonds he made. Katharine Hepburn might have been regarded in the industry as 'box-office poison', but Grant, who respected Hepburn's skill as an actress – 'Kate's a joy' he declared – had no qualms appearing with her again in *Holiday* immediately after *Bringing Up Baby*. And that despite the disappointing box-office returns on the latter film. He showed an even greater loyalty to the actress Ingrid Bergman after everyone else in Hollywood had shunned her following her decision to walk out on her marriage and child for another man.

Hepburn had bought herself out of her contract with RKO after *Bringing Up Baby* – without any protest from the studio, it must be said – and *Holiday* was made for Columbia.

The film had started life as a play by Philip Barry. Hepburn had understudied the leading role during its Broadway run and wisely bought the film rights after it had been made once before in 1930. She put together a package, with herself as star and George Cukor as director, and sold the whole lot to Columbia's Harry Cohn. There was little doubt in anyone's mind who should play the lead male role of Johnny Case, who becomes involved with the daughter of an uptight New York family only to then fall in love with her sister, played by Hepburn. The role of Johnny, an intelligent young man, making his way upwards socially into the idle rich but not uncritically, fitted Grant like a skin and it's obvious throughout the film that he identified with Johnny's ultimate rejection of the conventional. It's obvious, too, that George Cukor exploited much of Grant's own personality in developing the character.

Holiday (known as *Free To Live* in the UK) is not as widely remembered as *Bringing Up Baby* today but, at the time of release, the critics received it just as enthusiastically. Grant's performance under Cukor is, once again, an understated joy and relies heavily on his own natural sense of humour and comic timing. Although the screenwriters Ogden Stewart and Sidney Buchman made few changes to Barry's original play, they threw in a couple of scenes – or, maybe, Grant did – that allowed Grant to display his athletic prowess in backward somersaults, a legacy from his Pender days, of course. The film is interesting for purveyors of film trivia as well: the character actor Edward Everett Horton played the same role in both the 1930 and 1938 film versions.

Holiday was the precursor of an even greater success for Grant, Hepburn and the director, Cukor. Three years later, they collaborated on the screen version of another Philip Barry play, *The Philadelphia Story.*

After a run of three consecutive comedies, Grant felt it was time for a change of pace and his next movie, which was for RKO, was *Gunga Din* and was directed by George Stevens and produced by Pandro S. Berman.

Stevens, who also directed Grant in *Penny Serenade* in 1941 and *The Talk of The Town* in 1942, had worked for Hal Roach as an assistant cameraman in the early twenties on such classic comedies as the Laurel and Hardy two- and three-reelers before becoming a prolific director of standard Hollywood fare in the pre-war years. His films ranged from romantic comedies to action adventures and so-called 'women's pictures' and included the Fred Astaire–Ginger Rogers vehicle *Swing Time* in 1936.

In 1942, just after directing Grant in *The Talk of The Town,* Stevens left Hollywood to take charge of a film unit to cover the war in Europe. In his own way, he was emulating Leni Riefenstahl in Germany, but with less attention to the propaganda element of his work. Riefenstahl, a beautiful former silent-screen star turned producer-director-photographer, made stunningly evocative films of the rise and rise of the Nazi party, which were part of Hitler's sustained propaganda campaign.

On the other side of the conflict, Stevens witnessed and filmed some of the most significant moments of the Second World War, including the D-Day landings, the liberation of Paris and the opening of the Dachau concentration camps. Much of this colour footage only came to light after his death in 1975 and appeared on British television screens as recently as 1999 under the title *World War Two In Colour.* Narrated by English actor John Thaw, this highly acclaimed series was, rather poignantly, produced by Stevens' son, George Stevens Jnr.

Stevens' wartime experiences, coupled with his falling foul of the absurd McCarthy witch-hunts, meant that most of his post-war films became much darker: films like *A Place In The Sun* (1951), that magnificently cynical and brooding pairing of Montgomery Clift and Elizabeth Taylor, which many critics called one of the greatest films of all time; *Shane* (1953), the classic western starring Alan Ladd; *Giant* (1956), James Dean's swansong; and *The Diary of Anne Frank* (1959).

In 1965, Stevens directed the biblical epic *The Greatest Story Ever Told*. Alas, it felt more like the *longest* story ever told, dying at the box office and almost bankrupting its studio. Stevens was left virtually unbankable as a director and made just one more film (*The Only Game In Town* in 1969).

But Stevens, at 35, exactly the same age as Grant, was at the peak of his form when he came to *Gunga Din*. The screenplay, by Joel Sayre and Fred Guiol, was supposedly based on the poem by Rudyard Kipling, but any connection between the two was, in reality, purely coincidental. The screenplay was a rousing mix of adventure and bawdy barrack-room comedy and if it seems terribly jingoistic and politically incorrect now, it proved extremely popular with audiences then.

This was particularly important for Grant's career. Though *Bringing Up Baby* and *Holiday* had been great critical successes, neither had performed particularly well at the box-office. Grant was first to accept that critics do not make stars – box-office returns make stars. He needed, therefore, a resounding hit and, right from the start, he knew that a popular, rollicking adventure like this one was likely to provide it.

Furthermore, with a budget of two million dollars – RKO's biggest ever up to that time – *Gunga Din* was going to be a massive production. Again, Grant was shrewd enough to see that Hollywood needed to see him in a big budget action movie as well as the more homespun comedy vehicles.

Not only did his wisdom show in his agreeing to make the picture but again, when, after a couple of days of shooting had got underway, he recognised that he had been miscast. He was signed up to play Ballantine, a soldier determined to leave the army to marry and run a tea plantation. Douglas Fairbanks Jnr and Victor McLaglen had been cast as Cutter and MacChesney respectively, his comrades who try to dissuade him from leaving. But Grant quickly saw that he was more suited to the role of the cockney Cutter: the *second* lead.

Stevens and the producer, Berman, were astonished when Grant suggested what was tantamount to demotion by switching his role with Fairbanks. Had any major Hollywood star ever before sacrificed the lead in a motion picture? But they agreed, and it quickly became apparent that Grant's instincts were spot on: Ballantine was a straightforward, maybe even stolid, swashbuckling type – but Cutter had an undercurrent of humour that suited Grant. Berman even agreed with Grant's suggested in-joke: Cutter's first name was changed to 'Archie'.

Gunga Din gave Grant the major hit he wanted and needed. It was the second-highest grossing picture of the year and, more than sixty years later, still moves quickly. It remained one of Grant's personal favourites and, years later, he recalled it as being one of the most enjoyable jobs he'd ever had.

Gunga Din was followed by a more straightforward adventure story for Columbia. *Only Angels Have Wings,* a typically macho yarn from director Howard Hawks about the tough head of an air-freight service in Central America, gave Grant another massive box-office success in 1939. Paired with Jean Arthur, excellent in the thankless and underwritten part of stranded showgirl Bonnie Lee, Grant gave a surprisingly atypical performance – harder, and more cynical than previously, his moodiness wrong-footed everyone and served as a rehearsal for some of the darker performances he would later give for Alfred Hitchcock. Despite the success of *Only Angels Have Wings*, it was a somewhat dour and disappointing film – 'it's too bad an above-average cast had to be wasted on the story' thought the *New Republic*. But by the time of its release, that didn't seem to matter: by the end of 1939, everyone in Hollywood, like everyone everywhere else, was concentrating almost solely on world events. Particularly if, like Cary Grant, they happened to be English.

10

'I feel so damned helpless here. I feel I want to go back.'

Cary Grant

Grant was working on *In Name Only* – a romantic drama co-starring the ill-fated Carole Lombard (soon to die in an air crash) – for RKO, his third film of 1939, when Britain declared war on Germany in September of that year.

He had spent some time in Europe on vacation the previous autumn and these trips underlined to him just how far the place he now called home was from his actual roots. However, by 1939, Grant felt American, so much so that he had already begun the lengthy, wearisome process of becoming an American citizen, a process that would not be completed until 26 June 1942, when his name was changed officially to Cary Grant. But the outbreak of war put him in a troubling dilemma. Should he go back to do his bit, or should he stay put?

The first months of war were not too bad – this was the period of the so-called 'Phoney War', when many people in Britain were lulled into believing the war wouldn't be so bad after all because of the relative lack of activity. But when the war news became increasingly depressing during 1940, with Britain standing alone and seemingly vulnerable to invasion at any time, Grant, like the rest of the British expat community based in California simply didn't know what to do. The frustration and isolation such figures must have felt would have been quite considerable.

Their position was hardly helped by the treatment meted out to Grant's friend, David Niven. Niven had decided to join up as soon as war was declared and tried to enlist in the Canadian Army, reasoning, sensibly, that it was easier to reach Canada than London. Douglas Fairbanks Jnr and Grant threw a farewell party for Niven, who must have thought he was setting a good example to the rest of the British ex-pats. Alas, on arrival in Canada, the Canadian armed forces made it plain they neither wanted nor needed Niven.

Undeterred, and still desperately keen to make a contribution to the war effort, Niven then made a highly tortuous journey back to Britain – at his own expense – to join the RAF. But the RAF didn't want him either and, worse, the British press – the same press that castigated men like Cary Grant for not having returned to fight – accused the increasingly bewildered Niven of merely pulling a publicity stunt. This didn't stop them urging the ex-pats in Hollywood, whom they accused of being 'gone with the wind up', to 'come back home *like David Niven*' once Niven had been accepted as a subaltern in the Rifle Brigade.

It was an uncertain and messy few months. Perhaps more than any other British actor in Hollywood, the war forced Grant to confront the question of just who he was. Typically, he found it difficult to reconcile the many contradictory facets of his persona. On the one hand, he was seeking to become an American citizen and, given that America was to remain resolutely isolationist until December 1941, he did not feel compelled by American public opinion to return to England to fight. Added to this was the fact that, although he looked the epitome of athleticism on-screen, Cary Grant celebrated his thirty-sixth birthday in January 1940. That would have made him a more mature recruit than most. There was certainly no question of his being called up for active service.

However, he was still, fundamentally, a British subject and, as he listened to the ever-worsening news from Britain, his Britishness became as apparent to him as the *non*-Britishness of his American friends and colleagues. Indeed, years after becoming an American citizen, Grant would maintain he was 'very pro-British and terribly British minded.'

Grant was also acutely aware of the dangers faced by his family back in Bristol at this time – his mother, Elsie, still stubbornly refused to join him in California – and their circumstance worried him. He sent food parcels whenever possible and listened anxiously for any scraps of news about bombing raids on Bristol and the south west of England.

His concern proved tragically well founded. In 1941, under a deluge of bombs on Bristol, Dean Street in the St Paul's district of the city was hit. It killed three generations of the Leach family, including Elias's brother. Grant was devastated by the news and it seemed to mark the point where his resolve to do something hardened. In 1940, Grant's exasperation had already displayed itself in the remark, 'I feel so damned helpless here. I feel I want to go back. I could be an ARP warden. I could be a fire-fighter. I could do *something.*'

His frustration wasn't assisted when, after making enquiries about the possibility of his joining the Navy, Grant learned that the Foreign Office had advised the Admiralty against accepting him. A similar idea of volunteering for the US military also came to nought: he was rejected for the Army Air Corps in 1943.

Tired of being attacked in the British press for staying in Hollywood – Grant was a specific target – the ex-pats sought clarification from the British government on exactly what was the best way for them to serve the war effort. Many journalists might have been urging them home to fight, but this was countered by articles such as one early in 1940 which suggested that David Niven had done the wrong thing in joining up: 'The British film fan does not want David Niven in the army, the navy or the air force. We want him in his proper place, right up there on screen, helping us to forget this war a little.'

To clarify what the British government's stance was on British actors living in Hollywood, Grant and the actor Cedric Hardwicke flew to Washington in the summer of 1940 as representatives of their colony as a whole. They met up with the British Ambassador, Lord Lothian. His orders were straightforward enough. Echoing those published articles, he said, 'Stay put and carry on doing what you do best.'

This also echoed what Winston Churchill had told Noel Coward around this time; Coward having offered his services at the very outbreak of hostilities. 'You'd be no good in the intelligence service,' Churchill told him. 'Get into a warship and . . . go sing to them when the guns are firing – that's your job.'

Like Lord Lothian's, it was sound advice. Even if the likes of Grant and Coward were left feeling temporarily impotent, the maintenance of an influential British colony in Hollywood went far beyond the boosting of morale. The importance of such pro-British films as *Mrs. Miniver* in 1942 in swinging American public opinion against isolationism can never be overstated.

In his report of the meeting with Grant and Hardwicke to the British government, Lord Lothian appended a note which sounded a criticism of the British press: 'It's quite unfair,' he wrote, 'to condemn older actors, who are simply obeying this ruling, as "deserters".'

Unfortunately, his note was not made public until after the war, which meant that the British colony in California continued to be regarded as cowardly for the duration: 'All Englishmen still working in Hollywood should be filmed in black and white,' suggested *Picturegoer* in 1942, 'because Technicolor would show up the yellow of their skin.'

Grant could hold his head up, however. Having accepted the advice of the British government to continue making films, he contributed enormously to the war effort. He served on the Los Angeles Committee of the British War Relief Society and was instrumental in the sending of more than four thousand packets of seeds to the National Allotments Society in Britain – seemingly small fry to fighting combat war, but an absolutely vital contribution to the 'Digging For Victory' campaign that was helping to feed the beleaguered civilian population of Britain.

A little earlier, in 1940, in common with other Hollywood stars, he sponsored a child from the British Actors' Orphanage (whose president was Noel Coward) to be evacuated to New York.

In the manner of Bob Hope, he also took to touring service camps tirelessly, talking to GIs and proving particularly good at lifting the spirits of the wounded. On one month-long tour of military bases around America for the United States Organisations, Grant played straightman to Bert Lahr – best-known for playing the Cowardly Lion in the film *The Wizard Of Oz* – when they performed some classic vaudeville routines. Sadly, the event was not even partly filmed for posterity.

Grant also made several propaganda films: the most typical, perhaps, being the ten minute, star-studded *The Road to Victory* produced by Warner Brothers in 1944 to promote the Fifth War Loan Drive. And, in a pleasing gesture, he donated his entire $125,000 salary from *The Philadelphia Story* in 1941 to the British War Relief Fund.

When Gladys Cooper reported tensions between Grant and Niven on the set of *The Bishop's Wife* in 1947 whenever the subject of the war came up, Grant surely had no reason to feel awkward: he had contributed more than enough to the war effort. But was what Cooper perceived as awkwardness on Grant's part about his not having been in uniform actually a frustration about being unable to reveal the truth about the secret work he had been engaged upon during the war years? Had Cary Grant, as seems highly probable from recent revelations, been working for the British Intelligence Services all along?

The first hint that Grant's wartime career might have been more significant than anyone suspected came as early as 18 April 1947, when

King George VI awarded him the King's Medal for Service In The Cause Of Freedom. At the time, it was announced that Grant had been awarded the medal for 'outstanding service to the British Relief Society' and thus caused little comment. In recent years, however, it has come to light that this medal was generally awarded to individuals who had taken part in intelligence duties.

Of even greater significance was the revelation that Grant had links with Sir William Stephenson, the legendary head of British Security Co-ordination in the US – the euphemistic name for British Intelligence – and that he had liaised with Noel Coward and Alexander Korda on intelligence issues in Los Angeles.

Maybe most telling of all is the fact that all wartime British files on Cary Grant remain classified.

So what is the truth? Did Grant spy for Britain, both before and after he became an American citizen? Indeed, just how 'American' was he?

The FBI certainly regarded him with suspicion, though it is fair to argue they regarded *everyone* with suspicion. During the McCarthy witch-hunts of the 1950s, they even suspected him of having pro-communist leanings – a somewhat ironical notion considering other writers have labelled him as being rabidly right wing and others still have suggested he was entirely apolitical. But then, politically, as in every other facet of his life, Grant's make-up and beliefs were far from simple or simplistic.

If we can be sure of one thing, it is that Grant despised Nazism. Even if he did hold some right-wing views – his support of President Ronald Reagan in the 1980s suggesting as much – these were tempered by liberal instincts on matters of personal morality: everything the Nazis detested.

He might have been pushing his application for American citizenship through in the first two years of the war, but thoughts of England and his family in Bristol were never far from his mind throughout the whole campaign. Given that Grant was a perfectionist in all he did, it is entirely conceivable that, thwarted from making a contribution to the war effort in uniform, he would take up an opportunity to assist in a far more shadowy role. Riven with internalised hang-ups he may well have been, but Grant was no shirker when it came to duty. He had the ability to adapt and apply himself to any new role required of him with consummate skill. If he truly wasn't an agent, then he should have been, for who could possibly suspect Cary Grant of being a spy?

Nor is there anything fanciful about his discussing intelligence matters with Noel Coward. Despite Churchill's assertion that the most valuable contribution the playwright could make to the war effort was to sing 'Mad Dogs And Englishmen' to the troops as they came under fire – a suggestion Coward found insulting – Noel Coward *did* go on to work for British Intelligence, to a lesser or greater degree, during the war years and had established a Bureau of Propaganda in Paris before the fall of France.

Despite the scepticism of the British press to Coward's work – Max Beaverbrook, who loathed Coward, ensured the coverage of Coward in the *Daily Express* rivalled Hitler's in opprobrium – the British government was satisfied with what he had achieved. In 1940 the Ministry of Information suggested that a tour of the US by prominent British writers such as Coward could help explain the British position and assist in countering those vociferous opponents (such as Charles Lindbergh) of America entering the war.

Coward spent six weeks touring America, including visiting President Roosevelt on two separate occasions at the White House, and there was hardly any equivocation about his Intelligence contacts. On his departure, the *New York Times* calmly reported that 'Mr. Coward has been on a six-week furlough from secret British Government duties.'

During the Los Angeles leg of his tour, Coward stayed with Grant and Randolph Scott at their house and visited the set of *The Philadelphia Story,* which Grant was then making with Katharine Hepburn and James Stewart under the direction of George Cukor.

Given that Grant and Coward had, by then, been close friends for the best part of a decade, it is inconceivable that they did not discuss Coward's work for the British government. Grant, eager for first-hand news of the situation in Britain, would have pumped Coward for as much information as possible. And Coward, who had assured Roosevelt – 'beyond all logic and reason' – that Germany would never invade England, was likely to have been much more pessimistic in private with Grant.

If Grant was, indeed, a British agent, was this the moment when he was recruited? Did Noel Coward recruit Grant into British Intelligence or lead him to the appropriate figures authorised to recruit? The evidence is compelling.

Coward certainly worked for Sir William Stephenson, as did

Alexander Korda and Leslie Howard. Stephenson also liaised with Ian Fleming, later to become famous as the creator of James Bond, but then a commander with Naval Intelligence at the Admiralty.

Coward and Fleming were close friends – they would both build homes near each other in Jamaica after the war – as were, of course, Grant and Coward. Grant also knew Fleming, although the date of their first meeting is unclear. (Fleming made reference to Grant's film *North By Northwest* in his novel *Thunderball* in 1959; and Grant said that he was a great Fleming *aficionado* when 'Cubby' Broccoli approached him to play James Bond in the early 1960s.)

It was by all accounts a closely knit group of friends. Furthermore, both Stephenson and Fleming liked the idea of using celebrities as agents. With America still, officially, neutral, Stephenson could not operate British agents openly in the USA: but celebrities, supposedly on promotional trips, could move freely without raising too many suspicions. As Coward himself remarked, 'My major weapon is my celebrity – and my disguise is my own reputation as a bit of an idiot.'

Grant certainly fitted what Stephenson and Fleming required. It is likely that he commenced working for Stephenson from the middle of 1940, about the time that Noel Coward stayed at his house in Los Angeles in fact.

One of Grant's first assignments for Stephenson in 1940 seems to have been to report on anti-semitism in Hollywood. Whether Stephenson gave him this assignment deliberately will probably never be known but, either way, it was entirely appropriate because there is a tantalising suggestion that Cary Grant was himself Jewish.

Elias Leach is generally regarded as having come from a Jewish background, although he married Elsie in the local parish church, and Archie was circumcised at birth, something that Grant later believed was because Elias was at least partly Jewish.

Virginia Cherrill, Grant's first wife, certainly believed Grant to be Jewish and, while he denied it to some people, Grant gave the impression to others that he believed he was. And even though he told the late Walter Matthau in the early 1960s that he wasn't Jewish, Matthau said he believed he was. Certainly, if he *was* Jewish, it would help to explain why he contributed so much time and money to the defeat of Nazism – and why he might have been tempted to go that extra mile and become an agent for British Intelligence. But right-minded people of *all* persuasions are, and always have been, implacably opposed to the cancer of fascism and so Grant's opposition to the Nazis doesn't in itself resolve the issue.

Perhaps this is why some previous biographers have perpetrated a bizarre theory, one that even Oliver Stone would find difficult to swallow, that Grant was, in fact, the illegitimate son of a Jewish woman called Lillian who died or vanished. The main piece of evidence for this rests on the fact that, until the 1960s, the name given to Grant's mother in *Who's Who In America* is Lillian, and not Elsie. The possibility of a clerical error by the compiler seems to have unwittingly – or not so unwittingly? – been overlooked by these earlier biographers.

And yet, as with so many other aspects of Grant's contradictory and indeterminate personality, it is also true that he *did* support Jewish charities to a surprising degree for a man who once called himself 'a member of the Church of England' – an odd description in itself for someone who was now an American citizen.

In 1948, he donated a large sum of money to the newly established State of Israel and, in 1953, he attended two fundraising events to celebrate three thousand years of Jerusalem. Like doubts about his sexuality and rumours about his career as a British spy, the confusion over whether he was Jewish or not is yet another unresolved mystery in the enigma that is Cary Grant.

11

'Nobody plays Cary Grant like Cary Grant.'

Tony Curtis

In Name Only, which was made by *Gunga Din* producer Pandro Berman for RKO, was a disappointment to Grant. He had wanted to stretch himself by appearing in a dark melodrama, but the script was, essentially, an upmarket soap opera and he was somewhat wasted in the underwritten, passive male role and overshadowed by the more showy female characters played by Kay Francis and Carole Lombard.

Grant reckoned that *In Name Only* was a throwback to the weaker films of his Paramount contract days, and his disappointment was shared by the public who didn't care for it at all. Time has treated the film a little more kindly, however, and some contemporary critics now regard it as one of Grant's most underrated performances.

Interestingly, the script was better received as a radio broadcast, which Grant and his leading ladies performed for the CBS 'Lux Radio Theatre' on 11 December 1939. Grant appeared several times a year in radio adaptations of his films between the late 1930s and the early 1950s: it was a relatively easy way of publicising both himself and his work without having to travel.

If *In Name Only* was a disappointment, Grant had good reason to feel pleased about his next movie. *His Girl Friday,* directed by Howard Hawks and co-starring Rosalind Russell was not simply a triumph: it can lay claim to being the greatest, funniest screen comedy of all time. Actor Tony Curtis probably puts it more succinctly than anyone can when he says, 'In this movie, Cary is at his very best. He's brash, cocky and scheming. He switches from likeable to unlikeable in a blink. Yet he has so much charm despite the despicable character he represents. And still he keeps you smiling. Nobody plays Cary Grant like Cary Grant.'

Grant is at the very apotheosis of his career as a screen comedian in

His Girl Friday, but what makes the film so triumphant is that he was surrounded, both on screen and behind the camera, by colleagues who were also at their peak. Written by Ben Hecht and Charles Lederner, *His Girl Friday* was based on the scathingly cynical Broadway play, *The Front Page*, by Hecht and Charles MacArthur. It had been filmed once before in 1931 by Lewis Milestone. That version had starred Pat O'Brien and Adolphe Menjou and was produced by Howard Hughes. It was also re-made in 1974, disappointingly, by Billy Wilder with Jack Lemmon and Walter Matthau in the leads.

Howard Hawks's masterstroke when deciding to remake the movie with Cary Grant in 1940 was to make one fundamental change: he altered the sex of one of the main protagonists from male to female. Thus the story of the original play and first film version – of a manipulative newspaper editor using every cynical trick in the book to hold onto his ace reporter – retained its blackly hilarious and scathing commentary about the media, but also acquired the extra layer of a sophisticated battle of the sexes.

Grant plays Walter Burns, the editor of a major Chicago newspaper who is about to lose his best reporter, and former wife, Hildy Johnson (Rosalind Russell) to a boring insurance salesman, played by Ralph Bellamy. Using every trick in the book, Burns convinces her to cover one last big story – a man awaiting execution on Death Row – to win her back as his reporter *and* his wife.

Grant had the time of his life making this movie, and it shows. Not only was he reunited with Ralph Bellamy, who had proved such a perfect foil in *The Awful Truth*, but he found in Rosalind Russell a co-star who was absolutely on his wavelength and could respond to his ad-libs with retorts as lightning fast as his were to hers. And their ad-libbing was encouraged by Howard Hawks, who also instructed his actors to overlap their lines – at times it feels like everyone on-screen is talking at once – and to move faster than normal around the set to give the film a breakneck pace.

In one key scene, Russell improvised by hurling her handbag at Grant. Although he wasn't expecting it, Grant ducked with perfect timing – not bad as he wasn't facing her full on. As the bag flew over his head he ad-libbed, 'You're losing your eye. You used to be able to pitch better than that.' A delighted Hawks kept the whole thing in.

When Grant's character is asked to describe Bruce Baldwin, Bellamy's character, he replies, 'He looks like that fellow in the movies

– y'know, Ralph Bellamy.' And on another occasion says, 'Listen, the last man who said that to me was Archie Leach – just a week before he cut his throat.' Both were ad-libs, the latter being particularly telling. Grant even managed to ad-lib the last line in the movie. Reconciled with his ex-wife, he leaves her struggling to carry all their luggage. When she's in danger of dropping one of their cases from under her arm, Grant suggests, 'Why don't you carry that in your hand...?'

Pauline Kael described the characters in *His Girl Friday* as 'brittle, cynical, childish people rushing around on corrupt errands'.

But the astonishing thing is that we care about these characters, despite the 101 reasons not to and despite the gallows black humour which runs throughout the plot. One or two critics at the time might have described it as tasteless, but audiences loved it and it became a huge hit. It took Cary Grant at his inspired best to make this possible and it really has to rate as one of his finest moments in his long and distinguished career.

The film also provided Grant with a lasting friend in Rosalind Russell. They actually began an affair during the making of the movie even though he was, at this time, romantically linked to Mary Brian – a popular actress in the 1920s whose career had waned with the advent of sound – Ginger Rogers and the aspiring starlet Phyllis Brooks.

Though Grant's affair with Russell didn't lead anywhere, he was instrumental in her subsequent marriage to Danish producer Frederick Brisson. Brisson, who had worked mostly in Britain until 1939, was a friend of Grant's and was staying with him and Randolph Scott during the making of *His Girl Friday*. Grant engineered meetings between Russell and Brisson and was best man when finally they decided to marry.

More than twenty years after the making of *His Girl Friday*, Grant suggested that he had 'probably made too many films' during this period. But he was on a roll in 1940. And everybody knew it. There was no reason for him to cut down his workload – indeed, there was every incentive *not* to – and he went straight from *His Girl Friday* to *My Favorite Wife* for RKO, a sequel of sorts to *The Awful Truth*.

Although no one, including Grant, realised at the time, *His Girl Friday* had marked something of a watershed in his career, and in Hollywood comedy as a whole. And *My Favorite Wife* was the proof. The movie reunited Grant – who received a payment of $100,000 – with Irene Dunne and Leo McCarey, his co-star and director respectively from *The Awful Truth* three years previously. Dunne played Ellen, wife of Nick (Grant) who has been missing, presumed dead for seven years. In reality she's been shipwrecked on a desert island with Burkett, played by a somewhat stolid Randolph Scott. Rescued, Ellen returns home – only to find that Nick has remarried. As a premise for a re-run of *The Awful Truth*, the set-up certainly promised much. And had McCarey been able to fulfil his intended role as director, who knows? Sadly, McCarey was badly injured in a car crash before the shooting and, although he remained on board as producer, Garson Kanin took over the helm.

There is nothing actually wrong with *My Favorite Wife*. It moves briskly and the performances of Grant and Dunne, who also played together a year later on the tear-jerking *Penny Serenade*, are as polished as one might expect. The director Garson Kanin remembered Grant as a man who 'worked very hard – almost more than any other quality was his seriousness about his work. He was always prepared, he always knew his part, his lines, and the scene. And he related very well to the other players. He not only took his own part seriously, he took the whole picture seriously. He'd come and look at the rushes every evening. No matter how carefree and easy-going he seemed in performance, in reality he was a serious man, an exceptionally concentrated man. And extremely intelligent, too.'

Kanin's words were echoed by Douglas Fairbanks Jnr, Grant's friend and co-star in *Gunga Din*. 'Cary was the most generous player I've ever worked with,' said Fairbanks. 'He wasn't just taking his salary. He was concerned that the picture be a good picture. He believed that what was good for the picture was good for him. He was a master technician, which many people don't realise, meticulous and conscious of every move. It might have looked impetuous or impulsive, but it wasn't. It was all carefully planned. Cary was a very sharp and intelligent actor who worked out everything ahead.'

And yet, for all Grant's intelligent playing and planning, *My Favorite Wife* somehow never quite achieves the level of brilliance of *The Awful Truth* or *Bringing Up Baby* or *His Girl Friday*. *Time* magazine thought the film beneath Grant and even the director Kanin described it as 'mechanical'.

The truth ran deeper: Hollywood screen comedy was suddenly in crisis in 1940. *My Favorite Wife* was the first indication that the type of movie that had offered Grant the best opportunity for his comic abilities was no longer viable.

'The party was running down,' wrote Grant's biographer Richard Schickel in regard to the sudden downturn in Hollywood screen comedy at this time. 'Everyone was feeling talked out. Especially the writers. They were beginning to go soft and over-ripe in the LA sun. And some of them were beginning to feel guilty and to feel a pressure to say something significant, important, serious about the state of the world. They had glided through the Depression years on the wings of wit and manner borrowed from Broadway in the 1920s. Now, with a world war about to begin, they were not going to make that mistake again.'

Grant had proved that he could play everything from high farce to high adventure, but he was acutely aware that the kind of roles for which Cary Grant was best known would be much rarer in the years to come. He would have to adapt to the changing climate.

In itself, this didn't worry him too greatly. He had always liked to vary his roles as much as possible. His dispute with Paramount centred as much on the succession of similar, bland roles he was given as it did on his resentment of being regarded as a poor man's Gary Cooper. But he knew he would have to tread with care.

He would be 37 on his next birthday: hardly old, but approaching middle-age, and this would be an influence on the kind of roles he would be asked to play. The 1940s were going to prove perhaps his most challenging era.

As for his next film, *The Howards Of Virginia* (1940), (known as *The Tree Of Liberty* in the UK) 'challenge' was hardly the word. The biggest challenge was for the audience watching it. Put simply, it is probably the worst film of Grant's career as a major star. It was released through Columbia in September of 1940, just as Grant's homeland was fighting for her very survival in the Battle of Britain, and cast him in a rare costumed role as a Virginian backwoodsman who marries an aristocrat and becomes embroiled in the Revolutionary War. Quite what appealed to Grant about this screenplay is difficult to fathom. With his application for US citizenship still being processed, perhaps Grant believed it a judicious moment to star in a film set against the symbolic historical background of the break from the British Crown and that this would underline just how serious he was about becoming an American. It is not far removed from a similar situation involving the American film star James Cagney. Cagney came under scrutiny for allegedly being involved in un-American activities. The first thing he did in knee-jerk reaction was to go out and make the all-singing, all-dancing, all-stars 'n' stripes-waving movie *Yankee Doodle Dandy*.

Whatever Grant's real motive, *The Howards Of Virginia* was a disaster for him – a pony-tailed Cary Grant in buckskin just looks plain silly – and he gives his weakest performance in it.

'I was so bad in that movie,' he later admitted. 'I don't belong in costumes.'

Fortunately for Grant, his next outing returned him to urbane sophistication. Indeed, *The Philadelphia Story* was to prove to be one of his most memorable and best-loved films.

The film owed its genesis entirely to Katharine Hepburn who, with this one deal, proved just how astute and intelligent an actress she was. Regarded as unpopular with the public from 1938 onwards, Hepburn had found good movie parts difficult to get. The prevailing wisdom in Hollywood was that she had had her chance and blown it and that her star was definitely waning. The final straw came when David O. Selznick, who had considered her for the role of Scarlett O'Hara in *Gone With The Wind*, had passed her over for Vivien Leigh.

Undaunted, Hepburn approached the playwright Philip Barry – on whose play *Holiday* had been based – and asked him to write a new play for her. The result was *The Philadelphia Story*, which the Theatre Guild produced on Broadway.

Howard Hughes, an admirer of Hepburn since Grant had introduced the pair, bought her the rights to the play so that she could eventually make it into a movie with her in the starring role. This would not have been possible without her ownership of the property, as the 'box-office poison' label had stayed firmly attached. As she remarked with deliberate understatement of Hughes's gift, 'What a nice present!'

In passing, it is curious to observe that Hepburn wasn't the only leading lady to have an outlandish gift thrust upon her by the generous, if eccentric, multi-millionaire. Ingrid Bergman recalled Hughes ringing her at home. Again, it was Cary Grant who had introduced the actress to Hughes some time before this in New York. Hughes's adoration for the Swedish star was extraordinary to say the least and Grant played a sustained part in trying to convince Bergman she would be happy with Hughes. She simply wasn't interested, so Grant had to drop the matter and that was an end to it.

Hughes said on the phone to Bergman, 'This is Howard Hughes, and I've just bought a film studio for you.'

'What have you done?' asked Bergman, turning off her hairdryer having just climbed out of the shower.

'I've just bought a film studio for you. I've bought RKO. It's yours. It's my present to you ...'

That has to rate as even more remarkable than Hepburn being presented with a play. (Just for the record, Bergman extricated herself from Hughes – *and* the gift of the RKO Studio.)

Katharine Hepburn was a sensation in the play of *The Philadelphia Story,* in which she played the socialite Tracy Lord who discovers, on the day of her second marriage, that she's confused and possibly still in love with her first husband, K.C. Dexter Haven, who has, to her irritation, suddenly reappeared on the scene.

She won the New York Drama Critics Circle Award and the play was a smash at the box-office. Naturally enough, Hollywood was desperate to turn the play into a film and MGM beat off the competition to get first bite at the property.

It was then that MGM executives discovered – to their initial horror – that Katharine Hepburn owned a 23 per cent stake in the property and had had a clause written into her contract that guaranteed her involvement in any film version. In other words, any studio wanting the property had to cast her as Tracy Lord and pay her 23 per cent of takings. Revenge, as they say, really is a dish best served cold.

MGM bit the bullet because they were desperate to acquire the property. Hepburn wanted Spencer Tracy to co-star, but to safeguard their investment MGM insisted that Cary Grant and James Stewart be brought in as the leading men and that George Cukor should direct.

Hepburn was intelligent enough to go along happily with these plans. She had always enjoyed a good working relationship with Grant: they respected each other's talent and were friends. James Stewart was hardly going to hurt the box-office and *Holiday* – the previous Grant–Hepburn combination directed by Cukor in a Barry property – had been her last job in Hollywood before *The Philadelphia Story.*

Grant knew Hepburn needed him on the movie and he knew that MGM needed him more. Consequently, he was able to negotiate a big fee for the work, which he donated to the British War Relief. As well as steep financial demands, he demanded top billing: friendship or not, he believed he was also in need of a huge hit following the dreadful *The Howards Of Virginia.* That film had ended a good run of cinematic triumphs and he regarded it as nothing short of a personal disaster.

On the money front, he asked for $150,000 plus percentages. Finally, he insisted on having the choice of the two male leads – Dexter Haven, the ex-husband, or Macaulay Connor, the journalist infiltrating the wedding preparations.

The role of Connor would have been somewhat ironic for Grant who, even by the early 1940s, was becoming less of a party-goer and much more reclusive as his star rose. 'Despite his easy-going manner,' wrote the producer Cubby Broccoli, 'Cary was an introverted character who kept out of the mainstream of Hollywood social life.'

In contrast to the young twenty-something wannabe he had been in New York earlier, where he was quick to accept any party invitation going, Grant was now more likely to go to private dinners with trusted friends like Cole Porter, David Niven and, when he was in town, Noel Coward.

Grant affected to pretend surprise at the interest newspapers and the general public expressed in the private lives of stars. 'Why should a publicised person cause special excitement?' he once asked. 'Why is it not sufficient to see and enjoy the performance of a great entertainer or athlete and then leave him or her alone?'

He was always polite with the fans he encountered, although he hated autograph hunters. 'This autograph evil – and I do consider it an evil,' he said, 'has gotten entirely out of hand. Originally, it was charming and every player is grateful for admiration. To scrawl your name on a piece of paper does not seem the thing, but to be torn apart and insulted while you're writing it, several hundred times wherever you go, then it becomes intolerable.'

For once, Grant was being disingenuous. He knew perfectly well what the interest was in him. And however much he might have loathed columnists like Louella Parsons and Hedda Hopper, and their profession made them easy to loathe, he knew that his refusal to play their game merely fuelled their determination to find anything scandalous on him. Whatever basis in reality the rumours of his sexuality actually had, there is little doubt that they were propagated by columnists and journalists in whom Grant resolutely refused to confide.

'As a younger man,' he once said, 'it puzzled me that so many people of prominence seemed so carelessly eager to reveal intimate and private matters about themselves in print. Why did they do it? Was it vanity? Did they crave publicity at all cost? Were they desperate to correct or revise past impressions by telling what *they* thought to be the truth about themselves? Did they write about themselves rather than suffer a further succession of inaccuracies written by someone else? Or did they hope that by personally telling their own personal experience they might help their fellow men?'

Perhaps this, to a degree, explains why Grant did *not* do it: there were clear dangers in someone who had re-invented himself as assiduously as he had in giving too revealing interviews about his past. Journalism might not have been so deeply intrusive as it has now become, but journalists still pried into people's lives. And it was a no-win situation, for refusal to co-operate suggested something to hide. Grant was a 'will-o'-the-wisp' to David Niven – a man whose private character was 'as mysterious as the dark side of the moon', as Niven put it. It is entirely feasible that he took an almost perverse, masochistic pleasure in telling Hedda Hopper 'my personal affairs are none of your goddamned business.' Or perhaps an uncertainty about who Cary Grant actually was made it frustratingly difficult to explain himself with any credibility. And if the private Cary Grant was still fundamentally Archie Leach, he definitely wouldn't have wanted to expose the inner man to public gaze.

Whatever his motives, it was a dangerous game he played with columnists. Keeping them at arm's length, no matter how charmingly and stylishly he occasionally did it, was bound to generate resentment.

Still, it meant that the part of Dexter Haven, the character he chose to play in *The Philadelphia Story* was much more suited to Grant than the part of Macaulay Connor, whom James Stewart played. Like many of the characters Grant would choose to play subsequently, Dexter is wary of public scrutiny.

The Philadelphia Story proved immensely popular at the box-office and virtually resurrected Hepburn's career. Of her character, Tracy Lord, Hepburn said, 'I gave her life – she gave me back my career.' But it wasn't without its problems. From the start of shooting in July 1940, Cukor had deliberately kept a loose leash on the set. He was very aware that he had a superlative cast and he wanted to let them develop their own characters and, where appropriate, ad-lib their lines. As a consequence, the rehearsal periods were lengthy and the finished film was at least half an hour too long at nearly two and a half hours. Cukor had to cut, and there was some bitterness between the principals about what should go. Rumours that the arguments between Grant, Hepburn and Cukor got out of hand were denied – Grant was denying them still thirty years later! But it is undeniable, though possibly coincidental, that he never made another film with either one again.

The film was well-received at the box office and was 1941's most successful film bar *Sergeant York* which, ironically, starred the man who seemed to cause him so much irritation, Gary Cooper. (Cooper also won best actor Oscar.)

Grant still felt hampered by Cooper and would refer to this frustration in his one-man theatre shows at the end of his life. He would describe Hollywood as 'A streetcar named Aspire' because 'it fills up at the back and empties out at the front, and there's only room for a few. Gary Cooper got on just ahead of me, and Tyrone Power was just behind me. Cooper stretched out his long legs and let people trip over him.'

Back to *The Philadelphia Story*. The *Hollywood Reporter* thought that 'there are just not enough superlatives sufficiently to appreciate this show' and Grant's beautifully understated and restrained performance won plaudits – but, again, no awards.

Grant was bitterly disappointed. Hepburn, Stewart, Cukor, the screenplay and the film itself all received Oscar nominations (Stewart and the screenplay won), but Grant wasn't even mentioned. Was this another deliberate snub from the Academy? Had Grant been too successful for his own good? It is hard to know, just as it is impossible to understand, how a man now widely regarded as the greatest leading man the world has ever seen should have received nothing except an honorary award once his career had ended.

The Philadelphia Story remains a firm favourite with Grant fans worldwide and lingers in the memory of many others. It was such a success that MGM adapted it into the musical *High Society* in 1956, with Bing Crosby, Frank Sinatra and Grace Kelly in the lead roles and with Cole Porter's last great score. The film is also memorable from a cameo appearance by Louis Armstrong.

Even so, not everyone concurs with the general opinion that *The Philadelphia Story* is, in the words of Leslie Halliwell, 'Hollywood's most wise and sparkling comedy'. Some felt the script was far too talkative and Katharine Hepburn devotees insist that her performance in *Holiday* was far superior. Richard Schickel, while acknowledging the 'slick professionalism of everyone connected with it', believes that there is never 'a true Cary Grant moment' in the picture after the prologue. 'He never gets to whinny like a horse or turn a handspring, dance a jig or wear a dress,' Schickel complains. 'He never even gets to talk too fast. As he plays a man to both manner and manor born, one senses for the first time that the process of his becoming what he is playing is beginning to take hold.'

But then, as Schickel noted, Cary Grant was then just months away from marrying his own 'Tracy Lord'.

12 _____

'My wives divorced me. They said I lived too dull a life.'

Cary Grant (as Roger Thornhill) *North By Northwest* (1959)

Cary Grant had started 1941 with a box-office smash and, in many different ways, it was to be a year that he would always remember. By the time it had ended, America had been sucked into the war and Grant had given three very different performances in three very different movies, one of which, *Arsenic and Old Lace*, wasn't released until 1944 for contractual reasons. On a personal level, this was the year that Grant fell in love again and was heading for his second marriage.

Professionally, *The Philadelphia Story* had underlined – if it needed underlining – that he was Hollywood's consummate leading man. As Tony Curtis puts it: 'Women idolised Grant, and so did I. His casual masculinity also made him a favourite with the male audiences.'

His singular blend of wit and charm and sophistication had captivated the public imagination in every country where his films were screened. More telling was his universal popularity among his fellow actors – even the studio bosses seemed to like him despite his reputation for ruthless negotiation of contracts. The cynic could claim that this was purely because he was more or less guaranteed to deliver an audience and worked extremely hard to give every film an opportunity of becoming a big success. While that's true, Grant was the personable sort who had a presence, an aura, about him. When he entered a room people looked – even studio bosses.

He had some detractors, naturally. One particularly famous one was the actress Bette Davis, who refused to work with him. The notoriously unpredictable Davis, whose career waxed and waned more times than a harvest moon, had urged Jack Warner to buy the screen rights to the play *The Man Who Came To Dinner*, which she had seen on Broadway. The play told the scabrously funny story about a caustic drama critic who breaks his hip on a lecture tour and terrorises the inhabitants of the suburban home where he is forced to rest. It was a send-up of Alexander Woolcott, who, with Dorothy Parker *et al.*, was at the centre of New York's literati, and also contained a wicked spoof of Woolcott's friend, Noel Coward.

Davis's career was then going well. She had just finished *A Woman's Face* with George Cukor, who directed it straight after *The Philadelphia Story*, and she had regained some clout in the business.

She told Jack Warner that she wanted John Barrymore for the part of the stricken drama critic but Warner refused. Barrymore, known as 'The Profile', was once one of America's finest actors, but alcohol had done a spectacular job in putting a stop to such glory days. As a shadow of his former self, he was only able to act when cue cards were placed next to the camera. Instead, Warner hired Grant for the part. Davis was not exactly pleased.

'I'd rather work with John Barrymore drunk than play opposite Mister Cary Grant sober,' she snarled.

So Warner put Grant into *Arsenic and Old Lace*. He stuck to his decision not to use Barrymore and went with Monty Woolley as Davis's co-star. Bette Davis's jibe about Grant, widely circulated round Hollywood in 1941, was clearly designed to suggest she regarded him as a lesser actor than a known alcoholic. This was rather strange and unexpected. Grant had proved his ability and versatility in film after film since the door opened wide for him with *Sylvia Scarlett*.

Perhaps there was a hidden problem. *The Man Who Came To Dinner* was something of a departure for Davis. It was a comedy, designed to broaden and soften her public persona. But light comedy was Grant's forte: she would have been moving into *his* territory. Davis was not renowned for liking competition.

Moreover, Grant had, at that time, not only established a screen partnership with Katharine Hepburn – one of only two actresses Davis admired, the other being Garbo – but had shown his talent was every bit as great as hers. And maybe Davis, who was never as accomplished in her greatest films as Hepburn was in her lesser ones, was actually scared of appearing on-screen with Grant. Davis never admitted being scared to *anyone*, so her insulting remark could have been a camouflage to deflect attention from her own insecurities.

There may also be another reason. Davis's lifelong feud with actress Joan Crawford has been well documented (particularly in Shaun

Considine's book, *Bette & Joan: The Divine Feud*). Any friend of Joan's was an enemy of Bette's and Grant was more than just a friend of Joan's. He was supposedly one of her lovers.

Crawford's appetite for men has become the stuff of legend and, if legend is to be believed, it seems she had sex with virtually every man in Hollywood during the 1930s, 40s and 50s. She's even reputed to have stepped into the shower with Rock Hudson and, snaking her arms around him, murmured, 'Sssh, baby, close your eyes and pretend I'm Clark Gable.'

She was married to Douglas Fairbanks Jnr between 1929 and 1932 and pursued by Howard Hughes (one of the few men she turned down because she believed 'he'd fuck a tree if it moved'), so Grant was hardly likely to have been unknown to her after his arrival in Hollywood. If it is difficult to imagine the urbane Cary Grant making love to the grotesque caricature from the infamous *Mommie Dearest*, one must remember that Crawford was an extremely beautiful actress – and one of MGM's hottest rising stars – in the 1930s. And in 1940 her lovers were said to include Tyrone Power, Johnny Weissmuller, Van Heflin, Robert Sterling and Robert Preston – *as well as* Cary Grant.

Whatever the truth about Grant's alleged affair with Crawford (and no one has as yet provided any proof of its occurrence), Grant liked her and toured with her for three weeks (with James Cagney, Merle Oberon, Claudette Colbert, Judy Garland, Fred Astaire and many others) aboard the Hollywood Victory Caravan, a special train put on to carry stars from Boston to LA, via Washington, promoting war bonds. Grant's friendship with Crawford was probably enough for Bette Davis to refuse to work with him. But that was the last time Grant would ever be bumped from a film.

Penny Serenade and the ground-breaking *Suspicion*, Grant's two other film releases of 1941, proved important milestones, but in the seven months between the release of these films, Grant's thoughts were dominated by his love life. He had, of course, first met Barbara Hutton, forever destined to be referred to as 'the Woolworth heiress', three years previously in 1938 when they dined together aboard the *Normandie*. Re-introduced in the summer of 1941, there was an instant attraction between them. Within a month, Grant was spending all his free time with Hutton, and in August of what was turning into a truly exciting year for the actor, they spent a long vacation in Acapulco.

Much has been made of the differences between Grant and Hutton, not least by Grant himself: 'Our marriage had little foundation for a promising future,' he was to admit ruefully. 'Our backgrounds, family, education and culture, were completely unalike.'

And who can disagree? Hutton had inherited twelve million dollars at the age of seven, a personal fortune that had grown to twenty million dollars by the time she was twenty-one. The contrast with Archie Leach's Dickensian roots could not have been more profound.

There were, though, similarities. Both had been previously married – Hutton twice – and both had been damaged as children. Like Grant, Hutton had lost her mother at an early age. The circumstances of her death remain a mystery, though it is rumoured that she committed suicide, which was then covered up by the family. Grant's childhood had left him with an inherent inferiority complex and so, despite her wealth, had Hutton's. When she was six years old, a servant had told her: 'You're fat and ugly. When someone wants to marry you, it will only be because you're rich. People will envy your possessions.'

This cruel, yet easily imaginable, remark haunted Hutton for the rest of her life and she found it difficult to trust the motives of any of her seven husbands – although, at the end of her life, she concluded that Grant was the only one who *hadn't* been after her money. This is ironic considering Grant, always labelled a gold-digger in the press, was pilloried by some journalists when news of their courtship broke out.

As a couple, Grant and Hutton were labelled 'Cash 'n' Cary' and after they married he was called, to his understandable disapproval, 'Mr Barbara Hutton'. As Grant pointed out, he had amassed a personal fortune of some three million dollars himself by 1941, so he was hardly on his uppers. But his motives were still questioned even after it was revealed that he had signed a pre-nuptial agreement waiving any claim to Hutton's fortune in the event of their divorcing: cynics claimed that even if he wasn't fortune-hunting he was still social climbing.

Journalists were not the only ones who disapproved. Friends of Grant remained sceptical, too, though this was partly because *any* marriage involving Grant was likely to prove disastrous and those closest to him recognised that.

Noel Coward, staying at the house Grant and Randolph Scott shared when the love affair with Hutton became public, was particularly discouraging. He regarded Hutton, whom he knew, as a prototype for his song 'Poor Little Rich Girl', and, in one of his finger-waggings, lectured Grant that she was unstable. 'She's capable of great kindnesses,' Coward said, 'but her money is always between her and happiness.'

In many ways, they *did* make an odd couple. Hutton, a curious mixture of childlike wonder and bruised experience, was six years younger than Grant, yet looked a decade older. And although they were both riven with insecurities, Grant, at least, managed to be outwardly gregarious whereas Hutton tended to be rather withdrawn in public, and often found it hard to make eye contact with strangers.

Curiously, Hutton liked to live her life through the society diary pages of the press, something that was anathema to Grant. He exploded – arguably with fair cause – when one diarist referred to him as a 'former hot-dog salesman'. This was a reference to his stilt-walking days on Coney Island. And he railed at Hutton when she inappropriately chose to confide in Hedda Hopper, of all people, about their hopes to have a child.

Grant and Hutton were married on 8 July 1942, just two weeks after he had become an American citizen and changed his name legally to Cary Grant. It was a brief ceremony – six minutes – at the Lake Arrowhead home of Frank Vincent, who was Grant's agent at the time.

No one other than close friends was invited. Rosalind Russell and her husband Frederick Brisson – whose own marriage had been engineered by Grant – attended and the press were kept well away. A terse statement marking the occasion was all that was released, and the only photographs were supplied by RKO staff photographers. Sticking to the businesslike mood, Grant even returned to work immediately after the wedding (he was then making *Once Upon A Honeymoon*, appropriately enough).

The Cary Grant–Barbara Hutton marriage has often been depicted as a sorry mistake but, although it only struggled along for just two years, there were more compensations for Grant than in his previous marriage to Virginia Cherrill. Grant became particularly close to Hutton's son, Lance, from her previous marriage to Count von Haugwitz-Reventlow, a Danish aristocrat. And Lance adored Grant. Even after Grant and Hutton had finally divorced, Lance would go and stay with the actor and his third wife, Betsy Drake, and Grant would call Lance 'my son' in private. Lance even took to calling himself Lance Grant for a time, much to his real father's fury. Grant was devastated when, in 1972 at the age of thirty-six, Lance was killed in a plane crash.

The differences between Grant and Hutton were apparent more or less from the start, and gossip started up early on in their marriage to the effect that there were unbearable tensions. Grant, becoming rapidly more reclusive than ever, detested many of Hutton's friends – 'if one more phoney noble turns up, I swear I'll suffocate,' he complained – and he came to dread her many dinner parties for her titled friends. Often, he would refuse to come down at all, staying in his room reading. If he did deign to make an appearance, he would treat Hutton's guests to vulgar Cockney routines: walking in on one party he said, 'Now h' I comes from Lime'ouse. I'm just a bloody cockney. Where's me fish an' chips...?'

Grant clearly tried to go out of his way to antagonise Hutton's friends, with apparent success, for no one appeared very impressed. For his part, Grant couldn't have cared less. 'I was ostracised by all the people I hoped to be ostracised by and I couldn't be happier,' he said.

Their connubial situation wasn't helped by his long absences. Even when he wasn't working at the studios, fund-raising work for the war effort kept him away from home for long periods. Hutton would sometimes join him but she wasn't a natural fund-raiser and preferred to help the needy by writing out cheques in private.

One curious aspect of their married life – and of Grant's character – relates to his 1943 film *Mr Lucky* for RKO. Whether RKO executives approached Hutton or vice versa, there was a real possibility that the withdrawn Barbara Hutton seriously considered joining her husband as the co-star in the film. She had made a screen-test and had, apparently, photographed extremely well. When he heard of the plan, Grant was incredulous. He refused to take his wife's new ambitions seriously and, when she persisted, he refused to discuss it at all.

Grant's unhappiness and depression, as it became, increased throughout 1943 and the early part of 1944, and friends like Rosalind Russell frequently saw him on the verge of tears during what had descended into a very miserable period. He and Hutton separated and reconciled several times throughout 1944 and the first part of 1945 but their divorce was inevitable and no one was surprised when Hutton filed for divorce in July 1945. A month later, without fuss, it was all over.

If the marriage was a mistake, at least it was one that left no lingering bitterness. Their joint statement, issued at the time of their divorce, is an indication that, though their marriage was dead, their friendship was of more durable stuff: 'After much thought and with great consideration, we have decided we can be happier living apart.'

'All the unhappiness in my life has been caused by men,' said Hutton, who died, aged sixty-six, in 1979. 'I think I'm pretty timid about marriage, but I'm also too timid to live alone and life doesn't have any sense without a man. Cary Grant had no title but of all my husbands he is the one I loved most. He was so sweet, so gentle. It didn't work out. But I loved him.'

Grant was happy to reciprocate: 'Our interests were not the same,' he recalled. 'I was more interested in my work than I should have been, I suppose. But Barbara is a wonderful woman. I have only the best wishes for her happiness.'

The way things panned out matched with the public statements they issued and one wonders what they saw in each other in the first place. Cary Grant was a good catch – a very handsome leading man – and Barbara Hutton was rich, if not stunningly beautiful. But it wasn't money that motivated Grant, since he was excessively wealthy without needing to marry into more wealth. Could it have been that she met his requirements on another level? That she resembled his mother? After all, he claimed that for a time he was attracted to women who resembled his mother and Barbara Hutton's emotional frailty certainly matched Elsie's.

The failure of yet another marriage only left Grant as depressed as ever and equally disillusioned. Contemplating a future as a single man again, he must clearly have been wondering if he would *ever* find a woman with whom he could share his life.

13 _____

'Cary's the only actor I ever loved in my whole life.'

Alfred Hitchcock

Grant's disappointment at having been overlooked in the Oscar nominations for *The Philadelphia Story* was equalled only by his surprise at being nominated as Best Actor for his very next film, *Penny Serenade* (1941).

Released in April 1941, *Penny Serenade* is noteworthy for many reasons – it remains controversial among Grant devotees, loved by some, loathed by others – but is especially interesting because it is almost impossible to imagine a more atypical Cary Grant film or performance.

Penny Serenade reunited Grant with Irene Dunne, with whom he'd shared such success in *The Awful Truth* and, to a lesser extent, *My Favorite Wife*. The reunion was completed by the director George Stevens, who had directed Grant in *Gunga Din*. However, these reminders of previous Grant triumphs possibly only served to confuse his usual audience who were not used to seeing their hero in a tear-jerking, manipulative melodrama.

A brief resumé of the plot is enough to bring out the cynicism in the most sentimental of film-goers. Grant plays Roger Adams, a young and ambitious newspaper-man who, thanks to a legacy, has more money than sense. He meets and falls in love with Julie Gardiner (Dunne) and they move to Japan for a while. Julie becomes pregnant but suffers a miscarriage during an earthquake and is left unable to bear any more children.

Roger and Julie move back to the US and adopt a little girl. But when Roger's business collapses, the adoption agency threatens to take the child back. Roger is forced to plead with the judge to be allowed to keep the child. A few years later, the child dies and Roger and Julie's marriage crumbles. It's saved at the last minute, only when the agency sends them another child.

There is much to sneer at in the sentimental scenario and many did, even at the time of the film's original release. British critic James Agate wrote memorably: 'A tear-compeller showing how Cary Grant and Irene Dunne lose first their own baby then the one they adopt – which, as Lady Bracknell would certainly have observed, looks like carelessness.'

Richard Schickel regards the film as simply 'bad' and seems to rate it even lower in Grant's output than *The Howards Of Virginia* (which takes some doing). Several other critics have noted that the film-makers have thousands of Japanese extras 'die' in an earthquake just so that Irene Dunne's character can suffer a miscarriage!

It is certainly true also that the film sometimes lacks conviction in certain key scenes. The story as a whole is told in flashback and the device, at times clumsily handled by the usually reliable Stevens, becomes tiresome. Also, the death of the first adopted child occurs off-screen and is told only in a visually static exchange of letters denying the viewer any sense of genuine drama.

But there is still much to admire in *Penny Serenade*. As an example of how Hollywood was reacting and adjusting to the new bleak world order in 1941, it remains impressive: frivolous comedies were making way for tear-jerkers and classic 'women's pictures' that, like *Penny Serenade* especially, emphasised the importance of the family, every-thing that the Free World held dear and which was under outside threat.

Unsurprisingly, it was a movie that Grant had not wanted to do. Having one picture outstanding in the four-picture deal he'd cut with Columbia's Harry Cohn in 1937, Cohn had insisted that Grant make it. Cohn even refused when Grant, who didn't care for the script, begged to be allowed to buy himself out of the contract.

Resigning himself to having to do the movie, Grant at least could console himself that the shooting schedule was relatively short – and that he was being paid one hundred thousand dollars to do it.

While Dunne carries off her role in what is, essentially, a soap opera, there are moments in *Penny Serenade* when Grant has an uneasy air. Apart from a few, brief moments early on in the picture, there are no opportunities at all for Cary Grant to play Cary Grant: the story-line simply denies a single laugh. Having said that, Grant is supremely moving in the scene where he has to plead with the judge for he and

Dunne to be allowed to keep the adopted child they have had for one year. The devastation when that child dies is etched onto his face as he drives a car, mechanically and without thought for what he is doing.

If the film was mawkish and cynical, most critics enjoyed observing Grant in an entirely different kind of role. Its success – if nothing else, *Penny Serenade* was a *massive* hit at the box-office – also encouraged Grant to think that he could succeed in darker, more dramatic roles.

One critic summed up what many felt: 'Cary Grant is thoroughly good in the role, in some ways to the point of surprise, for there is not only that easy swing and hint of devil in him, but faith and passion expressed, the character held together where it might so easily have fallen into the component parts of too good, too silly...'

Grant had once said that 'I'd have to blacken my teeth first before the Academy will take me seriously.' He hadn't actually had to blacken his teeth but, metaphorically, the role of Roger Adams in *Penny Serenade* was the equivalent of his having done so. And the Academy *did* take him seriously when he was nominated for Best Actor, something Richard Schickel describes as 'an act of retribution against him for having so much fun in the past'.

He didn't win – gallingly, he lost out to the man he perceived as his thorn in the side, Gary Cooper. Cooper won it for *Sergeant York*, but Grant had served notice on Hollywood that he was its most versatile star.

His next film, *Suspicion,* was to prove it. *Suspicion* is highly significant in the career of Cary Grant: it gave him his most ambiguous and darkest role to date, and saw him working with director Alfred Hitchcock for the first time.

Like Grant, Hitchcock was a product of the lower end of the British class system. He was born on 13 August 1899 in Leytonstone, Greater London, and was every bit as much the loner as Grant, and just as independently minded. Like Grant, he also had the canny intelligence to know that his career was never in better hands than when it was in his own. Where they differed was that Hitchcock had already found his peak in the British film industry with films such as *The Thirty Nine Steps* (1935) and *The Lady Vanishes* (1938) before making his blistering Hollywood debut for producer David O. Selznick with *Rebecca* in 1940.

By choosing Grant as his leading man in *Suspicion*, Hitchcock revealed his own cinematic mastery. There had scarcely been a hint in any of Grant's performances of his suitability as a Hitchcock leading man but, in retrospect, it can be argued that there isn't a single leading male role in *any* Hitchcock movie which Cary Grant could not have played and made his own.

It is difficult to fathom quite what was the intangible, mutual fascination that existed between Grant and Hitchcock but, whatever it was, the unique chemistry between them made their association a particularly fruitful one. At a time in Grant's life when a sense of uncertainty in the direction of his career had begun to set in, plus a torrid marriage culminating in divorce, his liaison with a new director and new friend, as Hitchcock soon became, gave him an additional edge and sense of purpose.

Donald Spoto, author of what may be the most authoritative biography of Hitchcock, suggested that Hitchcock cast James Stewart in the role of the protagonists he believed himself to be and Grant in the ones he would have liked to have been.

Grant's relationship with Hitchcock was certainly a first for him. Grant had always mistrusted directors and a distance had lingered even with those, such as Cukor and Hawks, with whom he had worked more than once. But with Hitchcock, he had immediate faith and allowed the director to do whatever he liked with his screen persona.

Other actors working on the four collaborations between Grant and Hitchcock witnessed just how close the two men were. They seemed to operate with a kind of mental shorthand and some found this off-putting. James Mason, for instance, playing the villain in *North By Northwest*, found the closeness between the two made both men somewhat unapproachable and Martin Landau, playing Mason's sidekick in that movie, noted that 'James felt rather left out'.

The writer Peter Viertel, discussing Hitchcock's casting of Grant in *Suspicion*, has suggested that, 'Hitchcock saw in that face somebody besides a handsome leading man. I think he saw in that face the potential to be menacing; to be equivocal; to be mysterious.'

What is clear – and what Hitchcock recognised long before anyone else – was how few male actors in Hollywood at that time could incorporate the light and dark that effortlessly flowed through *Suspicion*'s Johnnie Aysgarth. And no other actor could pull it off with such a deft touch, mixing the exuberant youthfulness of the young Johnnie falling in love, with the threat of suppressed, ever-increasing, menace.

Grant cannily pulls us in, makes us feel comfortable, seduces us into believing we're enjoying yet another happy-go-lucky performance from the master of light comedy – and then he sharply pulls away the safety net. Suddenly we find ourselves believing that Johnnie, this roguish, flippant, fun-loving charmer he has shown us to be for half a movie, is capable of murdering his best friend and plotting the death of his wife. As a cinematic *volte face* it remains supreme, its impact diminished now only by familiarity with the film.

The plot of *Suspicion* is simple, as in all the best Hitchcock chillers, and kicks off in that recurring Hitchcock location, the train (*The Thirty Nine Steps, Strangers On A Train* and *North By Northwest* all contain significant train sequences). Johnnie steps into a carriage on a train and meets Lina, played by Joan Fontaine, who at first ignores him. Johnnie is nothing if not persistent and, despite her father (Cedric Hardwicke) warning her of Johnnie's reputation as a fast-living ne'er-do-well, Lina is very quickly swept off her feet by his worldliness and cheeky one-liners.

Johnnie and Lina marry and the first signs that Lina has married someone who is totally irresponsible come on their return from honeymoon: not only is the new house on the Sussex coast that Johnnie has acquired more suited to a millionaire, but he also confesses – with casual boyishness – that he had to borrow money for their honeymoon. He is flat broke.

Revelations in the months that follow lead Lina to have even graver suspicions about Johnnie. She is particularly concerned about his seemingly effortless ability to lie and embezzle. And when Johnnie's jovial friend Beaky (Nigel Bruce) suddenly dies just after financing a cliff-top building project with Johnnie, Lina has to confront the appalling possibility that her husband could be a murderer. Worse, little telling signals – such as her discovering Johnnie has secretly insured her life – convince her that she might be next.

The memorable scene in the film, and typical of the ambiguity which Hitchcock strove for in his work, is of Johnnie climbing the shadowed staircase, carrying a 'poisoned' glass of milk up to Lina. Hitchcock ensures that everything in this scene – the lighting, the photography, the set – conspires to make us feel Lina and ourselves are trapped in a giant web and helpless at the hands of a psychotic man. The *coup-de-grâce* is that the glass of milk itself, lit from within by Hitchcock, is supported on a tray, thereby making it the focus point of the scene. Hitchcock keeps Grant's face practically unlit and this, coupled with

Grant's superb, impenetrable expression, means that the audience is having to watch Johnnie while remaining uncertain whether he is a good, caring husband or a killer.

This point was emphasised in the film's publicity poster, which stressed: 'Each time they kissed there was the thrill of love – and the threat of murder!'

The is-he-isn't-he-a-murderer moment of the film is a wonderful bit of cinema, particularly since Hitchcock manages to convey, both literally and metaphorically, that the light has dissipated from Johnnie's character to be replaced with something altogether darker. Refusing the milk, Lina packs her bags and tells Johnnie that she is returning to her mother (May Whitty). He agrees but insists on driving her there along the coastal cliff road. And still the viewer doesn't know if this is the action of a caring husband or the opportunistic machinations of a man intent on murder.

During the reckless drive along the clifftops, we learn the truth. Johnnie confesses that he's no good but that he's no murderer, either. He wasn't with Beaky when his friend died, and he *had* been in search of an untraceable poison – to use on himself because he was beyond despair. The film ends with Lina realising that beneath Johnnie's foolishness – even ruthlessness – he is fundamentally sound and good. The car swings around and they head for home where Johnnie can face punishment for his financial deceit, and their life together can then start afresh.

But *Suspicion* wasn't supposed to end like that. In the original novel on which the film was based – *Before The Fact* by Francis Iles – and in early drafts of the screenplay, Johnnie is, indeed, a murderer. Hitchcock's intended ending had Johnnie poisoning Lina, but only after he had agreed to post a letter to her mother on her behalf, a letter revealing that Johnnie had murdered her.

This would have certainly made more sense than the filmed ending. As Richard Schickel points out, the implication that Johnnie is a murderer is 'implicit in scene after scene, so much so that we do not fully believe the film that was finally released.' Grant went along with that. He said, 'I thought Hitch's original ending was marvellous. It was a perfect Hitchcock ending.'

But executives at RKO supposedly wouldn't contemplate releasing a film in which Cary Grant was a wife-murderer. Legends have grown up about RKO's alleged interference in this movie, such as the one in which Hitchcock is supposed to have returned from a two-week break after *Suspicion* wrapped to find an RKO executive had edited out all the Grant scenes suggesting he might be a killer – and had left a film running less than one hour. Other writers have put forward the theory that secret test screenings with the original ending had had a very negative reaction.

Whatever the truth and extent of the interference, it is certain that RKO wanted the picture to end on a positive and not negative note, and John Russell Taylor explained why: 'We know that this is Cary Grant, so that however black the case may look against him, he cannot be a wife-murderer. The man he is playing might be, but he, Cary Grant, cannot be, because he never, ever, is. So Hitchcock's idea was to carry out the ultimate double-bluff, by making him turn out after all to be a wife-murderer, thereby administering a cosmic shock far beyond anything that the film story itself could be expected to give. Alas, this was going too far: the effect was too strong for the studio, who insisted that Grant must be exonerated at the end, as we knew all along he would be.'

This is the accepted wisdom, but is it possible Hitchcock really did pull off the double-bluff – on his actors and the studio? Years later, while not denying that RKO had imposed the ending on his film, Hitchock suggested that he believed the ending *as filmed* worked best. 'The sudden banishing of carefully built-up anxiety is more surprising and satisfying than the one we're logically prepared for,' he said.

Did Hitchcock direct *Suspicion* with his principals believing that Johnnie was a murderer to give them a conviction that made the ultimate twist even more surprising? He was notorious for getting the best out of his players – what better than to drive them along a path to a false conclusion? And it's certainly not difficult to believe, when watching the film today, that Grant was informed he was portraying a murderer. Perhaps Hitchcock got the ending he secretly wanted. And perhaps he goaded RKO into 'imposing' this ending on him, as a get-out explanation to his actors. He was definitely Machiavellian enough and it would have appealed to his manipulative sense of humour to behave every bit as ambiguously as his protagonist.

It must also be said that the contention that *Suspicion*'s happy ending mars, even fatally flaws, the film is relatively modern. It worried contemporary viewers much less and the film was received rapturously, with Grant's performance singled out for praise.

'Cary Grant finds a new field for himself,' thought the *New York Times*. 'The field of crime and the smiling villain without heart or conscience.' *Variety* noted that, 'Grant puts conviction into his unsympathetic but arresting role.'

Even those who did carp about *Suspicion*'s relatively happy and uneventful ending in 1941 didn't complain too much. Britain's *New Statesman* was typical of these: 'The fact that Hitchcock throws in a happy end during the last five minutes, like a conjuror explaining his tricks, seems to me a pity; but it spoils the film only in retrospect, and we have already had our thrills.'

Thrills were, of course, what Hitchcock was all about, and his famous quote, 'Drama is life with the dull bits cut out,' couldn't be truer in the case of this particular motion-picture drama.

Whatever the misgivings about the ending, *Suspicion* was a massive success at the box-office, which meant that Grant had appeared in three of the top ten grossing films at the US box-office in 1941, the other two being *The Philadelphia Story* and *Penny Serenade*.

Suspicion was nominated for several Oscars, including Best Picture and Best Director; and Joan Fontaine won the Best Actress Oscar for her role as Lina. Cary Grant didn't even get a mention.

'Cary Grant was unique,' said director Stanley Donen, who worked with him extensively from the mid-1950s onwards. 'You see it and feel it in the reactions and characterisations. There's not a false moment. And it seems like it's just happening, that he's experiencing it at that moment.'

Tony Curtis claims one can learn more from watching Cary Grant drink a cup of tea than by spending six months with a Method actor and reveals that he studied Grant himself to learn how to behave in civilised situations – such as at a restaurant or in important company – and how to wear the right clothes and appear comfortable in them as though they belong.

Grant told Curtis – and doubtless many others – that one has to believe in the role, no matter how banal the dialogue and unbelievable the plot, to *become* the person one is playing. Nothing else at that time is real: an actor *is* the person he or she is portraying.

'Just relate to the person you're working with, Tony,' Grant urged. 'Just be *with* them. Even if they can't play the part properly and you don't believe a word of the dialogue, you must *use* that. Use everything you hear and be ready to adjust like a good acrobat.'

But, as Stanley Donen was always quick to point out, this ability of Grant's 'wasn't a gift from God – it was the magic that came from enormous amounts of work.'

Grant applied Donen's own theory to Grace Kelly, arguably the co-star he most admired. 'She made it look so easy,' he said. 'Some people said that Grace was just being herself. Well, that's the toughest thing to do if you're an actor.'

In Grant's case, being himself was, indeed, the toughest part he played because 'Cary Grant' was entirely his own invention. He was in a unique position. Although Cary Grant was a movie idol whom every woman wanted to bed and every man wanted to emulate, Grant still hadn't got a handle on just *who* Cary Grant was. Because he was the creation of a mature man, there was an absence of background – of childhood, nation, evolution. In the space of one day, 7 December 1931, Cary Grant had gone from not existing, to being a handsome leading actor.

Many actors have had to wrestle with a fictional alter ego that has threatened to eclipse them. Sean Connery, for instance, walked away from James Bond – contractual disputes notwithstanding – because he was becoming indistinguishable in the public consciousness from 007. At a press conference in Tokyo in 1966 to promote the start of location shooting on *You Only Live Twice*, Connery was even asked such stupid questions as 'Are you going to open a detective agency?' It is little wonder that Connery – who was, and is, a fine actor – came to regard this one role as 'a Frankenstein monster' whom he 'wanted to kill'. But Connery could, and did, stop playing James Bond. Cary Grant's most famous creation was himself – and Cary Grant couldn't walk away from playing Cary Grant. Not yet, anyway.

At the 1979 Oscars, Grant presented Sir Laurence Olivier with a special Academy Award, calling Olivier 'the actors' most admired actor'. Afterwards, sitting through a hagiographical list of his achievements, Olivier leaned across to Grant and bemoaned, 'Oh, if only I *were* Laurence Olivier!' To which Grant replied, 'If only *I* were Cary Grant.'

So, the truth, perhaps delivered a little tongue-in-cheek, was that, even at the age of 75, Grant was still uncertain of who he was. But by then, of course, he must surely have realised it was a not a solvable problem. It is possible, however, that he had a much more relaxed attitude to his dilemma from the late 1950s when, in his own words, he was 'reborn', but his comment to Olivier proves, if nothing else, that Archie Leach never *quite* reconciled himself to the Cary Grant he had become.

Alfred Hitchcock's brilliance in *Suspicion* – and the reason why he can elicit from Grant a truthful performance that goes beyond mere acting – is that he was the first, perhaps only director to recognise this fundamental dichotomy in Grant's personality. And he was prepared to exploit it.

Thus, those critics who believe that Johnnie Aysgarth couldn't possibly be a murderer because he is played by Cary Grant are missing the point. If we don't know who a man is, how do we know of what he is or isn't capable?

It is Grant's ambiguity that gives Aysgarth's moral equivocalness such resonance and gives Hitchcock a free hand to layer the subtext of *Suspicion* with doubt and uncertainty. Hitchcock, for one, seems to have believed Cary Grant *was* capable of anything, which is why their very different collaborations, *Notorious* (1946), *To Catch A Thief* (1955) and *North By Northwest* (1959) after *Suspicion*, probe the inner reaches of Cary Grant more than any of his other films.

The problem seems to have been that the more successful and famous he became in the late 1930s and 1940s, the more confusing Grant found his inner ambiguity. Maybe this is the real reason why, coupled with his natural reserve and reticence, he did not actively seek publicity, even if he knew his silences frustrated journalists and fuelled the rumours about his private life. But how could he talk about himself if even *he* didn't know who, strictly speaking, he was? Far simpler to avoid the issue.

This would explain why, on the rare occasions when he did give interviews, Grant professed not to know the Cary Grant who came out of the article.

'Often, when I read about myself, it is so *not* about me that I'm inclined to believe it's really about the writer. Hardly a week goes by that I don't read about my proficiency in yoga, my fanatical attention to diet and my regular swimming work-outs. In truth, I know little or nothing about yoga and my diet is extraordinary only from the viewpoint of my close friends who have named me 'The Scavenger' because, after finishing every morsel of my own meal, I look around to purloin whatever little delicacies they've left uneaten on *their* plates. And about the only regular swimming I do is in my head around April fifteenth, when I'm confronted with these astronomical income-tax figures.'

Beneath the denial can one detect a defensive stance? It is as though, even regarding something as trivial as matters of his personal fitness, Grant is resisting any probing lest it should dent the reputation of Cary Grant which, so fruitful in what it had delivered, needed constant perpetuation if it were to survive.

What Grant actually did to keep fit remains a typical issue of conjecture about him. Apart from recurring insomnia, probably a legacy of his childhood, and a nasty bout of hepatitis and jaundice in 1948, Grant was healthy all his life. And he never considered the insomnia a problem: he coped with it by waking at three a.m. to read a book, going back to sleep at four and then getting up at about six-thirty.

Physically, he was in superb shape, always. He never lost the athleticism that had been honed during his days with Bob Pender's troupe. 'Cubby' Broccoli described his body as being 'like a Malibu lifeguard', and when he turned eighty in 1984, most commentators remarked that he had the body of a man at least thirty years younger. Just days before his death in 1986, journalist Roderick Mann, Grant's friend for many years, reported him as still looking 'spectacular'.

So, how did he manage it? According to Grant, himself, exercise played no part in his enduring good health at all. 'I never crook a finger to keep fit,' he remarked in 1981. 'I take no exercise whatsoever...If I have a secret at all it's that I do just what I want. I think that stops the ageing process as much as anything.'

Mann backed him up on this. 'In the twenty-five years I've known this man,' he wrote, 'he's hardly done any exercise at all and has always eaten like a timber wolf.'

David Niven, however, told a very different story. 'His perfectionist urge with regard to his own body was nothing short of mystic,' he recalled. And although Grant tried to convince Niven that 'I just think myself thin and it happens,' Niven remarked, somewhat caustically, in 1975 'but he conveniently forgot his frugal eating, his daily work-outs and his appointments with the masseur.'

Niven recalled Grant enduring gruelling lessons in how to swim the crawl and how to ride a horse. 'I want to do it perfectly' Grant is reported to have said when Niven asked him why he was putting himself through such pain. Niven, describing Grant as 'silhouette conscious', also tells of Grant's health-food obsessions, particularly one time when he was drinking only carrot juice.

Certainly Grant's professed indifference to his health is belied by his interest in hypnotism to cure himself of smoking: he kept repeating in his head 'your fingers are yellow, your breath smells and you only smoke because you are insecure,' over and over again for weeks. And he also became interested in the power of oxygen, telling friends that he'd healed a nasty gash on the back of his hand, sustained on the set of *The Pride And The Passion*, by applying oxygen to the wound and 'commanding my lungs to dissolve the useless tissues'.

On one hand, we have Grant's assertion he did no exercise and ate more than most people, on the other, we have Niven witnessing arduous swimming lessons, daily work outs and health food fads. Although it is fair to say that Niven was not a man who allowed facts to get in the way of a good anecdote, his memories of Grant 'conveniently forgetting' his healthy regime have the ring of truth, if only because he had absolutely nothing to gain by elaborating on the facts as he saw them.

If Niven's account is accurate, then why would Grant want to propagate the myth of his making no actual contribution to his undeniably superb health and physique? Did he believe that by acting as if it were something he achieved without input, the image of Cary Grant would appear even more remarkable? Or perhaps that the image of him sweating away in a gym was somehow disdainfully at odds with the suave, urbane sophistication for which he was renowned? Basically, did he want the world to believe Cary Grant was *naturally* fit because he thought the world *wanted* to believe that?

Like those Russian dolls that have another then another then another layer beneath, the more one digs into Cary Grant's life, the more contradictions, mysteries and ambiguities one unearths.

Alfred Hitchcock started peeling back the layers of Cary Grant in *Suspicion* in 1941. He would continue to do so, periodically, for the next eighteen years. Ultimately, all that Hitchcock would reveal would be more layers.

14

'Hello? Mother? Mother, it's your son ... '

Cary Grant, *North By Northwest* (1959)

Suspicion was a great Alfred Hitchcock film. It was also a tremendous Cary Grant film, perhaps the greatest of his career to that point, and hardly surpassed thereafter. But something curious happened to Grant's career after its release and the five intervening years until his next collaboration with Hitchcock on *Notorious* in 1946.

Although none of the eight films between *Suspicion* and *Notorious* is *bad*, this period sees some of the least remarkable and inspired work from his huge output, except for his days as a contract player at Paramount.

As the 1940s progressed, it was becoming ever clearer that there was a dearth of well-scripted vehicles for Cary Grant. As Pauline Kael noted sombrely, 'After 1940, he didn't seem to have any place to go. There were no longer Cary Grant pictures.'

Clearly the war, which America had entered in December 1941, was affecting the output of Hollywood and, like every other star, Grant had to adapt to the changing climate. His problematic marriage to Barbara Hutton, which was resolved in the divorce courts just weeks after the war in Europe had ended, also distracted him.

Grant, at least, had two things in his favour. Firstly, he was extremely versatile and his presence in any movie, no matter how banal, improved it artistically and commercially by a considerable amount. Secondly, he was a free agent, and as such did not have to obey the inflexible directives of studio heads. Nevertheless, the roles he was offered from 1941 to 1946 were simply not of the calibre of Walter Burns in *His Girl Friday*, Dexter in *The Philadelphia Story* or David Huxley in *Bringing Up Baby*.

At least *The Talk of The Town*, released by Columbia in August 1942, reunited him with the director George Stevens. Harry Cohn believed that Grant and Stevens were on a roll after *Penny Serenade* and he offered Grant the part of Leopold Dilg, a man wrongly accused of murder who takes refuge in the home of Michael Lightcap (Ronald Colman), a lawyer. A romantic triangle then develops between Dilg, Lightcap and Nora Shelley (Jean Arthur), Lightcap's housekeeper who becomes convinced of Dilg's innocence.

Again, as in *Suspicion*, there were problems with the ending of *The Talk of The Town*. The narrative throughout suggests that Grant will lose Arthur to Colman: Grant and Arthur even kiss and say their farewells. But then Grant returns and walks off with Arthur in the closing scene. To most critics, who believed the mix of subdued screwball comedy and legal polemic was awkward, this ending was inconsistent with all that had gone before.

If Alfred Hitchcock could plausibly argue that the revelation that Johnnie Aysgarth *isn't* a murderer made the twist denouement in *Suspicion* more effective, Stevens could not make the same claim for the resolution of *The Talk of The Town,* which smacked of playing to the gallery. This is precisely what Stevens had done: he had shot three alternative endings and tested each one on preview audiences.

Although some previous Grant biographers – most notably Graham McCann – regard *The Talk of The Town* as one of Grant's most underrated movies, it remains an uneasy blend and suffers from its terribly anti-climactic ending. It was, however, like most of Grant's movies, a big box-office success. This is undoubtedly a tribute to Grant's star power rather than anything the picture provided. However, it was nominated for *seven* Oscars. It won none.

The film was a liberal examination of, if not a full-frontal attack on, small-town American values: 'He's the only honest man I've come across in this town for twenty years,' one character remarks of Dilg. 'Naturally they want to hang him.'

Such subversive stuff was always tricky pre-1965, but during war-time, with the 'Boys' losing their lives defending the very values that *The Talk of The Town* was questioning, it was risky. This may be why the movie has a hesitant air, never quite seeming sure of itself. Stevens, directing his last film before joining the war in Europe, clearly wanted to have his cake and eat it, as is shown by his copping out and leaving the ending of the film to be determined by test audiences. Consequently, Dilg, potentially as interesting a departure for Grant as

Johnnie Aysgarth, is never fully used, and 'encouraged expectations that he was to satisfy only fitfully', as Lionel Godfrey wrote so perceptively.

Graham McCann argues that there is something admirable in Grant's willingness to work openly with screenwriters who were left-leaning or even card-carrying members of the communist party. Certainly we can admire Grant for rating talent above all else, even if, as was the case during the McCarthy witch-hunts, it led to awkward questions being directed at himself. But then, Grant always had a perverse instinct to side with the ostracised and the outsiders. Maybe it was to do with Archie Leach having entered Hollywood from the outside: he certainly remained very British despite becoming a US citizen. He publicly defended Marilyn Monroe when a scandal about nude photos she had posed for surfaced at the time their film *Monkey Business* was released in 1952 and championed Ingrid Bergman when Hollywood had shunned her, proving not so much that he was a loyal friend, as that he couldn't give a damn about convention or fitting in with prevailing opinions.

If *Suspicion* had shown that Grant could push against the parameters of his screen image given the right script and director, *The Talk of The Town* demonstrated, equally powerfully, that there were limitations. As Richard Schickel wrote of Grant's performance in this picture, 'That he is a man of mischief has long since been established: that he is a man of the serious left, a true radical capable of inflaming a whole community, no, that does not quite go down.'

If the film had at least been a courageous and intelligent one, neither *Once Upon A Honeymoon,* released in November 1942, nor *Once Upon A Time,* in May 1944, advanced Grant's reputation one jot.

In the former, a dreadful misfire from director Leo McCarey, whose judgement seemed to have gone into a tailspin since his glory days with *The Awful Truth,* Grant is teamed with Ginger Rogers in a witless and vaguely distasteful comedy-drama set against Nazi aggression in Europe. In the latter, a grim whimsy, he is an unsuccessful Broadway producer who discovers a boy with a dancing caterpillar and makes them both stars.

Fortunately, *Mr. Lucky*, which opened in 1943, was a cut above either of these two uninspiring efforts but, even so, the best one can say about this film is that it is 'interesting'. Having said that, Grant himself rated *Mr. Lucky* as one of his favourite movies because 'the character I played was more like the real Cary Grant than any before'. Given that the character he plays assumes another identity to escape one particular problem, only to discover that his new identity carries difficult baggage of an entirely different kind, this is quite telling.

Mr. Lucky, adapted by Milton Holmes and Adrian Scott from Holmes's *Bundles For Freedom*, has Grant playing the central character of Joe Adams, the co-owner of a gambling ship that he plans to sail to Havana. Being wartime, Adams's plans are thwarted by the arrival of his draft orders. In an attempt to dodge the draft, he assumes the identity of Joseph Bascopolous, a former crew-member who is now dead. What Adams doesn't know is that Bascopolous was an ex-con who had three convictions to his name: one more conviction and he would have gone down for life.

Against this background is the inevitable romance. Adams meets a charity fund-raiser called Dorothy (Laraine Day), to whom he is attracted. Adams develops the idea of a gambling concession at a forthcoming charity ball, although Dorothy and the good ladies of the War Relief Office take some convincing. Once they are content that his intentions are worthy ones, Dorothy is firmly on his side and even aids him in evading the police.

What she doesn't know is that he intends to con the War Relief organisation and steal all the gambling concession money. Unsurprisingly, of course, Adams just cannot go through with the con: Hitchcock might have *almost* convinced us that Johnnie Aysgarth could be a wife-murderer, but Joe Adams never once persuades us that he could embezzle charity funds. How ironic that audiences couldn't contemplate Cary Grant stealing from War Relief funds, when the young Archie Leach had been expelled from school for theft from a church!

Here again, though, we have a situation where Grant is pushing the boundaries of the accepted Cary Grant persona, only to discover that that persona is pushing back, resisting change. It is true that, from *Suspicion* onwards, we do get glimpses of the darker side of Cary Grant. But, apart from the three other pictures he made for Hitchcock, Grant's demons are never fully released on screen. Partly, this was a result of the times in which Grant lived and worked. The pioneering years of film-making in the 1930s had gone, and the 1940s, 50s and 60s were not always brave and ground-breaking. There was basically less artistic freedom and uncontrolled experiment.

Also, in January 1944, four days after his flagwaving *Destination Tokyo* was released, Grant turned forty. With so much under his belt, Richard Schickel isn't alone in believing that Grant had somehow slipped into taking a more conservative approach to his career choices. Perhaps this is why everything he did between *Suspicion* and *Notorious* disappoints most of us today and, in the case of *Once Upon A Honeymoon* and *Once Upon A Time*, often vaguely embarrasses us.

At least the dénouement of *Mr. Lucky* allows for a little ambiguity when Adams's ship sets sail not as a gambling ship, but carrying medical supplies. Dorothy reaches the docks in time to tell the reformed Adams that she loves him. On his return trip, the ship is sunk and the audience, and the hapless Dorothy, are left not knowing Adams's eventual fate.

Although several of the thematic strengths of Grant's career – redemption, being a fugitive from justice – pop up in *Mr. Lucky*, the film never quite seems to work, despite it becoming RKO's biggest draw of 1943.

'Grant makes a good fugitive,' wrote Richard Schickel, but his greatest innocent-man-on-the-run performance in *North By Northwest* was to come sixteen years after *Mr. Lucky*. Unlike *Mr. Lucky,* it was to capitalise brilliantly on mistaken identity.

However, *Mr. Lucky* is not without merit. It is, in many ways, a well-made film and Grant's affection for it means it deserves scrutiny. One or two moments in the film *do* seem particularly personal, not only to Grant but to Archie Leach. Almost every Grant biographer has noted that Adams's justification for dodging the draft – 'This isn't *my* war! I *had* my war: crawling out of the gutter – the hard way. I won *that* war!' – is Grant's way of dealing not only with his poverty-stricken childhood in Bristol but, more pertinently, his awkwardness at not fighting in the real war currently raging around the globe.

Whatever the nature of the secret work he was actually doing, it was, perforce, *secret*. This meant he was unable to respond to the flak he received about his not being in uniform throughout the war. The emphasis he puts on '*my* war' is possibly beyond the demands of the script and more indicative of how frustrated he must have felt during this time.

Furthermore, when Grant remarked that Adams was the on-screen character closest to himself, whoever 'himself' really was, it revealed the chippiness he sometimes displayed about coming from a working-class background in England. As we have seen, never was this more visible than when he was married to Barbara Hutton and *Mr. Lucky* was shot exactly halfway through that flawed relationship, when the class differences between them – his cockney touches, her 'phoney' nobles – had been contributing hugely to their disintegrating marriage. On this occasion, art really was mirroring life, and when Adams rails against the upper-class ways of Dorothy, no one familiar with Cary Grant's background can be in any doubt that, for once, Archie Leach is bursting through with near disdain for Dorothy and, surely, for Barbara Hutton:

> ADAMS: To people like you, folks like me are just like animals. We're so *bad* and you're so very *good*. What do you expect – credit for it? How could you be anything else with what you had to start out with? You ought to be horsewhipped if you *didn't* turn out right! And what are you so high and mighty about? What did you ever do? *He's* the guy who made all the dough for you [a reference to her ancestor], and he was born in a log cabin. Know where I grew up? In a one-room shack with a dirt floor. You talk about 'this side of your family' and 'that side of our family'. As far as I know, we only had one side, and it was awful poor! Lots of times there was what-for to eat. That's why I ran away when I was nine; I got tired of being hungry and seeing my old lady go hungry until she died.

RKO had, as we mentioned earlier, seriously discussed with Barbara Hutton the possibility of her playing Dorothy and those who believe Grant dismissed the idea because of her complete lack of acting experience or because he didn't take her ambitions seriously are only half right: his making that speech to Hutton would have surely been much too close to home.

The reference to 'running away when I was nine', almost certainly put in by Grant himself (he was always trying to be involved in every aspect of his pictures), is particularly telling. When he was nine, however, it was his mother, not Grant, who had done the running away.

It is possible – and certainly understandable – that Cary Grant was going through some kind of identity crisis between 1941 and the end of the war. Becoming an American citizen in 1942 and, therefore, cutting ties with the country of his birth, was possibly more traumatic than he had anticipated, considering Britain was fighting for her very survival. And his seeming unwillingness to fight, though it would become clear many years later not to have been the case, had brought him the most serious negative publicity of his career, all the more frustrating because to react might jeopardise whatever work he was doing for Sir William Stephenson. Furthermore, his marriage to Hutton had underlined, in the starkest possible way, just how humble his origins really were. Then there was the on-going anxiety of having to adapt to a Hollywood that just wasn't making 'Cary Grant' pictures anymore. Finally, he had hit forty – an age of reflection in any man's life.

Everything during the war was conspiring to make Cary Grant reassess just who he was, where he was going and where he had come from. Despite his visits back to Bristol between 1933 and 1939, when he was regarded as something of the returning conquering hero, Grant doesn't seem to have thought about his home town that often – at least, not when he was away from it. The war changed that. The difficult memories from his childhood, which he had packed away with Archie Leach, were now being pulled out from the locked closet at the furthest recess of his mind and re-examined, as he listened, daily, for news about bombing raids on Bristol. And the anxieties he felt for his mother's safety – she had refused to go to California at the start of hostilities – forced him to reassess his feelings for her, too. Supposing, like others in his family, she was killed by a passing bomb. How would he feel? How would he react?

Even though he had provided a house for her in Bristol and an allowance, both of which she never acknowledged, their relationship had, until the war, been awkward. It would always retain an ambivalence, right up until Elsie's death in 1973, for however forgivable the confusions and actions of a past era, they are not necessarily so forgettable.

Their enforced separation during hostilities did, ironically, bring them a little closer together. Somehow, after 1945, Grant and Elsie Leach managed to put the past to one side and develop an understanding and more mature friendship. It wasn't the kind of loving relationship most mothers and sons would recognise: Elsie was probably incapable of that after the breakdown that had led to incarceration, as Grant was to acknowledge: 'Perhaps no child ever feels the recipient of enough love to satisfy him or her. Oh, how we secretly yearn for it, yet openly defend against it.'

Furthermore, Elsie, it is clear, was not always an easy person to love. She remained uncompromisingly tough and independent and, whether because of guilt or envy – possibly a combination of both – she refused to accept lavish gifts from Grant or, indeed, anything associated with his fame. And there is no evidence that she ever expressed gratitude for his repeated visits to Bristol to see her or the financial support he provided throughout the second half of her life.

The war, at least, crystallised their feelings for each other. Elsie even wrote to Grant when the war prevented his flying home to say, 'Darling, if you don't come over as soon as the war ends, I shall come over to you...' And in one interview she proclaimed herself fiercely proud of his achievements: 'It's been a long time since I have seen him,' she said, 'but he writes regularly and I see all his films.' She even managed to tell Grant once, 'I am more than delighted you have done so well.' This may be a little ambiguous as it doesn't state for whom she is more than delighted, but it appears to be the closest he came to having his phenomenal success recognised by his own mother.

The logical reason why Grant and Elsie understood each other better after 1945 was that they saw that both of them were survivors of their own past and if their subsequent relationship was more like an emotional clinging to the wreckage after the ship has gone down, they knew no other way.

Towards the end of his life, Grant somehow managed to reconcile himself to his childhood and to accept his parents for what they were. 'They were products of *their* parents,' he said, 'who could know no better than they knew, and I've begun to remember them only for the most useful, the best, the nicest of their teachings.' Which is the honest way of saying that while he wasn't exactly content about his past, he now softened the impact by viewing it through rose-tinted glasses. However, it worked for him and explains a great deal about the happiness he would find so late in life.

This long and partial healing of Cary Grant's scars from childhood began during the war. From the moment Archie had run away from Elias to join Pender's troupe, he had lived life at a sprint, his feet hardly touching the ground and every so often taking nervous glances over his shoulder. When Archie Leach became Cary Grant with the stroke of a pen, Grant had taken up the torch for Leach. But now, older, wiser, he was more reconciled to his past, if not fully so: he had done with living life as though it were a racetrack. The war, his age, his mother, his success, his image – everything conspired for him to lay down the torch and stop running. Win, lose or draw, the race was over.

Accepting roles in *Mr. Lucky* and *None But The Lonely Heart*, in which he played a nomadic cockney – and even *Arsenic and Old Lace* with its resonances of vaudeville – show that Grant *did* now have the courage to confront his past, though only vicariously through his chosen roles.

15 _____

'I simply cannot do this kind of comedy.'

Cary Grant

It is, perhaps, going too far to suggest that Alfred Hitchcock rescued Cary Grant's career with *Notorious*, which was released in 1946. There is little doubt, however, that it is far better than any of the eight films Grant had made since *Suspicion* in 1941.

Curiously, one of these, *Arsenic and Old Lace*, remains one of the best-remembered Cary Grant films. This defies all logic considering Grant's huge body of consistently good, often great, work. Furthermore, Joseph Kesselring's Broadway farce never loses its theatrical roots: even on the occasional exterior shot, it remains wholly studio-bound.

Frank Capra wanted to make a movie of the stage play, but it had to be done extremely quickly. Not only had Capra volunteered for the US military and was due to join up at any time but, to use the services of some of the original Broadway cast, the film could only be shot in a brief (in movie-making terms) four-week break from the play, which was still running and would do for a long time. Indeed, it was the fact that it was continuing to run that had forced Jack Warner, when buying the film rights, to give an undertaking not to release the film version until *after* the Broadway run had finished. He had to wait three years, until the autumn of 1944, before he could actually release the picture.

Capra had already assembled key members of the cast for the movie, including Raymond Massey and Peter Lorre. Despite that, Warner was convinced that the project required a big name to swell the box-office. Warner first went to Bob Hope, who turned it down, and then to Cary Grant, who was unexpectedly free after Bette Davis had refused to work with him on *The Man Who Came To Dinner*.

Arsenic and Old Lace is the blackest possible farce you could wish to see on a stage, but, transferred virtually intact by Capra, it seems laboured, confined and claustrophobic on screen. One change in the film is that Grant's role was beefed up. While considering Warner's offer to make the picture, Grant had flown to New York to see the play and noted that his offered role of Brewster was a supporting one. He was also uncertain that it was a part he could add much to. But he cabled Warner to say he would do it if Brewster's role could be expanded. Warner agreed. He also accepted Grant's demands for a $100,000 fee which, again, Grant paid straight to the British War Relief (America did not enter the war until the last week of shooting on *Arsenic and Old Lace*).

Having come straight from the set of *Suspicion* and being directed by Hitchcock with whom he had established an immediate rapport, Grant found Capra a disappointment and he didn't much enjoy working on the film.

'I told Frank Capra I simply couldn't do that kind of comedy,' Grant said many years afterwards when singling out, rather harshly, *Arsenic and Old Lace* as the worst performance he ever gave. '"Of course you can, old boy", Frank said. And I went ahead and did it and I overplayed it terribly. *Terribly.* I was embarrassed doing it. It was a dreadful job for me. Jimmy Stewart could have done a much better job than I did. He would have been wonderful in the part. I told Frank Capra at the time but he just wouldn't listen.'

Ironically, Grant's 'overplaying' has delighted audiences ever since. The general perception has always been that he is overplaying Brewster deliberately and doing so particularly well. It is almost as if he is telling the viewer, 'I know this looks like a stage play – indeed, *was* a stage play – but let's suspend disbelief and have a few laughs together at what is a fairly acceptable farce.' So while Grant's personal dislike of his work on the film is understandable, it's negated by the fact that his public have always interpreted his performance differently. That he felt embarrassed by his performance would surely surprise if not confuse many of his fans.

On set for the film, Grant found Capra's insistence on shooting the movie in sequence – a highly unusual practice in the movies – an irritating and unnecessary distraction, which did little for their working relationship. But one mustn't make the mistake of laying all the blame for disharmony at the feet of Capra. We know now that Grant was a perfectionist and like most perfectionists could be a somewhat tricky individual to work with. Also, who is to say that Grant didn't keep telling Capra that, when recently working with Alfred Hitchcock, Hitchcock suggested this and Hitchcock suggested that? That would have been a perfect way to disgruntle any director. There are numerous scenarios here and the only certainty is that theirs was not a harmonious relationship.

A further disappointment to Grant was that the play/film was rooted in a world he knew and loved, British music hall and vaudeville, and should therefore have been a happier event. Grant always loved British comedy – he adored Sid Field, Tony Hancock, Arthur Haynes, Harry Worth and Eric Morecambe – and the part of Brewster owed much more to broad comedy than the immaculate suavity and sophisticated light comedy of his prevailing screen persona.

While the part of Brewster is one which Cary Grant *should* have loved playing, the problem with *Arsenic and Old Lace* is that he's called upon to do very little other than react to the rudimentary farce going on around him.

'Frank Capra has Grant performing in such a frenzied, dithering manner that throughout much of the picture he seems crazier than anybody else,' wrote an unimpressed Pauline Kael. The *New York Herald Tribune* noted that 'a fine actor merely mugs'.

Cary Grant was, of course, always the cinematic master of the reaction. As the author Donald Dewey wrote, 'Grant considered it professional self-protection to have his characters' exposition speeches broken up and reassigned to other actors so that his character would be free to dominate scenes through silent reaction shots.' And William Goldman recorded in his seminal book *Adventures In The Screentrade* that 'Cary Grant was famous in his films for trying to get the other actors in a scene to do the expository talking. Grant was a brilliant listener, and often scenes would be shifted to suit him.'

But there is much more to a classic Cary Grant performance than *just* reacting. Sadly, that is about all that is required of him in this particular picture. Its huge box-office success notwithstanding, Grant's enduring disappointment with the film hardened over the years to such an extent that he actually came to hate it.

If *Arsenic and Old Lace* was a project to which he wasn't truly committed, the reverse could be said of *None But The Lonely Heart* which, although made three years after the Capra film, was released, ironically, just *one day* before it in September 1944.

None But The Lonely Heart had been adapted from Richard
Llewellyn's novel by the American playwright Clifford Odets. A
previous adaptation of a Llewellyn novel, *How Green Was My Valley*,
had been extremely successful for producer Darryl F. Zanuck three
years earlier, and RKO executives were convinced that *None But The
Lonely Heart*, about a cockney drifter and petty criminal named Ernie
Mott who finds redemption only when he finds out his mother is dying
of cancer, would repeat that success.

Odets, whose previous plays had included *Waiting For Lefty* and
Golden Boy, was associated with the radical Group Theatre and an
outspoken member of the American Communist Party. And where
director John Ford had seen *How Green Was My Valley* as a
stereotypical Hollywood tear-jerker, Odets saw potential in *None But
The Lonely Heart* to push socialist propaganda in a mainstream movie.

Odets had originally conceived Mott as a young man, as in the
original novel, but RKO, already nervous of the box-office, insisted
that Cary Grant, who liked the script, should play the role. Odets agreed
and Grant repaid him by insisting that Odets, who had never directed a
picture before, should direct this one. RKO balked at this suggestion,
but Grant, who had now reached that rare exalted position of calling the
shots, stood firm. Odets remarked generously of Grant, 'If he believes
in you, he'll gamble his entire career with you.'

The studio executive Jack Haley Junior, whose father, the comedian
Jack Haley, had played the Tin Man in the Judy Garland classic *The
Wizard Of Oz* and had been one of Grant's first friends at Paramount,
agreed with Odets: 'Cary had a wonderful love of writers,' he said.
'That's why he helped several of them become directors. It was
extraordinary the way he put his career on the line to give all those guys
their first shot.'

But is it that typical of a man whose whole life had been one risk taken
after another? It is unlikely that people, even such good friends as Haley,
would be up to speed on Cary Grant's background. They would know he
had come from England and changed his name, but as the ultimate
human chameleon, it is doubtful they would have been given many other
details, unless romanticised heavily by Grant himself. They wouldn't
know for sure that this man had had to use any means at his disposal to
take him from a poor area in Bristol, England, to the top of the pile in
Hollywood, California. That sort of thing rarely, if ever, happens to
people who are not willing to continually take gambles.

Grant must have known that his championing of the notoriously left-wing Odets could have serious repercussions but, typically, he ignored any siren warnings. Again and again, Grant demonstrated a loyalty to those he genuinely believed had talent and he and Odets were to remain friends until Odets' death in 1961. Their friendship *did* cause the FBI to question Grant's political leanings in 1944. An official FBI report given the grand yet ridiculous title *Communist Infiltration of the Motion Picture Industry* identified Cary Grant, as well as Lucille Ball and Ira Gershwin, as having 'communist connections', while *None But The Lonely Heart* was deemed to be anti-capitalistic.

But it was character not politics that had drawn Grant to the film. Where Odets saw Mott as 'a man looking for a free, noble and better life in the second quarter of the twentieth century', as the rather serious voice-over tells us at the beginning of the picture, Grant regarded him as an opportunity to play another serious character – perhaps the most serious he had yet played – *and*, in a sense, to revisit his own past, the past with which he was still coming to terms.

'I was usually cast as a well-dressed, sophisticated chap,' said Grant. 'This time I was an embittered cockney. In many ways, the part seemed to fit my nature better than the light-hearted fellows I was used to playing.'

Unfortunately, for all their good intentions, *None But The Lonely Heart* did not work. London's East End, with its cockney rhyming slang and its pearly Kings and Queens, has always been a target for artistic condescension. From *My Fair Lady* and *Mary Poppins* (with the inspired Dick Van Dyke producing an *un*inspired cockney accent) to the BBC's long-running soap *EastEnders,* genuine East Enders have always been patronised by writers and directors. Despite the undoubted sincerity of Grant and Odets, their film falls into the same trap.

At a time when real East Enders were still burying their dead and picking their way through the rubble caused by Hitler's onslaught, there was something rather distasteful about Odets lecturing them from the safety of a California sound stage about how Mott, an ambitious Everyman, representative of every East Ender there has ever been, was constantly forced back into grime and crime by the evils of capitalism.

Artistically, the film is also a fake. Odets had a penchant for murky lighting and insisted that fog be pumped onto the set relentlessly. The result is that the supposed integrity of the staging of the film is no greater than Universal's long-running Sherlock Holmes series, starring

Basil Rathbone and Nigel Bruce. Worse, some of the dialogue goes wildly beyond self-parody and sounds as though it comes straight from Victorian melodrama and the world in which the master does the chambermaid wrong.

'Love's not for the poor, son,' says Mott's mother, who, as played by Ethel Barrymore, is surely the most robust cancer victim in cinematic history, but Odets presents it as though the line were written by Ibsen.

None But The Lonely Heart is, in many ways, an appalling film. It is overlong, poorly shot and earnest to the point of smugness. Its worst dramatic fault is that nothing actually *happens*. The film is an amalgamation of inferior sub-plots where people talk in strained cockney accents. It divided critics on its release: some loathed it so much that they mocked it openly, while most believed that Grant was simply miscast as Ernie Mott, which is fairly indisputable.

In fairness, it must be acknowledged that the film did have its supporters and continues to be controversial even today. Also, Ethel Barrymore – like many of Grant's previous and subsequent co-stars – won an Oscar for her performance. Even Grant himself was nominated for Best Actor. This time he really did believe he had done something that would win him the award. But Bing Crosby won it for *Going My Way*, which patronised the people of the New York slums even more than *None But The Lonely Heart* had done to the East End.

Curiously, Grant remained stubbornly proud of the film for the remainder of his days and its failure at the box-office disappointed and depressed him. What particularly galled him was that *Arsenic and Old Lace*, released fractionally before, was a smash hit and regarded by audiences as a proper 'Cary Grant' film. Thus, the public loved a performance of his which he loathed and had rejected a role of which he had been so very proud. The uncertainties that had clouded his career since 1941 showed no sign of clearing.

Grant started to believe that his failure to convert his second Oscar nomination proved that the Hollywood establishment still regarded him as an outsider and this, coupled with the failure of *None But The Lonely Heart* and the rapidly deteriorating situation between himself and Barbara Hutton at the time made him reconsider his whole life and career.

Apart from a short wartime propaganda film, Grant did not act again in front of a camera for more than a year after completing *None But The Lonely Heart*. Although eyebrows were raised in Hollywood at the time, no one took his absence too seriously. He had, after all, made nearly fifty movies in eleven years at an average of just over four movies a year. That was a serious output. So maybe he needed and deserved an extended break? It is quite possible Grant thought the same thing, and though his conscious mind didn't articulate what was happening, his subconscious was getting him accustomed to a life outside the studios for the first time since he moved to California. It would not be the last time, either.

When Cary Grant finally did step back in front of the cameras, it was to be in a role for which he was even more miscast than he'd been as cockney, Ernie Mott. This next role saw him as Cole Porter in *Night And Day*.

Porter vied with Noel Coward as the wittiest lyricist of the twentieth century and, intriguingly, Grant was a good friend of both. Like Coward, Porter was gay; unlike Coward, Porter had been born into a wealthy family in 1891 and not only surprised those closest to him by getting married, but getting married to an exceptionally wealthy lady, the socialite Linda Thomas.

Grant was particularly close to the Porters and when his social life mutated from the inveterate party-going of his younger days into the more reclusive intimate dinners with friends that he preferred from the late 1930s, it was with Cole and Linda Porter that he most frequently dined.

If there was one thing Grant admired more than talent, it was wealth. A combination of both therefore fascinated him and Cole Porter had both in abundance. Even if he hadn't been independently wealthy and then married a rich wife, Cole Porter's shows – typified by *Anything Goes* in 1934 – would have made him a rich man indeed. And as well as his Broadway shows, he also had a prolific and lucrative career in Hollywood. A riding accident in 1937, when Porter's horse had fallen on top of him and crushed his legs, had left him confined to a wheelchair. His left leg was amputated and twenty-one years later, in 1958, so was his right leg, which was when he decided to give up writing altogether.

The idea of doing a biopic on Porter's life had first surfaced in 1943 when it was suggested, somewhat fancifully, that Porter's story about overcoming his awful injuries would inspire wounded servicemen. But most of those servicemen would not be returning to the fabulous wealth that did much to soften the blow of Porter's physical handicaps.

Cole Porter never lost his sense of humour despite his personal tragedy. He thought the very idea of a film about his life hysterically funny. Linda, less amused, thought it a ghastly idea. Jack Warner, though, was determined to press ahead with the film and eventually paid Porter $300,000 for the rights to the story and Porter's songs.

Several screenwriters worked on the project, although the film is finally credited to Charles Hoffman, Leo Townsend and William Bowers, and they all faced the same problem: the riding accident apart, Porter's life wasn't exactly incident-filled. As Orson Welles famously remarked on hearing about the proposed film, 'What will they use for a climax? The only suspense is: will he or won't he accumulate ten million dollars?'

The final script – over which Porter's contract gave him full approval – made no mention of his homosexuality, hilariously substituting a tendency to overwork as a metaphor, and depicted him as walking with a slight limp following his accident instead of losing a leg. Porter laughed out loud when first reading the script. 'It ought to be good,' he quipped. 'None of it's true.'

Quite how Cary Grant came to be considered for the lead role has been open to conjecture but the most enduring, certainly most appealing, version is that Linda Porter, scathing about the project from the outset, had insisted that if the film *had* to be made, she wanted Alexis Smith to play her.

Porter said, impishly, 'In that case, I should be played by Cary Grant.'

Jack Warner, never one to see an irony – a character actor like Peter Lorre was far more suited as a lookalike for Porter – agreed immediately and set about signing up Grant.

Night And Day is remarkable in Cary Grant's life for one particular reason: it was his first colour film. It was also the talk of Hollywood because its budget was a then unheard-of four and a half million dollars. Grant's customary salary of $150,000, plus Porter's $300,000, accounted for one-tenth of the budget alone.

Jack Warner, however, saw little risk. He was soon proved right, the film making more than fourteen million dollars at the box-office. And Grant hadn't been taking much of a chance, either. Although he was experienced enough to have recognised that the script was fundamentally flawed and that he himself was hopelessly miscast, he also knew that a biopic of Cole Porter starring Cary Grant was bound for commercial success. Having, therefore, negotiated a share of the profits on top of his fee, Grant made an awful lot of money from *Night And Day*.

Even more importantly, he had used the film to reclaim his place in Hollywood. After *None But The Lonely Heart* had flopped, he had put down his marker to prove that, in the right vehicle, Cary Grant was still box-office gold.

However financially satisfying *Night And Day* might have been, it was a nightmare to make. For the director, Warner had turned to the Hungarian Michael Curtiz, who had helmed such classics as *Captain Blood*, *The Charge of the Light Brigade*, *The Adventures of Robin Hood*, *Yankee Doodle Dandy* and *Casablanca*. Warner had good reason, clearly, to value Curtiz and there's no doubting he was a director of real ability. Unfortunately, he was also sadistic and tyrannical – bawling his orders out at even the biggest of stars in his fractured English – and was said to be the most hated man in Hollywood after Harry Cohn.

David Niven revelled in repeating a story about the making of *The Charge of the Light Brigade* (1936), when Curtiz ordered that a mass of riderless horses should run into the scene.

'Okay,' he bawled into his megaphone, 'bring on the empty horses!'

When Niven and Errol Flynn doubled up with laughter, Curtiz had flown at them. 'You lousy bums,' he yelled. 'You and your stinking language. You think I know fuck nothing. Well, let me tell you – I know FUCK ALL!'

Niven so loved the story that he appropriated *Bring On The Empty Horses* as the title of his second collection of reminiscences which he published in 1975.

Grant knew all about Curtiz's ferocious reputation when he started work on *Night And Day*. Big name stars like Errol Flynn were already refusing to work with the director ever again. But Grant, mindful of Curtiz's impressive track record as a film-maker, was determined not to have any preconceptions. He resolved to have as good a working relationship with Curtiz as on any other film he had ever worked.

His resolve lasted less than a day.

Grant and Curtiz clashed immediately over every aspect of the film and within weeks a bitter joke was circulating around Warner Brothers that the only way the war between Grant and Curtiz would end would be if President Truman dropped an atom bomb on the set.

On the last day of shooting, Grant stood on the set and addressed Curtiz in front of the entire cast and crew present. 'If ever I'm stupid enough to be caught working with you again,' he announced, 'you'll know I'm either broke or I've lost my mind.' It was an uncharacteristic, unprofessional outburst, but it earned him the admiration of just about every actor in Hollywood at the time.

In a little-known coda to Grant's famous put-down of Curtiz, Grant sent Curtiz a telegram when *Night And Day* premièred, congratulating him on the completed film. Curtiz did not respond and Grant stuck by what he had said: he never did work with Curtiz again. He didn't even attend the première, preferring, instead, to attend an intimate dinner with Cole Porter, George Cukor and Jack Warner's wife.

Box-office success notwithstanding, *Night And Day* was a poor picture that hasn't improved with the passing of time, and Grant is decidedly under par as Cole Porter. But his next film was to prove to be one of his best and reunited him with Alfred Hitchcock. It was *Notorious*.

16

'I can't stand hypocrisy.'

Cary Grant

Notorious is more than a Hitchcock-Grant classic. Together with their final collaboration, *North By Northwest*, thirteen years later, it regularly features on critics' lists of the greatest films of all time.

But, just as *Casablanca* had had a troubled production, *Notorious*, too, had not been without its problems. The film has its roots in a short story, which David O. Selznick had shown to Hitchcock. The story told of a female counter-spy who bedded an enemy agent and afterwards believed the incident had ruined her chances of making a decent marriage.

Hitchcock didn't care for the story at all but, ever obsessed with sex, he *was* struck by the idea of a woman using her sex to gain information, and he agreed with Selznick that writer Ben Hecht should come up with a screenplay based on the idea.

From the outset, Hecht's take on the story differed radically from Hitchcock's concept. Where Hitchcock envisaged a deeply cynical love story, which he intended to make as sexually-charged and explicit as the censor would let him get away with, Hecht saw *Notorious* as, primarily, a spy drama. Although Hecht's first draft was very different from how Hitchcock had seen the story, Hitchcock couldn't fail to notice at once that Hecht's script was also superb. What he decided was to combine both concepts so that his own vision of a sexually-charged affair could be layered smoothly over Hecht's superb spy drama. The problem was Selznick.

Hitchcock and Selznick had had a reasonable working relationship on *Rebecca* (1941) and *Spellbound* (1945) but, while Hitchcock was developing *Notorious*, Selznick was obsessed with another film, *Duel In The Sun*, which was to star his lover, Jennifer Jones. Hitchcock felt that Selznick was not committing himself fully to *Notorious* and, as a result, he didn't fully respect Selznick's suggestions and ideas about the film. Indeed, he viewed them as little more than interference. Selznick instructed Hitchcock that he couldn't blend two stories, that he had to make one version or the other.

They also clashed over casting. Although Selznick concurred with Hitchcock that Cary Grant, a friend of both Selznick and his wife, Irene, should play the lead, he wanted Vivien Leigh to play Alicia, the leading female role. Hitchcock resisted this fiercely, believing Leigh to be utterly wrong. Selznick reluctantly compromised with Hitchcock that Ingrid Bergman, who had starred in Hitchcock and Selznick's previous collaboration, *Spellbound*, the previous year, should portray Alicia.

None of this made for a happy pre-production period and Hitchcock, who worked with Selznick the following year on *The Paradine Case*, never quite forgave the producer for what happened on *Notorious*.

But something even more extraordinary was to happen before *Notorious* began shooting. With the cast, which, in addition to Grant and Bergman, also included Claude Rains, and crew all in place, Selznick, under immense pressure from steering *Duel In The Sun* through its professional and personal minefield, sold the entire project – script, cast and director – to RKO for $800,000 plus half the profits. Given that *Notorious* ultimately made more than ten million dollars, RKO got themselves something of a bargain.

The merging of Hitchcock and Hecht's concepts made *Notorious* easily greater than the sum of its parts. Opening in Florida during the Second World War, we focus first on the promiscuous and alcohol-dependent socialite Alicia Hubbard, whose German father has just been convicted for treason. At yet another party, which Alicia uses to take her mind off the disappointments of her life, she meets T.R. Devlin, played by Cary Grant, who is a mysterious secret agent. Devlin persuades Alicia to go to Rio with him to spy against the Germans. Alicia and Devlin fall in love, but then Alicia is advised to become the lover of Alex Sebastian (Claude Rains), an old boyfriend, whose home shelters Nazi scientists and plotters.

Eventually Alicia, as much to prove where her loyalties lie and that she is as anti-Nazi as anyone else, agrees to the sordid plan, and Devlin – with understandable reluctance, as this woman was going to be *his* wife – fixes an 'accidental' meeting with Alex. Soon after this, Alex proposes and she accepts. Attending a party at the house of the now-married Alicia and Alex, Devlin discovers uranium ore in a cellar. Alex soon finds out that Alicia is a spy and, together with his unpleasant mother (Leopoldine Konstantin), begins to poison her – a plot device with shades of *Suspicion*. Ultimately, and inevitably, it is left to Devlin to rescue Alicia from the house and expose Alex, while they, reconciled, can hobble off into the sunset.

The suspense in *Notorious* is terrific and centres on a perplexing moral question: how far will Alicia go? And how far will Devlin *let* her go?

This basic premise has been copied many times since *Notorious* was released, and many critics pointed out that the script of the film *Mission Impossible 2* (2000) owed a huge debt to Hitchcock's film. It was also one of the first films to deal with uranium – a theme which, again, has serviced countless thrillers – and this resulted in the FBI keeping Hitchcock under surveillance for three months after the film's release.

As he did in *Suspicion*, Hitchcock ensures that Devlin is a supremely ambiguous character and he uses this ambiguity again to peel away the layers of Cary Grant. Unlike any other 'hero' of cinema at that time, Grant shows the occasionally petulant Devlin as having a near neurosis about women: it's clear that he's prejudiced against women, is frightened of them and never loses his suspicions. Again, Hitchcock triumphed in his choice of leading man because Cary Grant, by his own admission, had his own identical fears about women.

Devlin is the darkest, most complicated character Grant ever played. While not completely humourless, the film and its subject matter do not allow Grant to display any of his renowned comedy skills.

While comparisons with *Suspicion* are relatively easy to make, *Notorious*, in fact, demanded an even more constrained performance in which Grant has few opportunities to reveal the varying sides of Devlin in words and actions. There are very few Grant quips and none of the beguiling facial expressions audiences had, by this time, come to expect. Indeed, what *is* noticeable is the lack of them. When others in a scene are revealing some kind of human emotion – including Devlin's superiors – Devlin himself remains totally impassive and, therefore, very un-Cary Grant.

Devlin is a man in torment. Until meeting Alicia, he has never found it hard to stifle his inner emotions, but she makes him confront his demons and the sub-text of the film is about his taking the first tentative steps into a more humane world.

Graham McCann wrote that Devlin is 'a professional dissembler, secretive, deceitful, emotionally impotent and, beneath the cool exterior, acutely vulnerable. Grant himself was like that.'

Indeed he was. It is impossible to view *Notorious* today without seeing a vision of how Archie Leach might have developed in some parallel universe. One critic wrote that 'Grant reaches levels of mean-spiritedness that from any other leading man would startle an audience, but which from Cary Grant are almost devastating.' That reviewer would have been even more devastated had he known that Grant was, in many ways, tapping into his own store of mean-spiritedness to convey Devlin's potential moral vacuum.

The doubts and insecurities that usually lay beneath the urbane exterior of Grant are laid bare in the film. Alfred Hitchcock's genius whenever he worked with Grant was to see what lay beneath and to expose it. But then Hitchcock, more than any other director, found it easy to recognise Grant's insecurities. They were, after all, his own.

If *Notorious* was a more intense film than was usual for Grant, its production, once RKO had taken over, was a dream compared with the horrendous shoot he had endured with Michael Curtiz on *Night And Day*. Grant appreciated Hitchcock's sly humour and general love of amusement and, if anything, enjoyed working with him even more second time around. Whether it was for his love of amusement or for other reasons, Hitchcock always made a customary, very brief, cameo appearance somewhere in his own films. In *Notorious,* he can be seen drinking champagne at Alex Sebastian's party.

When Hitchcock made the film, the censors actually timed the length of a kiss to the second to ensure it came within the accepted running-time laid down by the censorship code. Hitchcock, always eager to push against the parameters, decided he wanted to have Grant and Bergman kiss for far longer than the censors would permit. His solution was to have them kiss on a balcony and then move inside. A telephone rings and Grant answers it. Thus, odd lines of dialogue punctuate the kiss which, ostensibly, had been going on since the balcony scene outside. Hitchcock got what he wanted; the longest, and sexiest, kiss on screen up to that time. The censors clearly knew what he was doing but, because the kiss was broken 'the censor couldn't cut it', a delighted Ingrid Bergman later explained.

Having to resort to such measures irked Grant who, in matters of personal morality, was a libertarian. He felt that many of those censoring films and who professed to uphold family values in public, were, in their own private lives, guilty of debauchery. More than once he voiced his loathing of such hypocrisy and he would time and again put himself, his career and his reputation on the line in defence of an ostracised friend. He was the first, for example, to defend Charlie Chaplin publicly when he became an object of hate in the US during the McCarthy witch-hunts.

From our viewpoint in the early 21st century, it is difficult now to appreciate just how courageous Grant's trait of rating personal loyalty above professional reputation really was. During the 1940s and early 1950s, a career in the movie industry could be destroyed simply if one were *suspected* – nothing had to be proved – of having communist sympathies. Simply being friends with a known communist was enough. Similarly, the faintest whiff of 'immorality' in one's personal life was enough to bring public opprobrium, though, again, it was part of the hypocrisy that Grant abhorred that the crime was not the immorality itself, but the getting caught.

Simply being perhaps the most successful leading man in Hollywood was no guaranteed defence. If a star as big as Chaplin could be driven into exile (he would leave California for ever and settle in Switzerland), there is no reason why Cary Grant should feel invulnerable. And given that he knew he was on the FBI's files from the middle of the 1940s onwards – he was extremely and inexplicably lucky to survive the McCarthy era unscathed – his insistence on sticking his head above the parapet in defence of friends is all the more impressive.

Grant was never more at odds with prevailing public opinion than the time when Ingrid Bergman was blacklisted by Hollywood. Although he later went on record as saying that Grace Kelly was his favourite leading lady, there is no doubt that Grant adored Bergman from the moment they met. He not only admired her talent, which was immense, but he recognised and possibly understood her inner complexities.

When Bergman shocked Hollywood in 1948 by leaving her husband and first child for the director Roberto Rossellini, by whom she was pregnant, she found herself denounced by senators and rabid religious groups as 'a powerful influence for evil'. The American movie industry turned its back on her and, like Chaplin, Bergman sought exile in Europe, not returning again to Hollywood until 1956.

Grant hated what people were saying about her and he was particularly incensed to hear men who had previously been her lovers denouncing her. But, given that she was such a figure of hate, it would be a brave man who would publicly stand up and totally contradict the vitriol. Cary Grant was the only one to do so.

'Ingrid Bergman,' he argued, 'is a fascinating, full-blooded yet temperate woman who has the courage to live in accord with her needs and strength enough to accept and benefit by the consequences of her beliefs in an inhibited, critical and frightened society. Ingrid needs no uninvited busy-body to proclaim her debts; she knows and pays them herself. I commend her highly to you.'

It was, by any accounts, a powerful speech and a savage snub to her many enemies, and Grant must have known he was doing himself little good by making it. But his principles were always very important to him and to the image of Cary Grant. Indeed, it is entirely what Cary Grant would have done in a 'Cary Grant' picture. He clearly cherished that image, so was not going to bury his head in the sand just because the action wasn't taking place on celluloid. Underpinning all the deceptions and confusions that went with the making of a massive cinematic self-creation called Cary Grant, there lay an immovable base of integrity.

Bergman, for her part, never forgot his support. 'For years,' she said later, 'Cary was the only one in Hollywood who contacted me. I had done no wrong in his eyes.'

While Grant and Bergman were always close friends, it is doubtful whether their relationship went any further. Bergman made it a policy not to have affairs with her leading men. She did, however, point out that she would get pretty close to her leading men before preventing it becoming something physical. She also remarked that it was not difficult to fall in love with the likes of Cary Grant. To underline the strength of their friendship, it is worth remembering that Grant said those well-quoted words: 'I think the Academy ought to set aside a special award for Bergman every year whether she makes a picture or not!'

If Grant's support for Bergman was absolute, his attitude to his past remained equivocal, at least until the summer of 1946. Although the war in Europe had ended in May 1945, he seems to have been in no particular hurry to return to Bristol and waited until after *Notorious* had been completed in April 1946 to do so. It had been eight years since Grant had last visited England. Now, in 1946, he was a 42-year-old American citizen and a very different, more mature, Cary Grant from the one who had first returned in the autumn of 1933.

But when he arrived at Elsie's house in Howard Road, Redland, he discovered that he was not the only one to have changed. Though still decidedly eccentric, Elsie had mellowed into a much more amiable, and occasionally downright amusing, lady. She was still extremely difficult and querulous, but she was someone with whom, quite unexpectedly, he could share a laugh.

He laughed especially on discovering that Elsie had another 'Cary' in her life these days: a spaniel, which she was convinced was more talented than Asta, the fox terrier from *The Awful Truth*. For the entire duration of his visit, Elsie was to badger Grant into getting *her* Cary into the movies!

By his own admission, Grant never quite reconciled his feelings for his mother after she had re-entered his life. He couldn't get a handle on precisely how he was expected to feel about her. But in these shared, conveniently brief, moments, when they could share a joke, the difficulties surrounding the bigger puzzle that was their relationship, seemed not to matter all that much. Grant was adept at concealing his true feelings, and would have had little trouble in deceiving his mother that all was light and happiness. His humour was the device which could protect the *real* him – which is a contradiction in terms as the real Cary Grant was a creation – from the rest of the world.

It would be fair to say that Grant was genuinely and utterly relieved that his mother had emerged from the war years unscathed. Although the war had been over nearly a year, Grant was shocked by his first glimpses of post-war Britain. Nothing could have prepared him for the level of devastation he witnessed. London, the city of his first marriage, particularly, had a curious effect upon him.

This visit home was, naturally, his first since relinquishing British nationality, and yet, during this two-month visit, he had never felt so English. Seeing just how close England had come to being invaded reinforced in Grant a latent patriotic fervour, which must have been terribly confusing for the man who was now an American.

From the moment he had caught sight of the Woolworth Building from the decks of the *Olympic*, he had willingly been absorbed by the star-spangled banner. Now, for the first time in a quarter of a century, Cary Grant was compelled to recognise just how much he missed that country from which he had escaped, the country that had offered him such an unpromising future, the country that had locked away his mother. The country that he called home. He missed the land of the Union Jack. He missed England.

The upshot of all of this was that he made the decision, then and there, to commit himself to making at least one film a year in Britain. This idea was never successfully executed, nevertheless, his return visits became more frequent after the war and after 1966, he would occasionally be spotted driving through the English countryside in search of that ploughman's lunch and sausage and mash.

His return to Hollywood in July 1946 coincided with the opening of *Notorious*. The critics were uniformly ecstatic, and Grant's performance, in particular, was hailed as his greatest triumph to date. *Notorious* opened at the same time that David Niven had begun writing a series of monthly letters from Hollywood for the *Sunday Express* in London. Niven's opinion of the film was typical of almost everyone who saw the masterpiece as he wrote in his column dated 17 September 1946:

> I have always made it a golden rule never to knock other actors, for the obvious reason that I am not nearly a good enough one myself to withstand the recoil. Conversely, I am ashamed to admit that words of praise, where other actors are concerned, usually flow from me like glue. I am, therefore, somewhat surprised to find myself gibbering and twittering with excitement over the performances of Cary Grant and Ingrid Bergman in *Notorious*. This Hitchcock picture is really good and the love scenes are the best, the most beautifully played and the best-directed that I have ever seen on the screen.

It was, without doubt, more than just another Hitchcock movie, more than even just another Cary Grant movie. It was an event – the movie *everyone* was talking about – and RKO, who had picked up the rights rather cheaply from Selznick, were understandably thrilled. Like every other studio, they recognised Grant's contribution to the box-office. His appeal was showing no signs of wavering as he moved into middle-age.

If Grant's career was seemingly unaffected by age, the same could not be said of another of RKO's stars, Shirley Temple. Temple, who was born in April 1928 in Santa Monica, had been everything Depression-hit America needed to help put smiles on faces through one of the country's darkest times. By the age of six, she had already made twenty films and, while on loan to Paramount, she had shot to international stardom with the film *Little Miss Marker*. Her grating signature song – guaranteed to set even the most sugar-tolerant teeth on edge today – was 'On The Good Ship Lollipop', which sold over half-a-million copies and earned its young star a special Academy Award.

The American movie industry and public just couldn't get enough of the curly haired, sweet-faced child-star during the 1930s – perhaps an indication of just *how* bad the Depression really was! – and even President Roosevelt got in on the act, praising her 'infectious optimism'.

By 1946, even Shirley Temple had reached an age where the sweet curls and rosy cheeks were looking vaguely misplaced and RKO began preparing her for a slightly older role in a film entitled *The Bachelor and the Bobby Soxer.*

Scripted, rather surprisingly, by Sidney Sheldon in the years before he struck gold as a blockbuster novelist, the film also starred Myrna Loy as Temple's sister – a highly unlikely piece of casting, this, given that Loy was forty-two and Temple eighteen.

But RKO, nervous about Temple's potential appeal as an adult – even if Sheldon's script did its best to emphasise her supposed 'college girl innocence' – felt they needed to protect the box-office even more. The executives decided that, for the older man on whom Temple's character develops a big crush, they required an actor who was a guaranteed draw. Not unnaturally they approached Grant.

One would think that after a dark, moody and hugely successful movie like *Notorious*, Grant would politely decline. That is where he remained such an enigma and possibly why Cary Grant could play screwball comedy and straight drama so successfully. And *definitely* why his peak years lasted over thirty years. Despite being cinematic froth, *The Bachelor and the Bobby Soxer* was a minor but unexpected delight despite its cumbersome title (it was known in the UK, rather more prosaically, as *Bachelor Knight*).

Grant played the part of an artist called Richard Nugent, with whom both Margaret (Loy) and Susan (Temple) fall in love. So, not for the first time, Grant finds himself the man in the middle, pursued by women – it was ever thus! What made this movie so different was the

An American in Paris. A relaxed Cary Grant enhances the skyline for photographers. © Bettmann/Corbis

Pensive and wary in London on his way to Bristol to see his mother, 1946.
© Bettmann/Corbis

Right: Don't ask, don't tell.
© Bettmann/Corbis

Above: 'Breast or leg?' The scene of *To Catch A Thief*'s erotic picnic, essentially unchanged in 2001. © Gary Morecambe and Martin Sterling.

Below: Grace Kelly's home in Monaco as it looks in 2001. Grant visited his former co-star at the Palace many times following her marriage to Prince Ranier. © Gary Morecambe and Martin Sterling.

The pursuit of happiness. Grant arriving in New York aboard the Santa Elena, 2 April, 1940. His love of travel never left him once he'd escaped his past in Bristol. © Bettmann/Corbis

She done him right. Grant poses with Mae West in a Hollywood nightclub despite his ambivalence towards her, 1955. © Bettmann/Corbis

Grant and a movie camera on location for *Father Goose* (1964): a 30-year relationship he was about to bring to an end.© Bettmann/Corbis

Grant and fourth wife Dyan Cannon with daughter Jennifer – 'My best production' – in 1966. © Bettmann/Corbis

Cary 'Man of the Year, 1982' Grant and his fifth wife Barbara Harris with Frank Sinatra at the Waldorf Astoria.

age gap between Grant and Temple, some 24 years. Not only are no attempts made to disguise this but, for the first time in his film career, Grant's age is alluded to on screen. Indeed, Grant's being so much older than Temple is used by Myrna Loy to get her man.

When Temple steers Grant into a compromising position, Loy, playing a rather unlikely judge, offers him Hobson's Choice – be charged with corrupting a minor or be Temple's date until she becomes disillusioned with him and turns her attention to boys her own age, thus freeing him for Loy to pursue without having to worry about sibling rivalry.

In her autobiography *Child Star* Temple recalls the experience of playing alongside Grant:

[One scene] was a close-up, with lights shining comfortably warm on my skin. We were slow getting started while director Irving Reis and Grant bickered about details of delivery and stage position. Their wrangles about words or stage direction were getting commonplace. Much of what Grant proposed was meritorious, mostly ad-libs and little routines. However, for every added embellishment, Myrna Loy would excuse herself to the portable dressing room and bring back suggestions to enhance her own role. Grant was known as someone obsessively concerned with nuance and detail and Loy as someone not easily finessed. In the middle was Reis, unwilling to be superseded by either of the two warring contestants.

Apparently, Grant went through the making of the picture in poor humour due to his repeated disagreements with Reis:

Although some residual disharmony continued to plague the set, (Dore) Schary (producer) coped with Grant's perfectionist tendencies and tolerated his abrupt absences to count or rewrite lines. As was my custom during such intermissions, I hung around joshing with the crew, far preferring some activity to nothing. That's how the trouble started. I started to mimic Grant. Egged on by the crew's applause, I soon was doing an impromptu show. Taking centre stage where the lights were ready for our next close-up, I tipped my head put on a quizzical smile and started a soliloquy in a deep-throated, cockney accent. Swaggering across the set, I executed a typical Grant double-take, careful to point out that I was showing only my right profile, a well-known minor vanity. The crew had been laughing and cheering, but suddenly turned silent as tombstones. Beyond the edge of the light's glare, I detected Grant's face. I was caught red-handed.

Again he stalked away, this time directly to Selznick, who sent word for me to come at once. Grant was quitting the film unless I went and Selznick was fuming at yet another personality clash on an already troubled set. Mimicry is immature, I was lectured, leaving a clear impression that if anyone left the film, it would be me... My only salvation lay in a personal apology, one fortunately accepted by Grant. By then his annoyance level had subsided, and with a grave nod of his head he accepted my remorse, turned, started off, then stopped. 'By the way,' he said, cocking his head in an exaggerated version of my mimicry, 'it was a pretty good imitation.'

As a comedian, Grant was always at his physical and verbal best in situations that bordered on farce. And if Sidney Sheldon's script was not quite the equal of, say, *Bringing Up Baby*, Irving Reis's assured direction coupled with excellent performances from Grant, Loy and Temple make the film fizz with pure entertainment. Basically, it is a hard film to dislike, even if unlike, say, *Notorious*, it was no cinematic landmark.

The most fundamental point that should be made about this picture, one made by many film historians, is that it is a watershed in Grant's acting career. One of the first to recognise this change, this dividing line, between what amounts to two different film careers, was Richard Schickel. 'This film,' argued Schickel, 'has a certain historical importance as the first in which Grant's former implicit capacity for bedazzlement was turned into a manifest quality.'

This is surely true. Grant's apparent effortless sexual charm – 'the man from dream city' as he was known among his female admirers – had, as Schickel saw it, only ever been implicit in previous films. Here, for the first time, though by no means the last, it is explicit. So explicit that, in one choice sequence, when Temple is daydreaming of her hero, he actually appears as a knight in full, gleaming armour. If ever we can pinpoint the truth behind Grant's oft-repeated phrase, 'I pretended to be somebody I wanted to be, and I finally became that person,' it is that sequence in *The Bachelor and the Bobby Soxer.*

Thus, history repeated itself. Just as *Sylvia Scarlett* had been vital in the development of Cary Grant's screen persona, so *The Bachelor and the Bobby Soxer*, an otherwise light and trite piece of fluff, was a turning-point in his on-going evolution. This is when the mature Cary Grant persona, the one he would play largely for the next forty years both publicly and privately, was honed.

The Bachelor and the Bobby Soxer was a major hit with critics and audiences alike. The *New Republic* thought that the film was 'sure-fire stuff guaranteed to do no conceivable harm. Cary Grant has now developed a characterisation that is constant, foolproof, engaging, hardy and warranted to be attractive. The audience laughed so hard I missed some of the lines.'

The box-office was doubtless boosted by the belief earlier that same year that Grant had been killed in a plane crash with his friend Howard Hughes. Hughes, whose passion for aviation eclipsed everything else in his life, had been developing a revolutionary reconnaissance aeroplane through his Hughes Aircraft Company. To facilitate development, he had invested over six million dollars of his own money in the project. The plane was ready by the summer of 1946 and Hughes was determined to make the first test flight himself. Seconds after take-off, the plane smashed into the ground in Beverly Hills. Hughes somehow managed to drag himself out of the cockpit and onto one of the blazing wings, from where he was pulled to safety by the first rescuers on the scene.

His injuries were horrific. In addition to a fractured skull, nine broken ribs and a collapsed lung, he had sustained lacerations all over his body, plus second-degree burns. Most sinister of all, his heart had been pushed out of alignment.

Hughes was barely alive when he reached the hospital. The doctors gave his chances of survival at one thousand to one. Believing death to be imminent and seeing the excruciating pain he was in, the doctors pumped him full of morphine, administering doses far beyond anything regarded as safe. No one can condemn them for this: Hughes wasn't expected to last the night.

But he did. And the next. And the next. Hughes's close inner circle – which included Grant and 'Cubby' Broccoli – kept vigil by his bedside and saw their friend come back from the brink of death to make an amazing recovery. The downside was that to deal with the dreadful pain that would last for several weeks, the doctors had no alternative but to pump masses of codeine and tranquillisers into Hughes's battered body. In 1946, this was uncharted territory and the risk of his becoming addicted was not fully understood.

In the 1960s and early 1970s, when lurid stories about the notoriously reclusive, supposedly drug-addicted, billionaire reached their zenith, both Grant and Broccoli were irritated that Hughes's addiction was not seen for what it was: a direct result of an awful tragedy. The great irony, as his friends knew, was that before the crash Hughes, if anything, had been fanatically anti-narcotic. But his reliance on drugs was not the only change his friends noticed. As 'Cubby' Broccoli wrote many years later: 'Before the crash, the Howard I knew had been a good-looking, boyish character, full of energy and high spirits. When I saw him afterwards, some of the spark had gone out of him. I wonder to this day which was worse for my late friend, the effects of that terrible crash or his increasing dependence on the massive doses of drugs he was given afterwards.'

The first recorded incident of Hughes's increased eccentricity following the crash involved Grant. Grant's own love of all things aviation had superseded his childhood fascination with those ships he'd spent hours observing on the docks of Bristol. 'I've flown for years in all sorts of weather in all sorts of aircraft,' he boasted. 'I've flown in open cockpits, in trans-continental Ford trimotors, in unscheduled small airmail planes in snowstorms, and, happily, many times alongside the most able pilot of them all, Howard Hughes, in his converted bomber.'

Like all Hughes's friends, Grant believed that the billionaire had made a full, if unexpected, recovery from his injuries. And Hughes, whose first goal on leaving hospital was to climb straight back into a cockpit, proved in the remaining months of 1946 that his flying skills had *seemingly* been unimpaired by his terrible accident.

So when in early 1947, shortly after his 43rd birthday, Grant climbed aboard Hughes's converted bomber, he had absolutely no qualms about the trip they were about to undertake to Mexico. It was, after all, a trip they'd made together many times before. But during this particular flight, Hughes did something inexplicably odd: he gave a single radio message, indicating they were somewhere over Indianapolis, and then severed all radio contact.

Nothing further was heard of Hughes or Grant for nearly 48 hours. The plane was posted as missing, and a search for wreckage was begun. Press speculation quickly grew that Cary Grant and Howard Hughes had been killed in Hughes's aircraft.

They had, in fact, headed for a remote house Hughes owned on the

Mexico coast. Whether Hughes had intended to create the incident as a sick joke, or whether it was, indeed, just a drug-influenced whim, we shall never know. It could also be cited as an early sign of a man who was fast beginning to rate personal privacy as a top priority. We will also never know to what extent, if it was a joke, Grant conspired in its execution. What we do know is that Grant had the rare, and dubious, privilege of reading his own obituary, published in many papers, on his return to Los Angeles.

If Howard Hughes's behaviour was becoming more erratic, Grant's, too – though less nihilistic – had become more unpredictable, this being clearly seen in the film roles he was accepting and those he was turning down. *Notorious* and *The Bachelor and the Bobby Soxer*, different though they were, had proved that he remained probably *the* foremost leading man in the business. Every studio head wanted Cary Grant because he could guarantee commercial success (*None But The Lonely Heart* had been forgiven because it was such an atypical Grant picture that it was dismissed as an aberration). Grant was, therefore, inundated with offers and scripts.

Grant, with his usual perceptive intelligence in regard to his own career, now became very choosy about the projects he accepted. From 1947 to the end of his film career in 1966, he was to turn down some of the most remarkable films in Hollywood history. He had, of course, turned down some notable films before this. If Hitchcock had had his way, their first collaboration would not have been *Suspicion* but *Foreign Correspondent*, which Hitchcock had made in 1940, his second American film after *Rebecca*. Joel McCrae eventually played the part of the American journalist, intended for Grant, who is sent to Europe in 1938 and becomes embroiled in spying. And Ernst Lubitsch's fabulous *Ninotchka* (1939) starring Greta Garbo and Melvyn Douglas, had originally been written as a Cary Grant vehicle until Grant said he wasn't interested in doing the movie.

In May 1948, David O. Selznick and Alexander Korda, the Hungarian producer who had been established as *the* leading producer-director in the British film industry since 1930, signed an agreement whereby they would make four films in Britain, which Selznick would distribute in the US, Canada, the Caribbean and Central and South America.

Among the four films was Graham Greene's *The Third Man*, which Selznick was particularly thrilled by. In Greene's original treatment, the characters who would become Holly Martins and Harry Lime were both Englishmen and Selznick wanted Cary Grant and Noel Coward in the roles (although he was prepared for Grant to insist on switching roles, not for the first time, and play Harry Lime).

The prospect of Grant and Coward together on screen whetted everyone's appetite, and good though Carol Reed's eventual movie was when it appeared with Joseph Cotton and Orson Welles in the Harry Lime role, it must be to the regret of every film buff that the original casting did not go ahead. From Grant's view, it was probably better that it didn't. Coward, by his own admission, was not the greatest actor in the world, but he could steal an entire film with just a couple of scenes, as evidenced ten years later in a different Graham Greene story, *Our Man In Havana*, in which he stole the movie right from under the nose of Alec Guinness.

The reason *The Third Man* didn't happen as originally planned was because of Grant. He knew his value to producers, of course, and although the artistic success of a film was of great importance to him, Cary Grant ultimately regarded the box-office as the main measure of success or failure in the film business. He was on record as saying that the business side of the industry interested him more than the actual acting. Consequently, his excellent business brain knew exactly how the profit and loss account of a movie added up. He was a man who knew the price and the value of everything. He knew how much a movie cost to make and he knew just how huge the sums of money a successful picture made actually were. He was also acutely aware of precisely how much his presence in a movie added to the returns: he could actually calculate it in dollars. He would until the end of his career, never allow anyone not to pay him *his* going rate.

By the time he came to negotiate with Selznick and Korda for *The Third Man* in 1948, he believed he was worth a basic fee of $200,000, plus half the net proceeds in Europe. These were very steep terms, but Selznick and Korda did, if reluctantly, agree to them. What scuppered the deal, according to the writer David Thomson in his biography of Selznick, was 'Grant's mistrust of everyone over money and the suspicion that Korda might fudge the calculation of "net profit".' This is very feasible, as net profit is only what the producers *claim* to be the profits. Grant would surely have wanted a percentage of the gross.

Money was also to undermine Selznick's attempts to cast Grant in the lead opposite Jennifer Jones in Selznick's long-delayed adaptation of F. Scott Fitzgerald's *Tender Is The Night,* which was eventually released in 1962. Selznick refused to pay the £300,000 that Grant demanded to do the movie, claiming it was excessive. It is quite possible, however, that Grant deliberately chose to out-price himself from doing the movie. As a good friend of Irene Selznick, David O.'s wife, Grant would not have been wholly comfortable appearing with Selznick's lover, Jennifer Jones.

Other roles he turned down for a variety of reasons in the remainder of his career are fascinating. He could have been the first James Bond in *Dr. No* (co-produced by his friend, 'Cubby' Broccoli) in 1962; the definitive Philip Marlowe, given that Raymond Chandler, Marlowe's creator, said, 'I always envisaged Cary Grant as Marlowe'; and he would have made an intriguing Hamlet in Alfred Hitchcock's pet project, *Hamlet* re-done as a modern-day thriller with Cary Grant in the title role.

Other films he turned down were *Roman Holiday* (meant as a Cary Grant–Elizabeth Taylor vehicle); George Cukor's 1954 remake of *A Star Is Born; Sabrina* (1954), in which he would have been far more at ease than its eventual star, Humphrey Bogart; and *Cleopatra* (1963), in which it was intended that he should play Caesar to Burt Lancaster's Mark Antony.

The Guns Of Navarone (1961), an all-star action adventure romp, which reached the screen with Gregory Peck, David Niven, Stanley Baker, Anthony Quinn and Anthony Quayle, was originally announced by its producer as starring Hugh O'Brien, Trevor Howard, Alec Guinness, Marlon Brando and Cary Grant (Grant and Brando on screen together – now *that* would have been something worth watching!). Grant also rejected the idea of his teaming up again with Ingrid Bergman to play the battling George and Martha in *Who's Afraid Of Virginia Woolf?*

He also turned down the role of Phileas Fogg in Mike Todd's mammoth production *Around The World In Eighty Days* (1956), in which he was replaced by David Niven, and the role of the Devil himself in Stanley Donen's film musical *Damn Yankees* (1958).

Professional courtesy prompted him to reject two other musicals offered to him: *The Music Man* in 1962 and *My Fair Lady* in 1964. There is little doubt he would have made a splendid Harold Hill in *The Music Man*, while playing Professor Higgins in Jack Warner's sumptuous movie of *My Fair Lady* – perhaps the greatest stage musical of all time – would have reunited him not only with director George

Cukor but also Audrey Hepburn, with whom he starred in *Charade*. In both cases, though, Grant believed that the stage originators – Robert Preston in *The Music Man* and Rex Harrison in *My Fair Lady* – should re-create their performances in the films.

Grant rarely professed regret at having turned down films that, subsequently, became huge hits. However, one exception was *The Bridge On The River Kwai,* which he regretted having turned down for the rest of his life. He had read the original book and talked with producer Sam Spiegel. But, typically, he had demanded script changes and balked at the extensive location work that would be required in Ceylon.

'Colombia,' he later noted, ruefully, 'knowing me, also sent the script to William Holden. Bill read the script, decided it was magnificent – which it was – and said he'd do it. By then, of course, I realised what a great part I'd lost.' Given that the film also made Holden an extremely rich man, it was also a hugely lucrative role and Grant had no qualms about admitting he was also irritated at the missed financial opportunity.

When David O. Selznick was prepared for Grant to switch roles if he made *The Third Man* he was, perhaps, thinking of Sam Goldwyn's experiences with the star on *The Bishop's Wife* in 1947. Scripted by Robert Sherwood and Leonard Bercorici, *The Bishop's Wife* was an agreeable piece of fantasy with shades of Grant's 1937 picture *Topper*. It told the story of an angel who is despatched from Heaven to intervene in the life of a bishop who, having become totally overworked because of his obsession with a new cathedral, has lost touch with his wife and parishioners.

Initially, Grant turned the film down. But Goldwyn persisted for six months in trying to secure the star and eventually Grant succumbed to playing the role of the Bishop. David Niven was already on board in the role of Dudley, the angel, and Loretta Young was cast as the bishop's wife.

Filming began with William Seiter as director. But the film was in trouble at the outset. Goldwyn hated everything he saw in the early rushes. The sets looked wrong, he complained, and the direction was atrocious. He didn't even care for Grant's performance. Seiter was sacked after just two weeks and replaced by Henry Koster. Goldwyn also had the sets scrapped and then rebuilt at a reputed cost of $900,000. And then Goldwyn tackled Grant – only for Grant to drop his bombshell. He wanted out of the picture.

Goldwyn knew that he faced disaster if Grant walked out. Not only had the sets been scrapped and rebuilt, but Henry Koster had now thrown out the script and insisted on it being rewritten from scratch. The trouble for Goldwyn was that he had already booked the film into theatres for the all-important Christmas season. If the film missed the deadline *and* didn't star Cary Grant, it could easily sink without trace.

But Grant was proving adamant, offering to return the astronomical $300,000 Goldwyn had paid him to acquire his services. Goldwyn made a counter-offer: if Grant stayed, he would pay him an additional $100,000. That would push his figure up to something that would be the talk of the industry.

Grant agreed to stay, but with one further condition. He had to swop roles with David Niven. Grant had been convinced from the outset that he was far better suited to play the Angel than the Bishop. Goldwyn put up token resistance, but knew he had to concede if he wanted his star.

Despite, or perhaps because of, the unsettling problems surrounding the production of the film, Grant found great consolation in working for the first and only time with his friend, David Niven. Although Gladys Cooper recalled 'a very faint feeling of tension between Cary and David on set whenever the subject of the war came up, which was not often,' Grant found Niven agreeable company on set. This demonstrates Niven's professionalism as his young wife, Primmie, had died of a fractured skull following a fall down some cellar steps just months earlier. Grant told Sheridan Morley many years later:

I don't think David and I ever thought of ourselves as rivals. We were such different types on the screen. I'd known him since the thirties when he was first in Hollywood romancing Merle Oberon and rather trying to model himself on Ronald Colman. I was about six years older than David, and I'd already been in Hollywood for a couple of years when he arrived.

My great heroes were the light comedians of the 1920s British stage, men like Ronald Squire and A.E. Matthews, whereas I think David was far more impressed by all the movie people like Errol Flynn. But we got on very well. We used to go riding in the hills and keep bottles of beer hidden along the route. He'd never talk much about himself or his background. He seemed terrified of boring or depressing you, felt he always had to be the entertainer.

He was more educated, I think more intelligent, than I was but you felt there was always something being held back. I admired him very much for going back and fighting in the war: that was a wonderful thing to have done.

When he came back he seemed, in some ways, to have changed, but I think that may have been because of that terrible accident to Primmie. He was still distraught about that when we were making *The Bishop's Wife*, and yet there was still that urge to entertain, to tell stories, not always true stories maybe, but marvellous rearrangements of the truth. He was a funny man and a brave man and a good man, and there was never too many of those around Hollywood.

If Grant found Niven congenial company on the movie, he retained a businesslike relationship with director Koster and producer Goldwyn for the duration of the shoot. His antennae were alerting him to the fact that the film, even as rewritten, simply wasn't good enough. This was borne out at a test screening when the reaction was terrible.

What happened next is a little confused. Grant said that he called Billy Wilder and asked him to take a look at the picture. Others maintain that it was Goldwyn himself who got in touch with Wilder. Whichever it was, Billy Wilder and his collaborator Charles Brackett sat through a screening. They confirmed the fears of Grant and Goldwyn – the film didn't make a lot of sense. But they had some good news. They claimed they could pull the whole thing round if they could add three new scenes. They did so and this potential flop ended up being a huge hit with audiences and moderately well-received by critics.

Nevertheless, it was with some relief that Grant travelled to London for a business meeting with Alexander Korda, with whom he had had on-going discussions about their setting up a production company together to make a film of a Daphne du Maurier story. The project was never to materialise.

Grant spent a few weeks in England, mostly in London, but with a visit to see Elsie in Bristol, before returning to the US aboard the *Queen Mary*.

Returning by sea rather than air was a capricious decision and Fate was to determine that it was also a momentous one. For also aboard was a young American actress called Betsy Drake who had enjoyed a hugely successful run at the Wyndham's Theatre in London's West End in the play *Deep Are The Roots*.

Drake would become the third – and longest lasting – Mrs Cary Grant.

17

'If I can understand how I became who I am, I can use that to shape my life in the future. I want to live in reality. Dreams aren't for me.'

Cary Grant

Betsy Drake changed Cary Grant. He knew it. She knew it. And all his friends watched her do it.

Grant was nearly twice her age when they tied the knot on Christmas Day 1949: he was almost 46 and she was only 26. But the irony was that it was Drake, not Grant, who was the more intellectual and spiritual of the two and she, therefore, who became more like his teacher as much as his wife. She helped him open his eyes to the wider world around; helped make him more questioning, more accepting and more relaxed.

'I owe a lot to Betsy,' Grant always acknowledged. 'She was good for me. Without imposition or demand, she patiently led me toward an appreciation for better books, better literature. Her cautious but steady penetrative seeking in the labyrinths of the subconscious gradually provoked my interest. Just as she no doubt intended.'

Although his getting to know Drake aboard the *Queen Mary* had echoes of his being introduced to Barbara Hutton aboard the *Normandie* a decade earlier, the circumstances were quite different. In any event, Grant had certainly seen her before: he had been to see her in *Deep Are The Roots*. He was so attracted to Drake that he appears to have returned several times to the theatre to watch her performing.

Drake was in many ways the antithesis of female Hollywood stars of the era. Although darkly attractive, she appeared to have very little interest in fashion and used make-up sparingly, something of which Grant wholeheartedly approved. She was also a very giving person, and this characteristic – something that even the most charitable could not apply to Virginia Cherrill or Barbara Hutton – was entirely new to Grant.

Certainly, the great Cary Grant of the screen was reduced to a nervous teenager when he discovered that, in addition to old mates like Elizabeth Taylor and Merle Oberon, Betsy Drake was aboard. She was returning to the US following an extended run of her play. Surprisingly – and endearingly – shy about asking her out to dinner, he lobbied Merle Oberon to intercede on his behalf.

'I told Merle to go tell Betsy she had to have lunch with a lonely man,' he joked afterwards.

Quite why Grant should have suffered from a lack of confidence at this moment is difficult to pinpoint. Apart from his screen image, his healthy sexual appetite, albeit never rapacious, was renowned among his friends. He never usually had much problem in seducing women.

The age difference worried him, certainly. Although he had been older than both his first wives, the difference had not been enough to cause comment. Drake, though, was a full nineteen years his junior. He saw qualities in her that were different from any other woman he had ever met and, like the inferiority complex that had manifested itself so obviously and destructively in his marriage to Hutton, he was overwhelmed by feelings of inadequacy at first. Her self-confidence challenged him and her knowledge and interests were clearly beyond his own ken.

A full two decades before such interests became the norm in Hollywood, Drake was into Eastern religions, psychology, and ecology. She was interested in such diverse subjects as yoga, astronomy, sociology and photography. Despite her being young enough to be his daughter, Drake was demonstrably more acute than Grant on almost any given subject. This must have been a strange experience for a man who liked to act as if he were in control.

If Drake's clear intelligence threatened Grant initially, he soon discovered that underneath she was an extremely selfless person who wore her learning lightly and, by the time the *Queen Mary* had docked in New York, they were spending much of their time together. The attraction was mutual.

Although the accusations were wide of the mark, Grant had faced the charge that he was pursuing a fortune when he was romancing Barbara Hutton. If anyone believed Drake was trying to further her own career by hooking up with Grant, they were equally mistaken. It is true that she had failed a screen test in Hollywood before going to London to pursue a stage career, but that career had proved successful and films were not on her list of priorities. Indeed, she was returning to the States to have talks about a number of Broadway roles that had been offered.

As the ship approached New York, Grant implored her to accompany him to Hollywood instead. He promised that he would do all he could to help her. Indeed, Grant was already signed-up to do a romantic film called *Every Girl Should Be Married* for RKO, after his next movie, *Mr Blandings Builds His Dream House*. And Grant assured Drake that there was an ideal part in it for her. She, however, insisted that she wanted to talk theatre projects with the appropriate Broadway producers, and they parted company in New York.

During production of *Mr Blandings Builds His Dream House*, a likeable comedy that reunited Grant on-screen with Myrna Loy, Drake contacted him. None of the Broadway parts had interested her and she wondered if his offer still stood. Grant assured her it did and Drake moved out to Los Angeles where executives at RKO were happy to give her a screen test. Given that Grant was RKO's biggest star – and a close friend of the studio's owner, Howard Hughes, to boot – cynics suggested that Drake was bound to pass the test. So it is only fair to point out that her test itself was actually very good and would have secured her work no matter who had introduced her to the studio.

Grant and Drake began working together almost at once in the slight romance *Every Girl Should Be Married*. Grant played a doctor, Madison Brown, who is pursued by a salesgirl (Drake) in a department store. Were it not for the fascination of watching Grant and Drake fall in love on screen just as they were doing in real life, the film would have been destined to be remembered as one of Grant's more forgettable moments. *Time* noted that 'in the past, Cary Grant has shown a talent for quietly underplaying comedy: in this picture, he has trouble finding comedy to play.'

If the critics were agreed on one thing, it was that Betsy Drake was a major new find. The *Newsweek* critic, almost alone in liking *Every Girl Should Be Married*, put it best: 'Most responsible for making it funny is a gangling, effervescent lass named Betsy Drake, whose previous film experience amounts to a Hollywood screen test.'

If the critics didn't care for the movie, audiences during Christmas 1948 did, and it made a decent enough profit for RKO.

By the time this film was completed, Grant and Drake had become inseparable. But, with two failed marriages behind him, Grant was wary of commitment. Drake, too, didn't want to rush into marriage.

Her parents had divorced when she was nine years old and it had affected her profoundly at the time. Thus, when Grant left Hollywood en route for location filming in Germany for his next movie, *I Was A Male War Bride*, Drake accompanied him as his girlfriend.

They stopped off in England so that Grant could introduce Drake to Elsie. He was curiously eager to get Elsie's approval for this match, and Elsie, who always apparently disapproved of her son's womanising, seems to have genuinely liked Drake. Her opinion was surely swayed by the fact that there was something decidedly un-actressy about the girl. And Drake accepted Elsie as an equal, while treating her with due respect. It was the same warm nature she would show towards Barbara Hutton's son, Lance, whenever he wished to visit Grant after he and Drake had married.

Once they had left England, they visited the set of *The Third Man* in Vienna before joining the *I Was A Male War Bride* unit. Production techniques were changing in the film industry. Films were leaving the studios as often as possible to get the gritty realism of location filming. Previously, the outside locations on a movie like *I Was A Male War Bride* – in which Grant played a captain in the French Army who marries an American lieutenant (Ann Sheridan) – would have been done on the studio back-lot. Audiences were expecting more realism now. Films were moving away from California to be shot at the appropriate location, and that could mean a massive transportation job to any single place on the globe.

This was not a development such leading men as Cary Grant particularly favoured. Location filming could be uncomfortable and, in some places, quite dangerous. And there was no going back to a cosy home at the end of a day's shoot.

Grant's experiences on this movie were not about to soften his attitude to location work, although, to start with, the film began auspiciously. He was again working with director Howard Hawks, with whom he'd worked on *Bringing Up Baby* and *His Girl Friday*, and in Ann Sheridan he found he had a co-star who, like Rosalind Russell before her, could appreciate and react to his ad-libs. As in *His Girl Friday*, Hawks retained much of the improvised dialogue between Grant and Sheridan. He even left in moments where Sheridan is 'corpsing' at Grant because it looked good in the editing room.

And, of course, Grant had Drake, to whom he was now devoted, right by his side.

It wasn't long, however, before the production began to appear a little jinxed. The weather turned nasty in Germany and outdoor scenes had to be filmed in heavy rain. Several members of the cast and crew fell ill, culminating in Ann Sheridan succumbing to pleurisy. As Grant ruefully pointed out to Hawks, it wouldn't have happened in California.

With location work completed, the unit moved to Shepperton Studio outside London for interiors. But now it was Grant's turn to fall ill. He had contracted hepatitis and he had got it very badly. In 45 years, Grant had never had cause to consider his health. Now, so weak he was unable to get out of bed and stricken with terrible jaundice, he was convinced that he was going to die.

There was obviously no way he could work, so production on *I Was A Male War Bride* ground to a temporary halt. At a lay-off cost of some $4,000 a day, Hawks had little choice other than to close the production down. The intention was to resume shooting in Hollywood when Grant recovered.

This decision caused a furore in the British press which, as always, comprised Little Englanders determined never to see the bigger picture. Pointing to the loss of more than 400 jobs at Shepperton (the real figure was nearer 200), journalists accused Hollywood of deliberately trying to sabotage the British film industry. The seriousness of Grant's illness seemed to pass them by unnoticed.

And Grant *was* in a bad way. Hardly able to eat, he had lost forty pounds in weight and looked very drawn. It was a month before he could even consider travelling back to Hollywood. When he did, he decided to do so by sea: a journey that would take him three weeks to reach Los Angeles. He could console himself with one thing: throughout his ordeal Betsy Drake had put her life on hold and nursed him selflessly. He convinced himself there and then that he was never going to find anyone quite like her again.

Everyone was appalled at the sight of Grant on his return to Hollywood, which was slightly ironic, as by now he was on the road to recovery. But to those people who had not seen him at his worst, he was a pale shadow of himself, gaunt and unusually pale. It would take a further four months before he returned to anything like his customary good health. And when he did return to work to finish *I Was A Male War Bride*, the effort exhausted him, and he booked himself into the Johns Hopkins Hospital in Baltimore immediately production wrapped for two weeks of complete rest.

Given the problems encountered during filming, one can forgive Grant for believing the film would be a disaster. This belief was reinforced when Hawks told him that the censor was causing problems and had demanded several cuts. But when Grant saw the picture he was delighted.

'I've just seen it,' he told the *New York Times*, 'and the audience laughed themselves sick. I've been in many comedies, but I've never heard an audience react like this one. I honestly feel it's the best comedy I've ever done.'

It was hardly that, as Grant himself must have known, but it was a precursor in many ways to *Some Like It Hot* in challenging and inverting sexual conventions through its male star dragging up to avoid detection. It was also 20th-Century Fox's biggest box-office hit of the year, grossing over four million dollars when it opened towards the end of 1949.

Christmas 1949 was even more memorable for Grant and Drake. On Christmas Day, Howard Hughes flew them to a small, remote ranch in Arizona belonging to one of Hughes's friends. In a brief ceremony, Grant and Drake were married with Hughes in attendance as best man.

Almost immediately afterwards, Hughes flew them back to Hollywood and the couple set up home in Grant's Beverly Hills home. His wedding present to Drake was a white poodle called Suzie. It had been, as Grant described it, 'an extraordinary day' and he was blissfully happy as he embarked on another attempt at finding the partner for a lifetime.

18 _____

'You spend all your time getting to be a big Hollywood
star. But then what?'

Cary Grant

Just as marriage to Barbara Hutton had coincided with the least
inspired period of Grant's professional life, so the first four years of his
marriage to Drake saw something of a downturn in his career.

He was as professionally accomplished as ever, of course – by this
stage of Grant's career, he was probably incapable of giving a bad
performance – but his five films released between 1950 and 1953 were,
frankly, not quite worthy of him, even if, in fairness, none was quite as
turgid as *None But The Lonely Heart* or as embarrassingly twee as
Once Upon A Time.

By 1950, Grant was halfway through his forties. While he did not
appear noticeably older on screen, his roles now began to reflect his
maturity. He played doctors in consecutive films, *Crisis* (1950) and
People Will Talk (1951), and a professor in the memorable *Monkey
Business* (1952).

Schickel writes of a 'harassed *paterfamilias*' to describe Grant's
roles at this time and cites the example of the strained comedy *Room
For One More* (1952) – his second and last movie co-starring Betsy
Drake – in which they play a couple who adopt five underprivileged
children.

In the hands of Hitchcock, *Crisis* could have been rich in
possibilities. The potentially powerful story tells how Eugene
Ferguson, a brain surgeon played by Grant, is kidnapped with his wife
while on holiday in South America and forced to operate to save the life
of a dying dictator. Although the film proved somewhat controversial –
it was banned in Mexico, South America and Italy – there remains
something relentlessly uninvolving about it. We never really care what
happens to the main protagonists of the piece. Much of the fault lies

with its writer-director Richard Brooks, whose directorial debut this was. But then, as with Clifford Odets before, Grant had insisted that Brooks, who had come up with the screenplay, should also direct.

Some contemporary critics did rate *Crisis* highly. One thought it 'original, arresting and considered' while another believed 'Cary Grant is more brittle and diamond-brilliant than before as the enlightened doctor. His sincerity in the story's guts is its premise for being believed.'

But time has not lent enchantment to the film. Modern reviewers are more apt to side with the cinema audiences of 1950, who positively loathed the film. It was, therefore, a massive flop – Grant's first since turning cockney for *None But The Lonely Heart* – and a memo from MGM's sales department noted sarcastically: 'we could've made more money with that picture if we'd cut the film up and sold it for mandolin picks.'

Ordinarily, the film's failure would have depressed Grant, who measured the success of any project by the box-office. But, for once, he was relaxed in his reaction, almost indifferent to the fate of the film. To many, this was the first outward sign of the change in his personality since marrying Drake. Grant was visibly more laid-back in the months following their marriage. He had become a more inquisitive and benign person altogether. It is likely that, in part, this must have been a direct result of Drake's interests in hypnotism and health foods and a more open-minded approach to his life.

'Betsy was very "in" to hypnotism,' said Deborah Kerr, who co-starred three times with Grant. 'I actually saw and heard her put him fast asleep. He awoke refreshed and full of energy. She also stopped him smoking. I remember him arriving on the set one morning at about ten a.m. busily consuming his lunch and he said to me: "that damn Betsy, she's cured me of smoking and now I'm so hungry I'm *already* eating my lunch!"'

Grant always maintained that hypnosis had cured his former 30-a-day habit and, similarly, that Drake had stopped his drinking hard liquor the same way. Although he had made a full recovery from the hepatitis he'd suffered in 1949, Drake insisted he was to take no chances with his liver and used hypnosis to wean him off the hard stuff.

Grant became something of an evangelist for the positive effects of hypnosis and never seems to have been concerned with what Hollywood might have been whispering behind his back. Hypnosis, he argued, helped him relax, learn lines and, of particular benefit to an habitual insomniac, to sleep for deeper, longer periods. It must have been difficult to argue with the man who was looking and behaving in such a positive way, and this must have been abundantly obvious to all those who knew him.

'We started talking about life, food, paintings, music,' recalled Billy Wilder. 'He became a man full of curiosity, always drinking everything in. Cary was a thinking person and he was proud of his work. He always pointed out to me in these discussions his humble beginnings. He wanted to impress his mother, I think, to be loved by her. I'm not sure she recognised how much he'd accomplished.'

'Like everyone else,' Grant once said, 'I shall die before accomplishing even an infinitesimal fraction of what my imagination will suggest to me. I'm not a Peer Gynt-like searcher, but I think if a man picks up knowledge, if he improves his tolerance, if he reduces his own impatience and irritability, if he can spare a listening ear to the other fellow – well, he can't help but find himself easier to be with.'

Grant's conversion to Drake's way of life also had its funny side. David Niven told of one incident during the time when Grant's friends were 'suffering stoically through his days of the carrot'.

Grant and Drake had had a machine installed in their Palm Springs home for the sole purpose of liquidising carrots. 'Today we'll have nothing but carrot juice,' Grant announced to Niven when he arrived for lunch. Having emptied many pounds of carrots into the machine, Grant and Niven left the kitchen for what Niven described as a 'pre-luncheon cocktail of buttermilk, wheat germ and molasses' while the machine got on with its work with 'fearful throbbings and crunchings'.

When the sounds died down, they went back to the kitchen and found that 'the machine had gone berserk and had redecorated the kitchen from top to bottom, covering walls, windows, ceiling and linoleum with a fibrous yellow paste.'

Much of what Grant was advocating at this point may sound as though he – aided and abetted by Drake – was wading through bogs of psycho-babble and false gods. But, in person, most of his friends found his new approach to life refreshingly open-minded. He had never been a man to prejudge anyone or anything, particularly in terms of personal morality, and now he was even more of a libertarian, more than ready to embrace change. For his career, Drake's influence on him couldn't have come at a better time.

Hollywood was undergoing seismic changes, which many of Grant's contemporaries were finding threatening. Television, which had once been dismissed by the film moguls as no threat to cinema, was now being blamed for the precipitous drop in weekly cinema admissions in the US (down from ninety million per week in 1946 to fifty million in 1950). And the 'scratch-and-mumble school' of Method actors, typified by Marlon Brando and Montgomery Clift, were grabbing the limelight from established middle-aged stars like Grant.

The failure of *Crisis* at the US box-office was seen by many as the first shot across Grant's bows that even *he* was not immune to the changes. His reputation as a guaranteed box-office draw was further dented when his next picture, *People Will Talk*, also flopped badly. No one could remember when Cary Grant had last had two flops on the trot.

Indeed, none of his five films between 1950 and 1953 did the kind of business that he was used to and many writers have suggested that this was the main reason why he took a two-year sabbatical from films, following the very disappointing *Dream Wife*, which he made with Deborah Kerr in 1953. Others have suggested that the reason he 'retired' was that he was bored with being Cary Grant. Both theories are specious. The truth, as it always was with Grant, was far more complex. Grant, perhaps uniquely among his peers, did not feel in the least bit threatened by the arrival of the new kids on the block. On the contrary, he was intrigued by them, curious to see what new ideas they were going to bring to films.

One of his co-stars in *Monkey Business* in 1952 was Marilyn Monroe, the star who was taking stardom to a new plane. The film, directed by Howard Hawks, and starring Ginger Rogers as Grant's wife, was not intended as a Marilyn Monroe film. It was conceived as a Cary Grant–Ginger Rogers film, a throwback to the screwball comedies of the 1930s. Grant even wears the heavy, professorial specs of *Bringing Up Baby*. It was written by Ben Hecht and Charles Lederer and had Grant playing a scientist whose experiments to perfect a rejuvenating elixir inadvertently 'succeed' thanks to the intervention of a chimpanzee.

Monroe had been hired to play the secretary to Grant's boss, but Monroe, who made appearances in *The Asphalt Jungle* and *All About Eve,* both in 1950, was being propelled into the stratosphere. In the end, a deprived childhood – she was brought up as Norma Jean Baker in numerous institutions, her mother having a mental condition and her father being a man whom she never met – plus a chain of failed relationships would lead to a very premature death ten years and one month after the release of *Monkey Business*.

Monroe's rapidly rising star resulted in Grant and Rogers being virtually ignored by the studio during the shooting of and publicity for *Monkey Business*. In fact, some commentators noted when the film was released that some members of the audience were not aware it was a Cary Grant movie at all.

Many actors would have been made insecure by this usurping of their position by Monroe, who was, to all intents and purposes, still an *ingénue*. But not Grant.

Howard Hawks recalled Monroe as 'the most frightened little girl on that movie, who had no confidence in her ability... A very strange girl. But when she got out in front of the camera, the camera liked her. Suddenly, she was a great sex symbol. Cary was a lot of help with her in *Monkey Business*. She listened to him.'

Grant could see what the studio was doing in promoting Monroe at the expense of himself and Ginger Rogers – the posters read: 'Marilyn Monroe in *Monkey Business!*' – and it would have been easy for him to have been difficult or, easier still, just not to help at all and to let Monroe get on with it. Instead, he identified with her insecurities and tried to help her through them.

Roger Moore, a good friend of Grant's for many years, said, 'During a Friar's Club Tribute to me, Cary made the most extraordinary speech. He said that "Hollywood is a bit like a street-car. When you arrive, you get on at the front and you gradually work your way to the back. In between time, at various stops, other people get on and we finally work our way to the back. Roger is nearly halfway there."'

Grant's likening Hollywood to a street-car was a favourite analogy of his and it explains why he was never jealous of emerging talent. He liked to help the new stars-in-the-making, if they would let him, particularly in avoiding the traps so well concealed behind the often ephemeral stardom of Hollywood.

One such example occurred just as *Monkey Business* was opening. With Monroe eclipsing everyone else in the film, a major scandal broke out when some nude shots that she had done for a calendar while still a model came to light. In the ultra-conservative moral climate of 1950s America, a climate that bordered on the fascist, such a revelation, which supposedly challenged 'family values', could easily have led to

Monroe's career being stillborn. The morals clause in her contract – a clause which every actor had to agree to – was enough for any major studio to drop her.

As he had with Ingrid Bergman before, Grant eschewed moral judgements and defended Monroe publicly saying, 'There are lots of models who pose in the art studio for hours. Nobody thinks wrong of that. What the hell is wrong with looking at a beautiful body if it really is beautiful? Marilyn is a very shy and a rather smart girl. A real person. A very dear person. She reads every book that comes out. The publicity about her is far in excess of her talents but not in excess of her sexual impact. They're all telling her to wear something revealing, and the child wants to be in blue jeans and an old flannel shirt. It's a good job I'm happily married!'

Immediately after *Monkey Business* there was talk of Grant and Monroe appearing together again in a movie called *Mother Knows Best*, in which Monroe and Jane Russell would play daughters of Mae West. West soon disabused everyone of *that* idea by stating, 'I don't play mothers!' That was quite a joke around Hollywood, but Grant knew where West was coming from: 'Quite right,' he said. 'I hope Marilyn will save her money and her sex appeal like Mae has. She must never play mothers, either, until she's a great-grandmother.'

There would be one further attempt to re-team Grant and Monroe. In 1959 George Cukor offered Grant the male lead in Monroe's *Let's Make Love*. Grant turned it down, albeit reluctantly, because by then, Hollywood had done its worst on her, and her 'difficult' reputation had become notorious throughout the industry.

By 1953, it is unlikely that, despite a lack of special films emerging from him, Grant had tired of playing 'Cary Grant'. He was first and foremost a businessman and he knew that his adopted persona was not only all he had to offer the world, but what had thus far made him a not inconsiderable fortune. But he was also acutely aware that the established writers and directors in Hollywood had penned themselves into a particular mindset and were thinking only of 'Cary Grant' type films to offer him instead of interesting characters 'Cary Grant' could play. And it was because of this that he came to loathe the word 'charming' as the popular description of him.

'I hate it,' he complained, 'because so often it's just used as a cover for someone who is really a sham. I just play me. To play yourself, your *true* self, is the hardest thing in the world. You're just a bunch of molecules until you know who you are. You spend all your time getting to be a big Hollywood actor. But then what? You've reached a comfortable plateau and you want to stay on it. You resist change.'

But Grant's greatest strength was that he never *did* resist change. Quite the reverse.

There was nothing wrong with having a particularly marketable screen persona. But the truth was that the 'Cary Grant' persona had been continually evolving from 1933, even if Grant had been so subtle throughout his evolution that very few people had noticed it happening.

The original 'Cary Grant' persona that he had discovered in *Sylvia Scarlett*, and which had carried him through *Topper* and *Bringing Up Baby* had reached its apogee in *His Girl Friday* and *The Philadelphia Story*. He had had to develop, just as Hollywood itself had after 1940, and his character became more dramatic, if less successful, with films like *Penny Serenade* and *None But The Lonely Heart*, and much darker through the two Hitchcock masterpieces, *Suspicion* and *Notorious*.

By 1953, if one were to ask cinema-goers to name a typical Cary Grant film, at least half-a-dozen titles might come back. Each one would, in a sense, be correct, but they would all be different. This was evidence of just how good an actor Grant was and how wide was his range. And if his seemingly effortless skill masked the true breadth of his talent – as late as 1986, the London *Times* obituary of Grant said, absurdly, 'he had limited range as an actor' – then that couldn't be helped. It was precisely his range and his willingness to constantly evolve that had kept him the most successful leading man for sixteen of his twenty years in Hollywood.

It wasn't boredom with 'Cary Grant' that kept him off-screen for two years between 1953 and 1955: it was his assessment that the 'Cary Grant' persona needed redefining to meet the challenge of the new faces and ways in Hollywood.

'To be a contemporary,' he once said, 'one has to mirror the tempo and beat of the time. You watch. You listen. And you reflect what you see and hear. It's fatal to freeze at any point in a career. Standing still means that the parade passes by.'

In that sense, *Crisis, People Will Talk, Room For One More, Monkey Business* and *Dream Wife* can all be seen as Grant exploring different avenues, seeing what would work with audiences and what they didn't want to see him doing. These five films, four of which had flopped, had proved that he had to be very careful what he did next.

'It was the period of blue jeans and the Method,' said Grant. 'Nobody cared about comedy at all.' Many have interpreted that comment as the words of a man resentful of his screen dominance being undermined. But it is wrong to do so. Grant was merely identifying the new realities facing him before deciding what to do next.

What Grant did next was to announce his retirement once he had completed *Dream Wife*. Again, it has passed into the accepted Cary Grant legend that this was a dress rehearsal for his proper retirement thirteen years later after *Walk, Don't Run*.

But, clearly, it was nothing of the sort. Grant's announced retirement in the summer of 1953 was a career move. It was the old music-hall tradition of 'leave 'em wanting more'.

And some 'retirement' it turned out to be. Grant continued to consider roles throughout the remainder of 1953, through 1954 and into 1955, when he agreed to make his 'comeback' for Alfred Hitchcock in *To Catch A Thief*.

Even as he was announcing his retirement, Grant was in intense negotiations with the director George Cukor to co-star with Judy Garland in *A Star Is Born*. He was Cukor's first choice for the male lead, Norman Maine – the alcoholic husband of Garland's character – ahead of Marlon Brando, Humphrey Bogart and Henry Fonda, who all said 'no'. Cukor settled on James Mason, who eventually took the part and received an Oscar nomination.

So much for Grant's supposed boredom with acting at this time: George Cukor maintained that Grant's reading of the part during their protracted negotiations was the finest thing he ever heard the actor do. Had Grant done *A Star Is Born*, there would have been no 'retirement' at all, as he would have had films released in consecutive years, 1953, 1954 and 1955. The much-touted turning his back on Hollywood rested, essentially, on his turning down this one film. And he turned it down partly because it was a bit too close to home – his father, Elias, had, after all, succumbed to the bottle. His primary reason, however, was that he believed his audiences would not want to see Cary Grant as a drunk. Such sensitivity to his screen image was hardly the mark of a man who had intended to jack it all in.

Grant was a victim of the era. The 1950s were a decade of transition for Hollywood and, therefore, Cary Grant himself. The eighteen-month break from films was more probably a carefully calculated rationing of his persona, aimed at giving himself a breathing space while he regrouped and reinvented himself for the second half of the twentieth century. He still had thirteen movies left to make, two of them for Alfred Hitchcock.

And one of these was to prove *the* highwater mark of both their careers.

19

'Regardless of a professed rationalisation that I became an actor in order to travel, I probably chose my profession because I was seeking approval, adulation, admiration and affection: each a degree of love...'

Cary Grant

When a man hits 50, his capacity to surprise has usually diminished. Typically, Cary Grant bucked the trend. He had used the time away from the screen throughout 1954 to redefine and re-tune his image.

As they travelled around the world – taking a circuitous route from San Francisco to London, via Japan, India, Africa and Europe – maybe even Betsy Drake had started to believe Grant's half-truth about having retired. He certainly told every journalist who interviewed him en route that his retirement was absolute, but at the same time he was confessing to a friend: 'I'd love to get back to those comedies I used to do. But where can I find one? Writers take themselves too seriously these days. Also, really polished dialogue is hard to write. It's much easier to write crude, everyday speech and writers can make a lot of money doing it.'

Back home in Hollywood, Grant had grown impossibly restless by January 1955. Initially, the extended holiday had left him more relaxed than at almost any other time in his life, and his marriage to Drake was ostensibly very solid. But Drake had also quit work, and was soon irritated by her husband's restlessness. The inevitable outcome of spending too much time together was that they began getting on each other's nerves.

Around this time, Hitchcock had begun pre-production on *To Catch A Thief*, a comedy-thriller that was to be much lighter in tone than most of his films. And Hitchcock could think of only one man to play the retired jewel thief, Robie.

But Cary Grant was retired – wasn't he?

Maintaining the pretence that he had, indeed, retired after shooting

Dream Wife in 1953, Grant always claimed that it was Hitchcock who enticed him back into the film-making arena.

'I really didn't want to do the film,' he always claimed. 'I told Hitch that I was too old to play a leading man and that I was old-fashioned. It was only when Hitch told me that I would be playing opposite Grace Kelly that I did accept.'

Hitchcock, who probably knew Grant better than anyone, including Grant, himself, dismissed his objections: 'There isn't a thing wrong with you, old man, that a first-rate screenplay won't cure.'

To Catch A Thief is not Grant's best film. But it is one of the most important because it marks the final stage of his evolving screen persona. Despite all his previous success, he now embarked on the most successful period of his life as an actor, a period that was to last for eleven years. Unlike most of his contemporaries who were visibly ageing on-screen and who were suffering from the competition of the current wave of screen idols, Grant's unique persona thrived better than ever. In 1948, he had been named fourth on the list of top ten male stars in Hollywood. In 1958, he topped that list. And in 1960, he was named the number one box-office attraction in America, male *or* female: an extraordinary achievement for a man aged 56, who had been making movies in Hollywood for almost 30 years.

In an era of tee-shirts and denim, Grant's immaculate tailoring, which Tom Wolfe has described as 'all worsted, broadcloths and silk, all rich and underplayed, like a viola ensemble', and his enunciation triumphed as never before.

Katharine Hepburn may have preferred the younger, plumper Grant, but she appeared to be in a minority. 'Grant had got better looking,' argued Pauline Kael. 'The sensual lusciousness was burned off: age purified him. Now the excess energy was pared away, his performances were simple and understated and seamlessly smooth. His glamour was now a matter of his resonances from the past and he wore it like a mantle.

'Unlike the macho actors who, as they got older, became strident about their virility, puffing their big, flabby chests in an effort to make themselves look even larger, Grant, with his sexual diffidence, quietly became less physical – and more assured.'

It's very difficult to come up with another actor of Grant's generation who could possibly have retained his position in the public consciousness a century after he was born, in anything approaching the same way as Grant himself has done. Just as we immediately think of a definite image when we hear the name 'Noel Coward' (and Coward's longevity depends chiefly on his career as a playwright and songwriter, *not* as an actor), so the name 'Cary Grant' is still synonymous with style, class and a certain elusive presence. Seventy years after Archie Leach invented Cary Grant, Grant is cool and relevant in a way that Clark Gable, Gary Cooper and Errol Flynn no longer are.

Most of Grant's contemporaries are now mere footnotes in cinematic history to all but dedicated movie buffs. Perhaps this isn't quite true of stars like Bette Davis, Humphrey Bogart or James Stewart. But even they are locked into an era that has passed.

While Grant is also a figure of the past, his best performances, which means *most* of his performances, have a timeless quality. The Cary Grant persona doesn't just belong in the past, but in the present and the future. He represents what decent, civilised men have always aspired to – and what women, of many kinds, have wanted to be around.

Grant had pulled back in 1953 to review his situation and decide how to meet the present and future Hollywood from a strong position. Those who claim that he didn't change after his extended break are surely wrong. He did change – but the changes he made were so subtle that anyone could be forgiven for missing them.

To many, he seemed to be doing the 'old routine'. If he was, there was a clear difference. Post-1955, Grant was playing himself not as Hollywood's leading leading man, but as an icon. And this was entirely an act of complicity in his performance: Graham McCann writes of Grant's 'arch awareness' in his later films.

Instead of playing down the essential conservativeness of his image to meet the Method actors halfway, Grant, in a brilliant, typically bold conceit, played it up. What this did was to reinforce – conversely – his uniqueness. No one could outplay Grant when it came to jockeying for position in the Hollywood pecking order of stars, and no one, but no one, could play 'Cary Grant' the way Cary Grant could play him. And never was this more apparent in Hollywood than between the years 1955 and 1966.

'He knew he'd perfected it,' one critic said of Grant's image in this last glorious decade or so of Grant's screen career. 'And not only perfected it, but patented it. And you'd never be able to spot the join between reality and illusion however much you strained your eyes.'

'No one else looked so good and so intelligent at the same time,' added David Thomson. '*But* there was always a mocking smile or impatience behind his eyes that knew being beautiful was a little silly.'

Other changes to Grant's screen persona were equally subtle. Despite his insecurities with women in his private life, or maybe *because* of them, Grant's relationship with female co-stars had usually been more complex than the industry norm.

Off-screen, he was reputed to have romanced many of the leading ladies, something he never denied, even if he was very discreet about which ones he had seduced: 'I try to make my leading ladies relaxed and at ease,' he once teased a journalist who asked him outright if his reputation was true.

On-screen, the relationship between Grant and his female co-star had always been more ambiguous and even-handed than many other actors would have been prepared to play. From 1955 onwards, this became even more apparent. Fifteen years before women's libbers started burning bras in Times Square, the women in Grant's films were easily his equal, often the instigators in creating a sexual situation.

So, he was still the seduced man of before, but as one critic wrote: 'The heroines of his later movies are all aware that he's a legendary presence, that they're trying to seduce a legend.'

It was a feeling shared by many of his later female co-stars off-screen.

'Cary was impeccably dressed,' said Leslie Caron, his co-star in *Father Goose* (1964), 'and yet he gave out a feeling of animal strength, like a jaguar ready to pounce. With his leading ladies he had this wonderful rapport, courtesy and tenderness, but with a great deal of humour – just like on the screen. It was really very pleasant. It was like going out with a gentleman.'

Grant's generosity was also appreciated. He had never lost his overwhelming appreciation of talent and his respect for a co-star's talent is obvious in all his films.

'You just felt he was with you every minute,' said Eva Marie Saint, Grant's outstanding co-star in *North By Northwest* (1959). 'Not just for *his* close-ups, but for your close-ups, too.'

When pressed by an interviewer to name his favourite leading lady, Grant had no hesitation: 'Well, with all due respect to dear Ingrid (Bergman),' he replied, 'I much preferred Grace (Kelly). She had serenity.'

Shooting *To Catch A Thief* with Hitchcock and Kelly on the French

Riviera was one of the most enjoyable and relaxed periods of Grant's professional life. Despite all his protestations that Hitchcock had practically dragged him out of 'retirement' to do the film, Grant was secretly delighted from the moment the director had called him up to pitch the project.

'Hitch and I had a rapport and understanding deeper than words,' Grant said. 'He was a very agreeable human being, and we were very compatible. I always went to work whistling when I worked with him because everything on the set was just as you envisioned it would be. Nothing ever went wrong. He was so incredibly well prepared. I never knew anyone as capable. He was a tasteful, intelligent, decent, and patient man, who knew the actor's business as well as he knew his own.'

One of the first films he had seen with Betsy Drake on their return from their round-the-world trip was Hitchcock's *Rear Window* and Grant had loved it. He confessed to friends how he envied James Stewart the lead, although it had never been offered to Grant.

And he had been mightily impressed with Grace Kelly, whom he had seen in Hitchcock's *Dial M For Murder*. All in all, he told Drake, *To Catch A Thief* was simply too good a film *not* to do.

Filming began in June 1955 and Grant and Drake made their way to the Riviera, stopping off in England to visit Elsie who was now nearly 80 but showing remarkably few signs of ageing. The south of France and Monaco locations are the highlight of the film, as are the scenes between Kelly and Grant. The crisp, well-written script (by John Michael Hayes) contains much more innuendo than was usual for a mid-1950s mainstream Hollywood movie.

Kelly represented Hitchcock's ideal female character: in his words, she belonged to 'the drawing-room type, the real ladies who become whores once they're in the bedroom.'

Perhaps one of the most beautiful women ever to adorn the cinema screen, Grace Kelly's private life was reputedly more colourful than her virginal screen image suggested. Hitchcock had, without irony, dubbed her 'the snow princess' when he cast her in *Dial M For Murder*. When he was informed that her past exploits were not so snow-white as he had envisaged, he never again referred to her in that way.

There was a story, apocryphal though it is, that concerned Grant and Niven at a dinner with Prince Rainier of Monaco, Kelly's future husband. Rainier is purported to have asked Niven 'Of all the women you romanced in Hollywood, who was the best?' Without pausing to think, Niven replied, 'Grace...er...Grace...Gracie Fields.' Grant apparently dined out on this story for years.

Unlike Grant, Kelly, who was born in 1929, came from a wealthy background. Despite the luxuriousness of her upbringing, she had decided on a career as an actress and moved to New York to attend the American Academy of Dramatic Arts after graduating from High School.

Having graduated, she appeared in various television and theatre productions before making her film debut in *Fourteen Hours* (1951). Her first major role came in the classic *High Noon* (1952), in which she co-starred, ironically, with Grant's long-time *bête noire* Gary Cooper. It propelled her to movie stardom. *To Catch A Thief* was only her ninth film and, although no one knew it at the time, she was to make only two more. She retired from movies the following year when, on 19 April 1956, she married Prince Rainier of Monaco, whom she first met while on location for *To Catch A Thief*. In a further irony, her last film would be *High Society*, a remake of *The Philadelphia Story*.

Despite all the ingredients, *To Catch A Thief* remains the weakest of the four Cary Grant–Alfred Hitchcock collaborations. As undemanding entertainment, it works just fine but as a comedy-mystery, it fails to grip in the way the Master of Suspense's movies usually do. There is a lack of real tension and we never once feel that Grant's ex-jewel thief character, John Robie, is ever in serious danger.

But what the movie lacks in suspense is more than made up for in Grant's scenes with Kelly. If one wishes to witness true screen chemistry, one need look no further than this film. Their dialogue crackles with unresolved sexual tension and, nearly half a century after it was filmed, these scenes remain more erotic than any of the more explicit Hollywood films which followed.

Nowhere is this more explicit than in the picnic scene, when Kelly offers Grant some chicken:

KELLY: Do you want a leg or a breast?
GRANT: You make the choice.
KELLY: Tell me, how long has it been?
GRANT: How long has what been?
KELLY: Since you were last in America.

The double-entendres continue just as suggestively when Grant and

Kelly are watching a firework display on the Riviera from the balcony of her hotel suite. Kelly is wearing a revealing evening gown and a glittering necklace.

> KELLY: If you really want to see the fireworks, it's better with the lights off. I have a feeling that tonight you're going to see one of the Riviera's most fascinating sights. (*Beat*) I was talking about the fireworks...
>
> GRANT: May I have a brandy? Would you like one?
>
> KELLY: Give up, John. Admit who you are. Even in this light I can tell where your eyes are looking. Look. Hold them! *Diamonds* – the only thing in the world you can't resist. (*She places his hand beneath her necklace as fireworks explode outside*) Ever had a better offer in your whole life?
>
> GRANT: I've never had a crazier one.
>
> KELLY: Just as long as you're satisfied.
>
> GRANT: You know as well as I do this necklace is imitation.
>
> KELLY: Well, *I'm* not.

Such was the rapport between Grant and Kelly that many of these intimate scenes were ad-libbed between them. And Hitchcock later admitted that, in the spirit of the stars' sexual ad-libs, he rewrote a lot of dialogue so that the other characters in the film could match them. Thus, when Jessie Royce Landis, playing Kelly's rich mother (she would later play Grant's mother in *North By Northwest* despite being almost a year younger than him) first sees Grant's character, her comment to Kelly is laced with double meaning: 'Mmm – handsome. I wouldn't mind buying *that* for you.'

The film teetered on the outermost edge of what censors would allow and Hitchcock fully expected to have to make cuts once filming had completed in August 1955. To his amazement, the film was passed without any demand for cuts: perhaps the censors were bedazzled by Grant's first film for two years.

When Grant had returned from the south of France to complete the interiors on the film in Hollywood, it was obvious that cracks were beginning to show in his marriage to Betsy Drake. She had not been at all happy about his visible rapport with the divine Grace Kelly while they were in France, and her displeasure had been fuelled considerably by French and British journalists who had compared Drake's looks with Kelly's.

Nevertheless, once shooting had been completed on *To Catch A Thief*, Grant and Drake settled back into some kind of domestic harmony until the movie opened. Grant wasn't in a rush to accept any new projects until he could be sure how well the film was going to be received. Having spent nearly two years tweaking at his screen persona, he wanted to be absolutely sure he had got it right before continuing with it.

Although the film itself received very mixed reviews, the entire world seemed to rejoice at seeing Cary Grant back on screen.

'The sad truth is,' wrote *Variety*, '*To Catch A Thief* is a disappointment. Billed as a comedy-mystery, it stacks up as a drawn-out pretentious piece that seldom hits comedy level. Grant, however, once again demonstrates he is a master of timing, getting laughs where a lesser talent would have drawn a blank.'

Grant himself was highly satisfied with the experience. He had put a lot into this movie and it showed in his performance. Such was his dedication to Hitchcock that he determined to make the climactic scenes, when John Robie is required to clamber over a villa's high rooftops, to be as realistic as possible. Drawing on his acrobatic history, Grant dispensed with stuntmen and safety nets and performed the scenes himself. He later recommended it jokingly as 'the most definitive cure for acrophobia'.

To Catch A Thief was a massive hit at the box-office. It became one of the top-grossing films of the year. By the mid-1950s, the studios had woken up to the fact that they could no longer expect audiences to leave their television sets and turn out for films just for the hell of it. Publicity was becoming more and more important and the selling of the film as a product had become as important as the actual making of it.

Ever the businessman, Grant quickly grasped this concept and when Paramount asked him to undertake a massive nationwide tour to promote *To Catch A Thief*, he agreed despite his antipathy to crowds. If Grant had had any lingering doubts about his popularity with the cinema-going public, this tour was to dispel them forever, and he drew massive crowds wherever he went.

Film offers had never stopped, not even during his supposed retirement, but now, with *To Catch A Thief* proving that Cary Grant was, again, box-office magic, the studios deluged him with scripts.

Mike Todd, who had recently married Elizabeth Taylor, and was regarded as Hollywood's new master showman, asked Grant to star as Phileas Fogg in the spectacular, if episodic, film version of Jules Verne's *Around The World In Eighty Days*.

Todd intended this film to be the most spectacular screen epic of all time, and was determined to assemble the greatest cast ever for a movie. Whoever played Fogg would be sharing the film with, among others, Ronald Colman, Noel Coward, Marlene Dietrich, John Gielgud, Trevor Howard, Buster Keaton, Beatrice Lillie, A.E. Matthews (one of Grant's heroes), John Mills, Robert Morley and Frank Sinatra. The film would eventually star David Niven.

Sheridan Morley wrote perceptively of *Eighty Days*: 'Fogg was to be one of the longest parts ever played by an actor on the screen, and in three full hours he was seldom out of shot. But Todd had already decided that this was to be his film rather than the property of any single star, and to underline the point, he was going to have fifty world-class stars all playing cameo roles. Fogg thus became the straight man who had to go through the whole picture having scenes stolen from under him by guests who were only in for a day's shooting.'

Cary Grant was far too conscious of his screen image to risk having several months' hard work on location being eclipsed by other stars. He turned the film down, quite rightly.

Grant was also inundated with offers to appear on television from the mid-fifties onwards. He didn't share the overt snobbery towards television felt by most of his contemporaries and actually claimed to enjoy watching the TV when he was at home. But he turned down all the offers. This was a pragmatic business decision. 'I won't do TV,' he insisted, 'because it's silly to set myself up in competition with myself.'

Given the quality of the work he was turning down at this point – *The Bridge On The River Kwai* being one of the big projects he prevaricated over – his acceptance of such a dreary film as *The Pride And The Passion* almost beggars belief.

Or does it?

On the face of it, Grant's choosing to do this stolid adaptation of C.S. Forester's novel *The Gun* is incomprehensible. The script, by Edna and Edward Anhalt, is all talk and very little action, and Grant's character, a British naval officer, gives him absolutely no opportunity to perform to his strengths. Most incomprehensible of all is the fact that *The Pride And The Passion* was a costume drama set in Spain in 1810 during the

Napoleonic Wars. Grant hadn't been in period costume since the disastrous *The Howards Of Virginia*, a full seventeen years earlier. If nothing else, that earlier débâcle had proved that Cary Grant did not belong in costume drama.

Perhaps that was the challenge. Was Grant trying to prove something to audiences and himself? It seems unlikely, however, as there would have surely been other opportunities to attempt a rectification of his first failed costume-drama outing during the previous seventeen years.

The real reason he accepted the film probably lay closer to home. As soon as he and Drake returned to Hollywood following Grant's promotional tour for *To Catch A Thief*, the niggling cracks in their marriage, cracks that had receded for a while during the tour, began to reassert themselves. If anything was clear at this stage in Grant's life it was that he was apt to become restless when he wasn't working – and when Grant was restless, he got on Drake's nerves.

Not for the first time in this and other relationships, Grant concluded that they were spending too much time together. It was not only time for him to go back to work – but time for Drake to pick up her film career.

Thus the prospect of several months' location work in Spain for *The Pride And The Passion* was what probably swayed his decision to do the movie. Significantly, Drake stayed in Hollywood, talking through possible film projects with 20th-Century Fox, while Grant travelled alone to Spain.

The Pride And The Passion was to create waves in Grant's life that were far more dramatic than anything its dull story-line was to provide. Originally, the cast was intended to be Grant playing the British officer; Marlon Brando as a Spanish guerilla; and Ava Gardner as the peasant girl with whom both men fall in love.

Brando, however, decided against doing the film and was replaced by Frank Sinatra who, from the outset, was unhappy, to say the least, at having been second choice for the role. Ava Gardner also walked from the picture to be replaced by the 23-year-old Sophia Loren, whose career was being masterminded by Carlo Ponti.

Ponti had discovered her seven years earlier and changed her name from Sofia Scicolone. Ponti and Loren had been more or less living together for nearly four years, even though Ponti was married to someone else and, given that divorce was then virtually impossible in their native Italy, was likely to remain so. Similar circumstances had turned Middle America against Ingrid Bergman not a decade before, so these were not the most propitious ways in which to establish a Hollywood career – and Loren knew it.

Thus, all three principals began the film with rather more than the film itself on their minds. Sinatra was resentful, Loren was concerned about her relationship with Ponti, and Grant was aware that all was not well in his marriage to Betsy Drake. Furthermore, neither Grant nor Sinatra was happy about Loren replacing Gardner. Both thought that she was too inexperienced and Grant, in particular, felt she was much too young for the role. From this point onwards, he was always concerned about the age difference between himself and his leading ladies. Once he had turned sixty, in 1964, he told the *Sunday Express* columnist Roderick Mann: 'I'm getting to the stage where I have to be very careful about love-scenes with young actresses. The public doesn't like to see an older man making love to a young girl. It offends them. I am well aware that I can't go on playing romantic parts much longer. After all, I'm quite an old fellow to some young people. But to be honest with you, I don't know what I'll do. Maybe I'll quit.'

Indeed, this sensitivity to his age does seem to have contributed to his decision to retire in 1966, but it wasn't something that occurred to him overnight. He had been sensitive to this issue for ten years at least – and it was co-starring with Sophia Loren in *The Pride And The Passion* that first alerted him to the dangers.

Ironically, if Grant was concerned about being seen making love to Loren on screen, he didn't have the same qualms in real life. Their affair, strongly rumoured for many years, was confirmed when Loren published her autobiography *Living And Loving* in 1979. Until then, Grant had always refused to confirm or deny his love for her.

'Where did those rumours start?' he said to a journalist in 1971. 'I know of only one leading lady with whom I had an affair.' Typically, Grant refused to say which, though we can safely assume it was *not* Mae West!

Grant's affair with Loren seems to have begun jokily and casually – he called her 'Miss Brigloren' – and when it developed into something more, it seemed to come as a surprise to both of them. Still, if he was one of the first of La Loren's co-stars to become infatuated by her, he most certainly wouldn't be the last.

The comic actor Peter Sellers initiated the break-up of his first marriage to Anne Levy because of his infatuation with the stunning Italian. In Sellers' case, it is believed, certainly by his family, to have been a figment of his imagination: Loren did not reciprocate and there was no physical relationship. That didn't stop Sellers lavishing her with gifts, ringing her every hour of every day, and talking to her spiritual 'presence' which, apparently, would haunt his bedroom on a nightly basis!

The Pride And The Passion was not a happy film to work on. The script was banal – and everyone knew it was – and the relentless heat in Spain put people under pressure, even more when they knew that, at best, they were striving towards a mediocre conclusion. Frank Sinatra was not getting along well with the producer Stanley Kramer – who died in February 2001 – and their constant fights were getting to everyone. These became so acrimonious that Sinatra eventually walked off the film before his scenes were completed and Grant had to shoot his close-ups, when he was supposed to be acting with Sinatra, talking to a coat-hanger off camera. Small wonder that Grant, thousands of miles from home, should fall under the spell of one of the most celebrated beautiful women of the time with whom he was working in close proximity. Grant once said that he only dated or married women who looked like his mother, but this affair surely disproves that: with the best will in the world, it is hard to believe that Elsie *ever* looked anything like Sophia Loren.

For her part, it is easy to see what Loren saw in Grant. Although now well into his fifties, he was, by general consensus, looking better than ever. He had scarcely aged at all in the last fifteen years and was enjoying perhaps the longest middle-age on record. His outer looks were now matched by an inner serenity. There was an old pro's grace about the way he walked, talked and conducted himself. Whatever insecurities and private fears still haunted him, they were buried deeper than they had ever before been and, consequently, showed themselves less frequently.

Loren despaired of Ponti ever being free to marry her and she knew she could not seriously contemplate living with him openly if she wished to pursue a successful Hollywood career. Of course, Grant was married too, but it was his third marriage, and if he truly loved her, Loren would have convinced herself that he was, essentially, a much better bet for lasting happiness.

Those who have accused Loren of behaving cynically at this point – David Niven described her as 'not the least ambitious of actresses' – have been a little unfair. There can be no doubt of her deep feelings for Ponti at this time, but with nothing but seeming years of frustration ahead – with no ultimate commitment – though she would always return to him, it is easy to view it as quite reasonable that she should remain a free agent in her relationships.

Although some have subsequently tried to play down Grant's infatuation with Loren – Niven tries to persuade us, rather unconvincingly, that Grant got over her with 'typical alacrity' – Loren herself had no doubts about Grant's attraction to her.

'I never doubted for a second that Cary loved me as much as I could hope to be loved by a man,' she said. 'I *knew* he loved me and that if I chose to I could marry him.'

The burgeoning relationship between Grant and Loren was painfully obvious to Ponti and to Betsy Drake when she arrived from Hollywood to visit her husband on the set of the film. It did not take her undoubted skills in parapsychology to discern what was going on, and it made for an uncomfortable stay.

Drake had, naturally, felt a little threatened by the rapport between Grant and Grace Kelly during the making of *To Catch A Thief.* But she had put that behind her and had happily attended Kelly's marriage to Prince Rainier in Monaco in April 1956 (the Grants had been among a party of guests which also included Ava Gardner, David Niven and Niven's second wife, Hjordis). But Grant's relationship with Loren was entirely different, as Drake knew only too well.

In effect, her visit to the location where Grant and Loren were filming was the beginning of the end of their marriage and, when she left to return to California, both of them knew it, although little, apparently, was said at the time. To make matters worse, Drake sailed for the USA aboard the ill-fated Italian liner the *Andrea Doria.* The fall-out of that particular incident was to see the Cary Grant story take one of its most bizarre turns.

But, first, there was the fall-out from the Grant-Loren-Ponti triangle, which was unresolved by the time filming had completed. Ponti was still desperately, but hopelessly, attempting to secure a divorce. Grant, meanwhile, was allegedly calling Loren every day and deluging her with flowers.

From *The Pride And The Passion*, Grant, rather appropriately, went straight into filming *An Affair To Remember*, in which he was working again with the director Leo McCarey and the actress Deborah Kerr.

An Affair To Remember – curiously released a couple of weeks before his previous picture, *The Pride And The Passion* – was a remake of McCarey's own 1939 picture *Love Affair*, which had starred Charles Boyer and Irene Dunne, and in 1993 had a new lease of life when it was the inspiration for Nora Ephron's *Sleepless In Seattle*, starring Tom Hanks and Meg Ryan.

The theme of *An Affair To Remember* is ironic, considering Grant's own private life at this point. Grant and Kerr play a couple who fall in love aboard a luxury ocean liner despite being engaged to other people. They agree to part for six months to make sure of their feelings for each other and then to meet again at the top of the Empire State Building. An accident, which leaves Deborah Kerr's character crippled and wheelchair-bound, intervenes and transforms the film from frothy romance to full-blown weepie.

The film came just at the right time for Grant, because it allowed him to concentrate on something other than his affair with Loren. He didn't expect much from the film, and only agreed to do it to help revive McCarey's career.

By this time, McCarey was in a mess. His days as a leading Hollywood *wunderkind* were well and truly behind him. His serious car accident just before *My Favorite Wife* in 1940, had begun a spiral into ill-health, which had, effectively, undermined his career. Having begun drinking heavily and become addicted to pain-killers – just like Howard Hughes – McCarey had been all but written off by the studios. He had made only one other film in the 1950s and that had been *My Brother John* in 1952, an appalling blend of sentimentality and anti-communism that had sounded the death knell of his career.

When McCarey sought financing for *An Affair To Remember* he was told, bluntly, he could make the film if, and only if, he could get Cary Grant to play Nickie Ferrante. Grant's loyalty to his old friends was demonstrated yet again. Where others had turned their backs on McCarey, Grant accepted the part in what, on paper at least, wasn't an exactly hot prospect.

As it turned out, *An Affair To Remember* is not a great movie. In every department bar one, the earlier Boyer-Dunne version is superior: the exception is the performances of the leads, Grant and Kerr. She recalled:

It was our most successful work together. Cary was not only the king of the 'double-take', but a superb ad-libber as well. He and I ad-libbed a lot on that film and Leo McCarey kept them in the finished film.

To this day *An Affair To Remember* is shown over and over again in the States and in England and on the continent, as well as Australia. Hundreds and hundreds of people tell me how *many* times they have seen the movie, and how they wept at every viewing.

It was also on this movie that I saw how Cary had an eye for detail in every aspect of the movie being made – not just *his* particular role. I remember well in the scene when the ship is docking in New York and our characters are ostentatiously keeping apart at the ship's rails, how he spotted one of the extras playing a woman passenger resting her bright red beauty-case on the rails. He insisted the case be removed because he said that in colour, on the screen, everyone's eye would automatically jump to the red case and be distracted from what was happening between the main characters. No one had thought of that before, and I think it demonstrates his utter concentration on detail.

As the suave international playboy Ferrante, Grant is absolutely sublime. He's witty and light-hearted in the early part of the picture and more poignant in the later stages: the transition from light to shade in his performance is seamless and, no matter how many times one watches this picture, it is impossible to see him making this transformation.

Moreover, there is perhaps nowhere else in the Cary Grant canon where the script plays up to the idolised 'Cary Grant' persona as much as it does here.

'As he makes his way along the passageway,' wrote Richard Schickel, 'in his perfect dinner jacket, people stop and stare and do double-takes – as any of us might do if Cary Grant came strolling along our path. He is almost languid in his self-assurance and self-amusement. He knows the stir he's causing. We're out of the realm of acting here, and into the realm of personal appearance.'

This is, perhaps, not altogether true. Grant maintained that playing yourself is the hardest thing in the world to achieve and, by that reckoning, his role in the film, when 'Cary Grant' is portrayed possibly more nakedly than anywhere, must have been deceptively difficult to pull off. Certainly, Grant delivers much of his performance with a self-aware irony and nowhere is this more evident than in the scene where Kerr tackles him about his attitude to women. Here, the material is fashioned so that the distinction between Grant and Nickie Ferrante disappears entirely.

GRANT:	Oh – *women* …
KERR:	You've known quite a few. And I suppose they've all been *madly* in love with you.
GRANT:	I doubt it.
KERR:	But you, er, you haven't had much respect for them.
GRANT:	On the contrary!
KERR:	Still, you've always been very *fair* in your judgements.
GRANT:	I've been *more* than fair. I idealise them. Every woman I meet I put up there. (He raises his hand up high.) Of course, the longer I know her (he begins dropping his hand) and the better I know her (his hand drops ever lower) …
KERR:	It's hard to keep them up there, isn't it?
GRANT:	Yes, isn't it!
KERR:	Pretty soon the pedestal wobbles … and then topples …
GRANT:	*C'est la vie!*

An Affair To Remember and *The Pride And The Passion* both opened in July 1957 and both suffered at the hands of the critics. The critic Paul Dehn, who later turned scriptwriter of films such as *Goldfinger* (1964) and *Murder On The Orient Express* (1974), thought the former was 'Ninety masterly minutes of entrancing light comedy and twenty-five minutes of beastly, melodramatic, pseudo-tragic guff'. *Time* said of the latter, 'the whir of the cameras often seems as loud as the thunderous cannonades – it evidently takes more than dedication, co-operative multitudes and four million dollars to shoot history in the face.'

But cinema audiences couldn't have cared less what the critics said and they flocked to both pictures. Grant had now made three blockbusting 'event' pictures in less than two years. If ever his status was in doubt, by the summer of 1957 he had underlined that he was the world's greatest – and most popular – leading man.

And everything in his private life appeared to be settled. There had been gossip about him and Sophia Loren, but there was *always* gossip about leading actors having affairs on location, so no one was paying too much attention. Besides, most of Loren's problems were centred around Carlo Ponti.

To all intents and purposes, then, all was well in the garden for Drake and Grant. But their apparent ease with each other masked a fundamental change in their post-Loren relationship. Grant was still in

love with the Italian beauty. And on the set of their next movie together
– *Houseboat*, made several months later – it was rumoured that the
married Grant proposed to Loren. He was heading, irrevocably,
towards his third divorce.

20

'Taking LSD was an utterly foolish thing to do but I was a self-opinionated boor, hiding behind all kinds of layers and defences, hypocrisy and vanity. I had to get rid of them and wipe the slate clean.'

Cary Grant

After careful consideration and long discussion, we have decided to live apart. We have had and shall always have a deep love for each other, but, also, our marriage has not brought us the happiness we fully expected and mutually desired. So since we have no children needful of our attention, it is consequently best that we separate for a while. We ask our friends to be patient with, and understanding of, our decision.

The Grants' joint statement in 1958, announcing their split, had a ring of familiarity about it. The wording was eerily similar to the announcement of Grant's split from Virginia Cherrill almost 25 years earlier.

The failure of the marriage was probably inevitable following Grant's association with Sophia Loren. However, though the marriage had failed, the deep affection between them remained long after their divorce – a divorce that was a long time in coming (it wasn't finalised until 13 August 1962).

When Drake did finally petition for divorce she cited mental cruelty, *not* infidelity, as the cause. Her petition accused him of disliking the institution of marriage itself, of loathing her friends, and of becoming bored with her. If the joint statement issued when they split was reminiscent of the one issued when he split from Cherrill, Drake's divorce petition was very similar to Barbara Hutton's in its accusations.

And yet there was a crucial difference this time. Neither Grant nor Drake was in any hurry to end the marriage. This had been the longest of Grant's marriages thus far and he doesn't seem to have had any appetite to precipitate its termination. Also he and Drake still genuinely cared for each other. A clear example is Drake's help in 'curing' Grant of an operation scar just prior to shooting *Kiss Them For Me* in 1957.

During his wartime tours with the USO, Grant had had to wear a steel helmet that had irritated, and then exacerbated, a small raised area on his forehead. This had developed into a lump and, subsequently, over the years, into a benign tumour, which a succession of directors and lighting men had had increasing difficulty in disguising. By the time he was about to begin work on *Kiss Them For Me*, Grant was advised that he really should have the growth removed. The trouble was, there wasn't time for the scar to heal if he was operated on under conventional medicine. Betsy Drake, though, had the complementary answer: hypnotism.

Grant said, 'The great British plastic surgeon Sir Archibald MacIndoe told me it would take about a month to remove and heal. I couldn't afford the time. I had Betsy hypnotise me before the operation. She emphasised that I had to stay calm and even enjoy the operation. I did just that. The surgeon used a local anaesthetic. He might have been cutting my hair for all I cared. It healed without a scar.'

Deborah Kerr was among Grant's friends who witnessed and marvelled at this. 'It resulted in an incredibly quick healing,' she testified. 'And left no mark whatsoever of where the growth had been.'

As for the film he was racing to get to work on, *Kiss Them For Me*, he would have been better served getting out of his contract and having a more leisurely operation. It was a witless and forgettable comedy that co-starred those most un-Cary Grant leading ladies, Suzy Parker and Jayne Mansfield. But it did, at least, introduce Grant to the director Stanley Donen.

Two decades Grant's junior, Donen had made his name as the choreographer and co-director on *On The Town* (1949) and *Singin' In The Rain* (1952) and as director of *Seven Brides For Seven Brothers* (1954), *Funny Face* (1957) and *The Pajama Game* (1957). He had never directed a non-musical before, and producer Jerry Wald wondered how Grant, who had already signed to do the picture, would react to Donen being hired to direct.

'I first met Cary in Jerry Wald's office,' Donen recalled. 'He'd already agreed to do the film while Wald wanted me to direct. I was a little apprehensive but the meeting went very well. Cary said he'd seen my work and wanted to work with me.'

Grant and Donen clicked immediately and, over the course of filming, they grew to respect each other enormously. Indeed, it is fair to say that Donen became, with Alfred Hitchcock, one of the two directors Grant admired most. And, in both cases, it was an admiration reciprocated.

'Cary was unique,' said Donen. 'You see it in the reactions and the characterisation. There's not a false moment. And it seems like it's just happening, that he's experiencing it at that moment. He projected ease and comfort, and he always concentrated. You never saw any fear in him when he was acting. His scripts were full of little notes to himself. The minute detail, that's what all art is about. The tiniest details, that's what he was great at. He always seemed real. It wasn't a gift from God. It was the magic that came from enormous amounts of work.' So often, that has been the description of Grant's skill as an actor – no God-given gift, just constant hard work.

Grant's relations with Donen were often much more volatile than his relations with the very calm – externally, at least – Alfred Hitchcock. Grant and Hitchcock were, more or less, contemporaries both in age and background, whereas the younger Donen couldn't have been more different from Grant in so many ways. They clashed chiefly over the making of the film, but these were positive confrontations which only served to better the end result they were seeking, even if that end result was perceived in a slightly different manner.

They must have got along famously, for they would go on to make another three pictures together, and also, more remarkably, set up their own production company – Grandon Productions (a fusion of their surnames) – to produce their own pictures. One of these, *Charade* in 1963, which was Grant's seventieth movie, would be recognised as one of his best films ever.

If Grant had found in Donen the perfect working partner, his private life was heading for disarray once more. Before their long-awaited divorce – Grant's and Drake's relationship at this time was described as that of a brother and sister – Grant was still infatuated with Sophia Loren.

But another mistress had entered Grant's life. She was an alluring, hallucinogenic siren whose beguilements have lured many into addiction, madness, and even death. But her dark side was largely hidden in the 1950s and to dally with her was to peek at new, unknown, potentially exciting vistas. This new mistress was no flesh and blood conquest: she was called, prosaically, lysergic acid diethylamide or LSD-25 and Grant was introduced to her by Betsy Drake.

When Drake had left the set of *The Pride And The Passion* and boarded the *Andrea Doria* to sail back to the US, her thoughts would have been full of the burgeoning love affair between her husband and Sophia Loren. Pretty soon, however, Drake, along with every one of her fellow passengers, had something more to concern themselves with – survival.

On 25 July 1956, in thick fog off the Nantucket coast, the Swedish liner *Stockholm* slammed into the *Andrea Doria*, causing her to sink with the loss of more than 50 lives. Drake was luckier than some. She managed to reach one of the lifeboats. She lost everything she had with her – a small price, perhaps – including the manuscript of a book she was writing and jewellery reportedly valued at a quarter of a million dollars.

Along with the other survivors, Drake was taken aboard the rescue vessel, the *Ile De France*, from where she cabled Grant: 'Aboard the *Ile De France*,' ran her message 'All is well. Not a scratch.'

Grant, who had heard nothing of the disaster, was mystified on receiving her message. When he finally realised just how close Drake came to losing her life, he was at once solicitous – and racked with guilt about his affair with Loren. Indeed, it has been claimed that the shipping disaster postponed Grant's and Drake's eventual separation. The reasoning goes that, having nearly lost her in the treacherous seas off Nantucket, Grant was in no mood to then cut her adrift from his personal life. Whatever the truth of this, one result of Drake's experience of which we *can* be certain is that she sought counselling from a Doctor Mortimer A. Hartman, who was then experimenting in Los Angeles in psychoanalysis. Together with a colleague, Dr Arthur Chandler, Hartman was researching – under licence from the US government, it must be stressed – the benefits of LSD-25.

Drake became almost evangelical about the positive effects of her LSD therapy sessions and her enthusiasm persuaded Grant to take sessions with Hartman as well. Grant's willingness to take part in medically-controlled sessions with the drug illustrates how marriage to Drake had opened his mind to wider possibilities. She had proved to him how hypnotism could be central to his life – 'hypnotism is complete relaxation,' he said in 1956, 'and relaxation is the key to everything from playing golf to acting to making love' – and his readiness to embrace LSD was, to Grant, merely an extension of his belief in hypnotism and Drake's greater intelligence.

Grant later estimated that he had undergone at least one hundred sessions of LSD therapy over a three-year period, most with Hartman in Los Angeles but others, too, in England, particularly when he was making *Indiscreet* in London in 1957: 'There was a country house where you could spend all week taking LSD and discovering about yourself,' he said.

From the point of view of our mixed-up, frequently hypocritical, modern perception of the whole drugs issue, the very idea of the seemingly ultra-conservative Cary Grant experimenting with LSD appears almost surreal, virtually unimaginable. Even more surreal is the claim by the late Timothy Leary, the godfather of the entire drugs subculture in the 1960s, that it was Cary Grant's enthusiasm for the positive effects of LSD that converted him to it. 'Cary Grant was my idol,' said Leary. 'When I was young I modelled myself on him.'

But Grant was no user who sought gratification for an addiction down seedy alleyways in downtown LA. And he wasn't to know that LSD – among just about all other narcotics – would fall foul of the US government from the beginning of the sixties to the present-day, nor that his professed enthusiasm for the drug would bring him negative personal publicity a decade later. All he knew, in a world that did not noticeably deal in or discuss drugs, was that his LSD sessions helped him enormously like the hypnotism he had undergone. For such a private man, he was particularly vociferous on the subject, as public quotes about LSD made during interviews demonstrate.

He certainly went into the sessions with his eyes wide open. 'I believe in caring for my health,' he argued. 'Physical health is a product of, and dependent upon, mental health. One nurtures and nourishes the other. And so, together with a group of other interested Californians – doctors, writers, scientists and artists – and the encouragement of Betsy, who was interested herself, I underwent a series of controlled experiments with LSD-25.' On the potential dangers of the drug he added, 'Men have also died testing airplanes and parachutes, vaccines and common cold cures. In attempting to traverse the next step into progress and knowledge, men have always died. But there is a difference between the man who knows what he is about with a high-powered airplane and an idiot who puts wings on a bicycle and takes off from the edge of Niagara Falls.'

During the sessions, Grant would take the drug and then lie on a couch with his eyes covered. He described what happened next as the drug took effect:

'The feeling is that of the lessening of conscious control, similar to the mental process which takes place when we dream. With conscious controls relaxed, those thoughts buried deep inside begin to come to the surface in the form of dreams. These dreams ... are fantasies and could be classified as hallucinations ... '

The effect of the LSD was to make Cary Grant – or Archie Leach, since in this soul-searching experiment, he was fundamentally Cary Grant in name only – confront his troubling issues. He became, he claimed, 'a battlefield of old and new beliefs' under the influence of the drug. He passed through 'changing seas of horrifying and happy sights', endured a montage of 'intense hate and love' until his 'terrifying depths of dark despair' were replaced by 'glorious heavenlike religious symbolism'.

The effect, Grant claimed, made him face all his inner demons head-on. He was forced to acknowledge that, apart from Elias and Elsie, there was one figure from his past he had never quite had the courage to confront: himself.

'I had lots of problems over the years,' Grant admitted, 'but they were Archie Leach's problems, not Cary Grant's. I had to rid myself of all my hypocrisies, had to work through the events of my childhood, my relationship with my parents and my former wives.

'At first I found it unbelievably painful and, in the beginning, I didn't want to go back. The first thing that happens is you don't want to look at what you are. Then the light breaks through. To use the cliché, you're enlightened. I discovered that I'd created my own pattern, and I had to be responsible for it. I went through rebirth. The experience was just like being born for the first time. I imagined all the blood and the urine and I emerged with the flush of birth.'

Grant's LSD sessions would last up to six hours each. 'I'd run the gamut of emotions,' he said, 'from deep pain with tears running down my face to light-headed, almost drunken laughter. I remember at one point lying on the doctor's couch, squirming around, moving around, in small circles, telling myself I was unscrewing myself. I told myself that I was getting un-screwed up. When each session ended I was drained. I'd go home to sleep. It took three years and it was horrendous. I had to face things about myself that I never admitted, that I didn't know were there. But it was necessary for my evolution.'

Grant claimed that he had been searching for peace of mind all his life and had never found it 'until undergoing this treatment'. He had learned 'many things' about himself, he insisted, particularly to 'accept the responsibility for my own actions, and to blame no one else for circumstances of my own creating. I learned that no one was keeping me unhappy but me – that I could whip myself better than any other guy in the joint.'

Throughout 1958 and 1959, Grant became increasingly open about what he believed he owed to LSD. Many of his friends and closest colleagues – who were 'half envious and half horrified by what he had willingly subjected himself to', according to David Niven – were alarmed not only by his use of the drug itself, but by his candour – some felt his *reckless* candour – when discussing it with journalists. During an interview on the set of *Operation Petticoat* in 1959 he said:

Thanks to LSD I now know I hurt every woman I loved, I was an utter fake. A know-all who knew very little. Now, for the first time in my life, I'm ready to meet people realistically. Every man's conceited, but I now know that in my earlier days I really despised myself. It's when you admit this that you begin to change. Introspection is the beginning of courage.

I was always professing a knowledge I didn't have. If I didn't know about a subject I would disdain it. I was very aggressive but didn't have the courage to be physically aggressive. I was a bad-tempered man but I hid it.

Now everything has changed. My attitude toward women is completely different. I don't intend to foul up anymore. I *could* be a good husband now. I'm aware of my faults and I'm ready to accept responsibilities and exchange tolerances. Now, for the first time in my life, I am truly, deeply and honestly happy.

Yet, despite this rhetoric, what changes were there? Cary Grant, the movie star, continued in the same wonderful fashion, making wonderful films and receiving wonderful notices. Cary Grant, the private man, would continue to screw up his marriages and end up back in the law courts. Perhaps what he was saying, but not recognising at that time, was that LSD had given him the opportunity to consider what he had been, what he had done and where he was going if he didn't alter his ways, but realising that and actually doing something about it are, of course, two very different things.

And did LSD really make Cary Grant a happier man? Many who knew him well claim that the effects were not that noticeable. 'Was there a difference?' said Stanley Donen. And Richard Brooks, the writer-director of Grant's film *Crisis* in 1950, believed that Grant was 'too placid – not his usual questioning self' under the influence of the LSD sessions, a somewhat negative observation of something which Grant could only claim as being positive in its reactions.

'All actors long to be loved,' Grant told his friend David Niven. 'That's why we become actors. But I don't give a damn anymore. LSD's made me self-sufficient *at last!*'

It was left to Niven to be the most publicly dismissive of Grant's LSD era. Niven just wasn't convinced. Years later, he wrote that 'it seemed to the rest of us a most hazardous trip for Cary to have taken to find out what we could have told him anyway – that he had always been self-sufficient; that he had always been loved; and that he would continue to give a damn about himself and, particularly, about others.'

On the other hand, no one could argue that the performances that Cary Grant gave while undergoing LSD therapy, coincidental or not, are the most relaxed, wryly self-aware of his entire career. In one of these roles, as Roger Thornhill in Hitchcock's *North By Northwest* (1959), Grant could claim to have given his greatest ever performance. Whatever the effect LSD had on his mind at this time, it was most definitely not to the detriment of his acting talent. Quite the reverse.

When LSD, along with a host of other pop-culture drugs, fell into disfavour and was finally made an illegal substance, Grant, never one to forget his *alter ego*, backtracked considerably, at least in public. To begin with, he stressed that he'd only ever taken the drug 'with the direct inspection and care of a qualified doctor,' and insisted his intention was merely 'to make myself happy – a man would be a fool to take something that *didn't* make him happy.'

Later still, when possession of LSD was an offence, he tried to distance himself even further from the drug: 'It was an utterly foolish thing to do,' he said. 'I wouldn't dream of taking LSD now. I don't *need* it now.'

Yet, somehow, he could never quite bring himself to condemn the drug completely after it was made illegal: he had found the benefits so positive, or so he believed.

'LSD is no longer available in America,' he noted, conveniently side-stepping the truth that it was always available, albeit *illegally*. For Grant, in private, this remained something of a regret and he blamed conventional thinking for its withdrawal and added, '...it's unlikely that it will be reintroduced unless some brave, venturesome and respected psychiatrist publicly speaks out in its favour.'

It is perhaps rather curious to note, if not altogether surprising, that many years later, Grant's will would reveal a $10,000 donation to Dr Hartman.

Grant certainly believed that taking LSD-25 had been necessary. 'I was a self-opinionated boor,' he described himself, 'hiding behind all kinds of layers and defences, hypocrisy and vanity. I had to get rid of them and wipe the slate clean.'

Of course, by 1961, when the Californian medical authorities had suspended Hartman from practising in the state, Grant's use of LSD was well-known and was used against him in his divorce from his fourth wife, Dyan Cannon, seven years later.

In 1968, with the drugs such as LSD having become a mantle worn by the Hippy movement, which was perceived as the greatest threat to the American Way, Cannon's lawyers believed labelling Grant 'An apostle of LSD' would damage him irreparably. That it didn't – and, in fact, did nothing to damage his reputation with the American public – reveals a curious quirk in the morality of Hollywood in the 1940s, 50s and 60s, and the extraordinary acceptance – even adoration – the public had for Cary Grant. One almost feels he could have assassinated the President and still been excused by the American public for one reason or another.

Also, drug-taking, unlike adultery and homosexuality, did not necessarily sound the death knell for a career. Morality clauses might be inserted in contracts to protect studios from any unpredictable violations by their stars, but drug-taking had always been viewed less seriously by the industry, and by the audiences, than by the Federal Authorities.

As far back as 1949, Robert Mitchum had been arrested for smoking marijuana at a party and the press had predicted the end of his career: 'Hollywood's laboriously contrived self-portrait is once again in danger of looking like a comic strip – and an ugly one,' tutted *Time* when Mitchum was sentenced to fifty days' imprisonment.

But the reverse happened. Howard Hughes, the owner and head of

RKO, stood by Mitchum and released Mitchum's movie, *Rachel and the Stranger*, within days of his coming out of jail. It went straight to the top of the box-office, the old saying that there's no such thing as bad publicity proving very true on this occasion.

'Mitchum, who was supposed to go to prison and suffer,' wrote Otto Friedrich in his Hollywood exposé *City Of Nets*, 'emerged as a kind of folk hero, still cynical, laconic, sexy and quite unreformed by his incarceration.'

(One can only wonder what private conversations Grant and Mitchum had on the subject of drugs, while working together in England in the summer of 1960 on the ironically titled *The Grass Is Greener*.)

Hollywood's ambivalence to drugs lingers to this day. When the talented, but troubled, actor Robert Downey Jr was jailed – with undue harshness by the Federal Authorities – for drug offences in 1999, the feeling was that, like Mitchum 50 years before, his career would be finished. Instead, Downey walked out of prison in September 2000 and straight into a plum role on *Ally McBeal*. Perhaps it is a case of the drop in standards we hear so much about – no one really caring any more about a fellow-human's misdemeanour – or, perhaps, it is a brighter scenario, a case of the hypocrisy having finally been sliced away. A third, more cynical, thought is that Hollywood, especially today, has always found itself very forgiving to stars who are the flavour of the month. Certainly Downey – and the English actor Hugh Grant, for that matter – did not suffer very much, or for very long, for their respective, if different, misdemeanours, although Downey's continued problems led to his leaving *Ally McBeal* in 2001.

Nobody understood Hollywood – or his own audience – like Cary Grant did. He wouldn't have jeopardised his image or sacrificed his career on a whim. One cannot help concluding, therefore, that Grant knew exactly what he was doing and just how far he could go with his experiments with LSD. With the benefit of hindsight, it is easy to see that whatever happened, Cary Grant was always going to emerge as the suave, tailored Cary Grant everyone knew and loved.

LSD, however, did nothing to cure his situation with Sophia Loren, with whom he was signed to star in the movie *Houseboat* immediately after making *Kiss Them For Me* in 1957.

Despite Grant having begun 'munching LSD', as David Niven amusingly put it, little else had changed in the Grant-Loren-Ponti triangle in the months since *The Pride And The Passion* had wrapped. Ponti was, seemingly, as far from divorcing his wife as ever, and Loren despaired of ever becoming the next Mrs Ponti. As for Grant, his feelings for Loren were as hot as ever. If nothing else, he must have known – probably relished the fact – that *Houseboat* was going to bring matters to a conclusive head.

Scripted by Melville Shavelson and Jack Rose, and directed by Shavelson himself, *Houseboat*'s scenario was derivative and owed much to Grant's earlier film with Betsy Drake, *Room For One More,* although *Houseboat* emerged as, undeniably, the more entertaining of the two. It was, the *Los Angeles Examiner* believed, 'the kind of movie to which you can take your stuffy maiden aunt, your wicked sophisticated uncle and your ten-year-old child – and they will all have a wonderful time.'

Grant played Tom Winston, a widower trying to get closer to his children after prolonged absences caused by his workload. His seven-year-old son brings home a beautiful young woman called Cinzia Zaccardi (Loren), and Winston persuades her to stay as their maid. Cinzia falls in love with Winston who, himself, believes he is in love with another woman, Caroline. Inevitably, Winston discovers that Caroline is as vacuous and phoney as her friends and realises that it is Cinzia he really loves.

Despite being a romantic comedy, the film has serious undercurrents, which, as such a versatile actor, Grant thrived on. Typical is the scene in which he has to explain death to his eldest son. As in *An Affair To Remember*, it is impossible to discern the technique in Grant's seamless transition from lightheartedness to tender seriousness and back again within this film. This is all the more remarkable given that Grant's proximity to Loren during shooting was making their real-life affair all the more difficult.

Both Betsy Drake and Carlo Ponti were aware of what was going on but didn't know the appropriate steps to take. Worse, the affair was beginning to be talked of – if in hushed tones – throughout Hollywood, and a rumour began circulating that Grant had actually proposed to the Italian actress, despite his still being married to Drake, just before they shot *Houseboat*'s love scene. Legend further has it that she turned him down.

What actually happened – and it appears more bizarre than any Hollywood plot – was that Ponti's lawyers managed to get him a divorce and, simultaneously, a marriage to Sophia Loren by proxy in Mexico. Two Mexican lawyers are said to have stood in for the bride and groom at the ceremony. The first Loren seems to have known about her 'wedding' to Ponti was when she read about it in Louella Parsons' column – just before filming her screen marriage to Grant in *Houseboat*.

In public, Grant gave Loren his very best wishes, but in private, understandably, he was devastated. They both knew that the marriage would not be binding in the USA and Grant privately believed that Loren's argument that she had to stick with Ponti because the authorities in her native Italy probably *would* recognise it was somewhat spurious.

As it turned out, the Italian authorities did, indeed, recognise the proxy marriage but, ironically, refused to recognise Ponti's divorce. This led to problems for Ponti and Loren in 1962 when they faced charges of bigamy.

Many marriages have survived, even thrived, after infidelity, but any pretence that Grant and Drake could make a go of it after Loren's marriage to Ponti were dispelled when Grant consoled himself not with Drake but with a defecting Yugoslavian basketball player called Luba, who just happened to be a ringer for Loren. Cubby Broccoli, who described Luba as 'strapping', remembered their affair as creating 'quite a sensation in Hollywood at the time'.

Grant took many years fully getting over Loren, and he always refused to discuss their relationship with journalists who tackled him about it.

When, in 1979, Loren published her account of his love for her in her autobiography, Grant retained a dignified silence. Some interpreted this as a sign he was relaxed, even amused, by the book. In reality, as he told close friends, he was incensed by it, which became clear in 1980 when a TV mini-series based on the book was proposed. Loren, it was announced, would play her own mother and an actor would portray Grant. Grant immediately threatened the producers with a lawsuit to prevent production. 'I can't believe that anyone would exploit an old friendship like this,' he said.

It is possible he was protecting his bruised passion as much as his pride. After all, he didn't get what he went after, and Cary Grant tended always to get what he went after. As Grant told Maureen Donaldson, who lived with him for a couple of years in the mid-1970s, 'Sophia broke my heart.'

21

'I guess I just love my fellow-man – and woman.'

Cary Grant

With Sophia Loren married to Carlo Ponti and thus lost to Grant, it was perhaps a relief to him that his next picture, *Indiscreet* – the first of Grandon Production's pictures – was made entirely in London.

The screenplay was written by Norman Krasna and was based on his own play, *Kind Sir,* which had been a recent hit on Broadway with Charles Boyer and Mary Martin in the leads. Stanley Donen, who knew Krasna, asked that the film be relocated to London – something that Grant had insisted upon. Krasna was happy to oblige. But, there again, most people in Hollywood were happy to go along with whatever Grant wanted by this time in his career. He had more power than any other star and, according to Stanley Donen, he knew how to wield it:

'If Cary wanted to make a film, it was not so much selling the idea, as which offer to take. He had the power to get pretty much what he wanted. His biggest concern was that the movie be made correctly and that we get the best people – not only in the cast, but in the crew also. He had the power to pretty much name his own deal. If one studio didn't want it, another half-dozen would. He could drive a very hard bargain.'

Jack Warner definitely wanted Cary Grant in *Indiscreet* and he was happy to pay whatever he had to secure it. In the event, Warner had to pay Grant a guaranteed fee of $300,000, allot the film a very generous budget and to guarantee Grandon Productions a large slice of the potential profits. Warner did not demur at these terms: he knew the benefits to his studio of having a Cary Grant picture and he even gave Grant a Rolls-Royce for his use whenever he was in England just to display goodwill.

By producing the film through his own production company, Grant was able to have the final say in every aspect of its making and, from the start, he was adamant about his co-star. 'The only woman on the list is Ingrid Bergman,' he stated.

Although relations between Bergman and the American public had begun to thaw with the passing of time, Donen seriously doubted she would be up to doing the movie.

Ever since her virtually compulsory exile by the rabidly moralistic motley coalition of press, religious fundamentalists, opportunistic senators and ultra-conservative middle-America, and anyone else who thought it was good to get angry about someone not native to their country, Grant had remained one of her few supporters – certainly her most powerful and vociferous. When, in 1950, she had given birth to Roberto Rossellini's son before her divorce from Peter Lindstrom, Grant had risked his own reputation by sending her a telegram: 'Ingrid dearest: it would not be possible in a single cablegram to tell you of all your friends who send you love and affection.' It was a deliberate, calculated and very public snub to her very many detractors and one cannot help but admire him for it.

Towards the end of Grant's life, he was asked *why* he had stood by friends like Bergman and others who had been hauled before McCarthy's witch-hunts and publicly defended them at the considerable risk to his own reputation.

'I've always found that the nicer you are to people, the nicer they are to you,' he said. 'So I'm receiving as much as I'm giving. If I can make someone happy, I'm making myself happy, too. It's all very simple. I guess I just love my fellow-man – and woman.'

During her exile, Bergman had been making smaller films in Europe, but had made a comeback in *Anastasia* for MGM in 1956. It had won her the Best Actress Oscar, but she had refused to travel to California to receive it. Grant had collected it on her behalf and, in the process, made a typically defiant speech:

'Dear Ingrid,' he said to the assembled royalty of Hollywood, most of whom had snubbed her just eight years back, 'wherever in the world you are, we, your friends, want to congratulate you and may you be as happy as we are for you.'

Thus, Bergman's attitude to Hollywood was still ambivalent – the massive success of her film notwithstanding – and this, coupled with the obvious difficulties the Bergman–Rossellini marriage was encountering, made Stanley Donen doubt that she would even consider *Indiscreet*.

'When Cary suggested Ingrid Bergman, I agreed,' Donen remembered. 'But I really didn't think we could possibly get her. It's like saying "Let's get Cary Grant". That's only possible if Cary Grant wants to do the picture ... But, in the end, getting her was simple. Cary called and talked with her, and then I flew over to Rome to meet with her and we talked about the film and she said yes immediately.'

Grant and Donen established a base at London's Connaught Hotel during the pre-production period, and, after all his emotional problems with Sophia Loren, being able to concentrate on producing and starring in his own film – and the added bonus of spending a great deal of time back in London – put a good distance between himself and the roller-coaster ride that was his emotionally-stretched, Hollywood-based life.

Grant always maintained that the making of *Indiscreet* in London during 1957 was one of the most enjoyable periods in his working life. He was in control, he was working with people he admired and trusted and, rightly or wrongly, he believed he was in better psychological health than ever before thanks to his LSD sessions. The only thing that could possibly mar his time in London was the British press.

Betsy Drake was in London during much of the filming. She was appearing in a West End play called *Next To No Time* during the evenings and working on a script for a film at Pinewood Studios in Buckinghamshire during the day. Despite being in the same city for several months, it did not escape the notice of the British papers that Grant and Drake barely met up at all. And naturally rumours began circulating again that all was not well with the Grants' marriage.

If Grant ignored press comments suggesting his marriage was all but over, he did not keep quiet when another potential scandal threatened to overshadow Ingrid Bergman's arrival in London to begin work on the film. Just before she flew to Heathrow from Rome, the news leaked out that she was separating from Roberto Rossellini.

This was a new sensation involving Bergman, and Grant knew it would be the only item of interest on the journalists' agenda when his co-star touched down on British soil. Knowing how much Bergman had endured at the hands of the press before, he took decisive action. He travelled out to Heathrow airport so that he could be with her during the press conference and deflect the inevitable pressure she would be subject to.

'I was taken into the transit lounge for a press conference,' Bergman said. 'And there was Cary, sitting up on the table. He shouted across the heads of the journalists, "Ingrid, you think *you* have problems – wait 'til you hear mine." That broke the ice. Everyone burst into laughter. He then held them at bay in such a nice way. "Come on, fellas – you can't ask a lady *that!* If you'll ask me that question I'll give you a better answer – I have a life twice as colourful as Ingrid's!" Then we escaped and drove to the Connaught Hotel. We were all laughing. I was telling him about my problems with Roberto and he was telling me his.'

Indiscreet, which was released before *Houseboat* in May 1958, is a pretty insubstantial romantic comedy and the screenwriter Norman Krasna never quite exorcises the inherent staginess of his original play. Nevertheless, there is much about the film to be enjoyed, not least the rapport between Grant and Bergman. And a definite highlight is Grant's bravura attempt at a Highland Fling. This was a particular favourite scene of his and he later said, 'I got a real kick out of dancing again.'

Although the film doesn't feature on too many cineastes' lists of favourite Cary Grant movies, it *was* one of Grant's personal favourites. This is perhaps because he produced it himself and, despite a slightly ponderous pace and a tendency to be over-talkative, it was the very model of intelligent, sophisticated and elegant froth. It was also a massive box-office hit – as Grant's pictures more often than not tended to be.

Once work on the film was over, Grant and Drake flew to Monaco to spend Christmas 1957 with the Rainiers. Whatever desperate measures the Grants were taking to try and give the impression they were still together – and it *is* possible that Grant believed that the marriage could be salvaged right up until the summer of 1958 – no one was really fooled, particularly Grant's good friend Princess Grace. It was generally accepted by those close to the couple that a parting of the ways was on the cards.

While the Grants enjoyed a festive season in the principality, Alfred Hitchcock was spending the Christmas period in warmer climes – Jamaica. He had with him the synopsis of a script he had commissioned from writer Ernest Lehman.

Hitchcock's brief to Lehman had been vague. He wanted to make a film about a man to whom extraordinary things keep happening about which he has absolutely no control nor knowledge. Hitchcock had no idea who the man was or why these terrible things keep happening to him. He made only two stipulations: the film was to be a series of chase sequences and Lehman was to think of the man as 'Cary Grant'. In other words, Hitchcock wanted to make a film in which he put 'Cary Grant' – and everything that name represented – through hell.

With little else other than a concept, Lehman struggled at first, and didn't mind telling Hitchcock so. But when Hitchcock settled down to read the synopsis, he knew Lehman had understood what he was trying to achieve. Hitchcock's working title for the project was *My Cary Grant Film* or, just as appropriately, *Breathless*. Lehman had put a rather more clumsy title on his first page: *In A Northwesterly Direction*. Eventually, both men would settle on a title inspired from a line in Shakespeare's *Hamlet*, Act 2 Scene 2 – 'I am but mad North-Northwest: When the wind is southerly I know a hawk from a handsaw.' This is appropriate given Hitchcock's long-standing desire to make a modern-dress version of *Hamlet* with Grant in the title role.

Legend recalls a second reason for the eventual title in that Lehman assumed the characters would be travelling North by Northwest Airlines.

The allusion in the title to madness is also apposite since at one point Grant's character, the urbane advertising executive Roger O. Thornhill, is asked whether he will give a simple answer, yes or no – 'A simple no for the simple reason I simply don't know what you're talking about' – an in-joke from Hitchcock who was gleefully aware Grant didn't understand the film's plot.

North By Northwest is Hitchcock's assault on the creation 'Cary Grant'. Not the Grant who was his friend and favourite actor, but the dashing, debonair and tanned 'Cary Grant' familiar to millions around the globe. On a superficial level, the chief pleasure of this picture, as one writer saw it, is 'to watch Grant's perfectly groomed, perfectly tanned, perfectly tailored gentleman get his suit dirty.' But Hitchcock was aiming for more than getting Grant dirty in the movie.

'Never did Hitchcock more brilliantly use comedy, romance and thrills to hide his true theme – the sadistic degradation of pride,' wrote Richard Schickel. 'The structure of the film is to humanise [Thornhill] through mortification, to keep chipping away at his smug self-confidence until finally he has expiated his original sin of superficiality, and knows in his bones, in his soul, how fragile our illusions are, how thin the skin of our social order, our civility is. The point of *North By Northwest* is to destroy Thornhill's arrogant innocence, strip him of the adult's artifice and illusion and to return him to the anxious state of a lonely child in a darkened room; to ask him to re-imagine himself and re-imagine the world; to make of him, if you will, Archie Leach.'

Nowhere else in Grant's films is his character so closely entwined with the 'Cary Grant' persona he had created several decades before, and nowhere else is that persona so violently stripped of all its certainties. So blurred were the edges between Grant and Thornhill that MGM's publicity for the picture establishes them as one and the same.

'You can't fight it, Cary,' says the voice-over on the original screen trailer. 'Someone's out to get you. By violence. Or by abduction. They'll even frame you for murder. So run for your life. Search for a man who doesn't exist. A secret nobody knows. And start a love affair in an upper berth.' Throughout the trailer, the voice refers to 'Cary' and not his character, Roger Thornhill.

'Cary Grant is the perfect actor for the part,' wrote Pauline Kael. 'He incarnates the directional confusion of the title.'

'Ostensibly a playful spy thriller,' said the British Film Institute in 1980, '*North By Northwest* is the American dream at twenty-four frames per second. Madison Avenue, Plaza Hotel, United Nations, Chicago, Mount Rushmore. Its geographical and spiritual trajectory – with Cary Grant at its centre, the shallow man of admass who breaks a spy-ring for the CIA – is a return to critical and cultural imperatives.'

'I'm an advertising man, not a red herring,' Grant protests to spymaster Leo G. Carroll. 'I have a job, a secretary, a mother, two ex-wives and several bartenders dependent upon me. And I don't intend to disappoint them all by getting myself slightly killed.'

Never had the inconsequential nature of the 'Cary Grant' screen persona been so brutally reduced to its most basic form. In arguing that he is more than a red herring, the Grant persona is having to justify his existence. The hoary old device of mistaken identity, so brilliantly employed by Lehman at the film's opening, has transformed Grant into the non-existent 'Mr Kaplan', who is the McGuffin of this particular Hitchcock film. Thus reduced, Grant's character is merely a skittle to be knocked down again and again, and this gives Hitchcock licence to employ his usual tricks in, arguably, his most perfect cinematic confection ever.

Grant, who had in real life been struggling with the concepts of identity and names all his life, was now in a film where his character was forever being stripped of identity by the villain of the piece, James

Mason, and his underlings. And there's something almost cheerfully malevolent about the way in which Hitchcock repeatedly puts 'Cary Grant' in a position where he has to quantify his existence.

GRANT: Wait a minute – did you call me 'Kaplan'?
MASON: Oh, I know you're a man of many names, but I'm perfectly willing to accept your current choice.

Later in the film, when Grant first encounters Eve Kendall, played by Eva Marie Saint, Hitchcock has brilliantly twisted events so that Thornhill has adopted the identity of Jack Philips, western sales manager for Kingsby Electronics, to avoid a phoney murder wrap, while *she* knows he is Roger Thornhill.

GRANT: I know. I look vaguely familiar.
SAINT: Yes.
GRANT: You feel you've seen me somewhere before.
SAINT: Mmmm.
GRANT: Funny how I have that effect on people. It's something about my face.
SAINT: It's a nice face.
GRANT: You think so?
SAINT: I wouldn't say it if I didn't.
GRANT: Oh, you're *that* type!

North By Northwest remains one of the greatest movies of all time and it is nigh on impossible to think of anyone other than Cary Grant in the role of Roger Thornhill – hardly surprising, perhaps, as Hitchcock, from the outset, intended to make a 'Cary Grant' picture. James Stewart coveted the role when he first heard about it. Although Hitchcock never really considered anyone other than Grant, he knew that, until Grant had signed, there was no guarantee he would get his man, so Stewart was kept in mind. Stewart badgered Hitchcock repeatedly and Hitchcock, who liked and admired Stewart enormously, had to keep him dangling 'with excuses for months thereafter' according to Stewart's biographer, Donald Dewey. Hitchcock told Stewart that Ernest Lehman's script wouldn't be ready until the summer of 1958 – which was largely the truth – but Stewart said he'd put all other projects on hold to wait.

'I didn't want to come right out and tell him I wanted Grant for the role,' admitted Hitchcock later, 'so I simply told him there wasn't much on paper yet. Then, when he called me to say he had to report to Columbia for *Bell, Book And Candle,* I was, of course, very relieved.'

Despite his wanting to work with Hitchcock again, Grant drove a very hard bargain with MGM on *North By Northwest.* He knew that the combination of himself and perhaps the world's greatest director on a spy thriller was the recipe for a box-office bonanza and, always a man who knew his own worth, he demanded, and received, an up-front fee of $450,000 plus ten per cent of the gross over eight million dollars. He also inserted a clause that gave him a bonus of $5,000 a day for every day he worked on the picture over seven weeks. Given that the film was delayed by two months, he was already one week into this profitable penalty clause by the time the first day of shooting arrived. And since the film's shoot took nine weeks, MGM had to pay Grant a penalty of almost $320,000 on top of his basic fee. He had made the best part of one million dollars from the film even before it hit the cinemas. It was a financial coup that sent shock waves through Hollywood but did nothing to assuage Grant's notorious parsimony. Martin Landau, playing henchman Leonard to James Mason's head villain Philip Vandamm, recalls lunching with Grant and Mason during filming. 'The only time Cary reached for the bill,' recalled Landau lightheartedly, 'was to declare, "It's Friday – that means we go Dutch!"'

He also jokes that Grant was allocated just one suit for the duration of shooting to underline the grimy struggle of a man on the run, while Landau, himself the same height and weight as Grant, was allocated several well-tailored outfits. At the end of the shoot, Grant tried to take home all Landau's suits.

MGM's financial investment in *North By Northwest* was well rewarded, even if there was a lingering resentment against Hitchcock for refusing to use Cyd Charisse in the female lead. Hitchcock had insisted on Eva Marie Saint, who was another of his 'ice blondes'.

Born in 1924, Eva Marie Saint had hitherto been primarily a stage actress, although she had won the Best Supporting Actress award for *On The Waterfront,* her first film in 1954.

In the final cut, it is hard to argue with Hitchcock's judgement. Saint has a wonderful inner serenity and the chemistry between Grant and Saint is electric. Her presence carries a sensual sexuality that rivals Grace Kelly's fire-beneath-the-ice *tour de force* in *To Catch A Thief.*

Where she really makes an impact is in capturing the conflict between Eve being attracted to Roger Thornhill and the need for restraint to avoid blowing her cover as Philip Vandamm's girlfriend. Thus, their first meeting aboard a train sizzles with ambiguity.

GRANT: Honest women frighten me.

SAINT: Why?

GRANT: I don't know. Somehow they seem to put me at a disadvantage.

SAINT: Is it because you're not honest with them?

GRANT: Exactly. What I mean, is the moment I meet an attractive woman, I have to start pretending I have no desire to make love to her.

SAINT: What makes you think you have to conceal it?

GRANT: She might find the idea objectionable.

SAINT: Then again, she might not.

GRANT: Think how lucky I am to have been seated here!

SAINT: Oh, luck had nothing to do with it.

GRANT: Fate?

SAINT: I tipped the steward five dollars to seat you here if you should come in.

GRANT: Is that a proposition?

SAINT: I never discuss love on an empty stomach.

GRANT: You've already eaten.

SAINT: But *you* haven't.

North By Northwest is a glorious cinematic treat that remains a triumph of style over content. The script is nonsense, and everyone involved in the film understood that, not least scriptwriter Ernest Lehman. He even throws in a joke at the film's expense by giving Thornhill a middle name beginning with 'O'. 'What does the "O" stand for?' asks Eve Kendall. 'Nothing,' replies Grant. But it does make Thornhill's initials on his company matchbook read: 'R.O.T.' – or Rot!

In other hands, the film could well have been rot. The plot doesn't make sense and many of the key sequences simply do not bare close inspection. Consider the celebrated crop-duster scene, which is, quite rightly, one of the most enduring images from cinema history.

Roger Thornhill has been lured out onto the Plains by the villains so he can be killed. There is a long, straight and dusty road, on which very little traffic ever passes. There are no witnesses. So how do they choose to kill him? By shooting him and hiding his body in the acres of tall maize alongside the road? Stabbing him and doing likewise with the corpse? Run him over in a car as he stands waiting and waiting for his imaginary contact to materialise? None of these. They try, instead, to run him down with a single-engined crop-dusting plane! How, precisely, do you kill someone by swooping low overhead in a small plane? And, having failed to evade the plane by hiding in the maize, Grant runs onto the road to flag down a passing petrol tanker. He is nearly run down by the tanker – this would have saved the imaginative and hopeful villains a great problem – which stops inches in front of him. And then the real mind-bender. The plane – which has perfect visibility up to about fifty miles – manages to contrive a way to fly straight into the tanker and cause a massive explosion. One can only assume that the pilot, who so adroitly controlled the plane up to this point, had a black-out of some kind. And furthermore, who *is* the pilot? We never see him, and nor is he referred to again in the entire picture.

Judged like this, any film is apt to collapse into absurdity. But this film bucks the trend. It doesn't fail because of the absurdities; it works *because* of them. The sheer visual quality of a single-engine plane in the middle of nowhere attacking a successful, well-dressed city executive across a field of maize, concluding in a spectacular explosion, distracts the mind from the fading logical progression of the piece. Hitchcock himself, referring to the crop-duster scene, admitted that he, too, had no idea who was flying the plane.

Although there are echoes of earlier Hitchcock films – Grant's flight from New York by train to flee the murder for which he has been framed is similar to Robert Donat's plight in Hitchcock's 1935 version of *The Thirty-Nine Steps*, and the ambiguity about just *whose* side Eve Kendall is on mirrors the question marks in *Suspicion* and *Notorious* – Hitchcock had never before mixed his recipe with so sure a touch.

Everything in the movie works perfectly: the insouciant witticisms, such as James Mason saying to Grant, 'Seems to me you fellows could stand a little less training from the FBI and a little more from the Actors' Studio' and Mason's own sublime performance as the faintly bisexual Vandamm, the blueprint of countless screen villains who would follow. And one mustn't forget Bernard Herrmann's pulsating score.

But the film's crowing glory is the fourth – and, as it turned out, final

– collaboration between the world's greatest director and the world's greatest leading man. Grant's trust in Hitchcock was absolute, as it had been right from the beginning of their association. It is difficult to imagine him having allowed any other director to raid the 'Cary Grant' persona to such an extent, to strip away all the flesh he had spent years acquiring and examine what was left on the big screen for millions to see. As for Hitchcock, nowhere else in his canon is there greater evidence of the insolent, irreverent, malevolent inner child that drove this man's bizarre imagination. Once Grant's name was on the contract for this picture, he knew he had got his own way and that he could make something special, something that would last longer than the protagonists on the project.

Appropriately enough, Hitchcock's finale to *North By Northwest* is perhaps one of his most accomplished sequences ever. By having the greatest American screen icon scrambling over the nation's most revered monument (Mount Rushmore), the savage wit of the director was given its freest rein. Denied permission to film the sequence on the monument itself by Mount Rushmore's less-than-playful guardians, Hitchcock, refusing to be denied his moment, recreated the monument, in part (the Federal authorities even refused permission for a complete studio reconstruction), at MGM's Studio. Grant wasn't about to complain. It was the last-minute necessity of having to recreate Mount Rushmore in the studio that delayed the start date and thereby filled his coffers. It also meant he didn't have to risk his neck leaping about the real thing. Not that working on the mock-up was without dangers.

Although Grant credited his previous Hitchcock film *To Catch A Thief* as finally curing his acrophobia, he looked back on his last two collaborations with Hitchcock and jokingly suggested the director had a hidden agenda to polish him off to gain extra publicity for the movies.

'In *To Catch A Thief*,' said Grant, 'I dashed over sloping rooftops of four-storied French Riviera villas with no net below, while trying either to rob Grace Kelly or to save her from being robbed; and in *North By Northwest* I heroically hung both up and down on replicas of sections of Mount Rushmore, rafter-high on the tallest stage of Hollywood. I've always felt queasily uncertain whether or not Hitchcock was pleased at seeing me survive each day's work. I can only hope it was as great a relief to him as it was a disappointment.'

Sadly, one scene Hitchcock had planned for the Rushmore sequence had to be scrapped for logistical reasons. 'I wanted Cary to slide down

Lincoln's nose and hide in the nostril,' Hitchcock said. 'Then he would have a sneezing fit...'

The loss of that scene is of minor importance. *North By Northwest* stands as Cary Grant and Alfred Hitchcock's legacy to the world. It was a massive hit at the box-office and critics almost wept with gratitude for the film. It was the collaboration that lived up to the promise of the previous three.

Despite the popularity of films such as *Psycho* (1960) and *The Birds* (1963), Hitchcock never quite matched – and certainly never bettered – the sheer verve and richness of *North By Northwest*.

And Cary Grant had, if he but knew it, given the performance of his career.

22

'Cary Grant is a living lesson in getting laughs without
lines. It is his reaction, always underplayed, that creates or
releases the humour.'

Variety, 1959

North by Northwest had established Grant as an almost god-like figure
in the film industry. His status had now eclipsed mere superstardom
and he was regarded with awe by audiences, critics and colleagues.

But to Grant himself, it sometimes felt as though he was in the calm
eye of a hurricane of success swirling around him over which he had
no control. While it was true that the LSD therapy of the previous three
years or so had given him the impression of being at ease with himself,
there was a deep sense of emptiness at his centre over the failure of his
marriage to Betsy Drake. Indeed, although he would always accept the
blame for the failure of all his marriages, Grant never seems to have got
over his puzzlement at how he and Betsy Drake actually came to split.
Obviously his affair with Sophia Loren was not going to help, but that
was more a symptom of something more profound and not the catalyst.
To find the catalyst one would have to look deeply into Grant's past and
the reasons as to why he was unable to stay attached to the women he
loved. And that was all wrapped up painfully in his relationship with
his mother – though, despite his marriage to Drake shortly coming to
an end, many of his problems involving his mother and women in
general, had presumably been adequately sorted in LSD therapy.

Being caught between the raging success of his career and dismal
failure, yet again, in his private life, Grant reacted by becoming more
reclusive than ever, retreating ever more into socialising with his very
close, tightly-knit circle of friends. His reclusiveness was never as
intensely loopy as the complete obsessive withdrawal Howard Hughes
retreated into but, nevertheless, Grant seemed to become more
untouchable than ever.

He remained, though, very true and loyal to his friends. Just before *North By Northwest* opened in the summer of 1959, he was best man at Cubby Broccoli's marriage to Dana Wilson, a beautiful actress and writer who had previously been married to Lewis Wilson, the screen's first-ever Batman.

Broccoli had enjoyed some success as a movie producer in partnership with Irving Allen – though nothing approaching the success he would later attain with the James Bond franchise – and their Warwick Films company had produced a series of solidly competent action-adventure movies in England since 1953, some of which had starred Hollywood heart-throb, Alan Ladd. But Broccoli had had personal tragedy. His second wife, Nedra, had died of cancer in 1957, leaving him a widower in his late forties with two young children.

Grant had been one of Broccoli's closest confidants throughout this period in his life and had proved a great sounding board particularly during Broccoli's wooing of Dana. (This is a role he seemed to enjoy playing. He supported and offered tips to Peter Sellers in his wooing of Countess Christina Wachtmeister.) 'He was an acknowledged expert in the game,' Broccoli recalled. 'He got his mileage out of a boyish exuberance and looking as tanned and healthy as a Malibu lifeguard.'

Describing a man, then aged 55, as looking like a Malibu lifeguard may sound unlikely, but the truth is Grant did indeed project and promote the image of a superfit man untouched by ageing. Has any actor – any man, come to that – enjoyed such a long middle-age? Grant's leading man middle-age lasted from 1944 (when he turned forty) to 1963 (when he starred in *Charade,* in which his character marries Audrey Hepburn's character, who was young enough to be his daughter).

Broccoli further described Grant's superfit state by saying that his midriff resembled 'flat steel' at this time. This surely gives the lie to Grant's insistence that he never did any exercise and supports David Niven's claim that, in reality, Grant's physical fitness was one of the three most important things in his life, the other two being film-making and women. Indeed, one starts to wonder if Grant ever ceased from training his body once he had found how beneficial it could prove to his future, which was undoubtedly at the moment he ran away to join Bob Pender. For several years he was an acrobat: he must have grown very accustomed to training and its benefits. Keeping in great physical shape had given him his first serious employment (with Pender) and was the basis for an opportunity to become a film star. His fitness and shape must have been a very significant part of his life. His 'Cary Grant' alter ego, as much as it didn't want to appear to have to fuss about taking prolonged bouts of sweaty exercise, certainly didn't want to appear jaded and flabby.

Broccoli's wedding to Dana Wilson took place on 21 June 1959. The previous day, Dana's sixteen-year-old son Michael – now producer of the Bond franchise with the Broccolis' daughter, Barbara – had arrived in Las Vegas and suggested a traditional stag night with Broccoli and Grant.

Grant backed out, claiming, 'I've got to get up early tomorrow, so I'm going to hit the sack early. And you'd better do the same.' The real reason was more to do with his not wanting to be out on the town as it would have been too public. In Las Vegas he would draw big attention, in fact, he could have been mobbed.

Broccoli and Michael Wilson ignored Grant's advice and hit the town. Both went for it big time and faced the morning with blinding hangovers. But not Grant who, according to Cubby Broccoli, 'had been up for an hour gulping in the desert air and doing maybe a hundred push-ups.' Even in Vegas, it seems that his secret exercise programme continued.

Just before the ceremony, Grant told Dana Wilson, with a twinkle in his eye, 'The groom has a hangover and your son has a hangover. I'm the only one to talk any sense. Y'know, I did a film once where the best man ran off with the bride. How about it?'

Dana laughed and said, 'As tempting as it might sound, Cary, I don't think it's going to happen this time.'

His genuine joy at watching friends like Broccoli settle into married life shows that Grant – if unable to get his own personal life on a contented footing – took vicarious pleasure in seeing those around him settled down happily.

In 1959, with the critical and commercial success of *North By Northwest*, Grant secretly knew that for all the plaudits, the film had given him something of a dilemma. The film had been a special event in his career and Grant, as astute a player as ever operated in Hollywood, knew in his heart this was so. Films that attain such success normally only come a handful of times in any star's career. Grant had been lucky. He had experienced more critical and box-office successes, and pure superlative pictures, than any other star. But *North*

By Northwest was easily his best since *Notorious* thirteen years earlier. At the age of 55, how many *North By Northwest*s did he have in him? And such a film, such a triumph, involved many others, not least a director of the quality of Alfred Hitchcock. Grant had a horror of declining in front of an audience. He didn't want them to see the grey hair go white, the teeth become slightly crooked, the skin more puffy and tired than before. He wanted to make his exit with the image of 'Cary Grant' intact. He had dedicated his life to that single creation; it could be no other way. And he had seen so many contemporaries out-stay their welcome, often ending up in little more than 'B' films – or worse, television specials.

Grant would give many different reasons for his retiring from acting in 1966 and, in reality, his decision was probably based on a combination of them all. Quite when he started to plan his retirement – if, indeed, he planned it at all – was only known to himself. But it's reasonable to suppose that the seeds might have been sown when *North By Northwest* proved his ultimate success.

All Grant's films thereafter have a whiff of commercial expediency about them. It's as though Grant was giving himself a five-year plan to exploit the 'Cary Grant' persona purely and simply for the box-office. That is not to suggest that he was not as professional an actor as ever. Quite the reverse. But only once in his remaining six pictures, *Father Goose* (1964), did he deviate from the tried-and-tested 'Cary Grant' formula.

If Grant was using these last five years of his screen career to swell his pension coffers – and no one can know for definite – he was remarkably successful. Five of his last seven films – all, except *North By Northwest* having been produced by his own companies – occupy the top five positions in the list of Cary Grant's biggest grossing films. They are, in order: *Operation Petticoat* (1959), *That Touch Of Mink* (1962), *North By Northwest* (1959), *Charade* (1963) and *Father Goose* (1964). Furthermore, his very last film, *Walk, Don't Run* (1966) comes in at number twelve, which, in a list of 72 movies, is also remarkable. Of these last seven pictures, only *The Grass Is Greener* flopped. He can, therefore, truly claim to have exited the business at the absolute pinnacle of his career. The fact that his consistent successes came right at the end of his career also makes him unique: no screen actor with such a long screen career – 33 years – has ever ended it on such a high note.

There was no gradual decline into lesser, supporting roles. His last hurrah as a screen idol was a golden age of Elizabethan proportions. And just as Elizabeth I transcended mere mortality to become a goddess in her realm, so Grant became a screen deity to his audience, studio heads and colleagues.

At the head of that list of admirers was Tony Curtis, Grant's co-star in *Operation Petticoat*, which Grant made immediately after *North By Northwest* had wrapped. 'I wouldn't take second billing to anyone else back then because I didn't have to,' said Curtis. 'But I made an exception to work with Cary Grant.'

Curtis's attitude reflected how many felt about Grant at this point and his sentiments are echoed by James Coburn, who co-starred in *Charade* four years later. Speaking on BBC television in February 2001, Coburn said: 'I was working on *The Great Escape* when my agent called and said they wanted me to do a film called *Charade* in Paris with Cary Grant. I said to them, "I'll do it. I don't care what the film is about or what the script is like – I'll do it."'

Working with Grant was now regarded as the ultimate accolade. He had been a big star since the late 1930s. His career had ridden every change Tinseltown had endured in this most insecure and uncertain of industries – every fad and fortune in the time he had been out there selling his wares as an actor. After his death, Grant would even be acknowledged as the star of whom other stars were in awe.

On paper, *Operation Petticoat* did not appear to be a worthy successor to *North By Northwest*. Produced by his own company, Granart, for Universal, and scripted by Stanley Shapiro and Maurice Richlin, the film was a jokey Second World War comedy about the commander of a decrepit old submarine (Grant) who is determined to get his vessel back into the war and agrees to the schemes of his wheeler-dealer first officer (Tony Curtis) to do so. Many of these plans go awry and the increasingly farcical plot sees the sub overrun by nurses, children and a goat. Due to a supply shortage the submarine even ends up painted pink.

Grant knew that the film was nothing more than a romp and his role of Admiral Matt Sherman was one that was hardly going to stretch his acting abilities. But he also knew it would be fun to do and his role would see him back in uniform which was something of a rarity for Grant after previous abortive costume outings. Furthermore, it would see him doing the light comedy routine on which his whole career had been founded.

As producer-star, Grant not unnaturally had a big say in casting and concerns of production. For his co-star, Grant wanted Tony Curtis, who had scored such a personal success alongside Jack Lemmon and Marilyn Monroe in Billy Wilder's magnificent *Some Like It Hot*.

In this picture, Curtis had memorably impersonated Grant. Wilder had told Curtis, 'After you have stolen the yachtsman's clothes and you begin your relationship with Marilyn, you have to speak differently – not the English of a Brooklyn musician. What can you do?'

'I can do Cary Grant,' replied Curtis.

Billy Wilder revealed afterwards that, 'I didn't know Tony could do such a perfect imitation – I discussed it with Cary afterwards and he was roaring with laughter. He loved it.' (And so must have Curtis. In Lew Grade's highly popular 1970s ITC series *The Persuaders!*, co-starring Roger Moore, he re-created the impression in two separate episodes.)

To direct the picture, Grant approved Blake Edwards, who had been in films primarily as a writer since 1947, but had been directing only for a comparatively short time. Although he went on to become one of Hollywood's most famous directors of comedy – most notably for the Pink Panther movies starring Grant's friend, Peter Sellers – *Operation Petticoat* was his biggest project up to that point in time. As with Clifford Odets, Stanley Donen and others, it demonstrates, again, just how keen Grant was to back emerging talent.

Everyone involved in the project remembered it as an enjoyable experience. Curtis, who was finally working with his mentor and role model, called it, 'A fabulous experience – there was much to admire in Cary.'

Curtis has never weakened in his vocal appreciation of his idol. In an interview in 2000 he noted that 'even today most of Grant's films have a contemporary feel. Because of this his films continue to be widely popular.' *Operation Petticoat* included, history records.

As Lieutenant Nick Holden, Curtis once again acted and spoke in the manner of Grant, albeit less overtly than in *Some Like It Hot*.

For his part, Grant didn't find his role of Admiral Sherman desperately challenging and he was somewhat taken aback when the *Hollywood Reporter* review identified it as one of the most challenging of his career. 'Though he gets many laughs,' the review went, 'Grant plays an essentially straight role and theatrical pros will recognise it as one of the trickiest acting jobs of his long and brilliant career. Throughout every inch of it, he makes you feel he is a dedicated captain determined to get his ship back to sea. He makes all that follows funny instead of silly.'

Variety agreed: 'Cary Grant is a living lesson in getting laughs without lines. In this film, most of the gags play off him. It is his reaction, always underplayed, that creates or releases the humour.'

Reviews such as these helped the picture enormously and, when it opened at New York City's Radio City Music Hall in December 1959, the queues waiting outside to see it were staggering. As Graham McCann observes, Radio City was 'the largest, most important and prestigious movie theatre at the time in the United States.' Twenty-eight of Grant's movies – a third of his output – played at the theatre. Queues there were the most visible sign of an actor's popularity and as soon as he saw them, Grant knew that he had struck gold with the film. He was proved right when his production deal with Universal guaranteeing him 75 per cent of the profits for *Operation Petticoat* eventually earned him more than four million dollars.

As soon as work was completed on the picture, George Cukor approached Grant to play the lead in *Let's Make Love* opposite Marilyn Monroe.

Grant had enjoyed working with the blonde goddess on *Monkey Business* and had genuinely liked her. But that was before fame had really set out to destroy her. Now she had become impossible to work with and Tony Curtis, who had co-starred with her in *Some Like It Hot*, had had some horrifying tales to tell about her behaviour, which, no doubt, he relayed to Grant during *Operation Petticoat*. Grant turned the film down – as did James Stewart, Rock Hudson, Charlton Heston, Gregory Peck and Yul Brynner after him.

Instead, Grant joined Stanley Donen again for *The Grass Is Greener*, which was shot entirely in England. Based on a play by Hugh and Margaret Williams, whose genteel drawing-room comedies had been successful enough in England, the film, produced by Grant and Donen's Grandon Productions company, told the story of Victor Ryall, an Earl, who opens his stately home to an American millionaire, Charles Delacro, played by Robert Mitchum. Delacro wants to learn how to behave like a gentleman but, in the process, falls in love with Ryall's wife, Hilary, played by Deborah Kerr. In an attempt to make Hilary jealous, Victor pretends to have an affair with a wacky family friend, Hattie, played by Jean Simmons. When that doesn't work, Victor fights a duel with Delacro, in which neither gets badly hurt.

Hilary realises she loves Victor and Delacro goes off with Hattie.

It was quite a lightweight and insubstantial picture. But the cast was impeccable and the actual production immensely enjoyable. Deborah Kerr said of this, her third and final outing with Grant, '*The Grass Is Greener* was a joy to work on, in that the cast included my other most favourite actor, Robert Mitchum, and my very good friend Jean Simmons, whom I have known since she was a very young girl in *Black Narcissus*.'

Although there had been various women reported in Grant's life since his affair with Sophia Loren, the most unusual being the defecting Yugoslavian basketball player Luba, Grant was still, officially, married to Betsy Drake. This caused much confusion in the British press, when Drake accepted his invitation to join him in England while filming there. Rumours spread that a *rapprochement* had taken place and that the Grants were staying together. These rumours were fuelled further when Grant and Drake turned up for a première holding hands. But both adamantly denied reports that they were getting together again and insisted that, while their marriage had failed, they intended remaining extremely good friends.

'We have spent more time together recently since separating than we did before,' confessed Drake to one bemused reporter.

Despite the fun that the cast had in making the movie, doubts about how the film would turn out began to surface pretty quickly. The truth is that the script just wasn't funny or sharp enough.

Noel Coward, whose back-catalogue of songs such as 'The Stately Homes of England' and 'Mad About The Boy' was raided for the soundtrack, and who wrote an original theme for Robert Mitchum and Deborah Kerr (for which he picked up a handsome $15,000), saw a rough cut on 12 June 1960 when helping Stanley Donen score the picture. He wasn't impressed. 'It's too slow and the colour is hideous,' he recorded in his diary. 'These defects, I hope, can be remedied.'

Sadly, they weren't, and the film, when it was released in January 1961 – it had been intended to open for Christmas at New York's Radio City, but had been pulled when the bookers had seen a rough cut – was savaged by the critics. One critic quipped, 'It's too bad Noel Coward couldn't have written the wisecracks, too.' The *Hollywood Reporter* said, 'The stars do not glitter or even glow. Instead of being liberated and propelled by the screenplay, they are chained and sunk. It is one of the year's most disappointing pictures.'

This last comment was a little unfair. Jean Simmons' performance was a joy, while Grant, himself, gave an assuredly humorous performance, which gently disdained Victor's aristocratic demeanour. He was particularly effective in his scenes with Victor's butler, Sellers, played by Moray Watson.

Time Magazine's review, which dismissed the film itself, was more a review of Grant's career and came to a rather bizarre conclusion. 'Actor Grant, as usual, is the mainstay of the show. He's the only funnyman in movie history who has maintained himself for close to thirty years as a ranking romantic star. He wears only one expression: the bland mask of drawing-room comedy. He plays only one part: the well-pressed, elegantly laundered masculine existence that suddenly finds itself splashed by love's old sweet ketchup. About that situation Grant has nothing important to say, no social or moral message to deliver. He creates in a vacuum of values; he is a technician only – but he is a technician of genius.'

The Grass Is Greener flopped and was patently Grant's most disappointing film since the awful *Dream Wife* back in 1953. But it did nothing to dent his own personal standing in Hollywood and still the offers poured in. One of these came from Jack Warner's office offering him the lead in *The Music Man*, which was based on the hit Broadway musical.

Grant turned them all down in favour of *That Touch Of Mink*, which Stanley Shapiro, who had co-written *Operation Petticoat*, and Nate Monaster had written specifically as a 'Cary Grant' vehicle. Robert Arthur, who had produced *Operation Petticoat*, approached Grant with the project as soon as he returned to California from London after *The Grass Is Greener* had wrapped. Grant read the script and recognising a typical 'Cary Grant' banker of the old style – one that could eradicate the disappointment of his last outing – he said 'yes' immediately.

That Touch Of Mink was made for Universal by Grant's company – now called Granley – in association with Stanley Shapiro's company, Nob Hill Productions Incorporated, and Arwin Productions Incorporated. This last company was owned by Doris Day and her husband Martin Melcher who, from 1952 until his death in 1968, was co-producer on all Day's films. If nothing else this proliferation of progenitors showed how the major studios had ceded much of their control to companies owned by the 'talent'. Cary Grant, the first major Hollywood star to become an actor-producer, had been a major player in this seismic shift in Tinseltown's economy. One cannot help but wonder if he took a great deal of pleasure from easing the power away from the studios who, in his opinion – certainly in terms of his relationships with Paramount in his earlier years – had 'done him wrong' to quote his former co-star, Mae West.

Grant had chosen his project wisely. The movie fused the tried-and-tested Grant formula – here he plays a bachelor tycoon – with the familiar Doris Day scenario of a virtuous secretary fighting to maintain her virginity through all kinds of innuendo-laden situations. Many found it a jaded sex comedy, and *Variety* was singularly unimpressed. 'Too often there's a hampering second-hand air about situation and joke,' wrote their critic. 'Throughout, the determination is to keep faith with the American sex mythology at all costs.'

But audiences disagreed. *That Touch Of Mink* was a massive box-office success. For once, though, there is a sense in which Grant is going through the motions. He has been down this avenue many times, and perhaps one can sense that this is one time too many. Once or twice during the film, he even manages to give out the air of being slightly bored with it all – as though it's just another movie, just another film set, just another large pay cheque. This wasn't helped by the fact that he had found a co-star with whom a shared tolerance is the clearest description of their relationship. He made it plain he had enormous respect for Doris Day's talent, and she reciprocated, but more recent industry gossip has suggested that, for all their professional courtesy, Grant and Day hardly sparkled in each other's company.

Financially speaking, the film was particularly satisfying for Grant – *and* for Day. Much comment was made in Hollywood about Day receiving $750,000 to Grant's $600,000. But Grant had negotiated his customary share of the profits, and so, in the end, he made as much from this picture as he'd done from *Operation Petticoat* – which was considerable. In fact, from the two pictures alone, he had pulled in around eight million dollars – a fortune for the time.

While Grant was filming, Cubby Broccoli approached him and asked if he would consider the role of Ian Fleming's James Bond in *Dr. No*. Broccoli, who had split from his former partner Irving Allen, had set up a new company with Canadian producer, Harry Saltzman. Together they had secured the rights to the Bond books.

Grant knew Fleming and greatly enjoyed reading the Bond novels. In many ways, Grant would have made the ideal actor to play 007. One commentator recently said, 'What is James Bond but Cary Grant with a gun?'

But Broccoli knew that it was unlikely his friend would accept the role. For one thing, United Artists, who would release the film, had allocated *Dr. No* a budget of less than one million dollars, which would barely cover Grant's fee. Also, Broccoli and Saltzman were hoping that the film would be the first of a series. Grant had never gone in for sequels, not even with *Topper* back in the late thirties. He certainly wouldn't have signed to a second Bond film. 'As a very important actor and world-class star,' said Broccoli of that time, 'he didn't feel he could lock himself into the Bond character.'

Dana Broccoli added, 'And that meant Cubby and Harry would have to start searching all over again for a James Bond.'

Grant was also aware that he was far too old to set out on what was intended to be a lengthy series. Filming was scheduled to commence on 16 January 1962: two days before Grant's 58th birthday. In terms of Bond, the rest, as they say, is history.

A month after *That Touch Of Mink* opened in July 1962, Betsy Drake finally got a divorce from Grant. Throughout it all, one senses that neither of them had much appetite for it, even if they recognised that divorce was the only sensible thing they could now do. Drake said, 'He appeared to be bored with me. He once told me he didn't want to be married. He showed no interest in any of my friends.' That is a sentiment that would have, no doubt, been shared by Barbara Hutton.

There seems a certain lawyer-speak to Drake's words, which perhaps shade her true feelings. In her later statement to the press, she set a far warmer tone: 'I was always in love with him – and I still am.'

Grant himself said little publicly at the time but, later on, he would, as ever – 'with great gallantry' according to David Niven – accept the blame:

Most women are instinctively wiser and emotionally more mature than men. They know our insecurities. A man rushes about trying to prove himself. It takes him much longer to feel comfortable about getting married.

I'm not proud of my marriage record and it's not the fault of Hollywood. It's down to my own inadequacies. My own inconstancy. My mistrust of constancy. My wives and I were never one. We were competing. When I'm married, I want to be single, and when I'm single, I want to be married.

It is one of the tragedies of Grant's life that he was to have to wait nearly another two decades – and another two wives – before he could finally acknowledge that he had 'learned that love demands nothing and understands all without reproach. I really didn't understand love. I wanted to be, you know, macho.'

In the autumn of 1962, with the ink still drying on his divorce papers, Grant prepared to make his fourth and, ultimately, last picture with Stanley Donen. *Charade*, written by Peter Stone, was to be filmed on location in Paris through the winter of 1962–63 ready for a Christmas 1963 première. No one knew at the time that this was to be the last great Cary Grant movie.

Just before flying to Paris to begin work on the film, Grant journeyed to Philadelphia to see the try-out of a play called *The Fun Couple*. He hadn't gone along with any genuine interest in the actual play itself – which was to flop on Broadway after just three performances – nor to watch its stars, Jane Fonda and Bradford Dillman. There was only one person Grant had gone to watch: a young actress, who had been born Samille Diane Friesen in Washington on 4 January 1939. She was 35 years younger than Grant. To put that into context, when she was born, Grant was working on the set of *Gunga Din* with Douglas Fairbanks Jnr. Grant had first caught sight of her the previous year in the soap opera *Malibu Run*, and had made contact. They had begun dating soon afterwards.

Friesen had, by the time she met Grant, changed her name. She was now called Dyan Cannon and would become the next Mrs Grant. Within five years, having partially destroyed each other, yet in the process managing to create his greatest pride and joy – a baby girl, the only child he would father – he would look back at the impact his fourth wife had had on his life with almost stunned disbelief.

23

'Cary Grant is still tall, dark, handsome, charming, lovable, considerate, dependable, an athletic day and night dream man who lurks deep in most women's fantasies.'

Look Magazine review of *Charade*, December 1963

As a swansong to the Cary Grant-Stanley Donen partnership, *Charade* could scarcely have been bettered. It is a stylish and beguiling comedy murder-mystery. It is also a film in which, for the first and last time, Grant is teamed with Audrey Hepburn in one of the most fascinating screen pairings of the 1960s. The fact that the supporting cast also included Walter Matthau, James Coburn and George Kennedy – all to have great careers and make their own mark on the film industry – that the script was the wittiest script Grant had been given since *His Girl Friday*, and that Donen's direction is impeccable was merely the gravy.

Peter Stone's script was a joy. He wasn't to know it at the time but he was writing the last great part for Cary Grant – or the established 'Cary Grant' persona. Grant's last two pictures would be atypical: in *Father Goose* he departed from his established persona completely and in *Walk, Don't Run* he didn't take the lead role.

Watching *Charade* now, it is as though Stone deliberately set out to anthologise Grant's strengths. Grant is irresistibly romantic; athletic (surely no man of 59, outside a marathon, has ever been seen to run quite as fast as Grant does in the climactic scenes through darkened Parisian streets?); funny; and even ambiguous in making us doubt, as in *Suspicion*, whether he is a good guy or a bad guy right up to the final *dénouement*. One sequence, early on in the picture, even gives Grant the opportunity to indulge in some pantomimic, vaudevillian mugging: compelled to take part in a party game in a nightclub, Grant must retrieve an orange from under the copious chins of an enormous woman and pass it to Audrey Hepburn without ever using his hands. These moments of screen time, when Grant says nothing and relies on facial expressions and body language to get laughs, are among the most memorable and enjoyable of his entire career.

As with *North By Northwest*, the script is beautiful and polished, rather than logical. It certainly doesn't bear too close an inspection and needs to be enjoyed for what it is – a pleasure to the senses and a feel-good experience. The hook on which the confection is hung involves the search for $250,000 (depicted as a huge fortune in the script but considerably less than Grant would earn from the picture) stolen from American agents during the Second World War. Regina 'Reggie' Lambert (Hepburn), a young widow, learns that her recently murdered husband has hidden the cash somewhere and his former buddies are prepared to go to any lengths, even murder, to retrieve it. Into Reggie's life comes the mysterious Peter Joshua (Grant), who may, or may not, be trying to help her.

Charade is clever but baffling and decidedly implausible. Again, as with *North By Northwest*, any attempt to pin it down is to miss the delicious joke and undermine its intended superficiality. The years were creeping by, and Grant, though having not announced his retirement, would clearly not have too many more opportunities as a leading man alongside a pretty young actress. This film therefore, is more a tribute to what Cary Grant created than just another title to add to the many under his belt.

Previous Grant biographers have suggested that *Charade* was an early attempt to jump on the spy bandwagon launched by the first Bond movie, but, given that the film was already shooting in Paris before Bond number one, *Dr. No,* had opened – to initial indifference – in the US, this cannot be correct. Besides, the suggestion insults the originality of the script and the integrity of Peter Stone and Stanley Donen and, ultimately, Grant himself. Grant may have sometimes chosen his roles – such as Roger Adams in *Penny Serenade* – to reflect changing tastes in Hollywood, and he had developed and protected the 'Cary Grant' persona with an assured touch for thirty years, but he had never blatantly jumped on any bandwagon.

One of the most enjoyable aspects of *Charade* is the rapport between Grant and Hepburn: all the more enjoyable in retrospect since Hepburn was his last leading lady in the class of Katharine Hepburn, Ingrid Bergman and Grace Kelly. 'Cary and Audrey had such chemistry,' said their co-star James Coburn. 'If you watch that movie today there's so much chemistry going backwards and forwards between them.'

No one, with the possible exception of Donen, had realised just how effective the chemistry between the actors would be and even Donen had to admit that the result exceeded his expectation.

Hepburn came to the film with an impressive movie history. She had been born Edda van Heemstra Hepburn-Ruston on 4 May 1929 in Belgium, the daughter of an English banker and Dutch baroness. Having begun her career in musicals and a few tiny roles in European films, her big break came when she was chosen by Colette – the author of *Gigi* – to star in the stage adaptation.

Her rise in Hollywood was rapid. She won her first Oscar for *Roman Holiday* (1953), in which she starred with Gregory Peck, who played the role Grant had turned down. By the time of *Charade* she was established as one of Hollywood's most intelligent and cultivated leading ladies – qualities that Grant admired even before working with her.

Donen, who had previously directed Hepburn in *Funny Face* (1957), recalled that the rapport between her and Grant was immediate. 'Except for *Kiss Them For Me* with Jayne Mansfield, where none of us knew each other very well, this was the first time I'd made a film with Cary where he had not worked with the leading lady before. With both Ingrid Bergman and Deborah Kerr, he already had long-established relationships of trust and I was the new person in the group, the outsider. Here, Audrey had worked with me before: we had the relationship and they both started out using me as their common bridge. But they were both absolute professionals and quickly developed a relationship and things went very well. It was as if they had worked together many times before.'

Hepburn agreed with Donen's assessment, commenting, 'I have never had so confident a feeling about a movie as I did about *Charade* after the first day of shooting.'

When work began on the film, Grant wasn't showing any real signs of having reached the age of 59. True, his hair was almost totally grey now, but he still managed to look about fifteen years younger than he was. The only giveaway of the passing years, and one that Grant was aware of before anyone else, was that his voice on a soundtrack was beginning to betray signs of ageing. It was becoming, almost imperceptibly, huskier; more gravelly and, basically, middle-aged. This is only evident in scattered parts of the film – although Grant, ever the perfectionist, picked it up when watching the daily rushes – and it added to, rather than detracting from his following movie *Father Goose,* where he plays a cantankerous ageing drunkard. Only in *Walk, Don't Run* did it become more obvious – and by then, it no longer mattered.

Grant expressed more concern over his playing Hepburn's love interest than anything to do with his voice. He might well have appeared younger than his years, but he, and, he felt, his public, recognised there was a 25-year gap between their ages. Grant was concerned that every one of those 25 years would show when they were projected onto cinema screens and were the size of houses.

Nearly forty years later, in 2001, Peter Stone said, 'Cary had problems with the script. He said, "I'm thirty years older than Audrey and I don't think it's seemly of me to chase her. So what I would like you to do is to have her chase me." He made me change the entire dynamic of the characters to make Audrey the aggressor. So she chased him and he tried to dissuade her. She pursued him and sat in his lap. She found him irresistible and ultimately he was worn down by her.'

'Cary was extremely sensitive about our age difference,' recalled Hepburn. 'He was afraid he would be accused of cradle-snatching if we had a full-blown romance. He just had this innate sense of good taste. The writer, Peter Stone, was wonderful about it. He changed his script to reflect Cary's concerns. He made it even funnier.'

Good taste notwithstanding, it is certainly ironic – not to say hypocritical – for Grant to have shown such concerns. It is difficult to reconcile his fretting over being regarded as a dirty old man by cinema-goers for making fictional love to the 34-year-old Audrey Hepburn on celluloid, with his being perfectly content to make genuine love to the 24-year-old Dyan Cannon in real life.

On that personal front, he said, 'I'm aware of the difference in our ages and the talk about it. But it's Dyan I'm interested in, not her age. She has brains, maturity and wit. What more could you want in a woman?' Certainly not a birth certificate showing her to be middle-aged, it would seem.

Audrey Hepburn also had brains, maturity and wit, both on and off screen – and was ten years older than Cannon. Indeed, worrying about romancing Hepburn on screen was clear double standards, but Grant was good at protecting his *alter ego*. From the moment he shed Archie Leach in favour of Cary Grant, not for a minute – if one discounts his LSD experimentation phase – did he let the public mask slip. If he had, there would have been so many disappointed fans.

In 1963, he had been working in Hollywood for more than 30 years.

For almost all that time he had been a major star and for much of it he had been Hollywood's biggest star. And Grant had achieved that success and longevity largely through his understanding of what he had created, plus his own business acumen.

Grant was perfectly capable of separating what Cary Grant did in private from what he did on screen. *He* saw no conflict there – no hypocrisy. He told Leslie Caron, his co-star on his next movie, *Father Goose,* 'Let the public and the press know nothing but your public self. A star is best left mysterious. Just show your work on the screen and let the publicity people do the rest.'

It could be argued that Grant's asking Peter Stone to alter the script to accommodate his age benefited the audience as much as himself, by presenting a better, more authentic relationship between the two stars. By shifting the emphasis, so that Hepburn is pursuing Grant – again a neat reflection of Grant's previous screen work in which he was often seduced by women – Stone gave *Charade*'s romantic elements a dark undertone. 'Reggie', still in her widow's weeds, is the sexual predator as well as the potential victim of the conspirators. Thus Hepburn's motivation throughout the picture is just as ambiguous as Grant's, adding an extra dimension to the puzzles within puzzles that Stone's screenplay revels in.

The result was the opposite of *North By Northwest.* If Hitchcock had managed the ultimate de-construction of 'Cary Grant', Donen and Stone now created the supreme cinematic commemoration of everything that had made him great. Once over his initial worries about age and voice, he revelled in the playful, teasing script. 'It was a question of rapport,' said Peter Stone. 'They hit it off immediately in terms of how to play it.'

HEPBURN: Uh-uh – here it comes. The fatherly talk. You forget I'm already a widow.

GRANT: So was Juliet. At fifteen.

HEPBURN: I'm not fifteen.

GRANT: Well, there's your trouble right there. You're too *old* for me.

HEPBURN: Why can't you be serious?

GRANT: There – you just said an 'orrible word.

HEPBURN: What?

GRANT: 'Serious'. When a man gets to be my age, that's the last

HEPBURN: word he ever wants to hear. I don't want to be serious. And I especially don't want *you* to be.

HEPBURN: Okay. I'll tell you what. We'll just sit around all day being frivolous – how about that? (She begins kissing him.)

GRANT: Now please, Reggie – cut it out.

HEPBURN: Okay.

GRANT: What are you doing?

HEPBURN: Cutting it out.

GRANT: Who told you to do that?

HEPBURN: *You* did.

GRANT: But I'm not through complaining, yet...

Other lines and exchanges, many a throw-back to Grant's earlier screwball comedies of the thirties and early forties, are equally sparkling, and Grant ad-libs like mad throughout the whole film.

He makes a clever reference to the movie version of *My Fair Lady*, which Hepburn was due to make straight after *Charade*. 'We're here,' he says, escorting her to her hotel room. 'Where?' she asks. 'On the street where you live.'

Perhaps the most telling line of all comes from Hepburn when, leaning against her hotel room door, she gazes at him adoringly. 'Do you know what's wrong with you? *Nothing,*' she sighs, thereby summing up not only her character's feelings for Grant's character in the film, but, seemingly, those of her entire sex – at least, those who hadn't been married to him.

The result is that the verbal interplay between Grant and Hepburn, a glorious fusing of their ad-libs and Stone's witty dialogue, ensures that *Charade* justifies Richard Schickel's assessment of it as 'as good a Hitchcock film as anyone not named Hitchcock ever made'.

'Audrey and I had a wonderful time making *Charade*, and I think it shows,' said Grant of that time.

And indeed it does, for there is hardly a film in which he had appeared before this where he had been more relaxed both on and off screen, even enjoying sending himself up. In one famous incident, he even gave credence to his supposed catchphrase 'Judy, Judy, Judy'. For a long time, Grant resolutely denied that he had ever uttered the name 'Judy' on screen. This wasn't true because in his very first screen appearance, in *Singapore Sue* in 1931, he called Anna Chang's character 'Judy' on screen and, in *The Eagle and the Hawk* in 1939, Grant's character, Jeff Carter, addressed Judith (Rita Hayworth) as 'Judy'. Nevertheless, it was true he had never said 'Judy, Judy, Judy' but, despite Grant's protests, impressionists had used the catchphrase to symbolise him from *The Eagle and the Hawk* onwards.

It became as famous – and as inaccurate – as Mae West's supposed 'Come up and see me some time'.

At the end of the last day of shooting on *Charade,* Grant turned to the camera and said, 'Judy, Judy, Judy – *there*, now you've got it on film!'

Even before the film had opened, the buzz in the industry was that the film was one of Cary Grant's best ever and that the rapport between himself and Audrey Hepburn was electrifying. Hollywood being Hollywood, there were frenzied attempts to re-team them as soon as possible. Howard Hawks was desperate to cast them in *Man's Favorite Sport*, a re-run of ideas from *Bringing Up Baby*, while Jack Warner implored Grant to play Professor Higgins to Hepburn's Eliza Doolittle in *My Fair Lady*. In the event, Hawks had to settle for Rock Hudson – not quite what he'd been looking for – while Grant, correctly, insisted that no one could play Higgins except Rex Harrison. Interestingly, Grant turned down Hawks' offer of *Man's Favorite Sport* by saying, 'I'm not going to play opposite a young girl.' Clearly, *Charade* had done nothing to dispel his fears about growing old on-screen. Hawks was later to regard that remark as prophetic.

Sadly, or maybe not, all attempts to re-team Grant and Hepburn came to nothing. Perhaps it was for the best. Anything they achieved together thereafter would only serve to reduce the value of what went before, in *Charade*. One of the chief reasons it works so well today, is that their screen union has a remarkable freshness about it – an underplayed, under-used coming together of two stars. A unique, indefinable cinematic alchemy is also very difficult to recapture and failure could also damage what had gone before.

When the film opened at Christmas in 1963 it broke all existing box-office records at Radio City in New York, taking more than $175,000 in its first week alone. And the critics were, largely, euphoric. *Look Magazine*, while clearly having failed to notice Grant's grey hair, was typical: 'He is still tall, dark, handsome, an athletic day and night dream man who lurks deep in most women's fantasies.'

Even so, there were occasional nasty elements in *Charade*'s violent moments that were indicative of the way Hollywood was moving and which summed up for Grant everything he disliked about the direction his industry was taking. As the critic Arthur Knight noted: 'One hesitates to be uncharitable to a film that seeks only to provide a little innocent merriment and make a pot of money. Of itself, it is a stylish and amusing melodrama, but in the context of the bloodlust that seems unloosed in our land, it is as sinister as the villains who stalk Miss Hepburn through the cobbled streets of Paris.'

Cary Grant found himself agreeing with such sentiments. Given that the film opened exactly a month after the assassination of John F. Kennedy, whom Grant had known – and who had once said he believed Grant would be his perfect *alter ego* – he was extremely aware of, and sensitive to, the brutalisation of movies that was beginning to happen at this time.

Indeed, Kennedy's assassination had posed a problem for Universal, who were distributing *Charade*. Post-production on the film had been completed by the autumn of 1963 in readiness for its scheduled Christmas Day opening. But the day after Kennedy was shot on 22 November, a Universal executive, viewing the film, was horrified by the following exchange between Grant and Audrey Hepburn in a key scene on the banks of the River Seine.

HEPBURN: We've got to do something. I mean, any minute now we could be assassinated. Would you do anything like that?

GRANT: What? Assassinate someone?

HEPBURN: No – swing down from there on a rope to save the woman you love. Like the Hunchback of Notre Dame.

Grant glances round and sees the Notre Dame cathedral across the river behind him and mutters 'Oh, who put *that* there . . . ?'

The flip use of 'assassinated' was perfectly in keeping with the witty Kiss-Kiss-Bang-Bang style of Peter Stone's screenplay for *Charade* and, in a wider context, indicative of the way western society and Hollywood – whether as a shaper or reflector of that society – was moving. Even so, Universal balked at risking negative comment that could harm the box-office and insisted the words had to be removed from the final print. This left Stanley Donen just two options: either the entire scene should be cut from the picture, which nobody wanted, or

Grant and Hepburn had to re-dub the offending section.

So, less than a month before the film opened, Grant and Hepburn were recalled to the production to re-record this section of dialogue. Peter Stone substituted 'assassinated' with 'eliminated' as having the same number of syllables as the offending words. The doctoring was only partially successful, however, and viewing the film in retrospect, the dubbing is painfully obvious.

Charade was always going to be a massive hit but, ironically, Kennedy's assassination probably helped it further. Just as the surprise British hit *The Full Monty* benefited from opening in the week Princess Diana died in 1997, its feel-good, life-affirming script helping to assuage national and international mourning, so *Charade*'s classy nonsense helped take shocked Americans' minds off the murder of their president.

The irony wasn't lost on Grant, whose ambivalence about Hollywood really began to become much more apparent from 1964 onwards.

For all the film's success, Grant was not only feeling his age, he was also feeling increasingly out of tune with the new Hollywood. And he was convinced the Golden Age was over.

Once *Charade* had been launched successfully, Grant flew to England for an extended break in the New Year of 1964, where he celebrated his 60th birthday without fuss. He spent a fortnight in Bristol, spending time with Elsie and meeting up with his extended family. 'I'm like the salmon,' he told local reporters. 'Or is it the elephant? I always come back to the spawning ground. I love Bristol, and always have done.'

Elsie was, by this time, over halfway through her eighties but, in spite of the years she had spent incarcerated, or maybe in defiance of them, her mental faculties showed no signs of succumbing to great age. If anything, she was more feisty than ever and one famous exchange between mother and son during this period was often repeated by Grant:

'We were driving along once and she said, "Archie, why don't you do something about your hair?" and I asked her why, what was wrong with it? She said I should dye it, that everyone was doing it these days. I said, "Well, I'm not doing it." She finally said that my hair made *her* look old!'

Gossip columnists, particularly those Stateside, were again linking

Grant with the young actress, Dyan Cannon. Grant, unavoidably aware of the age difference and also wary of commitment following three failed marriages, was determined to rush nothing. He remained circumspect throughout 1964, allowing his affair with Cannon to filter into the public consciousness slowly. Cannon's work during this period – she was touring the USA in the musical *How To Succeed In Business Without Really Trying* – kept them apart during the weeks, and this gave them space to consider how they really felt about each other. Certainly, when Grant visited Bristol in February 1964 – and again for a shorter visit just two months later – Cannon did not accompany him.

While in Bristol, Grant took Elsie to the Hippodrome to watch the annual pantomime. Grant had never lost his appreciation for British comedy and on his many trips to London after the war, he would make a point of seeing performers like Richard Herne, Max Miller, Arthur Haynes, Peter Sellers and Harry Worth. He was a particular fan of the unique Sid Field and, when Field went to Hollywood in 1948, Grant, along with Bob Hope, Jack Benny, Danny Kaye and Charlie Chaplin, fêted him. At a dinner held in Field's honour at the Hollywood Masquers Club, Grant performed an old music-hall routine – billing himself as 'Archie Leach' – especially for Field.

Starring in the Hippodrome's 1963–64 pantomime were Eric Morecambe and Ernie Wise. Morecambe and Wise had had a hit show on Lew Grade's ATV since 1961 and were establishing themselves as Britain's best-ever double-act by 1964. Grant went backstage to congratulate them after the performance. It was a mutual appreciation because Grant was not only one of Eric's heroes but, as Ernie Wise remarked, 'There was a part of Eric that longed to be a sort of Cary Grant figure and part of him that resented being the comic while the straight man had the style.'

Grant and Morecambe began a 20-year friendship that ended only with the comedian's death in 1984. During this period Eric Morecambe became widely regarded as the greatest British comedian of the twentieth century. Grant, as a great admirer, would have probably gone along with that.

When he returned to Hollywood in the spring of 1964, Dyan Cannon began spending more time with him and their relationship gradually deepened, even if Grant continued to prevaricate throughout the summer while he was filming his penultimate movie, *Father Goose*.

This film, again scripted by Peter Stone, together with Frank Tarloff, was a definite departure for Grant. 'I play an unshaven old grey-haired sot in sloppy denims,' he remarked of his character, Walter Eckland, a cantankerous drunk who is an unwilling look-out in the Pacific during the Second World War. He is forced, by circumstance, to look after a young Frenchwoman and a gaggle of refugee schoolchildren.

Although it would be unfair to accuse the film of being derivative, the script, based on the story *A Place Of Dragons* by S.H. Barnett, used elements similar to those found in *The African Queen* and *South Pacific*. Derivative or not, Stone and Tarloff did an excellent job and were awarded with the Oscar for best screenplay.

As usual, the film was produced by Grant's own company – called Granox Company Productions this time – for Universal. And in an interview during production, he left no one in any doubt just how much a hands-on producer he really was.

'I am the producer,' he stated. 'The executive producer, more accurately – because I hire a producer. I get the best director I can find. I obtain the service of an excellent scriptwriter and request his presence on the set in order to be on the scene if changes-for-the-better are necessary. I work along with a film editor, but I have the last word on the editing. Naturally, I choose the story and the cast. And I have no financial problems – Universal furnishes the money.'

For his leading lady, Grant hired 33-year-old Leslie Caron, the French leading lady and dancer who had previously found success in *An American In Paris* (1951) and *Gigi* (1958). His hiring of Caron appears, superficially, to contradict his telling Howard Hawks that he didn't want to play opposite younger women, particularly since Caron was more or less the same age as Audrey Hepburn.

That apart, Grant believed he had chosen his story well. By playing Eckland as written – grey, unkempt and with stubble – Grant was highlighting his age rather than trying to deflect attention away from it. Thus, the film can be seen not so much as an attempt by Grant to get away from his established image, as some writers have claimed – he is still, very much, the old, assured 'Cary Grant' under the stubble and grubby denims – but a more subtle experiment in seeing how 'Cary Grant' might be adapted to accommodate the fact he was getting older.

Central to the film were the children and Leslie Caron was struck by how much Grant enjoyed working with them.

'There were lots of children on the picture and he was very interested in them,' she recalled some time later. 'He was always asking me about mine and how I raised them. He had a very paternal attitude towards children. It was very touching.'

One of the biggest regrets of Grant's life was the fact that in three marriages he hadn't produced any offspring. He had told Irene Dunne during the shooting of *Penny Serenade* – the theme of which had been a couple's inability to have children – that, 'I know what my children are going to look like. They're going to be blond with brown eyes.'

At the start of his marriage to Barbara Hutton, Grant fully expected to have children and afterwards claimed the fact that they didn't was because, as he put it, 'Barbara was cut to ribbons long before I knew her.'

His long marriage to Betsy Drake had also proved childless and in 1962, with his marriage to Drake finally over, Grant publicly noted how Grace Kelly and Eva Marie Saint 'went on raising happy and beautiful children', adding, somewhat wistfully, 'I wish I could say the same.'

As we know, the closest he had experienced fatherhood was with Hutton's son, Lance. The dedication was mutual, Lance always calling Grant 'The General'. He appeared to regard him with more affection than his own father. Significantly, it was at Lance's own wedding in November 1964 that Grant and Cannon made a very public appearance together, deliberately displaying their own closeness to the world's media.

Throughout the latter part of 1964, Grant – with reason – was unusually anxious about how the public would accept *Father Goose*, even though he talked the picture up in endless interviews: 'I've often played the part of a spiritual bum,' he said, 'but this is the first time I've looked like one.'

Despite his confident assurance as a producer, Grant was increasingly concerned about his screen image and had openly raised the possibility of his retiring in an interview with Roderick Mann, published in the *Sunday Express* in June 1964. 'To be honest with you,' he said, 'I don't know what I'll do. Maybe I'll quit.'

Grant's uncertainty and ambivalence towards his career was becoming well known in Hollywood. William Goldman discusses his lack of self-confidence in *Adventures In The Screentrade*. 'A man who worked with Cary Grant,' wrote Goldman, 'told me: "Cary was at his peak. I did two pictures with him and both times it was the same fight: he was convinced he had no charm and couldn't do a lot of the scenes because the audience wouldn't buy him. It was madness. Here he was, maybe the most charming actor ever, and it was like pulling teeth. He was absolutely certain his charm had gone."'

On the face of it, Grant's fears about *Father Goose* appeared groundless. When it opened at Radio City at Christmas 1964, it broke the box-office record he had already set a year earlier with *Charade*. It took more than $210,000 in its first week alone. This prompted *Time* to comment mischievously, 'Cary Grant is now so rich he could join NATO.'

For once, though, the critics were not so impressed with a Cary Grant film, even if they could appreciate his attempts to present something a little different. One wrote, 'Grant makes a strong effort, partly successful, to subdue his usually sleek self in the whiskery curmudgeon; even when the old gloss shines through, he is still a very skilful performer.' But the critic Arthur Knight, who had been so perceptive about the undercurrent of nastiness in *Charade*, again put his finger on just what was wrong with the film. 'Cary Grant wrings what there is to be wrung from the role, but never quite enough to conceal the fact that *Father Goose* is a waste of his talent and the audience's time.'

For all the success of *Father Goose* at the box-office, Grant's instincts told him that roles like Walter Eckland were not what the public expected, or wanted. 'Cary Grant' was a product with a specific image. His dilemma was to know how to deal with the problem, as he was growing too old to play the roles for which the audiences had come to idolise him. There was genuine conflict here, and his comment to Roderick Mann ('I don't know what I'll do . . .') was heartfelt.

'I think he was very disappointed when the public made it clear they didn't want Cary Grant with a beard and sloppy and saying a few dirty words,' says Leslie Caron. 'That was very upsetting for him and he gave up soon after that and retired.'

The artistic failure of *Father Goose* – or what Grant perceived as its failure – was not the only catalyst in Grant's withdrawal from film-making. In the years following his last film, *Walk, Don't Run,* he would, typically, cite many different reasons, some jokey, others more reflective, for his decision to quit. Right up to the end, Grant often attempted to deflect too close an inspection of his inner motivation for quitting with smoke and mirrors, charmingly disarming many probing questions with the facile comment, 'I was tired of tripping over cables.'

At least he had his burgeoning relationship with Dyan Cannon to soften any disappointment with *Father Goose* – bearing in mind that his disappointment can't have been too extreme considering it was his 71st film – and he and Cannon flew to England straight after it opened to spend New Year 1965 in Bristol.

This visit was one of the happiest and most relaxed Grant had ever spent and was made more so because of how well Elsie and Dyan Cannon got on. In contrast to the uncertainties of his career back in Hollywood, Grant found he could take it easy and, in Cannon, he believed he had found someone he could take it easy *with*. For the first time in over thirty years, Grant felt truly detached from – and uninterested in – his movie career.

When he was with Cannon, Grant truly did not feel the 35-year age difference. Her youth and vitality were feeding his innate robustness and, if anything, he had started looking better off-screen than on. His friends were also commenting on how Cannon was enticing Grant out of his customary reclusiveness.

Certainly, Grant's reluctance to consider entering into a fourth marriage began melting away in the first part of 1965, no doubt assisted by Cannon's assuring him that she wanted a child every bit as much as he did.

On 22 July 1965, in a simple ceremony – 'marriage is a very private affair,' Grant said afterwards, 'and I prefer to do things quietly, without fanfare or intrusion' – he and Cannon were married in Las Vegas by a Justice of the Peace, James Prennen. Grant was 61 and Cannon was 26. She was, by a wide margin, nearer to the age that Virginia Cherrill had been when she had married Grant in 1934, than to Grant's current age.

Perhaps a little predictably, bearing in mind his record, the marriage was to last just three years. Its breakdown and subsequent divorce were to be the most acrimonious of all Grant's marital failures and would expose him to deeply embarrassing public humiliation.

But at least it gave him the one thing he had always wanted – a child of his own.

24

> 'Cary told me that he had stopped making movies because one day he was sitting in his trailer and heard a conversation outside which was aimed for him to hear. And it was completely sycophantic. He decided to get out. It was time.'

> Roger Moore

If there is one thing that actors are not good at, it's knowing when to quit – even the great ones.

Days before his death in May 2000, the 96-year-old Sir John Gielgud was reportedly bemoaning lack of job offers while Lord Olivier, gravely ill, threatened to eradicate the great memories of his career by appearing on British television in June 1987 to quaver through snippets of poetry. As the British comedian Kenneth Williams, who had worked with Olivier in his prime, rightly noted, it was 'depressing' and a 'dreadful exhibition of senility', which made Olivier look 'like some poor old sod being made to audition'.

In Hollywood, the pressure to carry on has, if anything, always been greater. Bette Davis, riddled with cancer for so long that she seemed to visibly diminish in the course of a single interview, accepted a succession of largely demeaning parts in her last two decades. Even Grant's former co-star, the admired and loved James Stewart, was reduced to bland fare like *Airport '77* and *The Magic Of Lassie* by the mid-seventies.

And those who had sensibly 'retired' from the screen could not resist a Norma Desmond-style comeback. James Cagney's swan song, *Ragtime* (1981), was his first movie in two decades and proved a big mistake. Mae West's returns in controversial *Myra Breckinridge* (1970) and the sleazy *Sextette* (1978), were so grotesque that audiences averted their eyes from the screen.

Marlene Dietrich, another former co-star of Grant's, virtually had to be supported to get her way through her final concerts. Frank Sinatra, yet another Grant co-star, and arguably, the greatest American singer of the twentieth century, became a pale shadow of himself during twenty years of 'farewell' tours.

Grant's refusal to attempt an unnatural prolongation of his career marks him out as unique in Hollywood history. By not only retiring at the peak of his career, but remaining in retirement until his death some two decades later, Grant ensured that his decline into old age was not recorded for posterity. His last films don't invoke in us pity. There is no tragic last screen outing to groan and wince over. Conversely, by watching Bette Davis's films in chronological order, one can observe the cancer eating her gradually down to nothing – year by year, film by film.

Like James Dean and Marilyn Monroe, the image of himself that Cary Grant left to cineastes was of a man forever in his prime – immortal. Unlike Dean and Monroe, he didn't have to die young and tragically to do so.

Quite when Grant decided that *Walk, Don't Run,* released in the summer of 1966, would be his last film – if, indeed, he actually did – and what his precise reasons for doing so were, only he ever knew. But to try and understand the dynamics of his retirement, we must examine the events of 1965 and 1966 in some detail.

Cary Grant's romance with Dyan Cannon was a gossip columnist's dream in the mid-sixties. Here was this matinée idol from Tinseltown's golden era falling in love with a girl less than half his own age who, in her miniskirts and boots, epitomised the Swinging Sixties.

If their affair was the talk of Hollywood, Grant knew that news of their marriage would be a sensation. This – coupled with his long-standing aversion to letting the press into his private life – was the reason he had married Cannon in private in Las Vegas on 22 July, and why he had asked for, and received, a promise from the Justice of the Peace, who had conducted the brief ceremony, James Prennen, to tell no one for 30 days.

Prennen was as good as his word and when Grant and Cannon arrived in Bristol on 30 July, no one outside Grant's inner circle knew they were man and wife.

Grant had not tried to hide his visit to his homeland: he advertised in the personal columns of *The Times*, using his own name, for a house to rent in the Bristol area. He and Cannon were chauffeured to Bristol in his black and gold Rolls-Royce with personalised plate, CG1. In doing this, we can assume Grant was intent on a double-bluff: by drawing attention to the visit, he was making it look like just another of his visits 'home' and therefore unimportant. Certainly, when he and Cannon arrived in Bristol, there was only a token interest from the press.

Booking into Bristol's Royal Hotel, it is also obvious that they were maintaining the charade of their not being married. He booked into the Churchill Suite – his customary policy whenever he stayed there – and Cannon took another room further along the corridor. So far, so good.

Then Grant did something inexplicable and entirely out of character. He blew the gaff to the press himself in an interview he gave to Roderick Mann.

Why he did this will never be known. Perhaps the rather quiet reception from the phlegmatic city of his birth rather disappointed him, and in an unusually careless moment he decided to release his news and stir up some reaction. Or maybe he suddenly felt he was in the right place to break the news – at 'home'. Definitely, his swearing James Prennen to a 30-days' silence and his booking separate hotel rooms demonstrate strongly that he never intended to give the game away.

His explanation to Mann was as follows: 'I'm only telling you now because you asked me. So many people have been hinting that we were thinking about marrying, were about to marry or were actually married, but nobody came right out and asked.' That's quite hard to swallow, because he had had plenty of time to equip himself with a response to this question should someone have come 'right out and asked' long before arriving back in Bristol, even if it had meant being a little frugal with the truth. One thing he must have known; *someone* was sooner or later going to pose the question.

As Grant became older and felt increasingly detached from Hollywood, it's clear he felt more connected with Bristol. This cannot be put down merely to the idealised romantic nostalgia that we're all prone to with advancing years. Grant's had been a wretched childhood in so many ways and his memories of Bristol were surely of emotional isolation and sadness. As a child, he had sat by the docks yearning for the day when he would make his own escape; as a teenager he had created the opportunity to escape via Bob Pender; and aged eighteen, he had rejected the nation of his birth in favour of the nation where he was to re-invent himself. Bristol should have held few memories for a man who had enjoyed so much success once having rejected it and all it contained of his past.

Yet, there is clear evidence that his feelings for the city became increasingly warmer from the late 1950s onwards. On one visit in the 1960s he even revisited the Fairfield Grammar School – a place one would think, all considered, he would not want to go near ever again. He didn't go back alone, opting to take a couple of Bristol friends: one of whom was Jack Garland, a press photographer. Unannounced, Grant and friends entered the school, with the classes in session, and Grant began mucking about, laying the tables for lunch while Garland snapped away. The visit, understandably, caused a sensation and when one teacher enthused, 'I've never met a film star before,' Grant blithely replied, 'Haven't you? Come over to Hollywood – they're two a penny, there.'

He also remarked to some pupils, 'I was chucked out of this school – goodness knows why.'

As publicity stunts, such visits worked extremely well – although, on this occasion, the irritated headmaster was overheard to ask Grant, 'Who gave you permission to do this?' – and proved how much he was willing to embrace the press so long as it was on his own terms.

His willingness to be identified as a son of Bristol throughout the 1960s and 1970s is also illuminating. Even in his sixties, Grant was still in search of his true identity. It is as though Grant, having been invented by Archie Leach all those years ago, was now returning the favour by re-inventing a more palatable past for Archie. Grant was transforming Bristol into a womb into which he could crawl to escape the outside world – significantly now, at the close of his career and the inevitable onslaught of age. Interestingly, once the need to perpetuate 'Cary Grant' was less compelling, he allowed Archie to peep out occasionally, even if he never quite had the courage to uncork the bottle into which he had banished Archie, or perhaps the bottle was tossed away long ago making the notion an impossible one.

Thus, it is likely that Grant had been caught up in the excitement of marriage to his pretty, vivacious young wife. Feeling safe in his Bristol 'womb', he broke the news to a journalist – 'a valued friend' as Grant put it – on pure impulse. The alternative – that he had planned his announcement in Bristol all along, seems merely perverse and, frankly, unbelievable.

Predictably, once the news was out, journalists besieged the Royal Hotel in a scrum not unlike the one parodied in *His Girl Friday*, with every photographer desperate to get that first, lucrative shot of Mr and Mrs Cary Grant together.

For once, the Bristol media – usually fastidious in giving Grant his space whenever he was in town – joined in the hunt, frequently using their local knowledge to trump their national and international colleagues in the cat-and-mouse chase that ensued whenever Grant and Cannon ventured outside the hotel. A reporter from the *Western Daily Press* on one famous occasion realised that the Grants were in a lift and ran up the staircase in an attempt to beat it.

The people of Bristol were appalled and Lionel Godfrey, in his excellent *Cary Grant: The Light Touch,* relayed how one local man, H.R.C. Buston, castigated the behaviour of the local press in the letters page of the *Western Daily Press:*

> We all appreciate that Cary Grant is a Bristolian and that to a certain extent he owes his popularity to a public demand in general, but surely this continual hounding of a man who is trying to spend a while in this city for the purpose of visiting his ageing mother is carrying reporting too far.
>
> How degrading to read that your man bounded up the stairs of the hotel in an effort to beat the lift. From this I can assume that he must be extremely fit or rather young in age and the heyday of Cary Grant is something that his parents related to him with a certain amount of pride.
>
> You have had your story that he is here in Bristol. Now forget it. The public would certainly like to. How nice it would be if he was allowed to walk through the town and acknowledge the nods and smiles of admiring people without the fear of molestation from over-zealous reporters. Let him, his wife and family try to live a normal life for a little while.

Grant, who read the letter, appreciated both Buston's sentiments and the underlying wit with which he had written of the reporter sprinting up the stairs. He sent Buston a telegram on behalf of himself and Cannon. A decade later, Grant thanked Buston again when Buston spotted him in Marks and Spencer in Bristol and introduced himself.

While under siege from reporters, Grant and Cannon *did* manage to snatch a visit to Bristol Zoo and Grant invited along the local photographer Jack Garland to take an 'official' honeymoon photo of the newly-weds. The picture of them, taken in the rain, with a laughing Cannon sheltering under a man's overcoat, may have been staged, but there's a wonderful sense of relaxed informality about it, which suggests that this would be the marriage in which Grant would find inner contentment.

They also managed a private trip to Grant's mother Elsie, who had recently been moved to Chesterfield Nursing Home in Clifton at Grant's insistence. He believed that, at 87, she would be better off being looked after. This is not to suggest that Elsie had suddenly become decrepit. She had, in fact, lost none of her vigour and Dyan Cannon recalls her as being 'incredible, with a psyche that had the strength of a twenty-mule team.'

Cannon's liking of Elsie was reciprocated. Of all Grant's wives she met, Cannon seems to be the one she preferred. Cannon was certainly an attractive personality. A vibrant young person who exuded health and good humour and who had none of Virginia Cherrill's selfishness, Barbara Hutton's poor-little-rich-girl insecurities, or Betsy Drake's psycho-babble and alternative, more spiritual, approach to life.

But if Dyan Cannon and Elsie adored each other, there were still underlying fault-lines in the relationship between mother and son. And most, if not all, of the emotional problems rested with the son these days.

It was now thirty years since Elsie had been released from the Fishponds mental institution and, in old age, the trauma of those 'lost' years no longer troubled her to any great extent. Whatever awkwardness she and Grant had had in coming to terms with their situation once reunited, it is clear that none of the awkwardness now lingered on her side.

So why did Grant still find it impossible to come to terms with his past, even now? It's certainly true he found it difficult to reconcile Elias's role in the enforced committal of Elsie to Fishponds with the other, positive, memories he had of his father and Elias's premature death robbed him of the opportunity of ever questioning his father directly about his motives.

It's also possible – indeed, highly probable – that Grant and Elsie didn't discuss Elias much at all. The private conversations between Grant and his mother in the years after her release were, and will remain, known only to themselves. But it's reasonable to suppose that the spectre of what Elias had done to Elsie 50 years earlier was so terrible that neither Grant nor his mother felt willing or able to talk about it.

Furthermore, in the few public statements Grant *did* make about his father, it's clear he retained persistent doubts about precisely *who* was to blame for his miserable childhood. This meant that Grant was destined never to repair fully the damage from his childhood, nor to find complete inner contentment. However much superficial smiles and good humour prevailed when Hollywood collided with Bristol, denial reigned in Grant's psyche and the objective outsider, looking at their relationship, *must* doubt the depth of Grant's unconditional love for his mother.

Elsie's love for Grant is a different matter altogether. It is certainly significant that she was now calling him Archie and doubly significant that he never corrected her, even though he had legally been called Cary Grant for 20 years. Archie and Cary were still being kept apart in his mind: he could – and did – divorce them utterly when it suited him. Elsie no longer could. To her, Cary and Archie were one and the same. She didn't distinguish between them.

All the evidence suggests that Elsie adored her only child, whatever he was called, and looked forward immensely to his visits. 'She'd dress up and sit by my office and look along the corridor toward the front door,' said Clarice Earl, a matron at the Chesterfield Nursing Home, when Elsie was a resident there. 'When she saw him, she'd give a little skip and throw up her arms to greet him.'

On the surface, Grant was a loving son, even if this was mostly achieved by going through the motions of what was expected from a loving son. He would sign his letters to her 'Archie' and would often end them with 'God Bless' and 'Love Always'. With the important pieces of their life together missing from the puzzle, it must have been very hard, particularly for Grant, to know with any certainty how he should act: and 'act' is the appropriate word. We have a confused, if no longer bemused, Hollywood film star, appearing in his longest, most demanding role with no director to lean upon.

The result was that Grant still felt stirrings of discomfort whenever he visited Elsie and in the early 1960s he confessed that, 'When I go to see her, the minute I get to Bristol I start clearing my throat.'

These ambiguities in his feelings for Elsie, if never fully banished, were certainly diluted when Dyan Cannon became pregnant with their daughter Jennifer. Shortly before her birth, Grant wrote to Elsie a letter in which all the uncertainties are blown away:

Watching, and being with, my wife as she bears her pregnancy and goes towards the miraculous experience of giving birth to our first child, I'm moved to tell you how much I appreciate, and now better understand, all you must have endured to have me. All the fears you probably knew and the joy and, although I didn't ask you to go through all that, I'm so pleased you did; because in so doing, you gave me life. Thank you, dear mother. I may have written similar words before but, recently, because of Dyan, the thoughts became more poignant and clear. I send you love and gratitude.

The love he feels for his mother at this point – though induced by a state of euphoria in anticipation of becoming a father at last – is clearly genuine. Fatherhood was going to change him in another way: he would feel less compulsion to be 'Cary Grant' and, by implication, more the Archie Leach that was cut off in his prime.

The Grants' honeymoon in Bristol, which had started peacefully and developed into a media siege, ended with a farce. When the pressure of the journalists became too much, Grant enlisted the help of his chauffeur, Anthony Faramus, to convince the press waiting in the lobby that they had already left while he and Cannon, somewhat ignominiously, climbed out of a window at the back of the hotel to make a getaway.

The honeymoon had been a bad omen for the start of a marriage but, for Dyan Cannon, worse was to follow. Grant didn't like her clothes and was vociferous in telling her so, once upbraiding her in public at an airport for wearing a miniskirt. If she demurred, he insisted he was right: *he* was the epitome of style and he knew what looked right and what looked wrong. It was an opposite dynamic to how he had reacted to marriage to Barbara Hutton. There his inferiority complex had manifested itself, but now he was overbearingly superior – one of the problems that came with such a gap in age. Having turned down the role of Professor Higgins in *My Fair Lady*, some friends now commented that he was intent on playing it in real life with Cannon.

Worse, having seemingly tempted Grant out of his reclusiveness during their courtship, Cannon now found that he seemed determined to revert to his old ways in marriage. Her husband, she soon discovered, liked nothing more than to have dinner in bed at eight p.m., after which he would watch TV for the rest of the evening. He also resumed his habit of accepting very few of the many invitations he received: if he *did* accept, the Grants soon became notorious for arriving late and leaving early.

For the young Dyan Cannon, it was not what she had been expecting from her marriage, and she became gradually frustrated by his obsessive privacy. Naturally, rumours soon began circulating that all was not well with Grant's fourth marriage. These, however, were quickly quashed when it was announced in October that she was expecting a baby in May 1966. As the *New York Journal* put it so succinctly: 'Cary's Fourth Expects First'.

News of Cannon's pregnancy overwhelmed Grant and would lighten any darkness within him forever. 'I've waited all my life hoping for children,' he said. Determined to be as good a father as possible, he devoted himself to studying childbirth and parenting. There was never any doubt that, financially, Grant's first child was going to be born into extreme comfort, but no one who saw how Grant reacted to the news of the pregnancy in the latter part of 1965 could doubt that the child would also be deeply loved.

Had Grant not already committed himself to making *Walk, Don't Run* before Cannon's pregnancy, *Father Goose* would have probably been his last film. His production company, Granley, made the picture through Columbia instead of Universal, since Universal had annoyed him by including his house on the official Universal Studios tour – not a wise move by Universal given that Grant was renowned for cherishing his privacy. When he heard the tour guides pointing out his house, his car and even the spot where he liked to sunbathe, Grant was understandably furious: 'I'm not an animal in a zoo!' he complained.

Emerging from the Golden Age meant that Grant, and most of his contemporaries, believed solidly in the mystique of film stars. Not only for the maintenance of his own privacy – though that was high on his agenda – but because he genuinely believed that to break through the silver screen, to take tourists round back-lots and show them how everything was done, was to erode the very foundations on which Hollywood had become great. It was like revealing how a magician does his tricks. Conversely, and some would argue hypocritically, he adored taking friends around the studios. The writer, Michael Sellers, and his father, Peter, who was a friend of Grant's, were two such visitors in the mid-sixties. Michael recalls Grant's 'great enthusiasm for showing us the back-lots where he'd made some of his own films, and talking about the past.'

The official studio tours were yet another manifestation of what Grant believed to be the vulgarisation of his industry. By the mid-sixties, he had become depressed by the low quality of the scripts he was being offered and particularly disliked Hollywood's new frankness in the depiction of sex and violence and use of bad language. It became clear to Grant that he had seen the best years of Hollywood and this, coupled with his own anxieties about ageing on-screen, meant that even without the unlikely prospect of his becoming a father for the first time at the age of 62, he was seriously considering his future in the movies.

With his wife pregnant, Grant could really have done without travelling to Tokyo to make *Walk, Don't Run* but, given his near-obsession with learning all aspects of parenting, it was probably a good thing he had the making of a movie to concentrate on as way of distraction. The schedule of the film meant that he would be back in Hollywood by February 1966, well before his wife was due to give birth.

Walk, Don't Run is an odd coda to Cary Grant's screen career. A virtual remake of the superior *The More The Merrier*, which George Stevens had directed in 1943, the film relocated the action from the Washington backdrop of the original to the 1964 Tokyo Olympics.

Grant plays Sir William Rutland, an English industrialist in Tokyo during the Olympics. Unable to find a room, he ends up having to share an apartment with a young woman, played by Samantha Eggar. While much of the comedy is based around their domestic arrangements, the dynamic of the story is Grant's attempt to sort out Eggar's love life with her American athlete boyfriend, played by Jim Hutton.

What made the film different – and, had he continued to make movies, it would have marked some kind of watershed – was that Cary Grant didn't get the girl. His role, instead, was to act as a kind of avuncular go-between to facilitate the romance between Hutton and Eggar, thus displaying similarities to *The Bishop's Wife*.

Despite the rather mild comedy that the screenwriter Sol Saks provides for Grant, his performance is as assured as ever. Saks, sensing Grant's ambivalence about his career at this time, even his possible boredom with actually sustaining 'Cary Grant', does provide one marvellous exchange that rings truer to Grant's own character than to Sir William's. At the beginning of the film, a sycophantic clerk gushes over Sir William much as fans gushed over Grant. 'Sir William,' says the clerk, 'may I say what a pleasure it is to meet you in person?'

'Only if you *must,*' sighs Grant.

Despite not being the romantic lead, the film couldn't ignore his matinée-idol past as an exchange between Grant and Eggar in the Tokyo apartment demonstrates.

EGGAR: Are you married?
GRANT: Yes. Why?
EGGAR: Well, I think you might have told me.
GRANT: Why? What did you have in mind?

Grant had lost none of his comedic skills. The delivery of that last line was as perfectly timed as any in his career. The scene in which he accompanies – and keeps up with – athlete Jim Hutton on a run (Grant dressed in his underwear) displays a fitness which belied his 62 years.

The only thing that was continuing to betray the ageing process was his voice. It sounds noticeably older and decidedly huskier on the soundtrack to this film – more so than when he had expressed concerns on *Charade*. There wasn't much he could do about it, even if the rest of his body was defying the passing years.

Throughout the making of *Walk, Don't Run*, Grant's mind was concentrated wholly on events back home with Cannon's pregnancy. And during this time, with the thought of oncoming fatherhood, he was wrestling with thoughts of his future. Life was clearly going to be very different from now on and he made it plain to all who mattered that he intended being a very hands-on father, which is understandable given the emotional and financial state of his own upbringing.

There were rumours abounding that Grant was planning to retire shortly, but these rumours had been coming and going for years, so people didn't know what to believe. Even Grant was giving out conflicting signals.

He said to one interviewer, 'By now, my choice of roles is very limited. I may wind up playing some old retired banker in a wheelchair. I want to go on and on, like Sir C. Aubrey Smith. I find the economics of this business very exciting because of the great sums involved. It's what I can do happiest. It's a profession like any other. If I knew of a better one, I'd do it.'

But to another reporter, while bemoaning the lack of 'high comedy and polished words' in modern Hollywood, he said, 'I said I would give myself a few years to see if a film career paid off. If it did, I'd give myself 40 years, God willing, and then I'd leave.'

One incident on the set of *Walk, Don't Run*, which he relayed to

Roger Moore a few years later, probably did more than any other to convince him.

Grant and Moore were close friends for many years and Grant liked the younger actor whose screen image of the perfectly tailored gentleman owed much to his own, and whose legendary sense of humour he appreciated. Moore remembers:

In the beginning of the 1970s, I tried my hand at being an executive for a while and joined Fabergé to run the European office for BRUT Films. Cary was on the board of Fabergé and we really saw a great deal of one another at that time.

Being an executive with a film company, I wondered whether there was any possibility of getting Cary to do another film for BRUT. When I approached the subject with him he was rather thoughtful and he told me he had stopped making movies because one day on *Walk, Don't Run* he was sitting in his trailer and heard a conversation outside which was aimed for him to hear. It was completely sycophantic. He came to the conclusion that he had now made his money so why did he have to go on making films? He decided to get out. It was time.

After hearing that from his lips, I could not bear to broach the subject again and never asked him again to do anything for the film company while I was on the Board.

Tony Curtis adds another reason for Grant's retirement, which echoes Grant's own words on the subject. 'He retired from show business voluntarily, while he was still one of Hollywood's most sought after stars,' said Curtis. 'He told me why. He said he didn't want to grow old on the screen.'

The combination of those two reasons – plus a third – is why Grant retired.

The 'third reason' arrived two months early on 26 February 1966. Grant only just made it back from Japan to be there for the birth. She weighed just four pounds, eight ounces and was to be named Jennifer.

Grant was overjoyed – as he had led the world to expect – and, for once, wasn't so guarded when he spoke to reporters at the hospital. 'I've waited all my life for this,' he told them emotionally. 'When you've waited for such a long time, you hope like mad that everything will work out all right. In my case, I knew the birth of my baby was the chance of a dream coming true. It's never too late to become a parent.'

After 72 roles in the movies, Cary Grant had now assumed the role he craved all his life: that of a father. And his performance would not disappoint.

25

'Some men cannot be married. Cary is one of them.'

Dyan Cannon

'I won't fight Dyan. After all, she's the mother of my child.'

Cary Grant

The headline of New York's *Daily News* on 21 March 1968 said it all: 'Life with Cary Grant a "Nightmare".'

When Dyan Cannon had started her divorce proceedings, Grant had been prepared for her lawyers to fight dirty, but even he was not expecting the humiliating claims made against him when the case began in Los Angeles on 20 March 1968. Its aftermath was to leave him, according to his closest friends, at the lowest point he had ever been in his life. His bitterness towards *all* women knew no bounds for a while afterwards, prompting him to tell one friend, 'Once the female has used the mate for procreation, she turns on him and literally devours him.'

One can well understand his cynicism. Accusing him of being 'cruel and inhuman', the picture Cannon's lawyers painted of her life with her husband of just three years was one of unmitigated hell – and one that he genuinely felt was grossly unfair.

According to Cannon's lawyers, Grant was 'an apostle of LSD' who had tried to cajole her into using the drug many times, and who was prone to fits of 'yelling and screaming'.

He was said to have spanked her and to have beaten her. On one occasion, he was accused of having imprisoned her in their house to prevent her going out for the evening: supposedly he commandeered all the car keys, bolted the gates to the grounds and then locked himself and the car keys in his dressing-room. After that, he was alleged to have started hitting her: 'He was laughing and screamed for the help to come and see what he was doing,' claimed Cannon. 'I was frightened and went to call the police.' The only reason she refrained from doing so was, she said, because Grant begged her not to.

Grant was said to often become 'violent and out of control'. More amusingly, Cannon's legal team described how, while watching the Oscars ceremony on TV, he 'jumped up on the bed and yelled that everyone on the show had their faces lifted. He was spilling wine on the bed.'

But rather more pathetic was the claim that Grant refused to allow Cannon to take along baby food for his daughter, Jennifer, when they travelled to England because, he insisted, 'the cows in England are as good as they are in this country.'

Even allowing for the exaggerated character assassinations routinely propagated by lawyers – the only true winners in any marital break-up that winds up in the courtrooms – this came across as a deeply unpleasant portrait of the much-loved film star.

But while he was deeply humiliated by the attendant publicity – the case was widely reported across America and throughout the world – he chose not to respond to the claims, although his lawyers did issue a statement that, beneath the blandly restrained prose of lawyer-speak, gave a hint of his seething anger: 'If Miss Cannon feels a need to seek public sympathy and approbation through a press agent, that is up to her. As Mr Grant's legal representative, we have good reason for our decisions, and each action is carefully considered, and taken in accordance only to what is best for his child's welfare.'

Many of his friends believed that this was not enough. They urged him to fight back and argued – reasonably, it seemed at the time – that his silence merely gave credence to Cannon's lawyers' assertions. But Grant refused to play dirty. 'I realise I've made mistakes with Dyan,' he said. 'I'll give her all the odds. I won't fight. She can have everything she wants. After all, she's the mother of my child.'

To many, it sounded like defeatist talk and people wondered if the car accident he had suffered in New York eight days before the divorce hearing had knocked the fight out of him.

Certainly, the accident at night in heavy rain had been a serious one. While being driven to Kennedy Airport, Grant's car was struck by a tractor trailer, which had crossed the central reservation having itself been hit by another truck. Grant looked horrendous when he was pulled from the wreckage and was rushed to St John's Hospital, Queens. His face was bruised and bloodied and it was suspected he had sustained a broken nose (though he hadn't). He also had three broken ribs and had difficulty in breathing. Although his injuries were not quite as serious as initially thought, he was still in hospital in New York when the divorce proceedings began in Los Angeles.

Perhaps the accident had knocked the fight out of him. Maybe his bewilderment about the vicious personal attacks in the court left him struggling to know how to respond. Grant's public image was dignity at all times and, since he wasn't contesting the divorce, he simply couldn't understand why Cannon's lawyers were attacking him and threatening his reputation with what he considered to be wildly embellished claims against him. But Grant's refusal to respond to the attacks was much more probably a very shrewd, if risky, strategy. By doing so, Grant denied the media the public spectacle of his wife and himself fighting, which had been eagerly anticipated. To the wider audience beyond – the audience to whom he believed he still had an allegiance, even if he had no more films to promote – he maintained the cool, urbane assurance that the name 'Cary Grant' conjured up. In other words, by keeping a dignified silence, he did just what the public expected of 'Cary Grant' and, simultaneously, blunted the attacks on his character and integrity and made them seem absurd and untrue.

If this was a deliberate strategy on Grant's part, it paid off. Grant was to emerge from the divorce with his reputation intact even if, in private, he was utterly shattered by the sheer nastiness that been thrust upon him.

How had Grant and Cannon come to this? How had a marriage that had begun with such mutual joy and promise in 1965 ended so bitterly less than three years later in the courts?

Ironically, the birth of Jennifer had acted as a catalyst to the fracturing of her parents' relationship. When she was born, Grant felt as though he, himself, had been reborn, at the age of 62. Accordingly, he focused wholly on his daughter's existence to the exclusion of everything – and *everyone* – else. He gazed at her in her cot for ages every day; he worried over every routine chill and stomach upset; he photographed her endlessly and used a tape-recorder to preserve every last gurgle: he even recorded a song for her, 'A Christmas Lullaby', which was released by Columbia in 1967.

Grant's friend, Peggy Lee – who was featured on the 'B' side of the disc singing 'Here's To You' – recalled, 'The wonder of having a child never left him. I've seen fathers look at babies but never the way Cary looked at Jennifer.'

For his part, Grant would tell anyone who would listen that, 'Jennifer is my best production' and 'she's the most winsome, captivating girl I've ever known.'

He became paranoid about Jennifer's security and was convinced – not without some foundation – that she was a prime target for kidnappers. After it was revealed that Grant was on Charles Manson's hit-list when Manson was arrested for the murder of, among others, the actress Sharon Tate, he became even more concerned about her and hired permanent bodyguards to watch out for her 24 hours a day.

Even so, and allowing for the fact that every parent's first child is more wrapped in cotton-wool than any subsequent ones, one can detect a family pattern reasserting itself in Grant's near-obsessive devotion. After all, was it not Elsie's compulsive over-protection of her little Archie – triggered by his brother John's death – that had been one of the manifestations of her mental frailty nearly sixty years earlier? And had not Grant put on record that Elsie 'was so scared something would happen to me that she tried to smother me with care'?

Grant's endless recordings of Jennifer and his staring at her in her cot for hours on end was really nothing more than Elsie's dressing Archie in baby clothes for years on end, her refusal to cut his cherubic curls and her determination to keep him in short trousers long after boys of his age had graduated into long trousers. Grant's attitude to, and treatment of, Jennifer uncannily parallels Elsie's for Archie. Does this suggest that, mentally, he was much more like his mother than he, or anyone else, cared to suppose? Was this something he was secretly afraid of – that he was vulnerable to a mental breakdown every bit as much as she had been? Reading between the lines, in all his divorces there is an air – and in Cannon's case, a direct accusation – of instability in his behaviour. There were unusual and unexpected moments in his life with his wives – specifically when the marriages were in their final throes – which demonstrate, if taken collectively, something rather less than the urbane 'Cary Grant' he managed to put across most of the time. Certainly if Grant's own emotional weaknesses were parallel to, albeit less obviously defined than, Elsie's, it would go a long way to explaining his inability to love her unconditionally for the rest of her life.

Whatever the motivation for his concentrating all his energies and thoughts on Jennifer, by the time *Walk, Don't Run* opened five months after she was born, Grant had become utterly immersed in parenthood. He was simply too preoccupied in his role as father to even consider any new film projects.

'I won't say I'll never make another picture,' he said when asked about his plans, 'because I can't look into the future. It's possible I might do another. I might make *ten* more. I just don't know.'

To close friends, though, he was sounding a more negative note with regards to his future as a screen actor. 'I'm too old to get the girl,' he said. 'It's time to climb off the celluloid and join the real world. I no longer care to see something that isn't happening. I don't go to plays or movies. I'm interested in truth, in reality.'

Although many friends speculated that domesticity would soon pall and would drive him back into a film studio, there was a growing realisation within Hollywood that this really could be the end of Cary Grant's long screen career. Perhaps this explains why the generally excellent notices for *Walk, Don't Run* were rather better than the film probably deserved: reading between the lines, it is possible to discern some critics urging Grant *not* to quit. Flattery was one possible way to keep him going.

'Cary Grant could not be unfunny if he tried,' believed *Newsweek*. 'He has watched the decline of Hollywood comedy first-hand and, in *Walk, Don't Run*, he tries almost single-handedly to prevent its complete downfall.'

The *New Yorker* went even further, all but urging him to carry on for another thirty-odd years: 'Grant's attempted abdication as a screen dreamboat is premature and will have to be withdrawn. He's a good ten years away from playing anyone's jolly, knowing uncle and as for lovable Mr. Fixit, he should be ready for that in about the year 2000.'

Grant was not indifferent to the fate of *Walk, Don't Run*. As producer, he naturally had more than a passing interest in its performance at the box-office and the businessman in him surely noted that, though successful, it wasn't doing anything like the business his recent films had done – *The Grass Is Greener* excepted – reinforcing his belief that the stock of an ageing 'Cary Grant's' was bound to fall and may have already started doing so.

Nonetheless, he promoted the film and, in August 1966, flew with Cannon and Jennifer to England to combine the London opening with showing Jennifer to her 88-year-old grandmother, Elsie, for the first time. 'She's lovely, and she looks just like Cary,' she declared.

While they were in Bristol, Grant told Cannon that he wanted to have Jennifer christened in the same parish church where he'd been christened – thereby raising serious doubts about whether he could possibly be Jewish – but the local vicar refused because Grant and Cannon, whose mother *was* Jewish, would not agree to the vicar's demand that Jennifer must be brought up as an Episcopalian.

This was, at least, one point on which Grant and Cannon stuck together. But there were precious few others. If Grant was absolutely bowled over by the arrival of his daughter, the twelve months between August 1966 and August 1967 saw his marriage to Cannon collapse.

'I somehow felt Cary was more in love with Dyan than she was with him,' the director, Peter Bogdanovich, a mutual friend, once said. 'Certainly, he doted on her and seemed to do whatever she asked. She appeared to enjoy showing him off. "Sing 'em that song, Archie!" she cried out on the way back from a ball game.'

Calling Grant 'outlandish, irrational and hostile', Cannon likened their marriage to a 'Pygmalion relationship' and claimed 'he dominated me completely, and I was so eager to please.'

Wherever the fault truly lay, Cannon finally walked out on him on 28 December 1966. Grant was horrified – more, it must be said, by the prospect of losing access to Jennifer than the failure of a fourth marriage – and tried many times to encourage her to help make the marriage work.

One of Cannon's disappointments was that Grant had expected her to give up her screen career when Jennifer was born. He *had* promised to help find her roles in the future, but only when their daughter was older. Cannon had reacted badly to this and, in an attempt to appease her, it was widely reported that Grant, who owned an interest in a screenplay by Isobel Lennart called *The Old Man And Me*, was going to make the picture with Cannon as his co-star.

Even after she had sued for divorce, Grant was attempting to save the marriage for some three months after.

That the divorce was bitter cannot be disguised, although Grant would surely find it rather touching that his first wife, Virginia Cherrill, appeared as a character witness on his behalf. With a personal fortune now estimated at ten million dollars, he also stood to lose a great deal of money as well as his reputation. Most heart-breaking of all, he was in danger of losing his one and only child. Cannon had demanded that his visits be limited to daylight hours and no overnight visits without an attendant nurse. Given Grant's obvious love for Jennifer, a love that seemed to have eclipsed everything else in his life that had gone before, this demand, to the impartial observer, does seem a little harsh.

In the event, Judge Robert A. Wenke demonstrated the judgement of Solomon in the case. Two expert witnesses had been used by the court to examine the allegations of LSD dependency made against Grant and much – especially his access to Jennifer – depended on their testimony. The Judge was told by Dr Judd Marmor that there was no indication of 'irrationality, erratic behaviour or incoherence' in Grant. He did, however, acknowledge that he had found the actor to be 'an emotional individual, but no more than other actors I have examined'. He said that he had discovered no lasting or pernicious fall-out from Grant's experimenting with LSD. 'He told me the drug had helped deepen his understanding of himself,' Marmor went on, 'and helped cure his shyness and anxiety in dealing with other people.'

The testimony of Marmor was enough to convince the Judge that Grant was far from being an 'apostle' of LSD and he said he was satisfied that the actor had not used the drug for at least a year. He dismissed the Draconian restrictions Cannon wanted to put on Grant's access to their daughter and Grant was granted two months visiting rights a year without any restrictions.

Judge Wenke also modified alimony payments to $50,000 per year, considerably less than Cannon's lawyers had been seeking and, it has always been maintained, much less than Grant had at first offered before the case was heard.

Grant had reason to be, if not cheerful, then relatively satisfied when Cannon's divorce came through. As well as his alimony payments being negligible – at least for a man of Grant's wealth – his reputation stayed in one piece. People had read the allegations, but somehow, probably because it was 'Cary Grant', they didn't believe them. Once one started believing that the sophisticated 'Cary Grant' beat up women and was perhaps less than perfect, something decent within one died and a fundamental tenet of human existence was shattered. So it was easier to ignore the issue and let it go away.

The legal skirmishes would continue for some time after their divorce and they were usually connected with Jennifer who, as in all good dramas, played the innocent in the middle.

Grant's habit of travelling to be near Jennifer whenever Cannon was filming on location – 'you get desperate to see your child,' he argued, 'absolutely desperate' – irked his former wife. On one famous occasion, Cannon was leaving Hollywood with Jennifer en route for New York where she was about to begin rehearsals for a new play, when she discovered Grant at the airport. She was even more amazed when he told her he had a seat on the same flight. When she challenged him, he admitted that he was making sure his daughter was going to be all right. His protection of Jennifer knew no bounds and he had even had the court stipulate that her face must never be photographed because of his fear of kidnappers.

As late as May 1975, Cannon was in court again, this time trying to get a court order to move Grant from his beach house in Malibu which was just three doors away from her because she didn't like him staring at her. The judge refused and ordered *both* parties to stop annoying each other.

Cannon seems to have been particularly irritated, and not without reason, by the way that the courts almost always seemed to rule in Grant's favour and complained that it was nearly impossible for her to get a fair hearing against an icon. On one occasion during yet another action centring on Grant's access to his daughter, the judge excused himself and left the court.

'What's the delay?' Cannon asked the clerk of the court.

'The judge's wife insisted he had to call home and tell her how Cary Grant looks today,' came the reply.

When one judgement *did* go in her favour, one can sense the bitter relief in Cannon's comment: 'I feel so good. It's the first time in three years I haven't lost.'

Of course, there was only one real loser in these on-going battles and that was, obviously, Jennifer. Gradually, it appears that Grant and Cannon began to see this for themselves and relations thawed between them, allowing flexibility and a little more consideration for the other to enter the equation.

'We had to work something out for the sake of this little girl of ours,' Cannon said some time later. 'Cary did some wonderful things for me and I for him. When he comes to see Jennifer and me now, the circumstances are very much the same as when we were dating. I can talk. We talk a lot about Jennifer. She knows she's loved.'

The idea that relations could improve between himself and Cannon must have seemed impossible to Grant in the weeks following the divorce in 1968. One friend recalled him 'staying in his house all day for word from the nurse as to when he could get to see his little girl for an hour or two. He'd just sit and hope the phone would ring...'

Typical of the contradictions in his life, however, it is worth noting that, even while he was still feeling extremely ill-disposed to Cannon in 1969, he used his influence at Columbia to secure her a part in *Bob And Carol And Ted And Alice*. At the same time, as he came out of his depressed state of mind, he was inclined, yet again, to shoulder the responsibility of his fourth failed marriage, while, concurrently, admitting his joy at it having produced his only child – 'my only ticket to eternity'.

'My marriage record is nothing to be proud of,' he admitted. 'I've had four wives and one daughter. Just think how much better my life would have been if I'd had one wife and four daughters. If I'd known then what I know now.'

A rueful Dyan Cannon herself put it more succinctly. 'Some men cannot be married. Cary is one of them.'

26

> 'The toiletries industry is very much like the motion picture industry. Distribution and marketing are much the same. Only percentages are different.'
>
> Cary Grant

When *Walk, Don't Run* opened in the summer of 1966, Cary Grant still had more than twenty years to live. That would be almost a quarter of his life and it is a sobering thought that, since he didn't make a screen appearance until he was 28, Grant, acknowledged as the greatest leading man Hollywood has ever known, spent the greater part of his life *not* working as a screen actor.

Very few major actors just stop acting at their peak. Fewer still switch professions in their mid-sixties. But this is precisely what Grant did and he was so successful that by the early 1970s he could legitimately claim, 'I'm a travelling businessman and it's the most successful role I've ever played.'

Again and again, throughout his life, Grant had avoided being pinned down through a combination of his many contradictions and ambiguities. Having officially announced his 'retirement' in 1953 when he was doing no such thing, he now, typically, made no formal announcement about the real thing. Although he still gave many interviews – and even embarked on a theatre tour talking about himself in the 1980s – he handled his privacy during these last two decades with such brilliance that, uniquely for a major cultural icon, we know less about what Cary Grant did between 1966 and 1986 than during any other part of his life.

Certainly, as the months ticked by following the release of *Walk, Don't Run*, it became obvious that he was not making any new movie. Being wrapped up completely in his daughter prevented him from considering new screen roles. 'We're put on this earth to procreate,' he remarked shortly after Jennifer's birth. 'To leave something behind.

Not films, because you know I don't think my films will last very long once I'm gone. But another human being. That's what's important.'

'When Cary retired,' said Billy Wilder, 'I started concocting stories for a man with grey hair in his early seventies. At any age, Cary Grant would still be a heartbreaker. He did not age one bit. His hair got grey, that's all. But he told me, "No, I'm not going to do it anymore." He guarded the last few years of his life brilliantly. But to the very end, I can assure you there were several pictures for which the studios wanted Cary, but he was just not available.'

Speaking in 1990, the legendary agent Irving 'Swifty' Lazar said, 'Cary didn't need the money so he wasn't even tempted. I once offered him three million dollars to do a movie – which today would be twenty million dollars – and he wouldn't do it. "It's not a question of money – I wouldn't do it for any amount," he said.'

If Grant's retirement exasperated and baffled some Hollywood insiders, it gained the immense respect of many others.

'I could never understand why,' said Stanley Donen, 'but he was determined. And I can't say I was surprised. He'd been saying he was going to do it for a long time. He didn't want to play old men on the screen. Of course, he wasn't an old man, ever, despite his age. But he just didn't want to turn into a caricature of himself... He had the class to simply quit when he thought it was time.'

Richard Schickel agreed: 'Having created 'Cary Grant' out of cloth as whole as that out of which Walt Disney created Mickey Mouse, he felt entirely free to dispense with him, erase him as it were. And in much the same manner that he had created him, that is to say in a subtle and seemly and slightly mysterious manner, without shock to his or to anyone else's nervous system, without regrets and without undignified appeals to nostalgic sentiment.'

Grant's messy divorce from Cannon did nothing to distance his public and his general reputation. In fact, two months after it had happened, on 22 May 1968, it was announced that Grant was joining the board of the cosmetics firm Rayette-Fabergé.

Grant had been introduced to the company's founder, the former jazz musician George Barrie, by Bob Taplinger, the publicist with whom Grant had lived for a short while in New York following his separation from Cannon.

Immediately after the divorce hearing in Los Angeles, Barrie – who had also recruited the songwriter Sammy Cahn to the company – flew

Grant back to New York aboard his private plane and the two men thrashed out Grant's new role during the journey. Not only was Grant joining the board, but he was to act as a consultant to and spokesman for Rayette-Fabergé.

It was clear what George Barrie was getting from the association: he was buying into the 'Cary Grant' brand, which he was convinced had not been sullied by the court allegations. But what were Grant's motives?

Joining the board of a cosmetics firm was, many believed, sheer hypocrisy on Grant's behalf. After all, was not this the man who had always loathed wearing make-up during his screen career; who had made no secret of his disliking women wearing make-up; and who had been scathing previously about men who did so?

Such a contradiction did not concern Grant too deeply. He argued that personal prejudices didn't come into business opportunities. He had identified, with great prescience, the potential growth for male toiletries – 'there's a big future in this,' he commented to a friend. 'The toiletries industry is very much like the motion picture industry,' he insisted. 'Distribution and marketing are much the same. Only the percentages are different.' And that was all that mattered. As far as he was concerned he was still using the brand 'Cary Grant'. All that had changed was the industry. Hypocrisy didn't come into the equation.

His salary was hardly on a footing with that of the 'Cary Grant' screen icon. He was paid $15,000 a year, plus a fee of $200 for every directors' meeting he attended. The million or two dollars a year pay cut didn't really worry him much, as that had not been the motive for making the change. Also, as everyone in Hollywood well knew, he didn't need the money any more, so it was never going to persuade him to do anything he didn't want to.

Certainly, the fringe benefits offered by his new employers were splendid. Not only was he given a sizeable chunk of Fabergé stock – which rose a full two points on the day the *New York Times* announced his joining the company – but George Barrie provided Grant with his own private jet, which came complete with a couple of bedrooms, a bar and even a piano and which was to prove most useful for reaching Jennifer at short notice no matter where she was. He also had use of the company helicopter whenever he was in New York, a room at Fabergé's New York headquarters and unlimited access to the company's town house in London's Mayfair, the renovation of which cost Barrie one million pounds in the early 1970s.

For a star of Grant's magnitude, such luxuries were hardly undreamt of. Nonetheless, they were agreeable extras for a man seeking a change of direction before his 65th birthday in the January of 1969.

'I accepted,' said Grant drily, 'because when it was offered to me, they threw in the odd bit of travel and a roof over my head.'

But he was also astutely aware of his own value. 'I regard myself as more of a public relations man. Most company presidents are men who've seen my movies, so it's easy to establish a liaison. I don't have to work for any other reason except that I like it. I wouldn't be doing this if I didn't like it. You shouldn't do anything you don't like. You wouldn't be any good at it.'

For his part, George Barrie was delighted with the work Grant was doing for the company and by December 1968 he was able to tell *Business Week:* 'When we purchased Fabergé five years ago, it was doing eleven million dollars. This year it will do fifty million dollars, and I attribute some of that to "Mr. G".'

On the surface, Grant seemed to relish his new role as a businessman. If any questioner suggested that the life of a glorified travelling salesman was very different from that of a movie star, Grant would disagree. 'Look, I was always a businessman,' he once said. 'It was just on a larger scale. Do you know any other business where a man can earn a million dollars in ten weeks?'

Grant didn't limit himself to Fabergé. He was made a director of MGM in 1975 and when, in 1980, MGM was divided into two separate companies he continued to sit on the board of both MGM Films and MGM Grand Hotels. He was invited onto the board by Kirk Kirkorian, a younger version of Howard Hughes whose fierce ambition had seen him build a business empire from nothing and who had made himself a gentleman every bit as much as Cary Grant had modelled himself from the rough clay of Archie Leach.

When MGM opened the MGM Grant Hotel in Las Vegas in 1973 – at a cost of over one hundred and six million dollars – Kirkorian requested, and received, Grant's help in publicising the opening. Grant presided over many of the promotional activities during the month-long celebrations. Many of Grant's friends muttered behind his back that being associated with the tacky Las Vegas set-up was not worthy of the 'Cary Grant' status, but Grant couldn't have cared less: business was business. Besides, he had always been fascinated by Vegas and had even befriended some of its most notorious characters, especially Bugsy Siegel whom he had first met in 1935.

Rather less happily, Grant also became a director in the ill-fated Shannonside land development project in the Irish Republic. This was a somewhat clumsy and curious attempt to establish an Irish-American community on the banks of the Shannon River. Launched in 1971, the cost was put at six million dollars but finance proved virtually impossible to raise and the project collapsed in 1974 when receivers were called in.

This, though, was a rare business setback for Grant and his numerous other interests succeeded, sometimes spectacularly. These included a directorship of Western Airlines, courtesy of Kirkorian, which afforded Grant the use of a private jet and which came complete with an office, a bathtub set in marble and an endless supply of Chateau Lafite and Beluga caviar; a directorship of Tamboo, an exclusive club in the Bahamas; and investments in and directorship of the Hollywood Park Racetrack.

But for all that he tried to convince everyone he didn't miss acting and preferred the life of an itinerant businessman, he did strike close friends as a somewhat melancholic figure, particularly in the early seventies in the immediate aftermath of the bitter divorce settlement with Dyan Cannon.

Insisting that he was happy, Grant said, 'I get up in the morning, go to bed at night and occupy myself as best I can in-between. I do what I want, when I want.'

Superficially, this was the statement of a man relishing a new freedom and new challenges that freedom brought. But the subtext – 'I occupy myself as best I can' – tends to imply a hollowness about the way his life now operated. It suggests a man who, in late middle-age, still possessing great looks, health and vigour, was forever searching for a purpose following a premature retirement from what he did best.

As the 1960s gave way to the 1970s, so Cary Grant was more than halfway between 60 and 70. This is an age when most men have done all their hell-raising, have built whatever empires they are going to build and are trying to fall into a contentment that will see them through their final years. Cary Grant, who had always belied his years, typically did not conform to this norm. He turned 66 in January 1970. He was a single man with four divorces behind him, he had a four-year-old daughter on whom he doted and he had recently exchanged a life-long career in acting for one in business and public relations. Despite the fact that he had by now partially come to terms with the negative repercussions from his traumatic upbringing, he was still somewhat emotionally handicapped.

The columnist Roderick Mann, the friend who saw him often in the last thirty years of his life, referred to Grant living 'a reclusive life' in the years immediately following his divorce from Dyan Cannon. His house along Beverly Grove Drive in Beverly Hills – 'a shack', Grant called it – was comparatively shabby and Mann recalled it as 'a tumbledown place indeed... Often when I went up there I would find him having his dinner on the edge of his bed. "It's the only comfortable seat in house," he would explain.'

Grant's slightly melancholic air was also recorded by the society photographer Allan Warren in his deliciously irreverent and racy autobiography *Dukes, Queens and Other Stories*. Warren, whose first professional client was Judy Garland and who has photographed every Duke in Britain as well as most members of the Royal Family, was recommended to Grant by George Cukor in the mid-seventies. They met when Grant was staying in London at the Royal Lancaster Hotel in Bayswater, a location that was to prove highly significant in Grant's private life in 1976.

Calling ahead to arrange a photo-shoot, Warren was put through to Grant's hotel and was surprised that Grant himself answered 'in that unique one-off Americanised Bristolian accent'.

Grant suggested they meet at a Fabergé convention currently being held at the hotel. When Warren arrived, he found the ballroom swarming with 'grey-haired businessmen dressed in shiny off-the-peg suits'. Grant was in the middle of them, 'much older-looking than the rest with thick black-rimmed spectacles and snow-white hair'.

Grant was surrounded by a group of sycophants who were 'hanging on his every word', according to Warren. Clearly Grant, who had always guarded his privacy and who loathed the inevitable crowds drawn by celebrity, had to compromise in his work for Fabergé. Perhaps when there was a profit and loss involved, Cary Grant was always happy to compromise.

Certainly Grant was happy to extricate himself to be photographed by Warren and the fact that he arranged for Warren to meet him at the conference suggests that Grant may even have been using the photographer as an excuse to get away from the nodding suits. 'Sorry about that,' Grant told Warren, 'I was surrounded. Thanks for rescuing me.'

Grant helped Warren set up the lights and seemed to genuinely relish the prospect of being in front of a camera again. Warren noticed how tired Grant seemed – although he was 'impeccably groomed, suited and sun-tanned' – but, requiring no make-up (working for Fabergé had not corrupted him so much he would abandon his lifelong aversion to wearing it), as soon as Warren's camera started clicking 'he posed happily' and the years fell away.

The results of the shoot were certainly impressive, and one shot, Grant's favourite, with his glasses dangling from his mouth boyishly, shows the seventy-something star looking closer to fifty-something. No wonder that Grant later wrote to Warren to tell him 'you've taken the best pictures of me in 25 years.' This was high praise indeed because Grant became increasingly tetchy in his seventies with photographers who failed to disguise what he, himself, acknowledged as the 'fatness in my face'.

Warren's encounter with Grant, coupled with his tetchiness towards lesser photographers, reveals yet another contradiction. Grant may have given up being a film star but he was still behaving like one. He was as well turned-out as he'd ever been, and his reacting to a camera – all the poses from Warren's session are a 'performance' – suggest he was still a movie star, but one who simply no longer made movies. It wasn't stopping him deploying 'Cary Grant' at any given moment, just in a different way, that is all.

Had Cary Grant been a nostalgic man, his later years would have doubtless been spent very differently. Had he suffered ill-health – his hernia operation in Santa Monica in the spring of 1976 (when he was registered as 'Cary Robins') hardly counted as a sign of frailty – he might have slowed down and completely disappeared from sight. But at seventy, he not only looked younger than his years but, it seems, he felt it, too.

The extraordinary longevity of his energy meant that he had no time, certainly no inclination, to look back and to wallow in past glories. He was no Norma Desmond: 'If you've enjoyed your life, why would you want to spend hours going over it again?' he argued, while denouncing those contemporaries of his who lived for chat-show appearances where they could roll out the over-familiar Hollywood stories one more time. In this, he was particularly critical of his old friend David Niven who had, in his 'anecdotage', turned raconteur. With many others, Grant was secretly peeved that many of the stories Niven claimed as his own in his light-hearted, irresistible memoirs had, in fact, happened to other people – Grant included.

Roderick Mann, friend to both Grant and Niven, and who helped Niven on both *The Moon's A Balloon* (1971) and *Bring On The Empty Horses* (1975), acknowledged this: 'Cary *was* a bit teed off with David,' he said. 'He said to me, "That happened to me, not him!" But everybody knew that David took stories that happened to other people and moulded them as though they had happened to him.'

Grant's lack of sentiment about his movie career showed itself in other ways, too. The contracts for his later films had included a clause that stated that ownership of the negatives reverted to him after a stated period. By the mid-1970s he owned the negatives of his last ten films, except *To Catch A Thief* and *North By Northwest*, and those of *Penny Serenade*. In 1975 he sold them all to television for a sum in excess of two million dollars. If he wasn't sentimental, nor did he regret a business decision once taken. A decade later, when VHS had made home ownership of movies popular, it was pointed out to Grant that he could have made considerably more from the negatives if he had held onto them. Grant shrugged this aside, insisting he had made the right decision: 'It was time,' was all he said.

As for the movies as a career, did he ever regret turning his back on making them? Friends like Roderick Mann insisted that he didn't, while Grant himself often said he didn't miss 'tripping over cables on movie sets'. But it's tantalising to speculate whether Grant would ever have made another film appearance if the right script had come along: although quite what would have constituted the 'right' script is hard to imagine.

Yet Grant did not cut himself adrift from movies entirely and by making rare, though well-publicised, appearances at testimonials and awards ceremonies, he maintained tentative links with the industry and creative community over which he had once ruled and which still regarded him with awe.

'I guess you can say that I'm retired from the movies,' he once remarked. 'Until some writer comes up with a character who is deaf and dumb and sitting in a wheelchair.' He rarely discussed the issue in a serious fashion, preferring to discard his decision with humour.

He often tried to suggest he was no longer interested in the movie *business* any more. 'I sold all the negatives of the last ten pictures I owned because I not only refuse to view any of my own pictures, I rarely go to any movie unless it's a Disney film that my daughter Jennifer wants to see. We all have our revolutions.'

But Grant was being somewhat disingenuous, surely. If such flippant pronouncements were to try and stem the flow of movie offers that continued to pour in, he must have known they would fail: how could he convince Hollywood he really was retired when a tiny part of Cary Grant was still not entirely convinced of it himself?

In fact, *Walk, Don't Run* was not quite the last appearance Grant made on the big screen. He can be glimpsed, briefly, attending an Elvis Presley concert in Las Vegas in *Elvis: That's The Way It Is* (1970) – 'Are you on?' he asks the cameraman of the documentary – while an excerpt from *The Philadelphia Story* was included in MGM's *That's Entertainment Part 2* in 1976. His voice was also heard in the 1977 TV movie *Once Upon A Time...Is Now* and extracts from *An Affair To Remember* were seen during the Tom Hanks-Meg Ryan weepie *Sleepless In Seattle* (1993).

There's no doubt that he *did* consider other parts after *Walk, Don't Run*. Even as late as 1983, as William Goldman states in *Adventures In The Screentrade*, Grant was interested in the legal drama *The Verdict* and, according to Goldman, 'let it be known in one way or another that [he] was aware of the project and [asked the producers] to please keep in touch.' And while in London in 1971 he saw Anthony Shaffer's excellent two-handed thriller *Sleuth*, which Joseph Mankiewicz, who had directed him in *People Will Talk*, was preparing as a film. Although he eventually didn't play the part in the film – 'I decided it would be too much work. I mean, I've done all that. Seventy times.' – and the role was subsequently taken by Olivier, no amount of backtracking could disguise the fact that he had been seriously considering the role.

These were not the actions of a man who had irrevocably turned his back on the film industry, but one who was caught between a decision made and the temptation to eat a bit of humble pie and re-announce himself to the cinema-going public.

Some of the roles he was offered during the seventies and eighties were, of course, eminently resistible. He did not have to think twice about turning down an offer to do a remake of Jimmy Stewart's old classic *Harvey*, with pop legend Elton John earmarked as the invisible rabbit, and he rejected Mae West's invitation – possibly with a shudder!

– to join the cast of her swansong *Sextette* (1978) in which the ageing actress was supported, in more ways than one, by Tony Curtis, Ringo Starr, Timothy Dalton, George Hamilton, Alice Cooper and Walter Pidgeon. If Grant ever saw *Sextette*, one of the most grotesque ninety-minutes-worth of celluloid ever to emerge from Hollywood, his reaction was not recorded.

Other projects were harder to reject out of hand. Until his death in 1980, Alfred Hitchcock cherished the idea of a movie based on *Hamlet* and written specifically for Grant. MGM, unsurprisingly, desperately wanted him to appear in a remake of *Grand Hotel*. And when Warren Beatty pleaded with him to do a tiny cameo playing God in *Heaven Can Wait*, a remake of *Here Comes Mr. Jordan* (1941), the offer of a straight million dollars for a couple of days' work surely whetted the appetite of the business brain in Grant. Eventually – and astutely, as it transpired – he decided it was 'not a good part. Long speeches. Stands around a lot. Everyone else gets the jokes.'

Even at Fabergé Grant complained that he could not escape his movie star past. 'I'm a target for people with a script who want acting jobs,' he said. 'Or shareholders who are convinced that their daughter is the prettiest in the world and should be in pictures. They all seem to want to get into pictures. I don't know why...' An interesting comment from the boy from Bristol who had exactly that ambition.

When Fabergé launched a movie-making division, however, Brut Productions in 1972, Grant was willing to bring his former expertise to aid the company: after all, this was *business*, and it was something definite that he could put into his nondescript role at Fabergé.

One of Brut's productions in which Grant took particular interest was *A Touch Of Class*, written by Melvin Frank and Jack Rose, and directed by Melvin Frank. Set in London, the film was a romantic comedy that told the story of a married American businessman who has an affair with a dress designer. George Barrie urged Grant to play the part of the businessman, a performance Grant could have telephoned in, so suitable was it. The temptation was clearly strong because the script, Grant believed, was tremendous. In the event, though, he decided against doing the film, telling Barrie, 'Ten years ago I would have made the film in a second but, no, not now.'

His faith in the film was well placed. *A Touch Of Class* was a huge box-office smash and the unexpected screen pairing of George Segal – in the role Grant declined – and Glenda Jackson proved very popular.

The film was nominated for four Oscars, including best film and best screenplay, and won one for Jackson.

Glenda Jackson herself, one of Britain's finest classical actresses until she became a politician and a minister in Tony Blair's government in 1997, had been unknown as a comedienne until appearing on *The Morecambe and Wise Show* in 1971. She herself has always said that the producers of the film saw her in *The Morecambe and Wise Show* and offered her the film as a direct result.

Since Grant and Eric Morecambe had been friends for the best part of a decade in 1971 and Grant was an avid viewer of *The Morecambe and Wise Show*, it is highly probable that it was Grant himself who first spotted Jackson's comic potential.

If so, this would prove – as does his spotting the potential of the entire project – that Cary Grant might have left the movies, but his knack of sensing a cinematic winner never left him.

27 _____

> 'Cary looked spectacular right up to the end. He kept himself busy and went to the races and attended board meetings and took trips and told terrible jokes and always, always made plans for tomorrow.'

> Roderick Mann

Cary Grant might not have had a picture locked away in the attic like Wilde's Dorian Gray but he was seemingly, miraculously, untouched by age. Friends, contemporaries and former colleagues were ageing and dying and succumbing to all the attendant frailties of passing time but Grant seemed invincible, his zest for life as strong as ever, his libido undiminished – and his desire for privacy even greater.

In March 1970, Grant was asked to present an honorary 'Tony' award to Noel Coward, who had just turned seventy and was newly knighted. Since Grant had known Coward for nearly fifty years and freely admitted that Coward's persona had had a profound impact on him when he was trying to mould his own screen image, Grant did not hesitate to accept.

At the ceremony itself, the contrast between the two men could not have been greater. Only four years separated them with Grant, at 66, the junior. But it might have been 24 years: Grant, tanned, erect and vigorous seemed decades younger than his hero, who was stooped, moving extremely slowly and heavily lined.

Afterwards, when Grant left the theatre, he was mobbed by the crowd outside.

'Grant stepped through the door,' recalled Bill Weaver, Grant's personal secretary from the late 1960s onwards, 'and in a second the police barricade was scattered as fans, young, middle-aged and old, erupted through the cordon, rushing to try to touch the man they still regarded as their idol, clutching out at him, shoving, pushing and kicking, tearing at his buttons in order to secure at least one small trophy of the star.'

This was the kind of frenzy usually only triggered by the arrival of the latest pop sensation and Grant, on the surface at least, gave the impression of having been horrified by the incident. Certainly he used it as the excuse to withdraw even further from public gaze thereafter. Not everyone, however, was convinced.

'Cary sometimes gave the impression of a man rationing his name and his time with a caution that owed something to natural shyness,' said his business associate William McIntosh. 'But also to a canny awareness of the heightened value that rarity confers.'

Again, Grant knew precisely how to market the 'Cary Grant' brand, though it is interesting that as a film star of several decades, he had managed to overcome a shyness that had probably been one of his most attractive attributes from the start of his rise to glory right up to his eventual death.

Also, Grant had never fully approved of awards ceremonies – perhaps having been slighted on so many of those occasions – still less the ritualistic backslapping that seems a permanent feature of show business.

'There's a banquet every night,' he once moaned. 'Every bloody night out here. There's one for Bob Hope, one for Jack Benny, one for every guy in the world. You can't do them all. I'd rather dine quietly down on the beach.' This said, it seems to be an attitude that diminished in passing years. Typical was Grant's tribute to Roger Moore and it is likely that any misgivings Grant had about these tributes was eclipsed by his loyalty to his friends. Certainly, Grant liked Moore and they saw a lot of each other during the 1970s when, like Grant, Moore 'tried his hand', as he put it, at being an executive and joined Fabergé to run the European office for BRUT films.

'During the following years, we saw a great deal of one another socially,' Moore recalls. 'And at Easter and Thanksgiving, we always found ourselves among the many guests staying at the guest houses on the Frank Sinatra compound at Palm Springs.'

The friendship was reflected at a Friars Club Tribute to Moore when, according to Moore himself, 'Cary very kindly made the most extraordinary speech.'

The Friars Club is an international show-business fraternity and Grant was named their Man of the Year in 1982. The occasion, held at the Waldorf-Astoria in New York was particularly memorable for George Burns' claiming in a light-hearted speech that he and Grant had been introduced by Abraham Lincoln's widow!

At the same ceremony, Peggy Lee serenaded him with *Mr Wonderful* and other musical tributes followed from Frank Sinatra, Tony Bennett, Cy Coleman and Sammy Cahn. Afterwards, Grant made an extraordinary speech which, perhaps more than any other, revealed his ambivalence about such tributes in later life.

'I feel myself tearful with happiness quite often these days,' he said. 'I cry at great talent. I'm deeply affected by the works of certain writers, by certain singers, phrases of music, the perfection of Fred Astaire. Such things can trigger off a complexity of emotions, but you see, to indulge in one's emotions, publicly and unashamedly, is a privilege permitted to the elderly...'

Leaving aside occasions that were tributes to him, one cannot help but sense a note of hypocrisy in his attitude to accepting invitations to public events. Throughout the 1970s, he showed further 'canny awareness' by attending several high-profile events which would do nothing to diminish 'Cary Grant' in the public mind.

He narrated Walt Disney's Candlelight Ceremony in December 1972 and Disneyland's Candlelight Ceremony in December 1973 and again in December 1974. He attended the Straw Hat Awards in New York in May 1975, when he was given a special plaque acknowledging New York's appreciation of his long career 'as a star and superstar in entertainment'. He introduced a speech by Betty Ford at the Republican National Convention in Kansas City in August 1976 and attended the Bicentenary dinner for Queen Elizabeth II at the White House also in 1976. He was 'dinner chairman' at a charity function in Beverly Hills for Prince Charles and attended a royal charity gala at the London Palladium in 1978. He hosted the American Film Institute's salute to Alfred Hitchcock in March 1979 and presented Laurence Olivier with an honourary Oscar the following month. And he was present in London for the funeral of Lord Louis Mountbatten, who had been murdered by the IRA, in August 1979.

Even before his marriage to Barbara Hutton, Grant had been accused of being a social climber and the acceptance of certain high-profile events in the presence of royalty, real or Hollywood, and presidents, led to more accusations of social climbing throughout the 1970s. It must be said, though, that for a man of Grant's wealth and stature, it was almost impossible for him to climb much higher socially and that any of his appearances at the events listed was, presumably, as much a thrill for those in attendance as he himself.

Twice, Grant himself was the recipient of honorary awards. Criminally overlooked by the Academy of Motion Picture Arts and Sciences, amends were made, of a kind, when Frank Sinatra, Grant's near-neighbour in Palm Springs and co-star from *The Pride And The Passion*, presented him with his special award on 7 April 1970. His Oscar was inscribed: 'To Cary Grant: For his unique mastery of the art of screen acting with the respect and affection of his colleagues'.

'It's presented for sheer brilliance of acting,' remarked Sinatra. 'No one has brought more pleasure to more people for many years than Cary has, nobody has done so many things so well. Cary has so much skill that he makes it all look easy.'

Rising above the years of injustice that Grant undoubtedly felt he had suffered from the Academy, he told the audience, 'Probably no greater honour can come to a man than the respect of his colleagues.' Paying tribute to all those with whom he had worked, he reminded his audience that, 'this is a collaborative medium. We all need each other.'

A consequence of receiving his Oscar was that Grant reinstated his membership of the Academy, having resigned in protest many years earlier. He explained his reasons in a letter to the Academy President in September 1970: 'Because of what may have since become outmoded principles, I deplored commercialising a ceremony which, in my estimation, should have remained unpublicised and privately shared among the artists and craftsmen of our industry. I'm not at all sure my beliefs have changed. Just the times.'

Nearly twelve years later, in December 1981, Grant was awarded a Kennedy Center Honour for Achievement in the Performing Arts, along with Count Basie, Jerome Robbins and Helen Hayes. Presenting Grant with his award, Rex Harrison said that 'audiences around the world have loved the civilised grace and brilliance of Cary Grant but not everyone has appreciated that he was also one of the most accomplished actors in the history of motion pictures because civilised grace and comic brilliance are two of the most unique and rare qualities within an actor's range. There have been descriptions of many newcomers as "young Cary Grants". The fact is there is only one original, the supremely gifted man, whom we honour tonight for a magnificent career on the screen.'

If the rare public events Grant did agree to attend during these last twenty years of his life were grand affairs, they were mixed with grief for friends who died. He might have been an essentially private man and, by his own admission, 'I've never been a joiner or a member of any – of a particular – social set', but those friends he did have were close and he felt their loss keenly.

Noel Coward once famously remarked about growing old that 'it's got to the stage when all I ask of my friends is they make it through lunch.' Grant, who looked like he would make it through lunch *and* supper for a long time yet, was saddened by the deaths of friends such as Hitchcock in 1980, with whom he had created such cinematic masterpieces, and Coward himself in 1973 – his first and lasting influence – and was devastated by the tragic loss of Princess Grace.

On 24 July 1972, Lance Reventlow, Barbara Hutton's son whom Grant came to regard almost as a son, was killed in a plane crash. He was 36. The actress Jill St John, a friend of Lance's who had met Grant through the younger man, recalls that, on the way to the funeral, Grant continually 'looked through a large manila envelope. Everything Lance had given him – cards, letters from camp, letters from school, Christmas cards, Easter cards – from the age of six to maybe twelve . . . '

The murder of Lord Mountbatten in August 1979 also hit him hard. The two men were friends of the same generation. Indeed, Grant had accompanied him on a visit to Las Vegas during the seventies and had introduced him to another friend, the singer and living legend Frank Sinatra. It was not just that Grant had lost another friend: the casual slaughter of a 79-year-old military hero by terrorists shook him to the very foundations in the belief – *his* belief – in human decency, and left him suddenly feeling out of sympathy with the modern world. It was his peer, Charles Chaplin, who had said that the older one became the more estranged one became to the real world. Grant was surely experiencing this as much as the perceptive comedian had done some years earlier.

'I'm absolutely pooped,' he remarked to a friend at the funeral. 'I feel so goddamned old. I'm just going to quit all next year. I'm going to lie in bed. I shall just close all doors, turn off the telephone, and enjoy my life.'

He didn't retire to his bed, of course, and even as he approached eighty, his stamina and vitality for life remained undiminished.

'He was quite simply never ill,' said his assistant Bill Weaver. 'He never seemed to suffer the palest traces of jet-lag and he showed exceptional resilience after long flights across the Atlantic: he was always eager to make plans rather than go to bed to rest and adapt to the change in hour.'

'I've got to live to four hundred to do all the things I've got to do,' Grant joked in the last year of his life. 'But even if I don't live that long – even if I die soon – it's been a wonderful life.'

On another occasion he admitted, 'I used to worry that when you reached a certain age, things stopped happening. But I don't worry about that any more because – and it's a real pleasure to say this – they don't stop happening. I haven't stopped doing anything simply because of my age.'

His remarkable resilience owed much, of course, to his mother who, despite the lost years in the asylum, had passed into her nineties with extreme aplomb. Nevertheless, no one – not even Elsie – could live forever. On 22 January 1973, just days before what would have been her 96th birthday, she died.

Grant had last seen his mother the previous June, when he made one of his regular visits to Bristol. Although there were still barriers between them, Grant and Elsie did have one thing that delighted them both equally – Jennifer. Elsie was delighted to have a grandchild at last and kept a photograph of her by her bed. During those last few visits between mother and son, talking about Jennifer was the one thing that truly, finally, brought them close. There had always been a missing link until that point, a gap where lay the hurt at her disappearance and the unimaginable shock of her re-emergence in his later life. But now Jennifer bridged that gap.

Although Elsie had begun to exhibit occasional bouts of mild confusion, Grant had found her to be as robust as ever: for one thing, she was insisting that she was only 93! And if her early years had been horrific, her 'second' life had been relatively contented. And in the end, when death came, it was mercifully quick.

'She died in a perfect way,' Grant reflected afterwards. 'She was served a cup of tea, and when they came back to see her, that was it. That's a nice way to die. I often wonder how I'm going to do it. You don't want to embarrass your friends.'

On receiving the news of her death, Grant at once flew to Bristol for the funeral. Mindful of the disgraceful press *mêlée* that had accompanied his father's funeral nearly forty years earlier and maintaining his now near-obsession for privacy, Grant did not inform the press of Elsie's death until after the funeral.

An indication that Grant's longevity was inherited from Elsie and not Elias was reinforced less than four years later when his half-brother, Eric Leslie Leach, Elias's other son, died from cancer at the early age of 55.

Though there is no evidence of bad feeling between Grant and Eric Leach, they rarely saw each other and Grant never mentioned him. Typically, he had helped his half-brother and his family financially although, again, this was kept absolutely private.

With his mother gone, Grant's visits to Bristol did not cease, but they did, understandably, lessen. He maintained his Bristolian links in the US when, in the autumn of 1974, he unveiled a plaque at the United Nations Building – a famous backdrop of *North By Northwest* – to mark the opening of a new landscaped area in New York's East Side called the Bristol Basin, so called because the development had used hundreds of tons of rubble from Bristol's pounding during the Second World War.

If some interpreted these rare public engagements connected with Bristol as a sign of nostalgia creeping into Grant's old age, they were absolutely wrong. Grant remained resolute in his rejection of any kind of nostalgia.

'You're only old when you forget to be young,' he told Ginger Rogers in *Monkey Business*. Grant himself seemed intent on remembering to be young for the rest of his life. He became determined not to look back and famously turned down a five-million-dollar offer to write his autobiography: 'No one's ever truthful about his own life. There are always ambiguities. I'd rather not be guilty of that. Besides, I'm much keener on living now than writing about the past.'

Part of this strategy was to distance himself from the movie industry, and the part he had played in it, as much as possible.

'At one time the movie industry was a fabulous industry,' he said. 'But now I feel that the public has grown up too much to believe in films any more. Their own lives nowadays are just as interesting as anything they are likely to see on the screen. I get scripts sent to me all the time, but I regard that part of my life as being in the past.

'You know, I can't even remember being on a particular set or making a particular film. Some I do. There were some. I may even have enjoyed working with a particular leading lady. But often I don't even remember being there. I sometimes see a film and say, "My God, is that me?"'

When it suited, Grant's recollection for the past could make a miraculous recovery, such as when he embarked on a series of one-man theatre shows he called, simply, *A Conversation With Cary Grant*. Perhaps, therefore, he was simply able to shut out the past from his mind, rather than having genuinely forgotten it.

If Grant rarely, if ever, succumbed to that most corrosive vice of the elderly, nostalgia, his youthful demeanour was occasionally undermined by a tetchiness with photographers or one of those odd obsessions old men get their teeth into with dogged tenacity. Somewhat literally, on one occasion, when he started a war about the English muffin as served at the Plaza hotel in New York.

Arriving at the hotel, Grant ordered English muffins from the room service menu and was appalled when he saw that he was served with three half-muffins. He demanded to know why, when the muffins were listed in the plural on the menu, he was served with 'a muffin and a half'. The waiter couldn't enlighten him, so Grant complained to room service. They couldn't help either, so they passed him over to the assistant manager who could only admit: 'I don't know why – but we've always served three halves ever since I got this job.'

Grant then called the managing director of the hotel who, again, didn't know why but said he would send up a fourth half-muffin with his compliments. This still didn't satisfy Grant, who then called Conrad Hilton – the Plaza being part of the Hilton group – at his home in Beverly Hills. But Hilton wasn't at home. So Grant tracked him down to . . . Istanbul, Turkey.

Hilton explained that the Plaza had in the past served four halves of English muffin, but a study had shown than nine out of ten people ate three halves and left the fourth. Thus, a decision had been taken to serve only three halves.

This still did not satisfy Grant, who argued that the menu was misleading. 'It should say a muffin and a half,' he insisted, 'not muffins in the plural.'

Hilton, to his credit, agreed and ordered a change in policy so that, in future, four halves of muffin were served. Grant's telephone calls about the amount of muffins – or lack of them – had, by his friends' reckoning, cost him over $100. But Grant maintained that it had been worth it. He also decided to form a society for English muffin lovers. There was just one rule: members had to insist on at least two muffins being served whenever they were ordered.

Some interpreted his rather obsessive muffin campaign as a manifestation of his legendary parsimony, but considering what it cost him in the long-term, it could be argued that it was a rather rarefied joke by a man with a particular sense of humour. It certainly wasn't a sign that he was a wealthy septuagenarian with too much time on his hands.

Quite apart from his numerous business interests and a young daughter, Grant continued to date and to be seen with some of the most beautiful women in the world. And if he, himself, was getting older, the age of his girlfriends remained constant.

His relationships in the first half of the 1970s tended to be brief liaisons. But they were liaisons with some of the world's most glamorous women and were evidence of yet another contradiction in his character. Even at this late hour in his life, Grant's love life was bound to be of interest to the press and, by being seen with women like Raquel Welch and Farrah Fawcett-Majors, this man who purported to cherish his privacy seemed to go out of his way perversely to pique press interest.

Bill Weaver, Grant's personal assistant, paints a picture of a man who still fascinated women and recalls that when Grant did attend a party there would be 'dozens of pressing women competing for his attentions'.

Grant, though, seemed unsure of his attraction and his failed four marriages clearly cast a gloomy shadow across his romantic inclinations. If Grant was attracted to a woman, he would send Weaver to make the first approach and enquire if she 'would like to have dinner with an ageing movie star'. Interestingly, Grant used the 'ageing movie star' tag as bait despite his insisting that he had given up the film business for good. Ever the pragmatist, he clearly saw the power that image had on those outside the industry. And it can hardly be called arrogance that he should recognise the truth that 'Cary Grant' still held a unique place in the collective hearts of women across the world.

'I often think my life has been a failure,' he once reflected. 'But whenever I drop into a movie theatre and hear women laughing at one of my films, I think, well, if I brightened their day before they went home and did the dishes, maybe my life hasn't been wasted after all.'

One of the relationships he had – with Victoria Morgan, who was later murdered in 1983 – he openly referred to as 'a strictly sexual relationship'. Even allowing for the revolution in sexual mores that had occurred in the wake of the Swinging Sixties, it was still bold in the 1970s for a man of Grant's age to be quite so blunt about his sexual relationship with a woman young enough to be his granddaughter. Grant, ever taking the liberal high ground in matters of personal morality, didn't judge – and didn't expect to be judged – until the end of his life.

That phrase 'strictly a sexual relationship' looks quite cold in print. To the uninformed reader it might seem cynical, as though Grant was not seeking anything more than physical gratification with each successive relationship. The truth appears to be that no woman seems to have regretted a brief fling with the 'ageing movie star'.

Raquel Welch, for one, has always spoken warmly of the influence Grant had on her. Welch, who once had the reputation for speaking her mind too plainly about those she disliked, explained a change of policy.

'I only say nice things about them now,' she said. 'It drives them crazy. It's a technique I learned from Cary Grant.'

Not all of Grant's female companions in the 1970s were famous, however. On one occasion, while he was staying at the Avon Gorge Hotel in Bristol, a fire broke out early one morning resulting in the evacuation of the place. Grant's fellow celebrity residents – the television naturalist David Attenborough and the underwater legend Jacques Cousteau – were forced to spend several hours out on the pavement while the firemen brought the blaze under control and searched the premises.

Consternation began to grow because Grant could not be found and rumours began to circulate – as they had thirty years earlier when he and Howard Hughes had 'disappeared' in Hughes's plane – about what had happened to him. Those rumours were quashed when Grant sauntered up to the hotel accompanied by a woman who was also a guest at the hotel and with whom he had been out all night.

Naturally, press interest was piqued as to the identity of Grant's new lady friend, but she remained a mystery. A Fabergé spokeswoman deflected all questions with a tectchily bland statement: 'She may have been one of the freelance ladies we use from time to time. Obviously, we look after him.'

Grant himself was even less forthcoming. 'The lady is a public relations consultant with the company,' he told them. 'That is all. There is certainly no romantic attachment. I am not prepared to say who she is.'

Bill Weaver said that women Grant asked out 'nearly always accepted' and has suggested that this was partly because 'his face, his voice, his manner, his charm, even his clothes were immensely familiar.'

But part of his charm was also that elusive vulnerability that he displayed from the bitter split from Dyan Cannon onwards. It was a vulnerability that centred, predictably, on Jennifer.

Grant's love for his daughter knew no bounds and his protection of her did not diminish as she grew older. Some have suggested that it bordered on the obsessive but, even if it did, it was an obsession that was entirely positive.

Jennifer did not get everything she wanted. At one time she pestered her father for a dog. Grant refused to get one, explaining he didn't like household pets. Given that his wedding present to Betsy Drake had been a white poodle called Suzy, this might be regarded as hypocritical: possibly it was a way of refusing Jennifer gently. He did, however, agree to buy her a horse and Jennifer eventually became a proficient rider.

It was the protectiveness he felt towards his daughter – together with disillusionment in the film industry – that compelled Grant to try and steer her away from any thoughts she might have had about becoming an actress. Almost from the age she could walk, Grant was inundated with offers for parts in movies for her. He turned them all down out of hand. He was determined that she would not follow in his footsteps and, if there was one thing he and Dyan Cannon were agreed upon, it was that she should have as normal an upbringing as possible.

Women, certainly, understood this – which is why his doting on his daughter, his emotional Achilles heel, merely added to his appeal.

'The miracle of having given life to someone is quite fantastic,' he said. 'I regard Jennifer as my ticket to immortality. I die off – she continues. All I want for her is to grow up happy. She'll have a better chance than I did, I should think. She's prettier.'

28

'What's good about being eighty? That one is living, I suppose.'

Cary Grant

When Grant licked his wounds in the months and years following his nightmarish divorce from Dyan Cannon, he never expected to marry again. And his relationships between 1969 and 1973, while mutually enjoyable, had been temporary and ephemeral.

Partly, this was because of his focusing on Jennifer. The regular, petty skirmishes with Cannon over access, which often could only be settled in the courts, meant that Grant felt that he simply could not commit himself to another relationship.

He was also wary of commitment. Even by Hollywood standards, four failed marriages was not a record to be proud of and he was acutely aware that to embark on yet another marriage might be to court another matrimonial disaster – not to mention further ridicule. Since the memories of what he still regarded as his public humiliation during the Cannon divorce proceedings were still raw, his reluctance to risk that again is entirely understandable.

There was another reason why he didn't want to risk another failed marriage: he was determined to set a good example to Jennifer as she grew up. He wanted some kind of emotional stability for her, taking into account the fact that her parents were divorced and that she would learn of his failures with relationships.

'I want Jennifer to give one man love and confidence and help,' he insisted. 'But I don't care what she does as long as she's happy. I advise her to love someone and be loved. The rest is a bonus.'

The emphasis he places on personal happiness is curious. It is as if he wants his daughter not just to be happy for *her* sake, but for *his* sake, which is often the way of someone who, to a greater or lesser extent, has been denied personal happiness for the most part in their own life.

There is a parallel again with Charlie Chaplin, who was desperately frustrated that all the money, the success, the properties, the swimming-pools, the accolades could not cancel out his mother having become unbalanced through chronic hardship before he arrived at his great status. In that sense, it is likely that all possibility of Grant finding true happiness died the day he returned home as a nine-year-old child to find his mother gone, seemingly for ever.

For a decade after his divorce from Cannon, Grant was attracted to women in their twenties. David Niven had noticed, thirty years earlier, his habit of 'repeating the pattern'. Once he had ended one relationship, he would immediately embark upon another with a similar woman. And there was definitely a Cary Grant 'type' of woman, as he himself acknowledged:

'I'm attracted to women who are secure. One gets secure as one accomplishes. A person tries to meet another on the same plateau, the same intellectual level. I like women without artifice. The social belles of my day, the long cigarette-holder types with little bonnets and jangling bracelets and all that stuff were artificial. I don't go for that.'

His brief relationships at this time were occasionally peppered by unconfirmed reports that he had proposed marriage, only to have been turned down. Given that he had been engaged several times previously in addition to his four marriages, these reports were not wholly unbelievable. But Grant never commented on the sporadic rumours of his being engaged and his pattern of uncomplicated affairs continued unabated until 1973 when his name became persistently linked with that of Maureen Donaldson, an English media correspondent and photographer. They met in August 1973 at Sun Valley, Idaho, when she was covering a film festival for a Hollywood magazine: Grant was then just five months away from his 70th birthday; Donaldson was just 26. It was also just over six months after Elsie's death and Grant, feeling unexpectedly hollow following the loss of his mother, initially regarded the affair as a diversion from his bereavement.

Despite the near 45-year gap in their ages, Donaldson had much in common with Grant. Like him, she had left a modest background in England at a relatively young age (her father was a retired fireman from Muswell Hill) to find work in Los Angeles. She first trained as a nanny before graduating into journalism and photography and had married the rock singer Dee Donaldson. Her divorce from Donaldson was finalised a little while after she met Grant.

Apart from a few snide comments in gossip columns, Grant's relationship with Donaldson attracted much press attention but very little real criticism and she subsequently moved in with him. This, not unnaturally, fuelled speculation that he was contemplating a fifth marriage. Grant denied it emphatically. 'The answer is no. I've been married four times. I'm obviously a failure at marriage. What went wrong? Who knows? But I'm not going to try it again.'

This did not stop the speculation and the *Daily Mail* in London ran a story that caused a great deal of trouble between the couple. The thrust of the story was that Grant was, indeed, considering marrying Donaldson – but only because it would enable him to fight for custody of Jennifer. Donaldson was, understandably, furious by the suggestion, and although Grant convinced her there was no truth in the story, the relationship appears never to have been *quite* the same afterwards.

The situation was not encouraged by a recurrence of the fault-lines that had fatally undermined his marriage to Cannon. He had, perhaps, learned one lesson from his fourth marriage: instead of stifling her ambitions, as he had attempted with Cannon's film career, he actively encouraged Donaldson – or at least apparently – to pursue her career as a freelance photographer by inveigling his celebrity friends to sit for her. But he couldn't resist the impulse to control and, just as he had with Cannon before her, his telling Donaldson what to wear, how to wear it, how to pronounce certain words and his endless lectures on etiquette undermined their relationship.

On one occasion, when Donaldson was resisting his lecture on social manners, he retorted by saying, 'I was going to parties with Noel Coward in the twenties, so I think you can accept *my* word as final on this matter!' It seemed that Cary Grant, despite his assertions of never looking back and claims of living purely for the moment, *could* refer to his past when it suited him. This can often be seen in his reference to his films and the film industry, once recalling most of his output as 'tinny'. Yet, he wasn't against sneaking into a theatre and catching a re-run of one of these same films and being hugely rewarded by the positive reaction of the audiences.

Donaldson's recollections of her time with Grant, which she published in 1989 under the title: *An Affair To Remember: My Life With Cary Grant* are essentially positive. Certainly, the picture of Grant she portrays show him still interested in the modern world, apart from the occasional tetchy reminders of his past, like the 'I was going to dinner with Noel Coward in the twenties':

'He clipped out everything of interest in the newspapers,' she recalled. 'He clipped coupons. He clipped news items. He clipped stories from magazines. No matter how trivial the "news" seemed to be, Cary would mark items to be included in his files.'

Donaldson's positive memories of Grant are echoed by almost every woman he loved, with the exception, ironically, of his wives. Forty years separated the women he romanced in the 1930s and those he dated in the 1970s, but their reminiscences are uncannily similar.

'Cary was beyond any question the most attractive, charming, funny, sweet, marvellous man I've ever known,' said actress Betty Furness, with whom Grant had had a relationship in the 1930s. 'And I haven't met his rival yet.'

Her words are echoed by Phyllis Brooks, to whom Grant was briefly engaged in the late 1930s. She recalled after his death that 'Cary was imperfect as are all we mortals, but he was my love. He was careful, gentle, kind, tender and fatherly to me. So far as I knew, he was a loving and passionate heterosexual. He had a strict moral code as to loyalty, fidelity and like virtues, and he lived by them when I knew him.'

Grant and Donaldson split in 1977. It was amicable and they remained friends to the end of his life. A measure of that friendship came some years after their split when Grant sent Donaldson a copy of a poem by Robert Browning called *Apparent Failure*. Grant had underlined one particular line: 'That what began best can't end worst'.

When he and Donaldson went their separate ways, most commentators believed that any prospect of him now re-marrying at his time of life was unlikely. He had spent four years with Donaldson. It had been a committed relationship – lasting longer than his marriages to Virginia Cherrill, Barbara Hutton and Dyan Cannon – and if he wasn't prepared to marry, or she him, he was unlikely, at nearly 74, to commit himself again.

What no one knew, including Grant, was that he had already met the woman who was destined to become the fifth, and last, 'Mrs Cary Grant'.

That woman was Barbara Harris who, having been born in 1950, was 46 years his junior.

They met in London in 1976 when Barbara was the PR officer at the Royal Lancaster Hotel and Grant arrived for a Fabergé conference. At first, their relationship was based on friendship and evolved into romance more slowly than perhaps any of Grant's previous lovers. This contradicts any suggestion that Grant, the ageing superstar, was merely looking for a young woman to comfort him during his last years – or that Barbara was a gold-digger. Although they maintained contact and saw each other regularly, sometimes in London and at other times in California, it was to be three years before she moved in with him at his Californian home as his 'constant companion' in 1979.

It wasn't as though Grant was unaware of how little time he might have left. Ever the realist, he knew only too well that he was already past the biblical three-score-years-and-ten and admitted at the end of the 1970s, 'I doubt if I have more than seventy-thousand hours left and I'm not about to waste any of them.'

In a way, this determination not to waste any time makes his gradual wooing of Barbara Harris all the more significant. If he had been looking for willing nubile company, he could have walked down Beverly Hills for about five minutes and attracted fifty applicants. This, therefore, was clearly something special.

As for Barbara herself, she was hardly the lucky hotel receptionist other biographers have attempted to portray. The daughter of a British Army officer, James Harris, who was a Colonial Officer in Tanganyika in Africa, she had been born in Dar es Salaam and had spent much of her earlier life in Africa. Thus, although she knew who Cary Grant was, she had actually seen very few of his films and, when they first met, consequently had few preconceptions about – and certainly no adoration of – him. It was this unaffected nature of their coming together that Grant really liked and appreciated.

While coming closer together in 1977 and 1978, they were also wary of getting *too* close, as Barbara herself acknowledged after they had married: 'I was worried at first about the age difference between us. Of course I was. And I had to think about it a great deal. I knew his reputation. But Cary, although a complex man, is extremely kind and intelligent and has a wonderful sense of humour. We appreciate one another more than young couples do because we both know that time is so precious.'

Barbara Harris's effect on Grant was extraordinarily positive and the relatively few disapproving comments about the age difference and number of times he had been previously married were blunted by the obviously genuine love they expressed for each other.

'He touched her all the time,' said Bea Shaw, a friend of Grant's. 'He touched her hand, he put his arm around her, he stroked her. And that said more to me than anything he could say about her. And she was that way with him.'

'Cary had never been happier,' agreed Prince Rainier of Monaco, who had been a friend of Grant's since marrying Grace Kelly in the principality in 1956. 'It was only when he met Barbara that he found what he had been searching for: the everyday happiness that lasted all day, all night, day after day, month after month, year after year.'

Grant's marriage to Dyan Cannon had given him the child for whom he had always yearned. Now Barbara could provide the settled family life he'd never had.

Barbara's mother, Mrs Lesley Harris, said after his death: 'He was not like a superstar. He never put on airs and graces for us. I treated him like my other son-in-law. We loved each other very much.'

Although there is something amusing about Grant's new mother-in-law treating him just as her other son-in-law when he was, in fact, fifteen years older than her own husband, there is something rather touching about the simplicity of Lesley Harris's words. So much had happened to Grant in his large and exciting life, so many emotional demons remained undefeated. And yet, at the end of his life, he had found the unconditional love and affection he had always been craving.

In 1979, Barbara moved in with him at his Beverly Hills home and it didn't go unnoticed he was like a man reborn at 75. Eschewing the reclusive habits of old, he became much more social and delighted in showing off the young and attractive lady now in his life. He became notably more benign, settled and humorous, and his Beverly Hills 'shack', which he had been having renovated for several years – 'I expect them to be putting the finishing touches just as I'm taking my last breath' – was finally transformed into a white Moroccan-style mansion. One of the workmen involved commented: 'I hope you don't mind me saying so, Mr Grant, but for a man of your age to be putting in additions shows a helluva lot of courage.' Grant pointed to an incline he'd requested to be put in next to the steps leading to an entrance and merely quipped, 'Don't worry – that's for when I'm in a wheelchair.'

Grant had always looked spectacular and tanned and the epitome of style. But now, perhaps for the first time, he was spectacular on the inside, too. It had been nearly a lifetime in coming, but he embraced contentment with open arms.

He had been concerned about how Jennifer would react to his relationship with Barbara and it is doubtful whether Cary Grant could ever fully love a woman without his daughter's approval. His adoration of Jennifer led him to moments of hypocrisy: for instance, having publicly scorned autograph hunters, he was happy to queue up and request them from stars – such as Woody Allen – whom Jennifer admired.

Jennifer was ten years old in 1976 when Grant first met Barbara Harris, and on her birthday that year he wrote her a letter that was unselfconsciously sentimental.

Writing of the ten years of 'being with you at every opportunity possible to me', he continues: 'I'm proud to know you. Proud to be seen with you. You are the dearest daughter a man could have. You have never caused me a moment's anguish or disappointment. Your qualities are of the best, and if you persist in these qualities throughout life, you will enjoy ever-growing happiness.'

Thus, Jennifer's opinion of Barbara mattered to him and as his thoughts of marrying again became more crystallised throughout 1980, he knew he would only do so if he had Jennifer's approval.

'Look,' he told her, 'how would you feel if I asked Barbara to marry me? I'm getting on. I need her.'

Jennifer was very happy about it and Cary Grant became married for the fifth and last time on 15 April 1981. It was a typically low-key affair – this time conducted at his Beverly Hills house and attended by Jennifer, Grant's lawyer, the judge and two servants acting as witnesses.

Equally typically, Grant kept the wedding secret although, since he and Barbara were regarded as inseparable in Hollywood by 1981, his reluctance to share the news is puzzling.

A few days after their own wedding, Grant and Barbara attended the silver wedding celebrations for Prince Rainier and Princess Grace at Frank Sinatra's Palm Springs home. Among a small, select group of old friends, Grant confessed that he and Barbara had married. Inevitably, the news leaked out and Grant professed himself disappointed. 'They're all old chums,' he complained. 'I thought they'd keep our secret.' Of course, since there really was no need to keep the wedding a secret, it is entirely possible that he had told his friends all about it knowing that it would be leaked. Had he not, after all, kept his marriage to Dyan Cannon a secret – with all the near-absurd measures to preserve the secret – only to blow it to Roderick Mann in Bristol?

If he was genuinely irritated by the leaked news of his marriage, then it didn't last for long: the new Mr and Mrs Grant settled down to an enjoyable, privileged and enviable life. They travelled extensively in Europe and the Far East and, in between trips, their Californian life was serene and untroubled.

Certainly, he became much more relaxed with the press in these later years, and an interview he gave in 1981 was an extraordinarily – for him – candid insight into his married life with Barbara.

'I suffer from insomnia,' he said. 'Always have done. I usually wake around three and read for an hour or so. I probably drop off about four and wake again between six-thirty and seven. If my daughter Jennifer is staying with us I have to get up and dress and drive her to school. My male secretary arrives at nine and we go through the mail, having to refuse a helluva lot of requests to this or that. I do most of my business on the phone. I go to board meetings but I've no illusions about why I'm there – it's always for my PR ability. Most mornings I deal with my solicitors. In the afternoon? More of the same, I guess. Certainly, I don't crook a finger to keep fit. I take no exercise whatsoever. Barbara thinks I'm fit now because I started life as an acrobat.

'We like a quiet life. We have a wonderful couple who look after us. Both are marvellous cooks, so we often have meals at home. We watch television sometimes. More often we play cards. Do you know Spite and Malice? Marvellous game. We go to bed sometimes at eight, sometimes at twelve.'

The emotional fulfilment in those words is palpable – and in stark contrast with his previous marriages. Virginia Cherrill had called him 'solemn and disagreeable', while Dyan Cannon labelled him 'outlandish, irrational and hostile'. Grant had always taken the blame for the failure of his previous marriages, and with certain justification: he was clearly a more troubled, less happy, volatile young man than he was to be in his later years. But it becomes more evident that he had had the genuine misfortune not to have met someone capable of fulfilling him, someone who could have brought him the happiness he had so easily acquired in his latter years.

'What's good about being eighty?' he was asked by someone in an audience in 1984.

'That one is living, I suppose,' was his flippant reply. But it was only half the truth. What was good about his life at eighty was that he'd finally found a partner who made his life *worth* living.

29

'I am happy. I do what I want when I want. Once, in St
Louis, I met a fellow who ran a whorehouse because it
made him happy. Well, I do what makes me happy.'

Cary Grant, 1985

Grant turned eighty in January 1984 and the anniversary, reported widely
against his wishes, seemed almost unlikely. For so long had Cary Grant
been part of all our lives that he somehow seemed ageless and timeless.
That timelessness was now the stuff of legend and was the thrust of
virtually every commemorative article written about him that January.

'Some men seek out lost youth and indulge second childhoods with
illicit drugs, with the purchase of sports cars, with face lifts and
dancing lessons,' one columnist wrote. 'Cary Grant needs none of these
things. Each generation or so he takes unto himself a young wife.
Young women, old tweeds and whatever mysterious flame that burns
within – these seem to be enough to keep him young. Cary Grant
eighty? Ridiculous.'

Grant, himself, claimed that he had no secret formula to explain his
longevity: 'I just breathe in and out. I don't smoke and I do everything
in moderation. Except making love. I don't feel my age. Not often,
anyway... I used to have a vodka before dinner, but I've given that up.
I still have a glass of wine with a meal. If I have a secret at all it's just
that I do just what I want. I think that stops the ageing process as much
as anything.'

As for the celebrating of his eightieth: 'I'm glad I've made it, but
there isn't any reason for a special celebration. I'm going to duck
everyone and keep a low profile.'

He was as good as his word although he did relent and allow MGM
to rename its studio theatre the 'Cary Grant Theater': apart from his
birthday, the honour was intended to mark his tenth anniversary on the
MGM board. 'No one's ever named anything after me,' he remarked.

'Oh, but my mother once named her dog Archie.'

However, he refused outright to co-operate with the BBC who approached him with a view to making a documentary about his background in Bristol as a way of marking his eightieth. For a man sensitive about his past, his childhood, the idea of returning to take nostalgic footage of the city of his birth and upbringing was understandably anathema.

His links with Bristol had, in any case, loosened since Elsie's death and his own ageing. When he did revisit, he remained enthusiastic for the old haunts. Perhaps he was still trying to exorcise the ghosts, or maybe it was all so long ago that he could simply rise above it all, as if his past belonged to someone else. After all, he considered himself to be fortunate to even be living after eighty years of an action-packed and eventful life.

One of his last visits 'home' occurred in 1983 when he drove round the city with a female journalist from the *Bristol Evening Post.*

'Anyone who knows Cary Grant will tell you that he does not spend time peering into the windows of his past,' Roderick Mann wrote to mark Grant's eightieth. 'Ask him a question about his career and he'll answer courteously. Though questions about his favourite film or actress are a sure-fire way to make his eyes glaze over.'

But on that 1983 visit to Bristol Grant, that least-nostalgic of old men, *did* appear – unexpectedly, one imagines – to be more reflective for once. Driving round the city, he reminisced about Elsie taking him shopping on Saturday mornings and his early memories of the Hippodrome Theatre, where it all began. He asked to be taken to his favourite fish and chip shop, even pointed out the cinema where he had seen his first Pearl White serial with Elias. When the memory-lane tour was complete, he expressed great sadness to the journalist. He would have liked it to go and on.

'Death? Of course I think of it,' said Grant in 1984. 'But I don't dwell on it. I must say, I don't want to attract it too soon. You know, when I was young, I thought they'd have the thing licked by the time I got to this age. I think the thing you think about when you're my age is how you're going to do it and whether you'll behave well.'

Intimations of mortality are inescapable when a man reaches eighty and no matter how immortal Grant might have appeared – even, at times, in his own mind – friends and colleagues were proving less so. Consequently, he often found himself part of yet another funeral cortège, or writing letters of sympathy to the family of someone close who had died. Alfred Hitchcock died in April 1980. Mae West, about whom he would always remain ambivalent – 'She did her own thing to the detriment of everyone around her' – but to whom he surely owed some of his early success, died in November of 1980. David Niven, who by this time was a familiar resident on Cap Ferrat in southern France, was next to go. His friendly face had often been seen boating on the beautiful Mediterranean waters, or taking lunch at the internationally acclaimed La Colombe d'Or at St Pauls above Nice – also a favourite retreat of the artist Pablo Picasso. Niven succumbed quite quickly to the dreadful motor neurone disease in July 1983.

It was in the summer of 1982 that Grant was stunned by a dreadful left-and-right when he lost his two favourite leading ladies within a fortnight of each other. Ingrid Bergman died of cancer in the August of that year at Chelsea, London. Fifteen days later, and more shocking and unexpected than Bergman's death, Princess Grace died following a mysterious car crash in Monaco on the very roads she and Grant had driven along 27 years earlier in *To Catch A Thief*. The suddenness shocked the entire world.

Grant and Princess Grace had remained close friends following this film and her subsequent marriage to Prince Rainier. 'Grace loved and admired Cary,' said the Prince. 'She valued his friendship.'

Grant had visited the Rainiers in Monaco many times and, at their request, had joined the board of the Princess Grace Foundation. Her sudden death, at the early age of 52, devastated him and when he attended her funeral with Barbara by his side, Grant was pictured distraught and, for once, looking every day of his 78 years.

But Grant's life between 1980 and 1986 was not all funerals and memorial services. Other old friends and contemporaries continued to thrive just as he did: Frank Sinatra was perpetually occupied by his never-ending series of 'farewell' concerts, while Cubby Broccoli, a close friend from those maverick days spent with Howard Hughes, was as busy as ever making movie history with the Bond series – now starring Roger Moore in the lead role. These three giants of the industry would often be seen together and Grant was particularly thrilled in 1982 to see Moore present Broccoli with the Irving G. Thalberg Memorial Award – the greatest accolade the industry can bestow and one rarely given – 'for consistently high quality of motion picture production'.

Above all else, Grant had Barbara and Jennifer, both of whom, he acknowledged, kept him young. Whatever fears he'd harboured about the effect his bitter divorce from Dyan Cannon might have had on their child, they were clearly unfounded as Jennifer reached her teens: as much credit for this must go to Cannon for that rare achievement in the frenzied climate of Los Angeles.

Of Jennifer he said, 'We love each other and we level with each other. And I know that when she's looking at me, she's not thinking, "I wonder if I can get this old goat for a BMW?"'

As for the fifth Mrs Grant, he claimed that 'my best piece of magic was marrying Barbara' and added: 'I want to remarry her every five years.'

Surely the clearest sign of the contentment he had found in this marriage revealed itself in his decision to embark on a series of one-man shows across America, something he wouldn't have remotely considered just a few years before.

Grant himself devised the show, which lasted approximately an hour and a half. It involved his reminiscing about his life and his career – working without a script – and taking questions from the audience.

He performed this one-man show, which he described as 'ego-fodder', nearly forty times between 1982 and his death in 1986, but he was as resolute about the bookings as he had been with the studio heads in the 1940s and 1950s. He kept the show decidedly low-key and refused to perform it in any of the big cities where the press and crowds would doubtless overwhelm the event. Nor would he allow any filming or recording. Each performance was purely for the moment, not something to be dragged up in later years on television screens around the globe so that commentators could remark how white was his hair by then, or how slowly he moved compared to his cinematic heyday. However, for someone so notoriously parsimonious, he took nothing as payment except his expenses from the box office and donated the large remainder to various charities.

Grant's enthusiasm for suddenly appearing in public again to do these shows wrong-footed everyone in the industry. Even at eighty, it seems that Cary Grant had the capacity to surprise.

Commentators speculated that, despite his eschewal of nostalgia, part of him still needed to know the audience loved him. 'And he had a need to show Barbara and Jennifer that he still had vitality and star attraction,' said one friend. 'He enjoyed meeting people and was truly interested in them. But if he hadn't had these two wonderful women in his life, I don't think he would have ventured out on that stage.' If these theories were true, they proved his old insecurities were still there, no matter how deeper they were now buried within him.

Whatever his motives, he approached the shows with the professionalism he had brought to his screen career. He took personal charge of all aspects of the evening, including lighting and sound, and a reporter from *Variety* in 1982 reported how he 'even supervised the placement of microphones in each aisle'. Memories of his days watching and learning behind the scenes at the Hippodrome, Bristol, remained as vivid as ever.

Grant, of course, had always been a professional, first in vaudeville and legitimate theatre, then in the movies, for well over sixty years. No one knew quite how to reach an audience like he did. It was how he had sustained popularity throughout his entire working life.

His shows were definite events: just as he had always done, he rationed himself perfectly. Never has a major star understood better the oldest show-business tenet of 'always leave 'em wanting more' than he did. Consequently, tickets for his shows were sold out within hours of being announced and sometimes changed hands for very large sums of money. Not that anybody could have felt cheated by his performance. Every audience seemed elated on its conclusion and the ovations were as long as they were loud. On one occasion, the only way Grant could bring a standing ovation to an end was to say, 'If you won't sit, *I'll* sit!'

The frank good humour with which he answered the audiences' questions showed he had lost none of his love to entertain. 'Grant's sharp, fast perceptive answers to questions belied his age,' marvelled *Variety.* They also displayed a self-mocking edge, especially about his age, which, perhaps intentionally, played on audience sympathy.

'Not bad for an old geezer like me, is she?' he joked of Barbara, who accompanied him on every appearance and arranged the PR. One questioner asked if he would do one of his famous pratfalls, to which Grant replied, 'It's all I can do to walk.' On another occasion, he told a member of the audience that 'I'm a fake. Watch me waddle off-stage – or catch me going upstairs sometime.'

His comic timing was as incisive as ever, as was his wry romanticism for which he was so renowned. 'What would you like for dinner if we were married?' asked one woman. 'The way you say that, I'd probably skip dinner,' he retorted, getting a huge, deserved, laugh.

The first indication that Grant was not immortal came in the autumn of 1984 when, following a bout of feeling vaguely unwell and generally out of sorts, he was checked out at the Cedars-Sinai Medical Center in Los Angeles. Grant had not really been ill since his bout of hepatitis in 1949. The results of his new tests showed that he had suffered a very mild stroke and, although there were no lingering effects, medical opinion was that he should cut down on his heavy schedule of business affairs and one-man shows.

At home, he played down his stroke and as soon as he was feeling well again, resumed his full programme. Privately, however, he acknowledged it as a warning sign. Significantly, he re-drafted his will in November 1984, just one month after his stroke had been diagnosed.

Having abandoned his lucrative film career in the mid-sixties without compunction, it seems perverse that he should want to sustain his stage performances when he was much older and following a health scare. Travelling around with Barbara must have been much of the attraction and showing her that he was still up to it: an even simpler answer was that he had come to realise he was back in love with performing after a lengthy, not always satisfying lay-off. Also, this time around, it was all being done very much on *his* terms with no producers, directors, co-stars, writers and so forth telling him what they wanted and what he could and could not do.

The clearest evidence of this came in one of his one-man shows he performed in September 1985. In one of his answers to the audience, he revealed, with profound simplicity, his attitude to life now:

'I'd prefer to be younger and know what I know today and to be able to apply it to life in every aspect. But, apart from that, I'm happy. I get up every morning and go to bed every night, and occupy myself as best I can in between. I do what I want when I want. Once, in St Louis, I met a man who ran a whorehouse because it made him happy. Well, I do what makes me happy.'

Cary Grant had often wondered how and when he would die. Not with any morbidity but with the rather detached, abstract interest of a man who had always taken his good health for granted. Had he been able to choose his own passing, it's doubtful he could have envisaged one quite so sudden, or hoped for one with no preliminary decline or decay.

In November 1986, Grant and Barbara were at the races at Hollywood Park Racetrack, where he was a board member. Roderick

Mann was with them that day and Mann recalled afterwards that his old friend was 'in fine form: laughing a lot and telling outrageous jokes – long convoluted stories. The kind he liked best.'

But the amazing adventures of Archie Leach were nearing their completion.

A couple of days later, on Saturday 29 November 1986, Grant and Barbara travelled to Davenport in Iowa for his next *Conversation With Cary Grant* show. They booked into the Blackhawk Hotel and then went straight on to the theatre, arriving just before three p.m. This was to set up and rehearse the show throughout the afternoon.

Grant had, in fact, been feeling unwell all day and this was something that the theatre staff picked up immediately they saw him: he looked very tired and he stumbled once in the auditorium. Nevertheless, as the photographer Basil Williams, who was also present that afternoon, points out, 'He still looked dashing and debonair. He was talking animatedly and was joking and hugging his wife.'

He was also, as ever, charming to the theatre staff. When he entered, the ushers broke into spontaneous applause. 'I hope I deserve that,' he quipped. But unusually he was less focused on the meticulous plans for the evening ahead and when the theatre manager said to him that he hoped everything would go all right, Grant's comment was a weary, 'Whatever happens, happens.'

Basil Williams took several photos of Grant at the theatre that last afternoon, some of Grant alone, some of him and Barbara together. The last photo of Cary Grant shows him looking much older but still striking. His eyes are closed as Barbara embraces him from behind, her chin resting on his left shoulder.

Grant rehearsed for about half an hour, then something changed. 'Something seemed wrong,' said Williams. 'He and Barbara disappeared backstage.'

What had happened was that he had begun to feel much, much worse. He and Barbara returned at once to the Blackhawk Hotel where, for a little while, she nursed him herself as he didn't wish to see a doctor. But she called for medical assistance, against his wishes, and the doctor discovered that Grant's blood pressure was reading 210 over 130. He knew that Grant was very ill and having a massive stroke and told him and Barbara that he must go to the hospital at once. Grant refused – perhaps he understood this was the end and that they would only be staving off the inevitable – despite increasing pain. He started suggesting that he should return to Los Angeles and see a doctor there, but the local doctor who had examined him knew that was simply impossible: Cary Grant was dying and had very little time left.

'The stroke was getting worse,' he said afterwards. 'In only fifteen minutes he deteriorated rapidly. It was terrible watching him die and not being able to help. But he wouldn't let us.'

By 8.45 p.m., Grant had started to slip into a coma and was no longer in any state to refuse medical assistance. As the doctor called for the paramedics, Grant somehow managed to glance at Barbara. 'I love you, Barbara,' he said. 'Don't worry...' Ironically, it could have been the end of the sort of weepie movie being made at the height of his career.

Another photographer, Greg Boll, was in the Blackhawk Hotel lobby when the paramedics brought Grant from his room. Barbara, distraught, was holding his hand throughout.

'He was barely visible under the blankets,' said Boll. 'They came up to his neck and he had towels placed over his face so that only his mouth and nose were visible. They sped him through the hotel lobby quietly and calmly, but obviously with great concern.'

Grant was taken to St Luke's hospital where, now comatose, he was admitted with the symptoms of a devastating stroke. The doctors worked on him for 45 minutes in the Emergency Department and he was then transferred to Intensive Care. But the stroke, as the medics understood, had been too severe, and he was pronounced dead at 11.22 p.m.

'Cary Grant was not supposed to die,' said a *New York Times* editorial. 'Cary Grant was supposed to stick around. Our perpetual touchstone of charm and elegance and youth.'

This editorial spoke for everyone around the world. There *had* been something immortal about the man and the news of his death took some time to sink in.

The tributes to him were, unsurprisingly, generous and fulsome. President Reagan led the honours from his adopted country: 'He was one of the brightest stars in Hollywood,' he said, 'and his elegance, wit and charm will endure forever on film and in our hearts.'

Eva Marie Saint, Grant's co-star from *North By Northwest*, said simply, 'Cary was the most handsome, witty and stylish leading man both on and off screen.'

But it was, perhaps, the actress and singer Polly Bergen, a friend of Grant's for more than thirty years, who summed up the feelings of those who knew him best: 'Cary was the one star that even other stars were in awe of. We have just lost the man who showed Hollywood and the world what the word "class" really means.'

Barbara Grant accompanied her husband's body back to California and his funeral was arranged almost at once. He was cremated in a secret, simple service, with only his immediate family in attendance, as was his stipulation. It had long been his wish – and deeply in character – that there should be no pomp and ceremony at his funeral, nor did he want a memorial service.

'Cary didn't want a razzle-dazzle funeral that would turn into a Hollywood circus,' commented a friend. 'He'd made all the arrangements himself years earlier. He insisted he was to have a private cremation away from the hordes of fans and TV crews.'

Grant had seen at first hand how prurient intrusion into private grief had marred the funerals of so many of his Hollywood friends and he was determined Barbara and Jennifer were not to be subjected to an unseemly media scramble when it was his turn. Even in death, Grant was the epitome of good taste.

He had requested that his ashes should be scattered over the Pacific Ocean. It was a long way from the docks of Bristol where the young Archie had first seen the troop ships heading out to sea, but it is what he wanted.

Cary Grant left an estate valued at around sixty million dollars. Jennifer received a third and, by granting her such a fortune, he perhaps was hoping it would dissuade her from ever becoming an actress. He had been delighted by her refusal to accept the movie offers which kept coming throughout her teens and even more so by her decision to go to Stanford University to study Law.

After Grant's death, Jennifer went against his wishes by dropping out of her final year at Stanford and enrolling in an acting class. Could Grant have really blamed her? She had lived with a man who had had a remarkable film career of his own – one that had started when he had run away from home to join Bob Pender in Norwich. With such an impulsive beginning to his career, it would have been difficult for him to be critical of his daughter's more structured approach. It appears to be a case of history repeating itself, if on a more secure, lavish scale. And it is hard to imagine that Grant would not have come around to supporting her decision, even helping where he could. If that was what truly made her happy, then it would surely have made *him* happy, too.

Leaving her a third of his vast estate is proof he wanted to look after her, despite no longer being around. Having been deprived both emotionally and financially throughout his formative years, leaving her so much wealth was an entirely natural decision to make.

Jennifer eventually found success in acting by appearing in the top sit-coms *Friends* and *Ellen* and with a regular role in *Beverly Hills 90210*.

The greatest irony of Cary Grant's life is that, as the veteran of 72 movies and the world's greatest leading man, he should only have found true happiness in his own life once he had ended his career. It was only when he was done with movies that he finally stopped looking for who he really was and found the contentment that had remained elusive for so many years.

Grant once said that 'in life there is no end to getting well. Perhaps death itself is the end to getting well. Or, if you prefer to think as I do, the beginning of being well.'

On another occasion, shortly before he died, he said, 'I'd be a nut to go through all that again, but I wouldn't have missed it for anything.'

He was once asked how he would like to be remembered by his family and friends. 'As someone who didn't rock the boat,' he replied. 'Someone who did moderately well at his craft and someone who was polite to his fellow man.' Somehow, one can't imagine them – or anyone – having difficulty remembering him that way.

And as the Pacific waves gently dispersed his ashes, Barbara and Jennifer could at least comfort themselves with one thought.

Archie Leach and Cary Grant were at peace.

Both of them.

Postscript

'Cary really wouldn't have liked to hear the nice things that are going to be said about him tonight,' said Roger Moore at a special gala tribute, benefiting the Princess Grace Foundation, on 19 October 1988 in Los Angeles. 'But what the heck – we'll say them anyway!'

Cary Grant did not believe that he would be remembered for very long after his death or that his films would endure. He was wrong on both counts: he will remain an eternal icon of twentieth-century popular culture.

Quite how he would have reacted to the news that a £35,000 statue of him was to be unveiled by Barbara and Jennifer in Bristol in September 2001, timed to coincide with the seventieth anniversary of his arrival in Hollywood, we cannot know.

But his ghost could be forgiven for smiling that characteristically wry, bemused and self-mocking smile for which he was renowned in life, in learning that Archie Leach was finally coming home.

Filmography

This is the Night (1932)
Director: Frank Tuttle

Sinners in the Sun (1932)
Director: Alexander Hall

Merrily We Go To Hell (1932)
Director: Dorothy Arzner

The Devil and the Deep (1932)
Director: Marion Gering

Blonde Venus (1932)
Director: Josef von Sternberg

Hot Saturday (1932)
Director: William A. Seiter

Madame Butterfly (1932)
Director: Marion Gering

She Done Him Wrong (1933)
Director: Lowell Sherman

Woman Accused (1933)
Director: Paul Sloane

The Eagle and the Hawk (1933)
Director: Stuart Walker

Gambling Ship (1933)
Director: Louis Gasnier and Max Marcin

I'm No Angel (1933)
Director: Wesley Ruggles

Alice In Wonderland (1933)
Director: Norman McLeod

Thirty-Day Princess (1934)
Director: Marion Gering

Born To Be Bad (1934)
Director: Lowell Sherman

Kiss And Make Up (1934)
Director: Harlan Thompson

Ladies Should Listen (1934)
Director: Frank Tuttle

Enter Madam! (1935)
Director: Elliot Nugent

Wings In The Dark (1935)
Director: James Flood

The Last Outpost (1935)
Director: Charles Barton and Louis Gasnier

Sylvia Scarlett (1936)
Director: George Cukor

Big Brown Eyes (1936)
Director: Raoul Walsh

Suzy (1936)
Director: George Fitzmaurice

Wedding Present (1936)
Director: Richard Wallace

When You're In Love (UK title *For You Alone*) (1937)
Director: Robert Riskin

The Amazing Quest of Ernest Bliss/Amazing Adventure (US title
Romance and Riches) (1937)
Director: Alfred Zeisler

Topper (1937)
Director: Norman Z. McLeod

The Toast Of New York (1937)
Director: Rowland V. Lee

The Awful Truth (1937)
Director: Leo McCarey

Bringing Up Baby (1938)
Director: Howard Hawks

Holiday (UK titles *Free to Live, Unconventional Linda*) (1938)
Director: George Cukor

Gunga Din (1939)
Director: George Stevens

Only Angels Have Wings (1939)
Director: Howard Hawks

In Name Only (1939)
Director: John Cromwell

His Girl Friday (1940)
Director: Howard Hawks

My Favorite Wife (1940)
Director: Garson Kanin

The Howards Of Virginia (UK title *The Tree of Liberty*) (1940)
Director: Frank Lloyd

The Philadelphia Story (1941)
Director: George Cukor

Penny Serenade (1941)
Director: George Stevens

Suspicion (1941)
Director: Alfred Hitchcock

The Talk of The Town (1942)
Director: George Stevens

Once Upon A Honeymoon (1942)
Director: Leo McCarey

Mr. Lucky (1943)
Director: H.C. Potter

Destination Tokyo (1944)
Director: Delmer Daves

Once Upon A Time (1944)
Director: Alexander Hall

None But The Lonely Heart (1944)
Director: Clifford Odets

Arsenic and Old Lace (1944)
Director: Frank Capra

Night And Day (1946)
Director: Michael Curtiz

Notorious (1946)
Director: Alfred Hitchcock

The Bachelor and the Bobby Soxer (UK title *Bachelor Knight*) (1947)
Director: Irving Reis

The Bishop's Wife (1947)
Director: Henry Koster

Mr Blandings Builds His Dream House (1948)
Director: H.C. Potter

Every Girl Should Be Married (1948)
Director: Don Hartman

I Was A Male War Bride (UK Title *You Can't Sleep Here*) (1949)
Director: Howard Hawks

Crisis (1950)
Director: Richard Brooks

People Will Talk (1951)
Director: Joseph L. Mankiewicz

Room For One More (1952)
Director: Norman Taurog

Monkey Business (1952)
Director: Howard Hawks

Dream Wife (1953)
Director: Sidney Sheldon

To Catch A Thief (1955)
Director: Alfred Hitchcock

The Pride And The Passion (1957)
Director: Stanley Kramer

An Affair To Remember (1957)
Director: Leo McCarey

Kiss Them For Me (1957)
Director: Stanley Donen

Indiscreet (1958)
Director: Stanley Donen

Houseboat (1958)
Director: Melville Shavelson

North By Northwest (1959)
Director: Alfred Hitchcock

Operation Petticoat (1959)
Director: Blake Edwards

The Grass Is Greener (1961)
Director: Stanley Donen

That Touch Of Mink (1962)
Director: Delbert Mann

Charade (1963)
Director: Stanley Donen

Father Goose (1964)
Director: Ralph Nelson

Walk, Don't Run (1966)
Director: Charles Walters

Other film appearances

Pirate Party on Catalina Isle (1936)

Topper Takes a Trip (1939)
(Grant was unavailable for this follow-up feature to *Topper*)

Polio and Communicable Diseases Hospital Trailer (1940)

The Road to Victory (1944)

The Shining Future (1944)

Without Reservations (1946)

Ken Murray's Hollywood (1965)

Elvis: That's The Way It Is (1970)

Once Upon A Time ... Is Now (1977)
(Voice only)

Cary Grant – the Leading Man (1991)

Sources

Cary Grant, A Celebration, Richard Schickel, Pavilion, 1983.

A Class Apart, Graham McCann, 4th Estate, 1996.

Archie Leach, Cary Grant (Autobiography, Cary Grant web-page on Internet, originally published as articles for a US newspaper, mid-1960s).

The Alfred Hitchcock Story, Ken Mogg, Titan Books, 1999.

The Other Side of the Moon, Sheridan Morley, Weidenfeld & Nicholson, 1985.

Grace, Robert Lacey, Sidgwick & Jackson, 1994.

Cubby Broccoli: When the Snow Melts (Autobiography), Boxtree, 1998.

Charlie Chaplin and His Times, Kenneth S. Lynn (Aurum 1997).

Katharine Hepburn: Me (Autobiography), Random House, 1991.

Tony Curtis (Autobiography), Heinemann, 1994.

The Moon's a Balloon (Autobiography), David Niven, Penguin Books, 1994.

Bring On The Empty Horses (Autobiography), David Niven, Hamish Hamilton, 1975.

James Stewart, Donald Dewey, Turner Publishing Inc., 1996.

Doris Day, Michael Freedland, André Deutsch, 2000.

Audrey: An Intimate Portrait, Diana Maychick, Sidgwick & Jackson, 1993.

Michael Caine: What's It All About? (Autobiography), Century, 1992.

Marilyn's Men: The Private Life of Marilyn Monroe, Jane Ellen Wayne, Robson Books, 1992.

Marilyn Monroe: The Biography, Donald Spoto, Chatto and Windus, 1993.

Showman: The Life of David O. Selznick, David Thomson, André Deutsch, 1993.
Cary Grant, Chuck Ashman and Pamela Trescott, W.H. Allen, 1987.
David Niven, Sheridan Morley, Weidenfeld and Nicholson, 1985.
James Mason: Odd Man Out, Sheridan Morley, Weidenfeld and Nicholson, 1989.
Bette and Joan: The Divine Feud, Shaun Considine, Century Hutchinson, 1989.
Noel Coward, Philip Hoare, Sinclair-Stevenson, 1995.
Cary Grant: The Light Touch, Lionel Godfrey, Robert Hale, 1981.
Dukes, Queens and other Stories, Allan Warren, New Millennium, 1999.

Index

Ball, Lucille, 158
Baltimore, 80
Bankhead, Tallulah, 42–3
Barnett, S.H., 261
Barrie, George, 288–90, 296
Barrie, J.M., 4
Barry, Philip, 103, 104, 120, 121
Barrymore, Ethel, 159
Barrymore, John, 127
Basie, Count, 5, 301
Bath, 13
Batman, 43
Battle of Britain, 119
Beatles, The, 3
Beaton, Cecil, 5
Beatty, Warren, 296
Beaverbrook, Max, 112
Beetlejuice, 91
Before The Facts, 138
Bell, Book And Candle, 234
Bellamy, Ralph, 87, 88, 91, 116–17
Bennett, Constance, 91, 92
Bennett, Joan, 81, 82
Bennett, Tony, 300
Benny, Jack, 260, 299
Bercorici, Leonard, 180
Bergan, Polly, 324–5
Bergman, Ingrid, 103, 120–1, 147,
    165, 167, 168–9, 171, 179, 194,
    201, 207, 228–30, 252, 253, 319
Berman, Pandro S., 104, 105, 115
Bette & Joan: The Divine Feud,
    128
Beverly Hills, 326
Big Brown Eyes, 81, 82
Big Business, 91
Bill Of Divorcement, 80
The Birds, 238
Birth Of A Nation, 35
The Bishop's Wife, 110, 180–2, 274
Black Narcissus, 246
Blair, Tony, 297

Blithe Spirit, 91
Blonde Venus, 43, 61, 66
The Blue Angel, 43
Bob And Carol And Ted And Alice,
    286
Bogart, Humphrey, 1, 2, 80, 179,
    196, 200
Bogdanovich, Peter, 94, 99, 283
Boll, Greg, 324
Bolton, Guy, 32, 33
Born To Be Bad, 75, 76
Boston, 128
Bouron, Cynthia, 89–90
Bowers, William, 161
Boyer, Charles, xi, 211, 227
Brackett, Charles, 182
Brando, Marlon, 179, 192, 196, 207
Breathless, 231
Brian, Mary, 117
The Bridge On The River Kwai,
    180, 206
Bring On The Empty Horses, 162,
    294
Bringing Up Baby, xv, 53, 92–5,
    103, 105, 118, 145, 174, 186,
    195, 257
Brisson, Frederick, 117, 130
Bristol, 2, 4, 5, 10, 13, 16, 17, 18,
    27, 28, 30, 34, 66, 68, 69, 76, 77,
    83, 84, 85, 90, 96, 108, 110, 151,
    157, 170, 182, 186, 259, 260,
    264, 266–70, 271, 283, 296, 303,
    304, 307, 315, 318, 325, 327
Bristol Evening Post, 66, 318
British Actors' Orphanage, 110
BBC Television, 243
British Film Institute, 232
Broadway, 31, 33, 38, 46, 50, 103,
    120, 126, 147, 154, 160, 185,
    247, 298
Broccoli, Albert Romolo ('Cubby'),
    102, 113, 122, 143, 175, 176,